Clear and Present Dangers

A Conservative View of America's Government

Clear and Present Dangers

A Conservative View of America's Government

M. STANTON EVANS

Chairman, American Conservative Union

Under the General Editorship of
James David Barber, Duke University

HBJ

Harcourt Brace Jovanovich, Inc.

New York   Chicago   San Francisco   Atlanta

ISBN: 0-15-507685-X
Library of Congress Catalog Card Number: 75-7683

Printed in the United States of America

Preface

There is no point, I suppose, in beating around the bush. The discussion that follows is an exercise in civil heresy. It is a challenge to the ruling orthodoxy of our times, and as such invites the reader to reverse conceptions that are widely held in American politics. The ideas advanced may therefore seem, on first inspection, a trifle odd.

To take some examples, more or less at random: It is generally believed (this is written in early 1975) that population totals here and elsewhere are growing much too rapidly; that the costs of American health care are prohibitively high; that Americans consume excessive amounts of energy; that the profits of petroleum companies are a scandal; that we are spending far too much on military matters; that we need infusions of Federal money and expertise to deal with problems of urban transit, environmental pollution, employment, poverty, and education—to name a few.

All these propositions and dozens of others like them are repeated daily in our political conversation and given almost universal credence—not so much explained or argued about as taken for granted. They are the axioms of the national dialogue, transcribing problem areas for us and implicitly defining the solutions. In the usual format, we are simply told that, *because* these things are so, we need to make a number of changes in our laws, impose some kind of regulation, or extend some kind of subsidy.

In addition to their wide acceptance, such notions have one other notable feature in common, as seen from the perspective of this book: the fact that they are not merely wrong, but exact inversions of the truth—so that in case after case the way to discover the actual situation is to take the conventional utterance and stand it on its head.

The ensuing pages contend, for example, that our population is growing not too rapidly, but much too slowly; that the problem with American health care is that it is excessively cheap; that high per capita energy use is a good thing, not a bad one; that petroleum profits could stand to be a good deal bigger; that the military, far from starving domestic services into penury, is itself, comparatively speaking, being starved; that outlays for public education, urban transit, pollution control, and poverty are, in the usual instance, counterproductive.

Similar heresies are committed on almost all the major issues of our time: inflation and taxes, corporate power, housing, unemployment, busing, social security, prison reform, capital punishment, pornography, abortion, drug use, child development, the Watergate scandal, and so forth. In almost all such cases, it shall be argued, the typical wisdom of the day—of the sort encountered in the *New York Times,* political Washington, and many college classrooms—has the whole discussion inside-out.

As is explained at greater length in the Introduction, this topsy-turvy pattern is intrinsic to the current orthodoxy. That orthodoxy is "liberal" in its value assumptions, and liberalism, for reasons to be noted, appears to be mistaken about practically everything. It has matters backwards in its basic philosophy, and because of this beginning error it almost always gets the essential facts of economic and political life reversed as well. It is therefore unsurprising that, under liberal guidance, our country has been lurching from one misfortune to another.

In attempting to cover a number of subjects in a single volume, I have necessarily had to treat each one with relative brevity. In most cases, I have cited data in some detail to back my argument, but it should be stressed that these are merest samplings from a burgeoning public record. To do justice to the evidence of liberal failure in any one of the areas covered would require a book-length dissertation on each and every topic.

To alter opinions at so deep a level on so many fronts is, of course, a difficult task, and I cherish no illusions that the arguments herein will make a lot of instantaneous converts. I know from personal experience that certain beliefs—such as the power of corporations or the sovereign evil of the Pentagon—are firmly planted and well-nigh impervious to correction. Still, I think the effort should be made—if not to turn society around in its tracks, at least to get a different view of all these matters out on the table.

As is by now apparent, I write from a definite viewpoint, generally described in the American political context as "conservative." I am an advocate and, in an ideological sense, a partisan. This being so, I do not ask that anything said here be taken at face value, or on the supposed authority of the writer. My hope is otherwise: that readers of this volume will at a minimum discover that there *is* another opinion on such questions—with evidence to back it up—and will be prompted to some independent study outside the categories of liberal discourse.

Thanks are owing to a number of people for assistance in the preparation of this volume: for help in various facets of the research, Don E. Cope, Stephen M. Davis, Alice Hartle, J. Danforth Quayle, Robert Ward, and George Watts; for typing the manuscript, Dorothy Lawrence and my secretary Carolyn Ronan, who also shouldered a heavy responsibility in trying to keep me relatively organized; for generally supportive activities, Alison Borland, Anita Korten, Becky Norton, and James Roberts of the American Conservative Union; for prodding a dilatory author to completion of his labors, Harrison C. Griffin, Virginia Joyner, and Andrea Halght of Harcourt Brace Jovanovich; and for reviewing the manuscript with a discerning eye, Benjamin I. Page of the University of Chicago.

M. STANTON EVANS

Contents

PART I The Politics of Power

PART II Policy and Planning: The Crisis Is in Washington

Part III Freedom Is As Freedom Does

Clear and Present Dangers

A Conservative View of America's Government

Introduction
The Death
of Liberalism

For the past four decades, the conduct of American politics has been chiefly guided by a social philosophy known in modern discourse by the name of "liberalism." Since the advent of the New Deal under Franklin Roosevelt, the political notions associated with this term havé shaped the major decisions of our nation both at home and abroad. There have been occasional digressions and setbacks, plus a chronic resistance by certain elements of our society, but by and large the liberal supremacy has been both obvious and continuous, and is generally acknowledged by political observers of every outlook.

Other aspects of the subject are considerably more controversial. What, exactly, this liberalism consists of, why it has come into being, and where it may eventually take us, are major items of dispute, both among the people who describe themselves as liberals and among opponents of the liberal creed. Most notably, there is disagreement as to whether the liberal ascendancy has been a good thing or a bad, and, if the latter judgment is offered, what political view should be brought forward in its place. On matters of this kind, all is in comparative confusion.

1

Concerning the identity of liberals in explicit politics, there is, of course, a kind of consensus. We know that Eleanor Roosevelt was a liberal, that George McGovern is a liberal, that the United Auto Workers stand for liberal views, that Americans for Democratic Action is a liberal organization, and so on. We can also identify types of legislation and stands on particular issues as "liberal," but even this remains unsatisfactory. Federal health care, legal services, and consumer legislation—to pick some random current examples—are known as liberal issues. But so are civil liberties for minority groups, rehabilitationist penology, and permissive abortion. Why are all these positions "liberal" (if in fact they are), and what, if anything, is the connection among them? Questions of this type are seldom raised in public discussion, and almost never answered.

Given liberalism's status as a reigning orthodoxy, such confusions should not surprise us. When critic Lionel Trilling said two decades ago that liberalism was "not only the dominant but the sole intellectual tradition" in America he was passably near the truth—and such a position of dominance generally discourages attention to first principles.[1] The ascendancy of the liberal worldview has accustomed all of us to think somewhat reflexively in the categories natural to that world-view, and it is no simple matter to replace these categories with something else.

By the same token, liberalism's unhindered sway has made the orthodoxy itself somewhat lethargic. Many devout liberals would be hard put to say exactly why they are liberals or what, at bottom, liberalism is. Not having been required to defend their position against sustained attack, they have settled rather comfortably into the belief that their particular way of viewing things is the correct one—a familiar syndrome among the orthodox. Until fairly recent times and the rise of an articulate conservative community, it has simply never occurred to many liberals that there was anything to argue about.

A striking example of this complacency may be found in the school of social science literature that arose in the 1950s and '60s and contended that people who deviated from the liberal orthodoxy were—well, crazy. Most charming in its directness was the assertion of Harry Overstreet, an eminent liberal psychologist, deploring the attitudes of people who were "angrily against race equality, public housing, the TVA, financial and technical aid to backward countries, organized labor, and the preaching of social rather than salvational religion." Such people, said Overstreet, "may appear 'normal' in the sense that they are able to hold a job and otherwise maintain their status as members of society; *but they are, we now recognize, well along the road to mental illness.*" [2] (Italics added.)

It is apparent that this judgment was rendered without particular malice. From his various writings, Dr. Overstreet seems to be an even-tempered fellow of rather conventional opinions. It was simply inconceivable to him that anyone could for good and principled reasons be opposed to programs that all right-minded liberals thought were necessary and that therefore enjoyed axiomatic status. What is axiomatic need not be defended; it is simply affirmed against the madmen who would question it.

Liberal Definitions of Liberalism

It is perhaps as a result of these factors that the term "liberalism" seems so remarkably amorphous. Being taken for granted, it never needs to be thought about very carefully. And certainly for a word that is used with considerable frequency, it appears to have an infinite variety of meanings, depending on who is using it and for what purpose. On etymological grounds alone, one would assume it has something to do with liberty, and indeed there is a great deal of talk about liberty in the literature of the liberal community; but talk is not the same as systematic argument.

One academic exponent of the liberal view, Salwyn Schapiro, informs us that "what has characterized liberalism at all times is its unshaken belief in the necessity of freedom to achieve every desirable aim. . . . The fundamental postulate of liberalism has been the moral worth, the absolute value, and the essential dignity of the human personality." [3] This is a representative statement, but it is also quite obviously a false statement. Liberalism certainly has *not* been characterized "at all times" by any such thing, and increasingly appears not to be characterized by it at all.

In certain formal and occasional statements, it is true, liberalism has never ceased to profess its belief in free speech, the competition of ideas, and the value of "dialogue." The liberal prides himself on an alleged tolerance of dissent, open-mindedness toward unfamiliar ideas, and readiness to hear something new and different. And while we shall have occasion in the course of our discussion to consider the consistency with which this view is applied, we may acknowledge that its ceremonial affirmation has been a regular feature of liberal discourse.

On other matters the liberal commitment to notions of personal freedom appears at best ambiguous. It is a cliché of such discussions that liberalism over the course of the last century has affirmed two seemingly contradictory opinions on economic issues. So-called classical liberals in the mold of Adam Smith, John Stuart Mill, Herbert Spencer, and William Graham Sumner assumed an essentially *laissez-faire* position on questions of political economy, arguing the view that that government is best which governs least. Their nominal descendants of the Schlesinger-Galbraith-McGovern school have taken exactly the reverse position: they are vigorous champions of the "affirmative state," urging constant resort to government and numerous restrictions on the scope of economic liberty.

Compare the lyric utterance of Professor Schapiro, for example, with this countervailing definition of liberalism provided by former Senator Joseph Clark of Pennsylvania, long a leading figure in Americans for Democratic Action. In an article for *The Atlantic Monthly* back in 1953, Clark put the matter quite succinctly. "A liberal," he said, "is here defined as one who believes in using the full force of government for the advancement of social, political, and economic justice at the municipal, state, national and international levels"—which seems more or less to cover the subject, and which has a distinctly authoritarian ring to it.[4]

Or consider the statements of liberal economist Robert Theobald (an early proponent of the guaranteed annual income), who says "we must recognize the fact the society's needs may be more important than those of a single person" and believes "a strict insistence on existing rights would lead to an intolerable situation for all." In the ideal situation, Theobald asserts, "each person and each pressure group would be willing to concede that the interests of the community as a whole—once they were known—should take priority over their own interests." He adds that "many of the policies now required by the situation have been described in the past as socialist and communist and therefore arouse widespread mistrust." He is happy to note, however, that such "doctrinal" considerations now receive less attention than they used to.[5]

Nor is the contradiction merely retrospective. It exists with regard to current issues as well. In discussions of free speech, or Communist Party membership, or something else of the kind, liberal rhetoric is strongly libertarian and, where questions of constitutional right are concerned, takes a position that is often described as "absolutist" or "strict constructionist." It will brook no interference with the rights of the individual, however great the provocation, because it believes First Amendment guarantees must be extended to the limit to protect the liberty of the person. (Thus liberal Justice Hugo Black: "I think the founders of our nation in adopting the First Amendment meant precisely that the Federal government should pass 'no law' regulating speech and press. . . .")[6] But on economic questions all this is reversed: rhetorical stress is on the primacy of the group, the fecklessness of the individual, and the undesirability of limiting the powers of government.

From the fact of such reversals and the various explanations provided for them, a number of conclusions emerge. Most obvious of these is that liberalism, whatever its lineage and whatever the usual definitions, quite clearly has to do with *something else* in addition to, or in preference to, the freedom of the individual. Other things have gotten in there, which at a minimum require some modification of the simple equation of "liberal" with liberty, and necessitate a bit of explaining.

Notable among these other things, suggesting itself in almost every phase of recent liberal action, is the idea of social uplift or improvement. Liberal utterance in the academic and political worlds is suffused with references to progress, reform, enlightenment, welfare, social justice, and assistance to the impoverished. On any candid reading, this aspect of the liberal outlook is more prominent nowadays than any commitment to individual freedom, though of course the ideas can be commensurated and various liberal spokesmen, such as Arthur M. Schlesinger, Jr., and James MacGregor Burns, have attempted here and there a kind of reconciliation.

In this dimension liberalism may be described as a sentiment rather than a program—a sentiment so strong and overpowering that at least one student of the subject, Kenneth Minogue of the London School of Economics, believes it to be the central feature of the liberal outlook. According to Minogue, the desire to alleviate suffering is the master principle of the liberal creed, and all its variations may be comprehended in this light.[7] Thus when greater government intervention diminishes suffering, liberals will favor that. When less intervention accomplishes the goal, liberals favor that. This view is similar to that offered by certain liberals who say the philosophy has remained consistent in its humanitarian goals, simply switching over from *laissez faire* to "affirmative state" when it learned the facts of economic life. For reasons to be noted, this explains very little, but it confirms the fact that liberalism, whatever it is, isn't quite the libertarian phenomenon its promoters like to suggest.

Beyond these issues, there is the deeper question of the liberal metaphysic—its approach to questions of basic value—and how this is related to the social ideas and political programs we have come to associate with the word. Here, too, the general outlines of the liberal view are fairly well-known from the statements of major spokesmen. At this level, liberalism may be described as essentially relativist and, in a general sense, materialist. Its principal affirmation is its belief in the changeableness of things, the tentative character of all conclusions, and the inadmissibility of moral absolutes.

There are numerous sources to illustrate this point, and the reader who is familiar with cultural, historical, or scientific relativism will doubtless have his own preferred examples. My particular choice is the statement of Justice Oliver Wendell Holmes, who told fellow Bostonian William James, "I can't help preferring champagne to dishwater—I doubt if the universe does." Holmes was an evolutionist who held that assertion of power was the law of nature and thus of life, and he had an evolutionist's insouciance toward questions of higher truth. He believed that "there are as many truths as there are men," and that an effort to project these conceptions on external reality, "to demand significance of the universe, etc., is absurd." [8]

The potential confusions in all this are obviously very great. It appears that liberalism might be described as anything or every-thing, depending on how you look at it. Is liberalism pro-freedom, or the reverse? Why have liberal views apparently changed on mat-ters of economics but not on matters of, say, speech? What *is* the liberal view toward concentrated political power? How are liberal "absolutist" views on the First Amendment reconciled with liberal "relativist" views on the Tenth—which affirms the rights of the several states? How does the liberal desire to diminish suffering square with an essentially evolutionist metaphysic à la Holmes? Such questions might be multiplied at almost indefinite length.

Until we have the answers to these questions, we will not really understand liberalism or its impact on the American nation. And the abiding error of such discussions in our time is that so many of the participants, both liberal and otherwise, do not attempt to trace the connections among these various subjects. Many liberal scholars discuss the transition from classical to modern, for ex-ample, but provide us virtually no enlightenment on divergent lib-eral readings of the Constitution. Conservative critics are hardly better, tending to isolate some characteristic of the liberal outlook for extended criticism, without providing an explanation of how that facet of the liberal world-view relates to various others.

It is my contention that each of the topics considered can be comprehended properly only in the light of the others. *Ad hoc* dis-cussions of liberal economics, liberal jurisprudence, or liberal value theory without some effort to interconnect these several matters may be interesting in their development of esoteric detail, but can-not provide much in the way of general understanding. An analysis that can account for one or two such manifestations but not the others has something wrong with it. Unfortunately, nearly all dis-cussions of the matter, both pro and con, appear to suffer from this defect.

The argument of this volume is that liberalism from the eighteenth century up to the present day has been a continuous and essentially homogeneous body of political thought, with conclu-sions following in natural sequence from the original premises. Far from being discordant, the several stances assumed by liberal spokesmen, as well as the relation of liberal opinions at various levels of discussion, are all quite logical if we grasp the essential nature of the philosophy at the outset and approach these seeming contradictions in terms of it. It all makes perfect sense, though the sense it makes is of a distressing kind.

Why Liberalism Has Failed

Most of the discussion in this volume is an effort to show that liberalism in America has failed, by every measure of the empirical record: not merely by the standards of its critics, but by all the criteria it has itself established for the assessment of social policy. I shall argue that the failure is total and conclusive—manifesting itself in every department of national life, wherever data are sufficient to permit definitive judgment. Virtually the only areas where such a demonstration is not possible are those where the data do not exist or have not been susceptible to full interpretation. Much of the narrative will be a survey of this lugubrious record.

Such a recitation would not accomplish much, however, if it were offered in a vacuum, without revealing why the liberal formula had failed, or what its failure signified beyond the tale of the empirical data. While it is possible to measure failure in one sense by matching political claims to political performance, that reading leaves us short of where we need to be. It does not tell us, except in a limited, operational way, *why* the failure has occurred, or why it has been so consistent. Nor does it tell us what measures should be taken to prevent recurrence in the future, or the direction in which we should move in quest of remedy. To arrive at affirmations such as these, we need criteria of judgment considerably broader than a simple discrepancy between advertising and performance.

The historical record, be it said, provides a remarkably uniform pattern: Time and again we shall observe that liberal policies are uniquely counterproductive, almost always promising one thing but delivering another. The regularity with which liberalism has not simply failed to realize the goals it has set for itself, but has produced effects precisely the reverse of those that were originally intended, is an arresting phenomenon. I would argue that it is in this phenomenon of reversal, rather than in any of the issues considered separately, that we may discover the character of the liberal creed: the very nature of liberalism is to generate results not merely different from, but directly opposite to, its stated goals.

We can understand this rather peculiar fact if we perceive that liberalism is a philosophy having to do only incidentally with any of the various issues referred to above—freedom, constitutionalism, progress, or anything of the sort. Liberalism touches on all these things in one fashion or another, but it does so only because they are aspects of a larger historical tendency, which defines and encompasses liberalism itself and establishes its relationship to all specific issues.

Reviewing the several values that have been affirmed by Western liberals from the time of Mill to that of McGovern, we encounter a rather familiar list: the idea of individual freedom, the volitional order of the market, limited government, constitutionalism, popular sovereignty, the rule of law, egalitarianism, progress, humanitarianism, the primacy of the person, freedom of speech and thought, the inviolability of the individual conscience, and so on.

These ideas are subject to differing construction, and not all of them are compatible with one another under all conditions. And some of them have been diminished in the liberal presentation as others have been brought forward or given different emphasis. Yet they all have one notable feature in common. Each is a product of the religious-cultural heritage of the West, far antedating the rise of liberalism. None was invented by liberalism itself, whether classical or modern, nor is any distinctive to modernity as such. In fact, all the characteristically "liberal" ideas derive from the Judaeo-Christian ethic, which sets off the strictly Western worldview from that prevailing in antiquity.

Unfortunately, the method by which we are taught our intellectual history tends to obscure this indebtedness to Judaic and Christian doctrine. We are instructed to believe that our uniquely Western values originated with the Greeks and Romans, and that these values were submerged by a thousand years of medieval darkness, to be recovered only with the classical revival of the Renaissance. This is not, as it happens, an accurate picture. Although the imprint of Greek and Roman thought on our political practice can hardly be denied, the fact remains that the distinctively *libertarian* (and thus distinctively Western) aspects of our politics are Biblical in origin.

All the ancient cultures, including the Greeks and Romans, saw the political state as a religious institution—a sacred agency by which the will of the gods was mediated into human society. The emperor or king, or the city-state itself, was the integrating principle by which the society made peace with the deities in nature; the state was divine, and hence unchallengeable. Since it was secular and religious authority rolled into one, there was no alternative source of loyalty, no challenge to its power, and no higher truth accessible to the average citizen by which its power could be judged.*

With the coming of Judaism and then of Christianity, all this was changed. When we enter the Old Testament, we are in a different world, both theologically and intellectually. We encounter a Deity who is not *in* nature, but above it, and who is not therefore to be propitiated by the magical rites of the ancient cities. The political state is no longer a compact religious-political institution, but becomes essentially a peace-keeping agency, incompetent to handle the higher orders of religious truth. Spiritual awareness enters society through a source (the prophets, the medieval church) quite independent of the kings and often sits in judgment *on* those kings. A tension is established between "church" and "state," alternative loyalties are possible, and a law is elaborated by which the political state itself is called to judgment.†

It is thus apparent that the early liberal vision of limited government is distinctively Judaic and Christian, utterly different from the opinion of the ancients. It derives from the Biblical conception of a transcendent Deity who lifts up the individual and scales down the assertions of the state. This view confers on us our Western notions of personal freedom, equal individual worth, privacy of

---

* Nor did the ancients place any particular value on the individual citizen. The idea that every person is precious in the sight of God, bearing the imprint of his creaturehood and possessed of an immortal, individuated soul—all this was foreign to the Greek and Roman philosophy. Thus human slavery was never challenged in these societies; it was accepted as a matter of course by that most libertarian and most congenial of the ancients, Aristotle. "Do not suppose," said the philosopher, "that any of the citizens belong to themselves; for they all belong to the state."

† It was precisely at the time of the "reception" of Roman law and pagan notions generally during the Renaissance that these distinctions became obscured, and the age of absolutism began.

conscience, the availability of public truth, and the spiritual limitations of secular politics.

It is also from the Christian history of the West that we derive such liberal ideas as checks and balances on political authority, a working federalism, and the idea of a spontaneous order arising from the mesh of individual volitions (the idea of the market). And it is from the Judaic and Christian conception of the created universe that we receive such liberal notions as "progress" over linear time, again a conception foreign to the philosophy of the ancients. Even our "rationalist" attitude toward nature and science, our rejection of magical conceptions of reality—all these and many other "liberal" positions are drawn directly from the world-view of Judaic and Christian religious culture.

In sum, the ideas that Americans and Europeans are accustomed to associate rather loosely with the word "liberalism" are actually by-products of their religious and cultural experience, as mediated by hundreds of years of medieval practice and the writings of Western sages from Paul to Fortescue and Althusius. Our notion of freedom and most of the other ideas attendant on that notion are a direct result of this religious heritage, and exactly the same is true of all the other conceptions we usually think of as "liberal," whether classical in the style of Mill or modern in the style of McGovern.

Considered in these terms, the liberal enterprise is always and everywhere the same: an effort to enjoy one or another of the secular by-products of Western faith, divorced from the theological content of that faith. The separation may be (and characteristically is) explicit, as in the case of the agnostic-relativist strain, which places its faith in doubt and which looms so crucially in liberal thought; or it may be implicit, as in the case of those who hold to their formal *devoirs* in matters of religion but shape their political program according to secular and humanistic teaching. In either event, the basic effort is to take some element of our religious-cultural heritage, set it up on its own feet, and make it purely self-validating.

The clearest statement of this formula appears in Mill's essay, the *Utility of Religion,* where he tells us that the ethical benefit of Christianity, however one might assess it, has entered into the permanent possession of mankind, and that we may preserve this benefit to ourselves while tossing overboard the theological aspects of the Christian religion, which to Mill's mechanical intellect were simply superstitious baggage.[9] Mill believed that he could establish rational, scientific, or utilitarian justifications for, say, individual freedom, and that this conception required no higher support. It was a simple matter of costs and benefits. Unfortunately, what seemed so natural and "scientific" to Mill, in the early dawn of the liberal epoch, has seemed less natural and scientific to succeeding generations who have drawn quite different conclusions from his premises.

The experiment suggested by Mill is a prototype for the liberal performance across the span of generations. And such an enterprise, by its very nature, is doomed to defeat. As British historian Christopher Dawson has instructed us, every religious vision creates its own distinctive culture, dictating certain ethical, social, and political ideas that shape one's attitudes toward everything else.[10] Although this notion is seldom stressed nowadays, it should hardly surprise us: one's vision of the cosmos necessarily governs one's view of subsidiary elements in that cosmos, including nature, the state, social institutions, and man himself. The ancients, beginning from one kind of world-view, came up with one set of political conclusions; the Judaeo-Christian world, beginning from another, came up with different conclusions altogether.

This being so, rejection of Judaic and Christian religious belief has brought a retreat from its secular by-products, too—not all at once, but, over time, inexorably. In the early stages of the process, the liberal believes he has perfectly good and mundane reasons for affirming the secular usufruct—the exercise of individual liberty, the limited political state, the volitional order of the market, and so on. It all seems very natural and obvious, even scientific. But in time the obvious arguments get harder to remember, or produce an entirely different result, as the world spins on away from the original source of inspiration.

One by one, therefore, the elements of this "natural" world-view begin to fall away; utilitarian arguments for *laissez faire* somehow get supplanted by utilitarian arguments for collectivism; evolutionist notions of libertarian struggle are replaced by evolutionist systems of rigid social engineering. We drift from Mill and Spencer to Holmes and Dewey and at last to such as B. F. Skinner, progressing by steady implacable phases from a world of libertarian feeling to a world of tight, collectivist controls—all under the general rubric of "liberal" social policy. The premises that impelled the classical liberals toward freedom push their descendants in quite the opposite direction.

This transition has become so commonplace that we often neglect the sequel—or, more precisely, the continuation. For the process of change that converted classical liberalism to modern has not yet ended. We are accustomed to think of modern liberalism as stressing democracy, progress, humanitarianism, science, and so forth, as social goals replacing the *laissez-faire* conceptions of the preceding century. But we forget that these opinions are also products of the Western religious heritage, and also subject to continued erosion. And these conceptions are vanishing, too, as Western liberalism careens with increasing velocity away from the religious-cultural heritage that gave it birth.

These reflections help explain not only the wandering from previous positions, but the amazing consistency with which modern liberal programs have produced the opposite of their intended effects. In essence, the liberal has chosen his social sentiments (freedom, equality, progress) from one brand of metaphysics, his political program (top-down coercive regulation) from another. He is trying to fashion humane results from conceptual materials that are essentially inhumane and hostile to considerations of human dignity and personal freedom. The attempt to tease a libertarian-humanitarian social product from the bleak assumptions of relativist value theory and the fearful potencies of the collectivist state is foredoomed to failure.

Where this process will eventually come out may be gathered from events in other societies, and from the thrust of twentieth century history in general. The liberal phenomenon is not, of course, confined to the United States, nor can liberalism itself be isolated from the larger movement of ideas that has affected the modern world, and that has given us all our collectivist "isms." This has been the hey-day of insistent secular ideologies that spurn the precedents and strictures of the past, and liberalism is rather plainly a subspecies of this general development.

Ours is the century that has most decisively "liberated" itself from asserted superstition, and we have generally considered ourselves to be more enlightened than our simplistic forebears. It is sobering to reflect, therefore, that we are living in the most barbaric century in the history of the human race. More people have been exterminated by despotic governments, killed in wars, locked up in dungeons, and starved to death in slave camps in the twentieth century than in any other epoch known to man. It is not improbable that 100 million human beings have been killed by the totalitarian regimes of our enlightened time, a result that ill fits the euphoric view modernity likes to take of itself, but fits very well with the fact that we have forgotten the premises from which such notions as human dignity and freedom are derived.

In the light of the totalitarian holocaust, we may see the phenomenon of liberalism somewhat more clearly. Liberalism is not, let it be said, the same thing as totalitarianism, which denies the Western religious heritage and its secular by-products all at once. Liberalism is different, softer, vaguer; a kind of halfway house. It, too, denies the Western heritage with varying degrees of explicitness, but is less eager to part with the by-products. These in one degree or another it finds attractive and wants to retain. Liberalism is nicer, and less brutal, than its totalitarian competitors—and less consistent—precisely to the degree that it retains some lingering attachment to Western value.

Viewing the matter in this fashion, we may say that twentieth-century liberalism is an attempt to embrace the collectivist and relativist premises of the modern totalitarian movements but somehow to avoid the totalitarian outcome. The result of this experiment, as we shall see, is that liberalism is drawn by the logic of its assumptions increasingly further from humanitarian social goals toward the repressive and elitist practices of the totalitarian governments. Severed from its roots in Judaeo-Christian inspiration, it is moving ever closer to the authoritarian rigors of the modern ideologies. How far this slippage has proceeded will be a major object of our consideration.

I stress these philosophical matters at the outset of the discussion because hereafter, for the most part, I must leave them unspoken. The essay that follows is documentary in approach, relying very little on theoretical argument. I seek to make my point by presentation of the factual record. Yet facts do not explain themselves; they must be approached and organized on some theoretical premise, and it is only fair the reader be acquainted with the conceptions that have informed my own particular handling of the data.

Having said all this, I should add that it is not required that one accept my interpretation of these matters to grasp their immediate political significance. Whatever explanation one chooses for them, the reversal and the failure are unquestionably *there,* and they are overwhelming. I believe the reasons set forward above explain their existence and tell us why it is that liberalism has failed. But *that* it has failed may be affirmed by anyone, of whatever outlook, who cares to examine the history of our times.

PART I
The Politics of Power

1
The American Design

Throughout the 1960s and 1970s there has been considerable discussion in American politics about the dangers of "extremism" and the need for all good citizens to combat extremists. As is the case with many other subjects in contemporary debate, discussions of this topic have been a bit diffuse. On careful examination, it appears that an "extremist" is someone the speaker or writer vehemently disagrees with and wants to disparage in the strongest language possible.

Such tossing about of political epithets generally serves its intended purpose of downgrading the person or party being labeled, but it does little to clarify the terms of public discourse. "Extremism," after all, is a term of relation—suggesting ideas or behavior that are unacceptably deviant from the norm. And unless we have a clear conception of what the norm *is,* we have no easy method of determining whether a particular group or person is really "extreme."

In certain cases the problem is easily disposed of. It is generally acknowledged, for example, that a desirable norm in most species of human conduct is the absence of violence or calculated infringement on other people's rights. So any group or person that routinely practices resort to violence or disruption of some sort may properly be called "extreme" in terms of normal common sense and manners.

When groups are analyzed according to their political philosophies, however, the matter is more complex. In this case it would appear that "extremism" depends almost entirely on the attitudes of the person using the term. From the standpoint of a dedicated Marxist, for example, the opinions of a *laissez-faire* capitalist are very extreme indeed, and precisely the same is true in the other direction. A democratic socialist would consider both of those positions quite extreme, and their proponents would return the favor. Conducted in such a manner, political discussion becomes a welter of subjectivities.

Matters of this type can be examined sensibly only if we have some notion of what our normative position is supposed to be. We can gauge degrees of deviance in any political philosophy only if we have some kind of standard by which the deviance can be measured. And for those who wish to have a politics conducted according to intelligible criteria, such a determination is of more than verbal importance. Most of us would like to believe that there are certain norms of proper government, and that the conduct of the political state will be guided by them as much as humanly possible. The attempt to establish such norms, indeed, has been the major crux of political philosophy down through the ages.

A volume of this sort cannot traverse so immense an issue as what the proper norms of government *per se* might be, or the arguments for and against particular norms propounded in the writings of Platonists, Aristotelians, legal positivists, or the *monarchomachi*. It is possible, however, to focus on a more limited range of issues, concerning the proper norms of conduct for our own American government. For it is widely understood that ours is intended to be a constitutional system, a nation of laws established on a fundamental law that governs all the components of our politics. If there is any accepted norm of proper conduct in our government, it is to be discovered here, in the American Constitution.

It is of course possible to argue that the American Constitution should *not* be the norm of our political conduct—and a number of people from varying perspectives have made just such an argument. But so long as we have the Constitution and a system of laws assertedly constructed under its aegis, everyone acknowledges that it is supposed to be the standard of official conduct, and is thus to provide the benchmark by which degrees of political deviance can be measured. For those who would understand the ebb and flow of American politics, the Constitution is the obvious starting point.

In seeking recourse to this standard, Americans in one respect at least are especially fortunate: There is nothing esoteric about the matter. The Constitution and the literature explaining it are all available on the open record, and may be examined by anyone who can read the English language and has entree to a reasonably well-stocked library. The literature is, of course, rather extensive, so many people do not get very far into it. Nonetheless it is accessible, and it is written in intelligible language, which means that anyone who wants to take the trouble can easily discover the intentions of our founders.

First Principles of the Founders

America's founders, whatever else they may have been, were not anarchists. They held that government was a necessary institution in the affairs of men, since it was needed to provide for the common defense and to maintain a regime of internal order that would permit its citizens to go in safety about their business. Performance of these functions, as the founders saw it, was a necessary precondition of a free society, and to this end they believed that a common government was required for the United States. Their object was to devise a political system that had sufficient authority to perform these basic tasks, but would be so constrained and limited in the reach of its power that it would not become a hazard to the freedoms it was instituted to protect.

This dual emphasis on personal freedom and the limitation of power to ensure the continuance of such freedom marks the entire formative period of American politics—including the pre-Revolutionary epoch, the Revolution itself, and the constitutional aftermath. From their colonial background with its continual stress on charter rights (by which the English government conferred title to the American lands), their British common law heritage as "free-born Englishmen," and their reliance on the higher law as descendants of the Puritan settlers, the founders derived not only their general notions of government, but very specific ideas about the way in which affairs of state should be conducted. These conceptions came together in climactic synthesis in the Philadelphia convention of 1787.

First and foremost in the founders' scheme of government was the idea of having a written instrument of authorization—a constitution. Such an instrument, it was believed, would provide a source of reference available to every citizen, make the scope of government powers plain beforehand, and provide a common benchmark of judgment thereafter. The instrument would define the total reach of governmental powers and, by implication at least, confirm the extent of the citizen's rights. Such a document, moreover, was essential to define the relationship of the several parts of the government to one another. This preference for written instruments was a double inheritance of the founders—deriving from their background in British common law and from their Puritan forebears in America who insisted on commonly available public authority as "men of the Book"—that is, of Scripture.

A second major feature of the founders' design was what might be described as its anti-majoritarianism. While they believed in the ultimate authority of the people, they also feared the notion that a majority in the legislature might be able to do whatever it wished. Such an arrangement, they believed, would be hostile to stable government and would endanger the rights of the minority. They therefore stressed the need for limits on what the Congress could do at any given time, built non-popular as well as popular elements into the government, and tried to impede the action of temporarily impassioned majorities. In this sense, their view was "republican" rather than "democratic," and as Lord Acton observed, "the views of pure democracy . . . were almost entirely unrepresented in that convention." [1]

In service to these ideas, the founders introduced a third major feature into their deliberations, a feature that may be de-

scribed as the leading principle of the whole experiment. This was
the separation and subdivision of power—parceling out the several elements of authority among different branches and extensions
of government so that no single branch could exercise despotic
authority. Insistence on this principle is by far the most pervasive
feature of our constitutional literature, expressed by nearly all the
participants and subject to endless modifications. No doctrine was
more familiar to the founders than John Adams' assertion that a
republic was "a government whose sovereignty was vested in more
than one person." [2] Indeed, James Madison called it "the sacred
doctrine of free government." [3]

The founders' thinking was influenced by, but not limited to,
the theories then prevalent in Western political writing—most
notably the works of William Paley and Baron Montesquieu. The
central teaching of these theoreticians, allegedly based on British
practice (but, as we shall see, something rather different), was
the tripartite character of governmental power: the legislative, the
executive, and the judicial. It was believed that governing authority
divided quite naturally into these three categories, and that each
in carrying out its natural functions would act as a counterpoise
against the others. If any one of them sought to get out of line, it
would bump up against another element of public authority that
had both motive and means for imposing restraints. Such is the
essential theory of checks and balances.

Accordingly, the tripartite division was written into the Constitution: a Supreme Court of the United States, a presidential
executive, and a national legislature. Each had a defined area of
responsibility, and each as well had an interlocking restraint on
the others—in some cases explicit, in others inferred from the
general design. Congress, for example, had participatory authority
in the conduct of presidential business: advice and consent in the
making of treaties, the appointment of cabinet members and ambassadors, and the approval of Supreme Court nominees. The
President in turn had veto power over legislation passed by the
Congress, which could be overridden only by a two-thirds vote
in both houses. The President and Congress together exercised
considerable authority over the Supreme Court through the
appointment process, and Congress had further power affecting

the courts through its ability to create inferior Federal courts (only the Supreme Court has original constitutional status) and to limit the appellate jurisdiction of the Supreme Court itself.

So much is explicit. The most important of the inferential restraints is that of judicial review, exercised by the Supreme Court with respect to acts of Congress and actions by the executive—a power not spelled out in the Constitution but simply asserted by John Marshall as the first chief justice. The power has been employed at different periods both to impede far-reaching social change (as in the epoch of the New Deal) and to advance it (as in the era of Earl Warren). It has in consequence been vigorously challenged by political theoreticians of both conservative and liberal persuasions unhappy with decisions of the court. Since it is not spelled out in the Constitution, the point is certainly arguable, and we may question various uses to which the power has been put.

These conceptions, moreover, were just the beginning. Not only were three branches of government established, but in keeping with the founders' republican notions these branches embraced distinctive principles of representation. The legislature itself was divided into two houses—only one of which, as it developed, was to be selected by direct popular vote. The President was to be chosen by a species of indirect election. And the court was not to be elected at all, but was to be appointed by the President and approved by the upper (non-popular) chamber of the legislature. All this testifies to the truth of Acton's observation, suggesting how far removed were the founders' intentions from ideas of "pure democracy." And all this refinement, balancing, and complication, remarkably enough, were just preliminary to the *real* complexity that the founders proceeded to build into their system.

Constitutional Complexity: States' Rights and Federalism

Up to this point the efforts of the founders had corresponded rather closely to their English background and their theoretical understanding of constitutional principle. If the matter had simply been theoretical in character, their labors might well have ended with the design sketched out above. They faced, however, a real-world situation that had to be dealt with if the new government was to come into being. For these were deliberations not simply of a single nation, but of thirteen separate and frequently jealous sovereignties—the thirteen original colonies, which were by treaty settlement distinct and individual nations in their own right. Each had come to the constitutional convention as a nation at international law, and could be made a part of the general design only by its own consent. This consideration introduced into the proceedings in Philadelphia the master complexity of them all.

The convention was not divided by ideologies or even regional associations so much as it was divided between the representatives of the large and small states. The larger states such as Massachusetts, Virginia, and Pennsylvania were rather sanguine about the prospects for a single American government and not very apprehensive about what might come of it. As the major powers in the new confederation, they had every reason for optimism. Representatives of the smaller states, however, took a different view of the matter. Delaware and Connecticut and other smaller states had reason to fear that in a national consolidation they would be "swallowed up" by their comparatively enormous neighbors. They would not consent to union unless they received some ironclad assurances.

To bring the smaller states into the new government, it was necessary for the convention to make numerous concessions to the idea of reserved state powers—states' rights, as we call them today. The crucial compromise of the convention occurred when it was decided by a narrow vote that the upper chamber of the Federal Congress would be chosen by the states themselves, with each state having an equal vote irrespective of population size. This principle of state equality was double-riveted into the Constitution by the provision in Article V, pertaining to amendments, that "no state, without its consent, shall be deprived of its equal suffrage in the Senate."

In the course of the ratification struggle, it was established that the states would retain the original powers they possessed under the Articles of Confederation, dealing with most of the ordinary concerns of day-to-day government, while the new central authority would confine itself chiefly to international dealings, military affairs, foreign commerce, and certain specified internal matters that were beyond the competence of the states. This understanding was written into the Tenth Amendment of the Bill of Rights.

The Tenth Amendment, which has been greatly disparaged in recent years, was crucial to the success of the Constitution. It put the states' rights emphasis very plainly, asserting that "the powers not delegated to the United States by the Constitution, nor prohibited by it to the states, are reserved to the states respectively, or to the people." A majority of the states ratifying the constitution insisted on some such formulation as a necessary precondition of their assent. It was intended as a rule of construction by which doubtful areas of authority could be interpreted. Where an issue was in question, that is, the rule suggested the presumption was in favor of the states.

The point was clearly driven home by Madison, the acknowledged "father of the Constitution," in *Federalist* No. 45. "The powers delegated by the proposed Constitution to the federal government," he said, "are few and defined. Those which are to remain in the state governments are numerous and indefinite. The former will be exercised principally on external objects, as war, peace, negotiation, and foreign commerce; with which last the power of taxation will, for the most part, be connected. The powers reserved to the several states will extend to all the objects which, in the ordinary course of affairs, concern the lives, liberties, and properties of the people, and the internal order, improvement, and prosperity of the state." [4] *

It is this *federal* element in our system, this sharing of authority by the central government and the states, that makes it so much more intricate than the English—even if our standard is the British constitution prior to the rise of parliamentary absolutism.

---

* The identical view was stressed, at least for purposes of the ratification debate, by Alexander Hamilton. "An entire consolidation of the states into one complete sovereignty," he wrote, "would imply an entire subordination of the parts; and whatever powers might remain in them, would be altogether dependent on the general will. But as the plan of the convention aims only at a partial union or consolidation, the state governments would clearly retain all the rights of sovereignty which they before had, and which were not, by that act, *exclusively* delegated to the United States." (Italics added.)

There can be no adequate appraisal of American government without recognizing this fact, without understanding that the states were the principal agents in founding the republic and maintaining its prolonged prosperity. The tension between local and general authorities, the diffusion of power, the necessity of a written constitution and of a pronounced legalism in weighing duties and prerogatives—all these ingredients of American liberty are strongly rooted in the institutions of federalism.

Finally, the founders closed the circle of complexities by interfusing the state governments into the operation of the central government itself—not only in the functioning of the Senate, but in the method of electing the President. Each state, it was decided, would choose a body of electors equal to its number of representatives in Congress—congressmen plus senators. The presidency would be decided by a majority of these electoral votes. This provision, in keeping with the founders' "republican" notions, further enhanced the authority of the states: it made them the intermediaries through which the popular will was to be filtered; and by awarding every state at least three electoral votes (two senators plus at least one representative), it strengthened the position of the states as such in the method of presidential selection.

Many other observations might be made about our "compound federal republic" as it emerged from the Philadelphia convention and the ratification process, some of which will concern us at a later stage of our narrative. For the moment, however, the point is simply to bring out as clearly as possible the immense complexity and balance of the American constitutional design, the importance of the federal element, and the intricate relationships among the several components of the system. The total effect was admirably described by John Adams in a letter to John Taylor of Caroline in 1814:

> Is there a constitution on record more complicated with balances than ours? [In the first place] eighteen states and some territories are balanced against the national government. . . . In the second place, the House of Representatives is balanced against the Senate and the Senate against the House. In the third place, the executive authority is in some degree balanced against the legislative. In the fourth place the

judiciary power is balanced against the House, the Senate, the executive power, and the state governments. In the fifth place, the Senate is balanced against the President in all appointments to office and in all treaties. This, in my opinion is not merely a useless but a very pernicious—balance. In the sixth place, the people hold in their own hands the balance against their own representatives by biennial which I wish had been annual elections. In the seventh place, the legislatures of the several states are balanced against the Senate by sextennial actions. In the eighth place, the electors are balanced against the people in the choice of the President. And here is a complication and refinement of balances which for anything I recollect is an invention of our own and peculiar to us.[5]

The Basis of the Complex Design

While a number of these balances have not survived and others did not work out as the founders expected, we may in general agree with Adams' description of the settlement. For balances within balances and counterpoises at every turn, there is hardly anything to compare with it in the annals of constitution-making. When we reflect that the men who drew up this design were hard-headed, practical men of affairs, involved in the very immediate business of fashioning workable institutions, we must naturally ask ourselves what might have been the point and object of all this complexity. And the answer to that question is as plain and simple as the design is intricate and complicated.

Quite clearly, our founders *feared the concentration of governmental power,* and were concerned to prevent any single man or group of men from accumulating authority that could endanger the freedom of the citizen. They had, after all, only lately emerged from a painful war of independence that had as its object freedom from interference by a distant center of governmental power. They were not eager to replace the untrammeled authority of London with another such authority of their own devising. They therefore sought to apply everything they knew about government and all the lessons they had learned from experience to the job of constructing the new republic. Specifically, they sought to avoid unilateral and unappealable actions by distant powers, government decisions that were quick and sweeping, and sudden assaults by "democratic" or other enthusiasts on the rights of the individual.

They were not pristine advocates of *laissez faire;* indeed, the finer modulations of that particular creed were little understood at the time the Constitution was written. But they were obvious libertarians, believing in the primacy of the individual and the need for limitations on the power of government. So much is manifest from their general design and from their numerous statements during the epoch of the Revolution and in the constitutional convention itself.

To reiterate, the founders looked upon the institution of government as a necessary evil. They saw it as an agency required by the nature of man to suppress disorder and maintain the peace. In more modern language, they believed that government was a *defensive* institution, required to neutralize the aggressive use of force but otherwise quite limited in its competence and often dangerous. The darker nature of man required the existence of government, but it also required that government itself be jealously hedged with limitations.

Madison gave the matter its classic formulation in *Federalist* No. 51, discussing the need for checks and balances. "It may be a reflection on human nature," he said, "that such devices should be necessary to control the abuses of government. But what is government itself but the greatest of all reflections on human nature? If angels were to govern men, neither external nor internal controls on government would be necessary. In framing a government which is to be administered by men over men, the great difficulty lies in this; you must first enable the government to control the governed; and in the next place oblige it to control itself." [6]

In keeping with this dual imperative, the object of the American constitutional settlement was to provide a government sufficiently vigorous to perform the necessary order-keeping functions of civil society yet sufficiently limited to safeguard the liberties of its citizens. The object of the Federal government, in particular, was to handle those defensive, order-keeping functions that were truly national in scope, surpassing the competence of the several states. Chief among these was the function of national defense, although the inventory of powers also included the ability to regulate foreign and interstate commerce, establish post offices and post roads, and adjudicate differences among the states.* Not, as noted, a *laissez-faire* conception (which would dictate free trade both overseas and between the states), but very much a limited-government, defensive conception.

The resulting norms of conduct for the American government are both affirmative and negative. That is, there are certain things that government is supposed to do—provide for national defense or prevent dispute among the states—and there are certain things it is *not* supposed to do—infringe on free speech or control the press. The various levels of government must perform their essential order-keeping tasks in proper fashion if the citizen is to be defended from incursions of violence and other disorders at home and abroad. At the same time these various levels of government must stay within their constitutional bounds if the citizen is not to be victimized by government itself. Violation of the constitutional norm is usually discussed in cases falling into the second category —for example, when government interferes with freedom of speech or throws someone in jail unjustly. But it is important for a balanced understanding to note that the purposes of the constitutional system can also be negated by government's failure to do the things it is supposed to do.

This intricate design, needless to remark, has been subject to many batterings. Fearsome battles were waged over the scope and plenitude of Federal powers—the Kentucky and Virginia Resolutions, which raised the prospect of state "interposition" against a Federal law; the Louisiana Purchase, which stretched the authority of the executive; the War Between the States, which settled the issue of secession. Yet, through it all, the design proved tough and durable. One hundred years after the drafting of the Constitution, the essential concept was remarkably similar to the system described in *The Federalist,* and the central government

---

* This conception was not limited to such republicans as Thomas Jefferson and James Madison, as is shown in the discussion offered by Hamilton, an ardent proponent of centralization, in *Federalist* No. 23. "The principal purposes to be answered by union," Hamilton wrote, "are these—the common defense of the members; the preservation of the public peace, as well against internal convulsions as external attacks; the regulation of commerce with other nations and between the states; the superintendence of our intercourse, political and commercial, with foreign countries."

remained comparatively modest in the reach of its authority. The description provided by British historian James Bryce late in the nineteenth century suggests how little the structure had been altered despite the upheavals of the preceding decades:

> An American may, through a long life, never be reminded of the Federal government, except when he votes at presidential and congressional elections, lodges a complaint against the post-office, and opens his trunks for a custom-house officer on the pier at New York when he returns from Europe. His direct taxes are paid to officials acting under state laws. The state, or local authority constituted by state statutes, regulates his birth, appoints his guardian, pays for his schooling, gives him a share in the estate of his father deceased, licenses him when he enters a trade (if it be one needing a license), marries him, divorces him, declares him a bankrupt, hangs him for murder. The police that guard his house, the local boards which look after the poor, control highways, impose water rates, manage schools,—all these derive their legal powers from his state alone. Looking at this immense compass of state functions, Jefferson would seem to have been not far from wrong when he said that the Federal government was nothing more than the American department of foreign affairs.[7] *

Today we may still recognize a number of features described in this passage—and that, too, is testimony to the resiliency of the system. Yet we notice, even more, the changes; various functions depicted here as pertaining solely to the state—schools, highways, the conduct of local trade, the application of the criminal

* A decade later, on the analysis of John W. Burgess of Columbia University, the situation had not changed appreciably. Describing the American system as of 1898, Burgess gave these as the leading characteristics of our national theory and practice: ". . . the doctrine of individual immunity against governmental power, the principle of the widest possible scope for free action on the part of the individual and of strict limitation in behalf of such action upon the powers of government . . . the requirement that local government shall have the maximum powers which it is capable of exercising, and . . . that it shall be the recipient of residuary powers. . . ." (*Recent Changes in American Constitutional Theory*, Columbia University Press, 1933, pp. 3, 6.)

law—are deeply affected by a Federal interest. Certainly it would be inaccurate to say, now that another hundred years have past, that the Federal government is merely our department of foreign affairs, or that it occupies the modest niche described by Madison in the eighteenth century or Bryce in the nineteenth. Our own particular century has brought a momentous transformation. How and why this change has come about will be considered next.

The Destruction
of the American
Design

If the major object of the founders was to establish limits on the reach of governmental power, the major object of modern liberals may be described as the removal of those limits.

American liberals have had and still have many other goals, of course, some of which run contrary to the general tendency. There has always been a counterpoint of limited-government verbiage in the liberal presentation, and the recent thrust of political events in Indochina and at the Watergate has provoked a renewal of liberal talk about the need to limit government power. The fact remains, however, that the prime objective of American liberalism over the past four decades has been the removal of constitutional limits to the exercise of political authority.

The Liberal Mind Set

Contrary to statements of Professor Schapiro, modern liberalism does *not* profess an "unshaken belief in the necessity of freedom to achieve every desirable aim." It would be far more accurate to

33

say that, with occasional exceptions, the modern liberal is profoundly distrustful of individual freedom and of arrangements arrived at through voluntary action. He believes that patterns of human behavior under such arrangements are usually wrong, harmful, stupid, or malicious, and that they should be prevented by the constant and pervasive attention of the government.

This fact is obvious enough to anyone who reflects on the general drift of American politics. It is difficult to think of a single problem area in our economic life to which the liberal response is not a demand for government intervention. If there be inflation, the liberal calls for wage and price controls. If we confront an energy crisis, the obvious answer is to regulate the relevant industries. If consumers want better products, establish a consumer czar with sweeping regulatory powers. If urban problems plague us, we need bigger and better Federal subsidies. Whatever the trouble, real or imagined, the reflexive liberal answer is to put more power into the hands of government.

That this has been the predominant liberal view for a period of decades is readily apparent from the political record. The writings of the most noted and respected liberal spokesmen reveal a profound mistrust of unhindered individual action, and yield repeated statements that a system of volitional exchange is destructive, both socially and economically. On countless occasions the liberal sages have stressed the need to put the values of the group above the freedom of the person.

A common theme in such discussions is the idea that individual liberty in economic matters might have been all right for the era of the founders, but is *passé* in a modern industrial society. We are continually instructed that economic conditions have changed, and that because of this alteration our views on individual liberty must change as well. Most liberal preachments urging the devaluation of individual freedom press hard on this theme, suggesting the manner in which historical relativism may lend itself to antilibertarian uses.

Writing in 1929, liberal scholar John Dewey provided a typical synthesis of these notions. Dewey attacked the alleged delusion of supposing that "the pioneer gospel of personal initiative, enterprise, energy and reward could be maintained in an era of aggregated capital, of mass production and distribution, of impersonal ownership and of ownership divorced from management." Changing economic conditions, according to Dewey, made traditional notions of liberty obsolete. In particular, depressions and unemployment were "a confession of the breakdown of unregulated individualistic industry conducted for private profit," while "the scandal of private appropriation of socially produced values in unused land cannot forever remain concealed." [1]

In offering this denunciation of unregulated private decision, Dewey gave utterance to a view widely held by liberals. It may be said, indeed, to be the characteristic liberal opinion on matters of economics. Compare, for example, the judgment offered by another liberal academic spokesman, historian Charles Beard, in 1931:

> The cold truth is that the individualist creed of everybody for himself and the devil take the hindmost is principally responsible for the distress in which Western civilization finds itself—with investment racketeering at one end and labor racketeering at the other. Whatever merits the creed may have had in days of primitive agriculture and industry, it is not applicable in an age of technology, science, and rationalized economy. Once useful, it has become a danger to society. . . . [2]

The conclusion drawn by Dewey and Beard, and many other prominent liberals, was that the "chaos" of individual decision must be replaced with a system of economic planning. Americans, according to Dewey, were victims of a "national habit of planlessness in social affairs," and it was time we developed a more systematic approach. In place of our individualistic economy, we must have planning to assert the "social interest":

> A coordinating and directive council in which captains of industry met with representatives of labor and public officials to plan the regulation of industrial activity would signify that we had entered constructively and voluntarily upon the road which Soviet Russia is traveling with so much attendant de-

struction and coercion. . . . In a society so rapidly becoming corporate, there is need of associated thought to take account of the realities of the situation and to frame policies in the social interest. Only then can organized action in behalf of the social interest be made a reality. We are in for some kind of socialism, call it by whatever name we please, and no matter what it will be called when it is realized. Economic determinism is now a fact, not a theory.[3]

Attitudes of this sort were frequently affirmed by counselors to Franklin D. Roosevelt, and became an important part of the official ideology when he ascended to power. Roosevelt was an eclectic without a systematic philosophy, so it would be wrong to suggest he was much of a collectivist planner himself. But his regime gave lodgment to those who were, and they managed to promote their ideas quite widely as a result. Among the most ambitious of the planners was a Columbia University professor, Rexford Guy Tugwell, who made no bones about the system he had in mind or what it meant for individual freedom:

The intention of 18th and 19th century law was to install and protect the principle of conflict; this, if we begin to plan, we shall be changing once for all, and it will require the laying of rough, unholy hands on many a sacred precedent, doubtless calling on an enlarged and nationalized police power for enforcement. We shall also have to give up a distinction of great consequence, and very dear to a legalistic heart, but economically quite absurd, between private and public or quasi-public employments. *There is no private business, if by that we mean one of no consequence to anyone but its proprietors; and so none exempt from compulsion to serve a planned public interest.*[4] [Italics added.]

That chill attitude toward the liberties of individual businessmen might be subjected to prolonged analysis in its own right. In particular, the notion that no business is "private" which in any way affects anyone but the immediate proprietors quite plainly threatens every type of liberty—including liberty of speech. Every form of volition, of course, has *some* effect on somebody else, if only indirect, and were this standard adopted across the board no conceivable aspect of our lives would be exempt from "compulsion to serve a planned public interest."

If we leave the epoch of the New Deal and come forward to our own time, we find the notions spelled out by Dewey, Beard, and Tugwell persisting as the major themes of liberal discourse. In 1958, for example, economist John Kenneth Galbraith brought out a volume called *The Affluent Society,* in which he argued that private interests were gobbling up America's resources and starving "the public sector" into oblivion. He has followed up this volume with two others (*The New Industrial State* and *Economics and the Public Purpose*) in which he plays variations on the original theme, though always to the same effect.

In all these writings, Galbraith recites, somewhat allusively, what purport to be facts about the American economy, usually sorted out in terms of inequality of performance or funding. On the one hand, he says, we have old and overcrowded schools, inadequate housing for poor people, terrible transportation systems, filthy streets, polluted air, and dubious medical services—to name a few. On the other hand, we have an enormous gross national product and a burgeoning output of consumer goods such as automobiles, television sets, soaps, deodorants, beer, and other products less important than the services we are neglecting.

The problem is symbolized, Galbraith says, by "the family which takes its mauve and cerise, air-conditioned, power-steered and power-braked automobile out for a tour" and "passes through cities that are badly paved, made hideous by litter, blighted buildings, billboards, and posts for wires that long since should have been put underground. . . ." Such people "picnic on exquisitely packaged food from a portable icebox by a polluted stream and go on to spend the night at a park which is a menace to public health and morals. Just before dozing off on an air mattress, beneath a nylon tent, amid the stench of decaying refuse, they may reflect vaguely on the curious unevenness of their blessings." [5]

What was required, according to *The Affluent Society,* was vigorous government action to reorder American priorities, suppress the greed of private interests, and shore up the public sector

38

with infusions of tax money. Galbraith's subsequent works elaborate these theories, arguing that large corporations have come
to dominate our economy and that their power must be countered
by the systematic compulsions of government. In his latest volume,
Galbraith pushes this analysis to the limit and says that nothing
will do but for the United States to accept the inevitability of
socialism that circumstance has thrust upon us.

"The new socialism," he writes, "allows of no acceptable alter-
natives; it cannot be escaped except at the price of grave discomfort, considerable social disorder, and, on occasion, lethal damage
to health and well-being. The new socialism is not ideological; it
is compelled by circumstance"—the crucial circumstance being
"the retarded development of the market system. There are industries here which require technical competence, related organization
and market power and related command over resource use if they
are to render minimally adequate service. Being and remaining in
the market system, these they do not have." [6]

There are a number of responses that might be made to this
analysis, foremost among them being that the "facts" Galbraith
invokes to prove his case on housing, transit, education, and health
care, are supremely unfactual. These subjects will be examined
in some detail in later chapters. For here and now, however, it is
enough to note the steady drift of his opinions—the pervasive
bias against private decision, the urge to increase the power of
government, and the final embrace of explicit socialism, albeit
"new socialism," as an alleged cure for what ails us. Here is devotion to personal liberty indeed.*

* The careful reader will perhaps have glimpsed another discrepancy. In
  Galbraith's original analysis, the problem with our "retarded" services was
  that they were consigned to government, and therefore starved for funding.
  In the later analysis, the reason given for retardation is that the services
  are in the market (that is, essentially private) system—thus allegedly showing the incompetence of free enterprise. Oddly enough, the industries and
  services sorted out in this way are in several cases the same—most notably,
  housing and medicine.
     We are thus successively invited to believe that services are retarded
  (1) because they are run by government, and (2) because they are not run
  by government, the answer in either case being vastly to increase the funding and authority of government. One may be forgiven for concluding that

Galbraith's division of economic society into a disgustingly opulent private sector and a deserving but withered public sector entered fully into the stream of modish liberal opinion in the 1960s, and supplied the premise for many a learned essay and oration. One of his imitators on this score was Harvard colleague Arthur M. Schlesinger, Jr., who prepared a memorandum on the evils of private greed for the edification of John F. Kennedy during the 1960 presidential election. These notions became a *leitmotif* of Kennedy's rhetorical thrusts about getting America out of its lethargy and moving forward to the better tomorrow.

In his memo, Schlesinger said that "while consumer goods pour out of our ears, while our cars grow long and our kitchens shinier and gadgets and gimmicks overflow our closets and our attics, the public framework of society, on which everything else rests, is overstrained by population growth and falls into disrepair." From these and other somber data, it was to Schlesinger apparent that "private interests and the public interest often come into harsh conflict. The test will lie in willingness to take on the private interests whose aggressive pursuit of their own advantage imperils the general welfare. . . . The assertion of the public interest will mean, in particular, a determination to prevent special interests from absorbing the communal surplus which ought to be dedicated to communal, not to private purposes." [7]

A few years later, the identical theme was sounded by another liberal spokesman already quoted—former Senator Clark of Pennsylvania—who came at the matter from the angle of employment. In Clark's opinion, our national job priorities were slanted in the wrong direction, toward trivial consumer goods or useless pleasures rather than toward the things that really mattered. He wondered, therefore, how we could get "young people trained and on the way to where they are really needed. How can we get more and better teachers, scientists, priests, politicians, rabbis, ministers and social workers? To get them we will have to settle for fewer brewers, night-club proprietors and lobbyists." [8]

What is noteworthy about these opinions from our modern

Galbraith has begun with the last-named point as a fixed assumption, and then set to work to see how many different explanations he could invent to support it.

liberals is how little they differ from what we were hearing forty or fifty years ago. The world has turned over many times since Lucky Lindy traversed the Atlantic, Babe Ruth called his shot, and the likes of Dewey and Holmes bestrode the intellectual universe. But the essence of liberal politics remains, in this particular if not in others, exactly as it was. In their preference for public employment and their attitude of menace toward private institutions, the statements of Schlesinger, Clark, and Galbraith are indistinguishable from the fustian of the New Deal era.

As the diagnosis remains the same, so does the cure: We must replace the "chaos" of private decision with rational economic planning—directed, of course, by government. The formula provided by Dewey and Tugwell back in the 1920s and 1930s has been repeated with amazing fidelity into our own era by all the reigning spokesmen for the liberal creed. From the liberal gurus encamped along the Charles River in Cambridge, Mass., to the veriest spear-carrier in the local chapter of the ADA, the faith in "planning" continues unabated.

Compare Tugwell's utterance of 1932, for example, with this 1963 statement by the late Walter Reuther, a major influence in the ADA, and an authentic liberal power in the world of elective politics: ". . . it is highly unrealistic to believe that one can find a rational way of harmonizing all the millions of private decisions flowing out of the exercise of power in the absence of some practical, workable democratic national planning agency. Therefore I believe we will eventually have to create some mechanism to bring a rational sense of direction into private decisions. It seems to me that only a national planning agency can provide this direction." [9]

Or, in similar vein, this statement by Americans for Democratic Action itself (in its 1964 platform): "The blind forces of the market place cannot be depended upon either to achieve full employment and vigorous economic growth or to direct economic resources in accordance with national priorities. For these purposes we need democratic national economic planning to evaluate our resources and our needs and to develop an order of priorities for the application of resources to our needs. . . ." [10] *

---

* Galbraith, for his part, informs us that we must "recognize the logic of planning with its resulting imperative of coordination. And government

I describe the persistence of such views as amazing because the intervening years have seen a fair amount of "planning," in fact as well as in the realm of theory, and the results have not been appetizing. The five-year plans of the Soviet Union and other collectivist societies have produced not only economic failure but incredible tableaux of human suffering. Yet the faith of the orthodox has continued, in many cases, undiminished—even down to citing the Soviet Union as an exemplar for America.*

An interesting feature of these discussions is the repeated suggestion that the liberal planners know what the people "need," even if the people themselves do not. Left to their own devices, supposedly, consumers will do stupid things like buying color TV sets, or beer, or cigarettes. They will pour their money into high-powered cars while neglecting to spend enough on universities or public parks. Or, in Senator Clark's scenario, they will choose

---

machinery must then be established to anticipate disparity and to ensure that growth in different parts of the economy is compatible. The latter on frequent occasion will require conservation—measures to reduce or eliminate the least socially urgent use. On other occasion it will require public steps to expand output. . . . There will have to be a public planning authority." (*Economics and the Public Purpose,* Houghton-Mifflin, 1973, p. 318.)

* Senator Clark has been a virtuoso on this theme. In a 1963 statement, Clark asserted that "they plan well in Russia. . . . There someone decides where little Ivan is going to work. If at the age of eleven he seems unresponsive, he goes back to the collective farm. If he shows promise, his education is continued at state expense. . . ." Why can't we do likewise, Clark wanted to know, using "persuasion" instead of compulsion? He wondered in particular "how we can use both the carrot and the stick to get these young people trained and on the way to where they are needed." This prospective use of carrot-and-stick to decide where people should be employed Clark described as "staffing freedom." ("Staffing Freedom," reprint from the National Civil Service League.)

Although Clark sounded a bit despondent about achieving the necessary planning to get people organized in the proper manner, he did see some affirmative elements in our situation. In an earlier article he had rejoiced over the general drift of American education, which he believed was preparing American youngsters for life in the planned society. "It is significant," he said, "that what used to be called 'history' is now 'social studies.' Spiritually and economically youth is conditioned to respond to a liberal program of orderly policing of society by government, subject to the popular will, in the interests of social justice." (*Atlantic Monthly,* July 1953.)

foolish jobs rather than sensible ones—a mistake the Soviets assertedly avoid with "little Ivan." In place of these unneeded things, the planners will give us what is truly "needed."

It takes only a little reflection to note that the issue of what is needed by somebody, beyond a certain threshold, is a rather "iffy" business. Who is to say a car or television set or detergent is less needed than the public spending projects preferred by Clark or Galbraith? One would suppose in a relativist world that conceptions of this type are hardly graven in stone. It is all, of course, highly subjective. So what we are really talking about is the desire of Clark or Schlesinger to make *his* subjective determination of what people "need" prevail above the determination of the people themselves.

All this implies, quite clearly, a considerable enlargement of government power. If we are to have the planning being talked of here, some authority must have the power to promulgate the plan and make it stick. It must be able to bring the dissidents in line and rearrange the pattern of choices that would be made through individual decision. Compulsory authority is needed to discipline the interests, and lay rough, unholy hands on sacred precedents.

We have noted Senator Clark's tough-sounding definition of "liberalism" as a view that favors government power in the interests of "social justice." A decade later he updated this sentiment with the assertion that "surely, we have reached the point where we can say, for our time at least, that Jefferson was wrong: Government is *not* best that governs least." [11] Suggesting Clark was by no means eccentric in offering this view is the similar statement of liberal scholar Robert Hutchins, who tells us "the notion that that government is best which governs least is certainly archaic. Our object today should not be to weaken government in competition with other centers of power, but rather to strengthen it as the agency charged with responsibility for the common good." [12]

Thus the liberalism that started out as a limited-government phenomenon has become, in economic matters, exactly the reverse. (We shall consider noneconomic freedoms at a later point in our narrative.) The change, we are told, is regrettable but necessary. Under rustic conditions we could afford a system of limited government and individual freedom. But under the stress of modern economic and technological change we require a government that is powerful and vigorous, that can coordinate matters, and that is generally capable of handling the problems of this century. We must therefore switch over to a regime of top-down Federal planning.*

So much, to the liberal intellect, seems obvious. There is, however, a bit of a problem. It may be clear to all right-minded liberals that the economic stresses of the modern era call for centralized and very powerful government, but the same had not been clear at all to the founders of the United States. The founders, on liberal premises, had been sadly lacking in foresight. They had left us this eighteenth century Constitution which, in its general design and several particulars, was intended to forestall the very concentration of power that the march of events so urgently required.†

* Schlesinger puts it this way:

> American anti-statism was the function of a particular economic order. Jefferson had dreamed of a nation of small freeholders and virtuous artisans, united by a sturdy independence, mutual respect and the ownership of property. Obviously strong government would be superfluous in Arcadia. But the industrial revolution changed all that. The corporation began to impersonalize the economic order. It removed the economy, in other words, from the control of a personal code and delivered it to agencies with neither bodies to be kicked nor souls to be damned. . . .
>
> The state consequently had to expand its authority in order to preserve the ties which hold society together. The history of governmental intervention has been the history of the growing ineffectiveness of the private conscience as a means of social control. The only alternative is the growth of the public conscience, whose natural expression is the democratic government. [*The Vital Center,* Houghton Mifflin, 1962, p. 176.]

† "We have," notes Senator Clark, "inherited from our forefathers a governmental structure which so divides power that effective dealing with economic problems is cumbersome. Local, state, and national governments each have their responsibility in housing and urban renewal, in the appropriate uses of water, in transportation, labor-management relations, and education. . . . At each level, the responsibility for appropriate action is divided between the executive and the legislature, and the judiciary is prepared to step in at a moment's notice to declare unconstitutional whatever notion the other two may decide upon." Under the circumstances, he sighs, it is a miracle we get things done at all. (*Challenges To Democracy,* Frederick A. Praeger, 1964, pp. 104–05.)

How Liberals Enlarged Federal Powers

If all that planning was to occur on schedule, it was necessary to figure out some method of getting around the founders' complexities and limitations, and across the decades a number of subtle minds have devoted themselves to this important mission. The struggle to secure enlargement of Federal powers has gone through a number of phases, which for want of an accepted terminology will here be labeled the subliminal, the explicit, and the brazen. These phases are not mutually exclusive, of course, and are quite capable of operating simultaneously. Yet they are distinguishable.

At the first or subliminal level, the liberal effort has been and continues to be an attempt to find the requisite powers *within* the Constitution—by seeking out selected phrases that can be interpreted as conferring plenary powers on the Federal government. Most favored by the centralizing interest from the time of Hamilton on has been the phraseology in Article I, Section 8, wherein Congress is given "power to lay and collect taxes to provide for the common defence and general welfare of the United States," "to regulate commerce . . . among the several states," and "to make all laws which shall be necessary and proper for carrying into execution the foregoing powers. . . ."

In this group of phrases, it has been argued, may be found all the powers necessary to put the planning state into effect. Under the general welfare clause, Congress may enact all sorts of public subsidies and controls, engage in business enterprises, conduct vast programs of Federal aid, dispense medical services, build housing, and what-not. Under the commerce clause, it is deemed to have powers to set wages and hours, regulate businesses, cartelize transportation, fix prices, establish regulations, control rents, and so on. All that is needed is to take particular phrases here and there and interpret them as sweeping grants of power.*

---

* Undoubted master of this sort of reasoning was liberal historian Irving Brant, who went so far as to suggest that, through the commerce clause alone, the Federal government could do whatever it wished. "What could be done," Brant asked himself in 1936, "under a power to establish government monopolies in trade and commerce? Anything . . . it would per-

By gradual stages these arguments have suffused the decisions of the Supreme Court, permitting expansion of Federal power in almost every direction. In 1936, for example, the court turned up with a latitudinarian reading of "general welfare," asserting that "the power of Congress to authorize expenditure of public moneys for public purposes is not limited by the direct grants of legislative power found in the Constitution." [13] The next year it affirmed that the choice of such expenditure was almost wholly within the discretion of Congress.

Soon the floodgates were really opened. In 1937 the court construed "interstate commerce" as anything that remotely affected the flow of business, whether it actually crossed state lines or not. Next "due process" as a barrier to regulation was disposed of. By 1941 the court discovered the Tenth Amendment was a meaningless truism, and by 1942 it was affirming that the Federal government could regulate whatever it subsidized. Since by previous rulings the government could subsidize almost anything, common logic suggested it could therefore regulate almost anything.

Such rulings would have been sufficient to transform our limited-government system into its own negation, but for good measure there have been added as well the direct and explicit regulatory powers asserted under the Fourteenth Amendment, which has in recent years become the sovereign instrument of centralization.* By means of the Fourteenth Amendment the Federal government over the past two decades has intervened in matters of education, prayer in the schools, conduct of the criminal law, reapportionment of state legislatures, pornography, and several other matters once held to be within the competence of the states and now staked out as Federal jurisdictions.†

---

mit the erection of a completely socialized state." (*Storm Over the Constitution*, Bobbs-Merrill, 1936, pp. 134–35.)

* This amendment says, among other things, that no state shall "make or enforce any law which shall abridge the privileges or immunities of citizens of the United States; nor shall any state deprive any person of life, liberty, or property without due process of law; nor deny to any person within its jurisdiction the equal protection of the laws."

† Conservative justices of the early part of this century bear a considerable responsibility for this development, since they freely used the Fourteenth Amendment as a device for overturning industrial regulations enacted by the states.

Through these openings, the liberals have requested, and the Supreme Court has by degrees affirmed, extension of Federal authority into every zone and echelon of American life. Since the Supreme Court has approved it all, this studied conversion of our limited-government system into its opposite can be presented as a perfectly normal and justifiable series of actions. The circle is squared, and negation of the Constitution's central precepts is rendered "constitutional."

Yet this ingenious achievement, by itself, rests a bit uneasily. The founders' stated intentions, after all, make it rather clear that the job of centralization, however cleverly one works the phrases, is contrary to the real design. As Madison quite logically inquired (concerning "general welfare"), what sense would it make to construct a limited and balanced system, with a painstaking distribution and enumeration of powers, if a single phrase or sentence conferred enormous plenary powers to do virtually anything? Obviously, not much.

The founders' intentions, in sum, were a standing rebuke, and so long as people could read the English language and had access to the records, the discrepancy would continue to suggest itself. And that was annoying. It was therefore needful to go another step—to move beyond the subliminal alteration of the Constitution and tackle the problem somewhat more openly. The founders' intentions, quite simply, had to be disposed of.

Here, as in other cases, the theory of value relativity stands the liberals in good stead. On liberalism's basic premises, after all, there are no universals that persist over time, no axioms of belief impervious to the flow of circumstance. As conditions change, so do our attitudes and values. It follows that the American Constitution would have to change as well—that its "meaning" would have to be different in the twentieth century from what it was perceived to be in the eighteenth.

Justice Oliver Wendell Holmes was an eloquent spokesman for the crystallized essence of these arguments—the doctrine of the "living Constitution." As he put it in *Missouri v. Holland* (1920), "when we are dealing with words that also are a constituent act, like the Constitution of the United States, we must realize that they have called into life a being the development of which could not have been foreseen completely by the most gifted of its begetters." [14] The Constitution had to be defined from epoch to epoch, according to the flux of circumstance.*

Justice Felix Frankfurter made the point with even greater clarity. The words of the Constitution, Frankfurter said in 1940, are "so unrestricted by their intrinsic meaning or by their history or by tradition or by prior decisions that they leave the individual justice free, if indeed they do not compel him, to gather meaning not from reading the Constitution but from reading life. . . . Members of the court are frequently admonished by their associates not to read their economic and social views into the neutral language of the Constitution. But the process of constitutional interpretation compels the translation of policy into judgment. . . ." [15]

The logic here is deeper and a bit more difficult, but adds up basically to a more sophisticated version of what was argued at the subliminal level: The Constitution's "meaning" is a product of economic and political forces of the age, and therefore changes as these forces change. One way or another, therefore, the conversion of our Constitution into its own negation is entirely proper, and nothing to worry about. The average citizen might find it a bit baffling, but he may rest assured the scholars and learned judges understand it very well. Everything remains perfectly "constitutional."

Occasionally, however, a franker appraisal is offered, lifting the argument from the merely explicit to the high plateau of the brazen. At this level, the liberal view is simply a bold assertion: We did it and we're glad. We found ourselves up against this old-fashioned Constitution, and we simply decided to dump it. We did what had to be done and we might as well admit as much. This third, and fundamentally most honest, of the liberal answers to whatever-happened-to-the-Constitution is presented with remarkable candor by Rexford Tugwell.

In a 1968 article, this veteran New Dealer reflected on the transformations that had come over the American government. Rehearsing themes already noted, he opined that American society

* While at this point I am merely expounding the liberal view rather than critiquing it, a passing observation may be in order, namely: If the Constitution is to be changed from age to age merely by interpretation, why does it contain within itself a rather elaborate process for formal amendment?

had changed enormously between the eighteenth century and the twentieth, but that our political institutions had not kept pace. "It was a genuinely different society," Tugwell said, "but it had the same Constitution. . . . The Constitution had been meant for an age not only with a different physical environment but with a different notion of men's relation to the government and to each other." The crux of this difference was, precisely, the question of limited government:

> The Constitution was a negative document, meant mostly to protect citizens from their government, not to define its duties to them or theirs to it. . . . It would have been thought fantastic to suggest that individuals ought to be made secure from the risks of their occupations or to be protected from the hazards of life. . . . The Founders lived in the age of Adam Smith's economics and Montesquieu's politics. Above all, men were to be free to do as they liked, and since the government was likely to intervene, and because prosperity was to be found in the free management of their affairs, a constitution was needed to prevent such intervention. . . . The law would maintain order, but would not touch the individual who behaved reasonably. He must pay taxes to support a smallish government, and he must not interfere with commerce; but otherwise laws would do him neither good nor ill. The government of the Constitution was this kind of government.[16]

Such a Constitution, according to Tugwell, was inappropriate to the times. In recognition of our altered situation, the government had assumed new responsibilities, asserting powers it hitherto had not possessed. It had seen to the requirements of stability, discipline, the curing of depressions, and "the expression of mutuality . . . through government." Such changes, in Tugwell's view, were altogether necessary, but certain problems had to be admitted:

> . . . No constitutional amendment had acknowledged the progression from competition to mutuality. None legitimized stability and discipline. To the extent that these new social

virtues developed, they were tortured interpretations of a document intended to prevent them. The government did accept
responsibility for individuals' well-being and it did interfere to
make secure. But it really had to be admitted that it was done
irregularly and according to doctrines the framers would have
rejected. Organization for these purposes was very inefficient
because they were not acknowledged intentions. Much of the
lagging and reluctance was owed to constantly reiterated intention that what was being done was in pursuit of the aims em-
bodied in the Constitution of 1787 when obviously it was in
contravention of them.[17]

This says it pretty well. While we may disagree with the
rationalizations provided for this condition and with Tugwell's
suggested remedy (a new constitution to fit our new practice), we
may fully agree with his description of the change itself. While
pretending to interpret and adhere to the principles of the founders,
the proponents of centralized power have effectively turned the
American Constitution inside-out.

3

The Power in the President

The latter 1960s and early 1970s were a time of trauma and confusion for Americans in general, and for American liberals devoted to big government in particular. The convulsion of Vietnam, the rigors of Watergate, and the resulting agonies of the Nixon administration were treated in the media as a major crisis for the nation and derivatively for the Republican Party—and they were all of that. Less noted, perhaps, was the fact that these historic events also signified a crucial watershed for American liberalism, a period of testing for its stated principles and favored political formulas.

Constant readers of the daily press need hardly be reminded that the years of the Vietnam-Nixon-Watergate furor found most American liberals aligned against the power of the presidency and in favor of an augmented role for Congress. Wherever one looked in political discourse he encountered the charge of swollen executive power and the asserted need to bring that power under control: the cutoff of aid to Cambodia, the war powers bill, impoundment of funds, executive privilege, and the climactic struggle over impeachment. In every case, the liberal complaint was that the executive was out of line and needed rebuke by a righteous legislature.

51

Most of this got started in the days of Lyndon Johnson, when Senators William Fulbright, George McGovern, and others began promoting amendments to halt the Vietnam war and liberal publicists such as Walter Lippmann bombarded Johnson for usurpation of congressional authority. The fire in liberal breasts grew even hotter in the Watergate debacle when President Nixon refused to deliver up to courts and Congress tapes of certain conversations in the White House, claiming executive privilege as his sanction. Liberal journals such as the *New York Times* and *Washington Post* denounced the Nixon position as a manifestation of presidential arrogance.

Spurred by these disputes, Fulbright, Arthur Schlesinger, Jr., and various other authorities took to describing Nixon as a would-be monarch, whose claims to power were a menace to our freedoms. The most systematic exposition of this view was offered by Schlesinger in *The Imperial Presidency,* published in 1973. Most of Schlesinger's discussion was devoted to attacking the enlargement of presidential power in the conduct of our defense and foreign policies and marshaling evidence to suggest this power had extended far beyond the mandate of the nation's founders.

"Imperious," "piratical," and "Messianic" were among the choicer epithets employed to describe the conduct of various presidents—with Nixon the ultimate and obvious target. The American executive of the 1970s, according to Schlesinger, "had become on issues of war and peace the most absolute monarch (with the possible exception of Mao Tse-tung of China) among the great powers of the world." [1] Schlesinger's polemic synthesized the emerging liberal view of presidential power, and could be duplicated at length from the utterances of other liberal spokesmen and from the final spasm of distaste and fury that harried Richard Nixon out of office.

I describe the epoch producing these assertions as a watershed for American liberalism because the thrust of them runs so directly counter to the position staked out by liberal scholars previous to the 1960s. Although latecomers would hardly know it from the manner in which these opinions have been offered, the emergence of an anti-presidential rhetoric on the liberal-left is a stunning reversal of intellectual and political form.

For a span of decades beginning with the New Deal, liberal spokesmen in government, the academy, and the media had argued long and loud for an increasingly powerful executive and denounced the futility and absurdity of Congress. Indeed, the very people quoted above had applauded the heaping up of power in the executive and argued that the problem in the American system was that we hadn't done nearly enough of it. The stumbling block to effective government, they said, was the impertinence of Congress.

As late as 1965, for example, Schlesinger was telling the world that "Congress through its enlarged use of its powers of appropriation and investigation had become increasingly involved in the details of executive administration, thereby systematically enhancing its own power and diminishing that of the President." In the good old days of FDR, the historian recalled, you could get lump sum appropriations with few strings attached. But an interfering Congress had started imposing a "tangle of stipulations and restrictions" on things like foreign aid. The result, according to Schlesinger, was that "contemporary Presidents, hedged around by an aggressive Congress and unresponsive bureaucracy, had in significant respects considerably less freedom than their predecessors." [2] *

The about-face by columnist Lippmann was equally abrupt. In a 1955 essay called *The Public Philosophy*, Lippmann had lu-

---

* A favorite pastime of Schlesinger and his father, an equally distinguished historian, has been the rating of Presidents for their alleged "strength." In the Schlesinger rating game various historians are polled to find out which of our chief executives were "great," which near-great, which were average, below average, and failures. The results on two different occasions were remarkably uniform: The "great" Presidents turned out to be Lincoln, Washington, Franklin Roosevelt, Wilson, Jefferson, and Jackson. The comment of another liberal historian, James MacGregor Burns, is to the point:

> From extensive reading of the work of many of these historians, I believe that the criteria set forth by Professor Schlesinger represent the criteria of the great preponderance of the respondents. And these criteria seem to boil down to one crucial characteristic—strength in the White House. The great Presidents were the strong Presidents, and by "strong" the historians meant their mastery of events, their influence on history, their shaping of the country's destiny, their capacity to draw talented men to their side, their ability to magnify their own department, and their own powers, at the expense of the other branches. [*Presidential Government*, Houghton Mifflin, 1966, p. 81.]

formed us the nation was sorely threatened by the ambitions of Congress, which had tried to usurp the rightful powers of the President. Lippmann argued that the executive branch of government had "lost both its material and ethereal powers" to the legislature, popular opinion, and "the misrule of the people." What was needed was a strong executive regime that could, among other things, "resist the encroachments of assemblies and mass opinions." [3]

In similar vein were the assertions of Senator Fulbright, later such a vigorous foe of executive arrogance. Far from being too great, he asserted in the Kennedy era, the President's power in foreign affairs "falls far short of his responsibilities." Fulbright said "the overriding problem of inadequate presidential authority in foreign affairs derives . . . from the 'checks and balances' of congressional authority in foreign relations. . . . Public opinion must be educated and led if it is to bolster a wise and effective foreign policy. Only the President can provide the guidance that is necessary, while legislators display a distressing tendency to adhere to the dictates of public opinion, or at least to its vocal and organized segments. . . . The United States is under the most pressing compulsion to form wise and farsighted policies. . . . *The essence of this compulsion is the conferral of greatly increased authority on the President. . . .*" [4] (Italics added.)

That liberals should hold opinions of this type is not, of course, astonishing, but only seems so in the light of all the recent protest engendered by Vietnam and Watergate. By logical extension the expansive liberal view of government would imply a considerable enlargement of the President's powers, if only because he is the chief presiding officer of the government to be expanded. This is, however, but part of the story. As the preceding quotations suggest, there are specific factors in the planning outlook of the liberals that militate in favor of an immensely strong executive.

Origins of the Expansive Presidency

In the main, the expansive presidency with which we are familiar is a product of this century—utterly different in outlook and in powers from the office conceived by America's founders. That the intended role of the President was fairly modest is evident from the fact that the Federal government as a whole was thought to be severely limited. As commander in chief and in other respects, of course, the President had broad originary powers, and was expected to employ these with vigor in the proper circumstances. But essentially he was the head of the executive and administrative aspects of the government, and there simply wasn't that much to be administered.

The modern conception of President-as-Caesar did not, therefore, occur to our forebears. Although there were variations in the influence and power of different Presidents—Jefferson as party leader, Jackson's battle against the National Bank, Lincoln's assertion of sweeping war powers—the norm of government throughout the nineteenth century was that of a modest, limited presidency. The leading role in terms of policy was taken by Congress, and the President saw to the carrying out of the laws the Congress passed. It remained for our particular era, with its liberal Presidents, global wars, and zeal for collectivist planning, to establish the imperium.*

The triad of causes suggested in the preceding sentence is not deployed for rhetorical effect. The emergence of our liberal Presidents, our global involvements, and our collectivist planning on the home front are indissolubly linked together as aspects of a single

---

* As noted by Professor James Burnham, the major political figures of the nineteenth century—Webster, Clay, Calhoun—were members of the Senate. It was then considered perfectly natural for a former President, John Quincy Adams, to hold a seat in the House of Representatives. And for more than a century, from 1801 to 1913, the formal division of powers was so discreetly observed that the President's annual state of the union message was delivered to Congress in writing, not by the chief executive in person before the assembled members.

The reality of presidential power in the nineteenth century was summed up by Alexis de Tocqueville in 1832: "Hitherto no citizen has cared to expose his honor and his life in order to become the President of the United States, because the power of that office is temporary, limited, and subordinate. The prize of fortune must be great to encourage adventurers in so desperate a game. No candidate has yet been able to arouse the dangerous enthusiasm or the passionate sympathies of the people in his favor, for the simple reason that when he is at the head of the government, he has little power, little wealth, and little glory to share among his friends; and the influence in the state is too small for the success or ruin of a faction to depend upon his elevation to power." (*Democracy in America*, Vintage Books, 1955, Vol. I, p. 133.)

movement toward augmented Federal power. The liberal Presidents referred to are Woodrow Wilson and Franklin Roosevelt, although one could make a cogent case for including Franklin's cousin Theodore, the maverick Republican who had a considerable impact on both his Democratic successors.

Wilson and Franklin Roosevelt were different in many respects, but in those attributes that presently concern us they were remarkably alike. Each professed an enlarged conception of the executive office and labored to expand its powers. Each also cherished certain objectives in the international arena that contributed greatly to the growth of executive power, and each fostered programs on the home front that served to make this power overwhelming. This chapter will attempt to trace, in abbreviated fashion, how this transformation occurred; the next will try to determine why.

Woodrow Wilson was the most scholarly of all our Presidents, and as a working ideologue the most committed to expansive theories of presidential power. A former president of Princeton, he had long lamented the sway of "congressional government" (the title of his doctoral dissertation) and urged the strengthening of the presidency as the proper focus of American statecraft. The President, he said, was our "only national voice," beholden to no special constituency, and when he articulated the "national thought" he was "irresistible." [5] As President himself Wilson got a chance to put these notions of irresistibility into practice.

During his first term Wilson succeeded in pushing economic measures through the Congress, most notably tariff legislation and the Federal Reserve Act. He revived the custom, dormant for a century, of appearing personally before the legislature, and he lobbied the lawmakers in diligent fashion. When his major opportunity came—the advent of the war—he sought to make the most of it. The daily conduct of foreign policy and war is by definition an executive and administrative function, so that the degree to which the nation's resources are diverted to such efforts will also be the degree to which the power of the President is enhanced. In addition, wartime has provided the pretext for exerting presidential power on the home front—co-opting industries and imposing economic regulations.

All this occurred, exactly according to schedule, under Wilson's administration. He persuaded Congress to give him broad and sweeping powers over the organization of the American government, and proceeded to deploy controls on industrial production, agriculture, private investment, communications, and transport facilities. His power was enormous, and generally unchallenged. Criticism of his conduct became extremely inadvisable since, as historian Wilfred Binkley puts it, "to doubt Wilson was to invite proscription as pro-German." [6]

At war's end, the President and his men had little difficulty converting their planning enthusiams to the requirements of peace, although Congress had some different notions. When the legislature repealed some sixty wartime measures conferring emergency powers on the President, Wilson promptly vetoed the bill, retaining these powers for another two years. He and his subalterns were desirous of continuing government ownership of the railroads and of radio communications, and Wilson expressed the further view that there should be government dominion over water power, coal mines, and oil fields.

Liberal opinion on the wisdom of our involvement in the "war to end war" had been divided, but those who favored the notion of the planning state were alert to the opening sensed by Wilson. John Dewey, for one, expounded the "social possibilities of war" —the idea that the communal solidarity, top-down planning, and techniques of control that war brought with it could be converted to peacetime uses. Private property, he thought, had been given a welcome *coup de grâce*. As a writer in the *New Republic* put it, "What we have learned in war, we shall hardly forget in peace. . . . The new economic solidarity, once gained, can never again be surrendered." [7]

These visions of glory, however, were premature. The time for an American imperium was not yet ripe, and the balance wheels of the system were still in relatively good order. Government efforts to control communications were defeated, for example, and the League of Nations went down to defeat in the Senate. An era of relative conservatism was about to commence; what Wilson had begun would have to be completed by another liberal President.

It was with the coming of the second Roosevelt that conversion to the planning state and a system of full-fledged "presidential government" became decisive. If Wilson was the Aristotle of executive power, then Franklin Roosevelt was its Alexander. Taking office during the crisis of the depression, he became not merely the head of the executive branch, but in effect the nation's legislator in chief. In the so-called "hundred days" beginning in March 1933 he pushed his legislative program through Congress with hardly a whisper of opposition, and was acclaimed as a national hero for having done so.

It was under Roosevelt, indeed, that the practice of "executive legislation" came into extensive and regular use. He secured emergency powers to reorganize the government as he pleased, subject only to a veto by the legislature—a reversal of constitutional functions that has become quite customary since. His agents drafted bills and carried them to Congress for enactment. At one point executive staffers took a piece of legislation to Capitol Hill that was passed without a single member's having read it. During the war, Roosevelt made the humiliation of Congress explicit when he demanded action on emergency price controls by a date certain, saying that unless he got the bill he wanted, he would act on his own. Congress scurried to do his bidding.[8]

Roosevelt artfully used the resources of his office to keep potentially recalcitrant congressmen in line. He was particularly adept at using his patronage powers to obtain congressional cooperation. His regime created special agencies by the dozens and new jobs by the tens of thousands, and these were filled by people loyal to his program. Congressmen who voted FDR's way could get their friends appointed; if not, then not. "When a congressman was asked to vote for a presidential measure in the face of local opposition," we are informed, "his support was given the President on the frank basis of a *quid pro quo*." [9]

As it had during the Wilson years, the coming of warfare accelerated the transformation of the presidency into something resembling an American kingship. Even though he had pledged to keep America out of the war, Roosevelt and his advisers were moving strongly behind the scenes to secure American involvement —a fact well-documented by the anti-Roosevelt "revisionist" historians but also acknowledged frankly by the pro-FDR interventionists. James MacGregor Burns, for one, describes the Roosevelt policy in this era as "the struggle to intervene," a struggle which, of course, turned out to be successful.[10]

One of the most crucial of Roosevelt's steps to bring us into the war on the side of the British was the destroyer deal of September 3, 1940, consummated by executive agreement. This transaction violated existing "neutrality" statutes but was defended by Attorney General Robert Jackson as a proper exercise of the President's powers as commander in chief.* Of similar kidney was the battle over Lend Lease, advertised as a method of keeping us out of the war but in fact establishing an enormous discretionary reserve from which FDR could assist the allies. Most crucial of all, perhaps, were Roosevelt's endless quest for a naval "incident" with the Germans, his effort to get the Japanese to "fire the first shot," and the misstatements fed out by the administration concerning its foreknowledge of Japanese attack.[11] †

(In assessing all this, it is not required that we determine whether America's involvement in the war was either wise or necessary. It is possible to affirm that Hitler should have been stopped, and that America should have declared itself on the side of the allies, but also to affirm that our involvement should not have been achieved by clandestine or irregular means. This latter view was argued by some prominent liberal spokesmen, most notably Charles Beard, but in general the liberal stance has been otherwise. President Roosevelt, according to the Burns-Schlesinger analysis, did what he had to.)

At the wartime conferences, Roosevelt gave vent to further unilateral action, pledging the United States to various secret agreements, with little input by Congress and not much more by way of congressional leverage after the fact. (Indeed, to this day there are aspects of the Yalta, Teheran, and other conferences of the Second World War that are still locked up in government archives.) When all this had been accomplished, we were well down the road to executive supremacy. By the time Roosevelt

---

* And once the war was fully on us, further extensions of executive power occurred as Roosevelt simply created some 35 brand-new government agencies—also under his authority as commander in chief.

† The United States had broken the Japanese code, and on the evening of December 6, 1941, Roosevelt was given Japanese communiques detailing the declaration to be made the next day. Roosevelt's response was "this means war." The 7th fleet gathered at Pearl Harbor, however, was not notified. In his speech to the nation December 8, Roosevelt asserted that Japanese advices "contained no threat or hint of war or of armed attack."

had appointed himself legislator in chief, become the regulator of our economy, donned the mantle of global leader, and been quadruply elected, the notion of the President as American Maharajah was indelibly printed on the consciousness of the nation.

The change from the old conception was decisive, and apparently irreversible. Roosevelt's successors have worn the cloak of power with varying degrees of relish—but worn it they have. President Truman, for example, entertained his own exaggerated notion of the presidency—committing the United States to war in Korea without congressional approval and attempting to seize the steel mills. Truman explained his conception of the matter by saying that "when Congress fails to act or is unable to act, in a crisis, the President under the Constitution must use his powers to safeguard the nation." (As James Burnham drily observes, Truman failed to specify what constitution he was referring to—since there is no such provision in our own.[12])

President Eisenhower professed a more modest conception of the office and wanted to pull back from the assertive and expanding executive role of the Roosevelt-Truman era. Yet it was under Eisenhower that the Department of Health, Education, and Welfare, the most bloated of all the civilian bureaucracies, had its genesis—by executive order. And it was also Eisenhower who staked out a sweeping claim to executive privilege that would have permitted the President and his agents to deny anything at all to Congress if disclosure was not in "the public interest." President Kennedy's tenure wasn't long enough to bring about appreciable changes, but it is clear from the record that his view of the office was fully in keeping with that developed from the time of Roosevelt forward.*

---

* Historian Eric Goldman gave an interesting and sympathetic assessment of the Kennedy style in comparing the New Frontier executive to his predecessor, Ike. "The outgoing President," Goldman wrote, "believed that the chief executive should not attempt to run things too much and especially should not try to whiplash Congress and the nation into line. John Kennedy took office with whip brandished high." The Kennedy men, Goldman wrote, were "students—and products—of the new managerial America, a managerial world that includes political campaigns and universities as well as business corporations, and they are acutely aware that a managerial world is one in which men and ideas are made or broken by

In the epoch since the New Deal, therefore, the presidency has become something quite different from the office conceived by America's founders. Its mighty sway is suggested by Burns, who tells us the modern presidency "has absorbed the cabinet, the executive department, the vice presidency. It has taken over the national party apparatus. Through consistently liberal appointments over the years it has a powerful influence on the doctrines of the Supreme Court. . . . [A] tendency that may bring Congress more into the presidential orbit is continuing congressional reform. . . . As the elected leadership continues to gain strength in Congress as compared to the committee chairman . . . the President will gain added influence over the legislature." [13]

The Liberal Position on Expansive Presidency

If it should be supposed that commitment to the presidency is one thing but opposing its "abuses" quite another, we may add that liberal devotion to executive power has included support for sweeping authority in almost every specific policy area, including those that excited horror under Nixon. It has been noted, for example, how "secret" diplomacy and involvement in foreign conflict was considered reprehensible in the case of Vietnam and Cambodia, but perfectly acceptable when the ends pursued were those favored by the liberals themselves, such as involvement in the Second World War.

Typical of once-prevailing liberal attitudes about such matters was the stance assumed by liberal spokesmen toward the so-called Bricker amendment, named for Senator John W. Bricker of Ohio. This measure was a topic of steaming debate in the early 1950s, with conservative stalwarts such as Bricker, his Ohio colleague Robert A. Taft, and numerous other Republicans and Southern Democrats lined up in its behalf. The idea of the amendment was to protect domestic American law from being overridden by a

---

subtle configurations of power." The "new moralism" of the Kennedy regime, he concluded, "is the more striking because it is accompanied by the most unabashed power-consciousness that the Capital has ever known." (*Let Us Begin*, Simon & Schuster, 1961, pp. 9, 15.)

treaty (a possibility under the Supreme Court's decision in *Missouri v. Holland*) and to put a halt to secret diplomacy conducted through the device of executive agreements.*

When the amendment was originally proposed, it was massively attacked by most of the liberal organizations in America, including Americans for Democratic Action, the American Civil Liberties Union, the United World Federalists, the CIO, and so on.† So intense was the liberals' opposition that they demanded —and got—the scalp of Clarence Manion, then chairman of the Commission on Intergovernmental Relations and a principal spokesman for the amendment. Manion's official status was galling to the ADA, the *New York Times,* the *Washington Post,* and other outposts of liberal opinion. President Eisenhower finally yielded to the hue and cry and in February 1954 dismissed Manion from his post.

Of equal interest is the previous liberal record on questions of "executive privilege," which was anathematized as an excuse for cover-up when President Nixon invoked it in the battle over Watergate.‡ In the 1950s and early 1960s, when the executive

---

* At the time of Bricker's original motion, it was estimated that some 1,500 executive agreements had been put into effect. In the intervening two decades, the growth rate has been truly exponential. As of January 1, 1973, there were 4,589 such agreements on the books, compared to 910 treaties. Some 846 of these executive agreements had been put into effect by President Nixon, compared to 65 treaties—a ratio of 13 to 1.

† It is particularly intriguing to note Senator Fulbright's attitude toward the Bricker amendment. "Our enemy," he said, "is not the President of the United States, whether the incumbent, his successor to come, or his predecessors. . . . The Constitution charges the President with conducting our foreign relations by and with the advice of the Senate. It makes him the leading actor; not a spectator and mere witness. And this role has been discharged by successive Presidents of the United States throughout the nearly two centuries duration of the Constitution. It was never intended by the Founding Fathers that the President of the United States should be a ventriloquist dummy sitting on the lap of the Congress." (Haynes Johnson and Bernard Gwertzman, *Fulbright the Dissenter,* Curtis Books, 1968, pp. 328–29.)

‡ "A . . . refusal to produce the evidence as it pertains to Watergate," said the *New York Times,* "would only create other problems for Nixon of a far more consuming nature—problems of leadership and credibility which might well be fatal to his presidency. The alternative is delay, which could not help but appear self-serving. Suspicions would only redouble,

was relatively more congenial to the liberal interest than was Congress, the liberal view was militantly *in favor* of executive privilege. This attitude was manifest on several occasions up through the Kennedy administration, but emerged most clearly in the apocalyptic battle against Senator Joseph R. McCarthy of Wisconsin.

The climax of that struggle occurred during televised hearings concerning charges and countercharges between the Senator's staff and the Department of the Army. In the course of these proceedings, McCarthy attempted to obtain administration records of monitored phone calls in which disputed conversations had occurred. McCarthy said these records would vindicate his claim of administration pressure to call off a sensitive investigation of possible subversion, and would disprove the administration's counterclaim of McCarthy pressure on behalf of a former aide who had recently been drafted.

It was when the monitored phone calls appeared to be proving McCarthy's point that presidential secrecy was invoked, and the chief magistrate issued a stiff-necked decree laying down the doctrine of "executive privilege." In a sweeping claim to presidential secrecy, President Eisenhower asserted that Presidents historically had "withheld information whenever [they] found that what was sought was confidential or its disclosure would be incompatible with the public interest or jeopardize the safety of the nation." [14]

In that instance American liberals saw no need whatever for the President to bring forth the relevant evidence, and certainly

___

presidential pretensions to leadership would shrivel up in doubt. There can be no practical justification for failure to make this evidence publicly available. In the interests of the American presidency, and Nixon himself, the sooner it comes out the better." (*New York Times,* July 18, 1973.)

The *Washington Post* was of a similar opinion. Nixon's refusal to deliver up the tapes to the Senate investigating committee and the special prosecutor's office, according to the Post, "have precipitated a constitutional crisis for no real constitutional or legal reason. . . . What is at issue here is not a question which may be resolved by legal needlework, as, for example, it would be if the issue concerned how far the legislative branch can inquire into the thought processes and confidential exchanges within the executive. . . . What is at issue is only to what extent those crimes we already know about have corroded and compromised that high office." (*Washington Post,* July 24, 1973.)

they did not suggest he was doing something illegal or unconstitutional. The *New York Times,* for example, did not concern itself with the fact that the evidence in question concerned a major security dispute, a potential cover-up, and possible perjury by people high in government circles. The *Times* was strictly interested in preserving the principle of executive privilege.

On May 17, 1954, the *Times* commented that "if a congressional investigating committee could compel a presidential agent to reveal what went on at a Cabinet meeting, the constitutional separation of powers would be ended. Congress could then in effect have its delegates and spokesmen at every gathering of the presidential advisers." Such procedures, the paper said, would "seriously weaken" the "constitutional separation of powers." It added that "congressional committees have been increasingly tempted into lines of inquiry which are legally and morally none of their business. A limit had to be reached sometime. Maybe it has been reached." [15] *

---

* The next day the *Times* put the issue of executive privilege in even broader context, as part of a struggle between the Congress and the presidency— and the *Times* was all for the latter:

> From the outset of the fight between Senator McCarthy and the Eisenhower administration this newspaper has maintained that the fundamental issue is an attempt on the part of the legislative branch in the person of Mr. McCarthy to encroach upon the executive branch in complete disregard of the historical and constitutional division of powers that is basic to the American system of government.
>
> The President has been late but not too late in recognizing the deep significance of this issue and standing up to it while the committee itself has apparently swallowed Mr. McCarthy's contention that he and it are entitled to know and pass judgment upon every word, every thought that transpires within the executive department.
>
> The committee has no more right to know the details of what went on in these administration councils than the administration would have the right to know what went on in an executive session of a committee of the Congress.

Responses by the *Washington Post* to these disparate cases have been in substance identical to those of the *Times.* The *Post* and its weekly adjunct, *Newsweek* magazine, were in the forefront of the media belaboring Nixon over Watergate, deploring executive secrecy and expressing

The claim of executive privilege asserted by Eisenhower was extended even further by President Kennedy. In the early 1960s the Kennedy regime became embroiled in a number of controversies with committees of Congress involving Cold War policy and internal security. One such case concerned the so-called muzzling of military officers. State Department and Pentagon censors had gone over speeches by military officers, deleting statements considered provocative to the Communists.

The Senate Armed Services Committee wanted to call the government censors as witnesses and question them as to why they were embarked on this activity and why they had made particular deletions. Defense Secretary Robert S. McNamara refused the request under a claim of executive privilege by President Kennedy. McNamara provided the Senate with a letter from Kennedy, dated February 8, 1962, in which the President stated: "I have concluded that it would be contrary to the public interest to make available any information which would enable the subcommittee to identify and hold accountable any individual with respect to any particular speech that has been reviewed." [16]

As noted by investigative reporter Clark Mollenhoff, this claim to executive privilege was even broader than that asserted by Eisenhower. In the earlier case, the claim had been applied to

---

horror about the cover-up of the Nixon tapes. Compare with this position the comment of the *Post* (May 18, 1954) on the Eisenhower claim of executive privilege in 1954:

> . . . it would be absurd to suppose that any congressional body could compel this testimony if the President should decide to forbid it. . . . It is a settled principle, moreover, a principle enunciated by George Washington and adhered to uniformly by his successors in the presidency, that it is a matter of presidential discretion to determine whether it is in the public interest to give Congress executive documents which it may request. No useful purpose can be served in any case by a conflict on this issue.

And again:

> The President's authority under the Constitution to withhold from Congress confidences, presidential information, the disclosure of which in his judgment would be incompatible with the public interest is altogether beyond question. His obligation to do it in vindication of the American constitutional system is clear.

the communications and testimony of high officials in the executive branch. But in this episode, Kennedy extended the claim to lower-level officials of the government as well. As Mollenhoff recalls, this move "won overwhelming support from the nation's editorial pages. . . . Many segments of the press completely lost sight of their long-standing self-interest in freedom of the press and thereby endorsed the broadest possible interpretation of 'executive privilege.' " [17]

A second case was even more sensational and even more closely parallel to the Watergate scandal. State Department official Otto Otepka, protesting what he considered lax security practices in the Department, had provided information supporting his charges to the Senate Internal Security subcommittee. In retaliation, State Department officials broke into his office, ransacked his desk, and bugged his telephone. When called to testify about these matters, the relevant officials perjured themselves, denied that the bugging had occurred, and later recanted only when the subcommittee secured independent evidence of what had happened.

While the subcommittee attempted to dig out the facts of the Otepka case, Secretary of State Dean Rusk issued a blanket order forbidding any State Department employee to testify in the matter —another claim to executive privilege on the broadest possible scale. Again the Kennedy administration was applauded by the liberal media. Both the *New York Times* and the *Washington Post* opined that Otepka was the culprit in the drama, and that the Kennedy administration was properly concerned about preventing "leaks" of data to the Senate investigators.[18]

So the liberals have supported past instances of what is now labeled presidential "abuse." Nor is this the whole of the story. For if one gets past the recent outcry over Watergate, he finds that many of the liberals haven't learned their lesson even now. Despite the obvious meaning of the Watergate debacle, and despite their own emotional rhetoric, they still favor an enormous concentration of power in the Federal government, and still favor an immensely powerful executive. The only message that certain liberals seem to have derived from Watergate is that Richard Nixon should not have been in the White House.

Consider in this respect that widely touted liberal "reform"— the demand for direct election of the President. Under this proposal, our Presidents would no longer be chosen according to electoral votes cast state by state, but by direct popular plebiscite. Such a move, whatever else might be said of it, would clearly diminish the authority of the states in the federal balance, enhance the voting power of the major urban centers, and transform the presidency even more decisively into a "national" plebiscitary executive.

How does this proposal to convert the presidency into a mass-base "national" executive fit in with liberal rhetoric about the need to restrain the President? Quite obviously, it doesn't. It is a holdover from the era in which strong executives were held to be the salvation of the country, and it became a staple of liberal discourse in that period. To the extent that liberal publicists and lawmakers continue to promote such notions, we may be certain their conversion to a limited view of executive functions is purely superficial.

In similar vein is the liberal reaction to Watergate itself. If this series of scandals established anything, it was that the Federal government had gotten too big and arrogant and that fallible or venal men in Washington could not be trusted with so much untethered power. But what has been the liberal response? That we should concentrate still *further* power in the Federal government by imposing restraints on private participation in the electoral process and by financing political campaigns with government money.

The call for this alleged remedy was prompted by contributions to the Nixon reelection effort by the milk interests and the International Telephone and Telegraph Company—supposedly showing that private interests needed stricter government control. But the actual lesson of these episodes was precisely the opposite: The common feature of these two cases was that both ITT and the milk interests were *already* subject to government control, and thus had reason to solicit favor with the controllers. Pile on still more government regulations, and the motives of business or other interests to influence the regulators will obviously be enhanced, rather than diminished.

Or consider the case of wage and price controls. Standby presidential authority to impose controls on wages and prices was pushed through by liberal Democrats in 1970 in the face of

Nixon's protestations that he did not want and would not use such powers. When the ravages of inflation became increasingly painful in 1971, there was a tremendous clamor from the liberal community that they be imposed—and Nixon obliged, to liberal plaudits, in August of that year. In March of 1973, the self-same Senate that was supposedly aching to rebuke the White House had a chance to end this enormous grant of executive power. By a hefty margin, it voted instead to extend the President's price control authority for another year.

Then there is the energy crunch, which came so painfully to public notice in the latter part of 1973. The best response the liberal "opponents" of executive power could think of in this instance was to propose an "emergency" energy bill to give the President still more sweeping powers over the economy—including fuel oil allocation, export controls, and authority for rationing. Despite the rhetoric about restraining the President in matters pertaining to Indochina and Watergate, the liberal instinct when confronted with a serious problem in American society was to make the President's power even greater.* Other such examples might be recited at length.

If we screen out Watergate and Indochina, therefore, we find the normal thrust of liberal advocacy continuing exactly as before. In Schlesinger's recent treatise on the "imperial presidency," for example, nowhere does he tackle the original source of the prob-

---

* It is also worth observing that, on numerous domestic issues, the executive branch has often ignored the will of Congress, with no discernible protest from the liberals. Congress has repeatedly voted, for example, that employes of the executive are not to dispose of Federal funds or take other actions designed to promote the cause of busing for racial balance. Such stipulations are included in the Civil Rights Act of 1964 and in various appropriation bills from 1966 on.

In defiance of this legislation, executive agents in the Department of Health, Education, and Welfare and in legal services have systematically withdrawn funds to compel adoption of busing programs, prepared busing plans to be imposed on local communities, and brought suit to compel augmented busing. As noted by Senator James Allen (D-Ala.), the bureaucracy in this instance has converted "a limitation of its power into a grant of power to do precisely what the statute said it could not do." Liberals who presumably want the executive to obey statutory commands of Congress have had little to say about this sort of defiance—except to suggest that funds for all the relevant agencies be increased.

lem, namely, the build-up of economic and political power within the federal government, and particularly within the executive branch. Somewhat incredibly, he even reiterates suggestions that the presidency be made *more* powerful through grants of authority to raise and lower taxes and to initiate public works spending (although, of course, the President doing such things would not, in Schlesinger's scenario, be Richard Nixon).

If the President is to be made even more powerful, how does one go about preventing the exercise of an "imperial presidency"? Schlesinger's answer is a muddle. The presidency must be strong, but it must be "a strong presidency within the Constitution." What, if anything, this may mean in view of liberal teachings concerning the infinite pliability of our fundamental law is anybody's guess. Schlesinger's only hint is to suggest there must be self-control on the part of the President, who has "to believe in the discipline of consent." [19] In other words, rather than cutting down executive power, we should leave it as it is, or even increase it, and count on the President to be a reasonable fellow who will behave himself. Roosevelt and Kennedy were such good fellows and are in general to be commended; Nixon was not and therefore needed to be thrashed.*

The writings of Schlesinger, Burns, and other liberal spokesmen abound with such hair-splitting. It was correct of FDR to amass the power he did, to maneuver us into war, and to engage in secret diplomacy after the war—but wrong for Nixon to conduct a secret bombing of Cambodia. Executive privilege was right as rain when invoked by Eisenhower against McCarthy or by Kennedy against Strom Thurmond, but wrong when invoked by Nixon against the Watergate investigators. It is good to have some kind of restraints on the the power of executive diplomacy, but we cannot and should not pass the Bricker amendment.

---

* Schlesinger's desire to maintain and enlarge presidential power and his fear of any real restraint on that power despite his rhetoric are apparent in passages referring to the New Deal and New Frontier. Commenting on a proposed reform to establish a collegial six-man presidency, he says: "One wonders whether a six man presidency would have prevented the war in Vietnam. It might well, however, have prevented the New Deal. The single man presidency, with the right man as President, had its uses; and historically Americans had as often as not chosen the right man" (p. 385).

So, what was axiomatically right under one set of circumstances is said to be completely wrong under another. The intellectual machinery is thrown into screeching reverse, and in Orwellian fashion we are told to forget today what we were instructed yesterday to learn by heart. It has been a curious spectacle, and one that at a minimum should cause us to question the steadfastness and acuity of people who contradict themselves so readily on so immense a topic.

After one has encountered enough such distinctions, their common thread becomes apparent: When the exercise of presidential power conflicts with what liberals want, then it is both immoral and illegal; when the exercise of presidential power conforms to what the liberals want, it is right and proper. The rule of thumb is therefore not a constitutional guideline, counterpoise of powers, or diminution of presidential authority: *It is simply to have officials who do what the liberals want.* Such is the liberal conception of "a strong presidency within the Constitution." The founding fathers had another name for it—a government of men, and not of laws.

One question seems especially baffling. Why did liberal spokesmen who so blithely favored the concentration of executive power across the years have no apparent thought that someone they didn't like would get hold of it? Why couldn't they see the possibility that the authority they were heaping up, and vehemently defending on every conceivable pretext, *might* someday be used for purposes other than their own? The answer to those questions perhaps resides in what may be called the liberal political theory of the presidency.

Under this theory, it is assumed that certain elements in our political system will nearly always make the executive branch more liberal than the Congress. There are institutional factors that support this view, and the political considerations were thought to enhance the logic of the institutional balance. On this analysis, no one could get elected President unless he carried the electoral votes of the largest states in the union—California, New York, Pennsylvania, Michigan, and so on—and to carry these states it was generally necessary to carry the largest cities.

Since the big-city vote has for most of our recent history been a liberal vote, the dynamics of the electoral college were thought to dictate continuous liberal power in the White House. Burns and numerous other liberal theoreticians (along with some conservative spokesmen) have joyfully chewed this thesis over for years, using it to explain the necessity of liberal nominees for president in *both* political parties as a matter of "realistic" politics.

As recent events have amply demonstrated, this notion of inevitable liberal triumph in contests for the White House is badly off the mark, and there is really no guarantee whatever that the more liberal candidate will win, say, the Republican presidential nomination, or the subsequent general election. Indeed, a good deal of evidence suggests precisely the opposite. That revelation has come rather late in the day, however, and only recently has it dawned on a number of liberals that someone other than themselves might get control of all that enormous, overweening power.

In this respect, some further comments from Burns are apropos, and not a little ironic. Evaluating the concentration of power in the presidency, the erosion of checks and balances, and the possible danger in all this for American civil liberties, Burns (as of 1966) had the following reassuring comment:

> The old and accepted fears of presidential power . . . do not seem justified on the basis of actual experience. Increased authority and scope have not made the presidency a tyrannical institution; on the contrary, the office has become the main governmental bastion for the protection of individual liberty and the expansion of civil rights . . . the office has attracted neither power-mad politicans nor bland incompetents but the ablest political leaders in the land, and these leaders in turn have brought the highest talent to the White House.
>
> We must, under modern conditions, reassess the old idea that the *main* governmental protection of civil liberty, social and economic rights, and due process of law lies in the legislature or the courts or state and local government. The main protection lies today in the national executive branch. As a general proposition the presidency has become the chief protector of our procedural and substantive liberties; as a general proposition, the stronger we make the presidency, the more we strengthen democratic procedures and can hope to realize modern liberal democratic goals.[19] *

* If those sentiments read somewhat strangely in the light of Watergate, consider Burns's further observations on the possibility that an American

It is necessary, of course, to distinguish cases. Certain liberal spokesmen—Irving Kristol, Nathan Glazer, Daniel Moynihan—are authentically disturbed by the steady accretion of presidential and other governmental power. To the extent that these and other liberal scholars have attempted to think through the dangers of concentrated power and have moved toward a consistent opposition to arbitrary authority, their efforts should be commended rather than disparaged, and nothing said here should be interpreted as a negative comment on such developments.

Liberal spokesmen of this type, however, are still very much a minority, and increasingly find themselves described in public comment as "conservatives" (Kristol is the most obvious case in point). The normative thrust of liberal policy and liberal statement—as represented by the *New York Times,* the *Washington Post,* Schlesinger, Fulbright, McGovern, Kennedy—continues to be in favor of concentrated power in general, and concentrated executive power in particular. The "change," in sum, is not a change at all, but a tactical shift of partisan rhetoric. The liberal commitment to enormous and expanding power in the President remains as before.

President might do something seriously zany because he is no longer subject to restraint. There is a problem here, Burns concedes, "but it is not a problem that can be met by tightening the old constitutional restraints on the presidency. The only people who could actually restrain the President from erratic, irrational, or psychotic action are those close to him—and not senators or congressmen or judges. . . . These checks do not operate in the making of war or even in the making of foreign policies that could precipitate war—for example, Franklin Roosevelt's instructions to the Navy Department in the months before Pearl Harbor. . . . The only protection possible is the one the White House already affords: a group of men closely related to the President who can restrain him if need be" (pp. 306–08). (Like, for example, Haldeman and Ehrlichman?)

4
The
Decline
of Congress

On the evidence examined in the preceding chapter it is apparent
that the liberal rhetoric emerging from the Watergate debacle and
the struggle in Vietnam should be taken with a grain of salt. Yet it
should be equally plain that these confusing events and the general
reaction to them contain the seed of potential good. If they have
led us to do some serious rethinking on the subject of executive
power and produce consistent rather than merely partisan efforts
to bring that power under control, then the agony experienced by
the nation may eventually prove worth the cost.

In particular, the costs will be effectively amortized if the recent tendency of Congress to reassert itself as a coequal element
in the determination of national policy persists and is applied
across the board. For the decline of Congress has been among the
most dolorous of political developments in the twentieth century.
It has contributed greatly to the erosion of our institutions and
our liberties. Although denied on occasion by such as Lippmann
and Fulbright, this enfeeblement is generally acknowledged by our
political scientists. Some think it is a bad thing, others think it
rather good, but nearly all are agreed that it has happened—and

73

that ascendancy over both our foreign and domestic policies has passed into the hands of the executive.

An easy way to measure the relative scope of our supposedly coequal branches of government is to examine a copy of the United States Government Organization Manual, which sets forth the titles and duties of all the various agencies of the Federal government and the principal officials thereof. Exclusive of introductory matter and supplements, this is a book approximately 500 pages in length. Of that 500 pages, exactly 26 are devoted to listing the major personnel and principal agencies of the legislative branch, with another 11 devoted to the judiciary—a grand total of 37 pages. The remaining 463 pages are devoted entirely to the executive branch and its swarm of agencies, councils, offices, commissions, departments, divisions, secretariats, boards, administrations, authorities, services, corporations, forces, staffs, colleges, commands, and institutes.[1]

Unsurprisingly, the same disproportion is evident in the distribution of employes. As of March 1973, there were 2,768,000 workers on Federal payrolls. Of these, exactly 2,726,000, or 99 percent, were employed by the executive, compared to 33,000 employed by the legislature (which includes all the employes of both the General Accounting Office and the Government Printing Office). The annual payroll for executive employes stood at $32 billion, compared to $428 million for employes of the legislature. So, both in numbers and in cost to taxpayers, the executive force today is about 80 times as large as the contingent employed by the Congress.[2]

A similar view emerges if we compare the total budgets disposed of by the component elements of our government. In fiscal 1973, outlays for the legislative branch, all told, came to slightly over $500 million—from a total Federal budget of $246 billion. This compared to $4.1 billion in "funds appropriated to the President," $11 billion for the Department of Agriculture, $75.9 billion for the Department of Defense, $78.9 billion for the Department of Health, Education, and Welfare, and so on—all these enormous sums being dispensed, of course, by agents of the executive bureaucracy.[3] *

* For purposes of long-term comparison, it is noteworthy that, back in 1822, expenditures for Congress were larger than those for the executive—by a margin of $455,000 to $449,000.

Such aggregate figures do not tell us all we need to know. Despite its meager 26 pages and 80-to-1 employment deficit, Congress still possesses the original legislative power. It could, if it chose, assert much greater authority in areas that are now the uncontested fiefdom of the administrators. And the courts, needless to remark, have exerted an enormous shaping power on our society despite their relatively scanty allotment of personnel. So numbers aren't everything. Still, the fantastic imbalance between the growth of the executive and that of the other branches suggests the direction in which we have been heading. Ours has become, preeminently, an administered society, run by executive agents, social planners, and members of the permanent bureaucracy.

The clearest indication of this development, perhaps, is the phenomenon of "executive legislation." Nothing could suggest the alteration of the constitutional balance more plainly than the contemporary assumption that the President should invent "his" legislative program and present it to Congress, that the legislators should thereafter decide whether to support the President's proposals, and that congressmen should be routinely gauged according to their degree of backing for the executive program. (The respected *Congressional Quarterly* research service, for example, issues periodic ratings on "presidential support" by senators and representatives.)

Liberal scholar Stephen Bailey comments on this development in the usual rhetoric of the executive force. "If the executive branch now exercises a virtual monopoly on the drafting of major bills," he says, "it is because the complex agenda of modern public policy necessitates an expertise and a coordination which only the executive branch can provide." He adds that "the President is an omnipresent force in congressional life. In legislative terms, it is his view of national necessity which is overriding in setting the congressional agenda. . . . In many areas of foreign affairs and national security policy, his prerogatives and constitutional authorities are so substantial as to make Congress little more than a shadow or an echo." [4]

Executive legislation has in fact proceeded so far that in certain cases Presidents pass laws and Congress is called on to veto them in the event of disapproval—a complete inversion of constitutional functions. This practice, as noted, first came into extensive use with President Roosevelt, when Congress delegated to him the task of reorganizing the Federal government. President Kennedy sought authority of this type with respect to tariffs, agricultural programs, and taxes. Liberal writer Joseph Harris, in a bland rhetorical twist, describes this procedure as "a new and highly significant form of control of the executive branch by Congress." [5]

Nor is this all. It also turns out that executive agencies engage in daily legislation of their own. Once they decide that some prohibition or sanction is needed, say, in the realm of occupational safety, they simply publish a regulation to that effect in the *Federal Register*. Within thirty days of publication, the "reg" becomes a Federal law—without Congress having lifted a finger, without a word of public debate, and without the average citizen's having the faintest idea of what is going on. The administrative bureaucrats then enforce the law they have themselves promulgated, and sit in judgment on citizens who violate these new and often highly confidential regulations.*

The Founders' Perspective on Legislative Power

A review of the nation's constitutive literature suggests the present state of affairs is very different from the scheme intended by our founders. In contrast to the government organization manual, the Constitution is rather prolix in giving authority to the Congress, laconic in describing the powers of the President. The duties of the legislature are set forward in some 3,200 well-chosen words,

---

* A principal horror story in this department has been written by the Occupational Safety and Health Administration—OSHA for short. This agency has been given sweeping power to fine businesses and in some cases shut them down for every kind of alleged violation concerning toilet seats, guard rails, stairways, ladders, garbage cans, window shades, doorways, furnaces, air conditioners, and countless other items. Employers are subject to surprise visits by compliance officers and may be heavily fined for alleged violations by their employes, even if these violations are concededly beyond the power of the employer to control. In pursuit of these objections, OSHA one day in 1971 published 375,000 words of rules and regulations in the *Federal Register*—laws that small businessmen all over America, most of whom have never heard of the *Register,* are supposed to know and adhere to on pain of instant punishment.

more than twice as many as are devoted to the executive. And, it should be noted, the legislative power is defined in Article I, the executive power in Article II. Both in scope and order of presentation, the Constitution suggests that Congress is "the first branch of government."

This impression is confirmed if we examine the various powers conferred on Congress. Foremost among these is the provision that "all legislative powers" are to reside in Congress, and nowhere else—a provision routinely violated by the actions described above. Specific powers of Congress include the raising of revenue and levying of taxes, borrowing money, regulating commerce, coining money, establishing a post office, issuing patents, establishing courts, declaring war, raising and supporting armies, and providing and maintaining a navy—among other things.

The President, in contrast, is given authority as military commander in chief and is empowered to execute treaties and appoint ambassadors (both with two-thirds concurrence in the Senate), veto bills (with the proviso that Congress can override), grant pardons, recommend measures to Congress, and "take care that the laws be faithfully executed." On the face of the document, it is rather plain that Congress was supposed to *make* the laws, the executive to carry them out—just the reverse of the prevailing modern view in which the Congress is exhorted to carry out "the President's program."

Why this emphasis on legislative as opposed to executive power? The founders had no illusions about the virtue of legislators as such, and they were as concerned to limit potential abuse of legislative power as abuse of any other kind. Having little faith in human beings armed with compulsory authority, they sought to limit the damage that might be inflicted on society by anybody so equipped.* Nonetheless, their background, experience, and philosophical bias caused them to view the legislature as the principal forum of popular liberties within the tripartite central government. And history suggests their view was altogether proper.

From Magna Carta forward, after all, the effort of the British

---

* Madison, for example, warned against "the danger from legislative usurpation, which, by assembling all power in the same hands, must lead to the same tyranny as executive usurpations." (*Federalist* No. 48.)

"whig" or libertarian interest had been to limit the reach of kingly power over the lives and property of the citizens. English kings were constantly in need of revenues to conduct wars, build fleets, construct new residences, arrange a marriage or an alliance. Since they often didn't have sufficient wealth to do these things themselves, they had to ask for contributions from their subjects assembled in Parliament—assembled, it might be added, in most reluctant fashion. For their part, the subjects were not anxious to fork over their substance without receiving something in return.

Parliament grew up, therefore, as an institution that could and did obtain redress of grievances and defense of popular freedoms as a condition of granting funds to the crown. Because revenues were the principal lever by which the king was held in check, taxation became the leading issue of British politics and the precipitating issue of the American Revolution. The theory was that the revenue of the crown was a free gift of the commons, and it is from this tradition that revenue bills in England, in our Federal Congress, and in state legislatures always originate in the lower house of the assembly, where the "commons," the people generally, are directly represented.

Enforcing these considerations was the fact that America was founded by Puritan settlers who were the most emphatic partisans of the parliamentary interest in the climactic struggles with the Stuart kings, settlers whose covenantal theology told them every form of human authority rose through the popular will—the congregation in the church, the free-born citizenry in the body politic. Add to this the fact that the colonial intelligentsia was steeped in John Locke, the apologist of parliamentary revolution, and the motives impelling the founders toward a reliance on the legislature are apparent.*

Beyond these historical data, there are other factors suggesting that Congress is the logical redoubt of the libertarian interest. In the last analysis, America's founders favored Congress because they favored a system of limited and essentially modest govern-

---

* As law professor Edward Corwin put it: "The colonial period ended with the belief prevalent that 'the executive magistrate' was the natural enemy, the legislative assembly the natural friend of liberty" (*The President: Office and Powers,* New York University Press, 1962, pp. 5–6.)

ment, bound by constitutional restraints and held accountable to the will of the people. They did not want an autocracy or an elite handing down directives from on high. Their bias in favor of Congress fitted in with these conceptions. For a reliance on Congress presupposes, at bottom, a reliance on the popular capacity for self-government.

The Liberals' Perspective on Legislative Power

What pleased the founders, however, has not been pleasing to the friends of economic planning. From the liberal perspective, as described in Chapter Two, a dependence on Congress is something to be devoutly avoided. If the job of government is to plan things, to execute immense designs according to a social blueprint, and to deal with economic problems on a national scale, then Congress in general will be an uncongenial institution. The executive branch, and the administrative bureaucracy in particular, will be much better suited to one's purposes.

To the planning intellect, the handling of socioeconomic problems appears to be essentially a matter of applying means to ends. We have this much poverty or unemployment, that much poor housing, this other amount of substandard medical care. What seems to be needed is the will to "do something," a proper plan of action, and sufficient expenditure of money to get the job done. We must marshal our facts, establish our priorities, and apply our resources. Such is the burden of countless liberal platforms, programs, agendas, manifestos.

Other things being equal, these considerations militate in favor of executive government and against the Congress. In theory at least, the executive sees the total picture and is thus equipped to establish *national* priorities—as opposed to local or parochial ones. Its power is centralized and administered according to hierarchical principles; it can, again in theory, apply the planner's vision uniformly, without a lot of haggling. Its civil service bureaucracy is presumably hired and advanced on principles of professional worth, rather than political leverage, and it is teeming with specialists who don't have to worry about the next election and thus can devote themselves to polishing their expertise.

Congress, by way of contrast, is not adept at applying means to ends, at least as social planners view such matters. The social engineer who casts an eye on our national legislature is usually disheartened by what he sees. Instead of one will at the pinnacle of a hierarchy, he finds an assemblage of 535 different wills, several hundred of whom must be persuaded to a social program before it can be accomplished. Instead of a uniform design in which priorities are graded on a single scale, he discovers a clash of state and local interests. Instead of a permanent cadre of experts, he encounters a motley group of laymen with differing capacities, all supremely interested in pleasing constituencies back home less expert than themselves.

All this is bad enough, but there are other flaws as well—flaws that go to the very nature and spirit of legislative institutions. For congressional government is essentially open-ended, and thus a bit untidy. There is no grand design and very seldom a linear progression toward fixed goals. There is a great deal of backing and filling, as initiatives taken at one time are countered at another or allowed to lapse somewhere along the way. The essential features of the system are its indeterminate quality, its fluidity, and its measured pace—all accompanied by an endless process of discussion. It is above all a *political* system, in which the guiding imperatives are not the findings of the "experts," but the common sense, the judgment, and the aspirations of the average citizen.

Congressional Flaws—from the Liberal View

In addition to these generic traits of legislative bodies, there are other specific aspects of the Federal Congress that excite the hostility of liberal spokesmen. Each of the two houses has attributes of its own that the reformers have subjected to criticism, sometimes with contradictory implications. Certain aspects of the House of Representatives make the reformers angry, while some directly opposite features of the Senate make them mad as well.

The basic problems with the House, as seen by liberal theoreticians, stem from size and the shortness of tenure. The House exemplifies to the utmost the "political" features that seem to the planning intellect so hostile to progress. Its 435 members are elected every two years. Since Congressmen are more or less constantly running for office, their major concern at any given moment is likely to be the mood of their own particular districts.

The House is thus the most intensely parochial and pluralist element of the Federal government, the least inclined to take an over-all view of the "national interest" as defined by the liberals, and therefore the least likely to be smitten by utopian visions for making over the country according to some grandiose design. Moreover, the fact that there are continual fluctuations in its membership means that in any given Congress a considerable portion of the members will be fresh from private life or state-level politics, not particularly "expert" on national issues.

The Senate is quite different in many respects, but from the liberal ideological perspective not appreciably better. Its six-year terms give members a greater interval to adopt less "parochial" views of things (and this does happen) and to develop a bit of expertise. So in these respects a conscientious planning type would have to prefer the Senate to the House. But there are other ways in which the upper chamber, if anything, is even worse than its popular counterpart.

The very makeup of the Senate is manifestly contrary to the ideology of the liberal-left. Despite the recent enthusiasm for the Senate in its combat with Nixon, it is apparent that this chamber violates one of the most cherished precepts of liberal orthodoxy—equality of suffrage. The Senate is a uniquely federal institution, where the states are represented *as* states, not according to population. In its deliberations, the two senators from Wyoming have equal weight with the two from California—which means that 345,000 people have just as much representation as 20 million.*

---

* This consideration is aggravated by the practice of the filibuster, in which senators can go on talking as long as they wish unless there is a two-thirds vote for cloture (cutting off of debate). Since one third plus one of the chamber can keep debating almost indefinitely, the filibuster is frequently used to prevent a vote on a given measure that otherwise would obtain passage (the civil rights bills in the 1950s and early 1960s provide the most prominent examples). When this tactic is employed, it violates democratic orthodoxy twice over: *one* senator from Wyoming can actually cancel the votes of *both* the senators from California. And, of course, it accentuates the major liberal complaint against the Congress—its supposed inability to "get things done." Interestingly enough, liberals in recent years

The work of the congressional committees is a particular irritant to liberal reformers. Indeed, the list of complaints against the committees is almost endless. There is, for one thing, the diffusion of responsibility. Each committee pursues its own objectives in independent fashion, often with seeming disregard for what is being done by somebody else. Jurisdictions overlap, and as many as a half-dozen different committees at a time may be found inquiring into the identical subject matter. Although the final results are melded together somehow, there is no master plan of action.

In addition, choice committee assignments and the powerful chairmanships have traditionally been handed out on a seniority basis, according to length of service. This arrangement has in general proved enormously distasteful to the reformers (although of late their objections have softened a bit as the liberals have accumulated seniority of their own). First, resort to seniority tends to reward age, especially in the Senate, and older legislators are less given to sudden departures and planning initiatives than are the younger ones. Second, the idea of "merit" seems to be subordinated. And, third, the system tends to favor members with "safe" seats, which means in particular the South (although of late this too has been changing), whose members are generally more conservative than their colleagues from the North and East.

Finally, the committees exemplify the open-ended nature of the congressional routine. There is considerable speechifying, debating, and questioning. Witnesses give testimony and are interrogated by congressional staff and by the legislators. There is an ambiance of talk. Bills are watered down, rewritten, or killed entirely, as the process of discussion, horse-trading, protection of local interests, and compromising takes place. The problems from the standpoint of the planner are apparent.

The differences between what a legislative committee and a member of the executive branch can accomplish are vividly set forth by Joseph Harris, a prominent liberal writer on the supposed failings of Congress. "The factors that influence the decisions of legislative committees," Harris tells us, "are often quite different

---

have themselves resorted to filibusters—to block funding of SST aircraft and anti-busing legislation—suggesting the mutability of liberal principles on this as on other matters.

from those that influence department heads. The department head is expected to take into account government-wide policies, the program of the President, how a particular action will affect the policies and operations of other departments and whether it will promote the national interest. He should be prepared to accept responsibility for the policies and actions of his department when they are attacked in Congress and elsewhere."

This noble mandate, Harris asserts, "has a sobering effect upon [the department head's] judgment. His decisions are ordinarily not his alone, but the product of conferences in which many specialists and administrators participate; practical considerations of administration and timing are given great weight. Department decisions are subject to review, consultation, and clearance by other government agencies affected, and often by the central staff agencies of the President."

Measured against this picture of judicious responsibility, the activities of Congress seem downright shameful. "Decisions by congressional committees," according to Harris, "are based on considerations in which provincial, partisan, and personal factors often play key parts. Committee participation in executive decisions, especially when formalized to the extent of giving the committee the final determination, divides responsibility for administration and in essence enables a few members of Congress, who are accountable only to their own constituents, to direct department activities." It is not hard to see where Harris's sympathies lie, or why they lie there.[6] *

Liberal hostility toward the committees has been most vividly

---

* The exasperation of the liberal intellect with legislative idiosyncrasies is expressed with even greater vehemence by Senator Joseph Clark, quoted in earlier chapters. "Whether we look at the city council, the state legislatures, or Congress of the United States," says Clark, "we react to what we see with scarcely concealed contempt. This is the area where democratic government tends to break down. This is where the vested-interest lobbies run riot, where conflict of interest rides unchecked, where demagoguery knows few bounds, where political lag keeps needed action a generation behind the times, where the nineteenth century still reigns supreme in committees, where ignorance is often at a premium and wisdom at a discount, where the evil influence of arrogant and corrupt political machines ignores most successfully the public interest, where the lust for patronage and favors for the faithful do the greatest damage to the public interest."

exemplified, perhaps, in the continuing ideological war against the investigation or hearing. This is the principal *modus operandi* of the committee—the method by which it gathers the information it needs for legislation, decides whether there should be new laws enacted, inquires into executive handling of the laws already on the books, and determines whether any changes or corrections are needed.

With the investigations of Senator Ervin's committee and the House Judiciary Committee in the matters of Watergate and impeachment, the idea of congressional investigations has enjoyed a comeback of sorts in fashionable opinion. Prior to these inquiries, however, congressional investigations were held in generally low repute. They were reviled on a number of counts—as "witch hunts," quests for glory by posturing windbags, "exposure for the sake of exposure," efforts to crush dissent and destroy reputation, unwarranted attempts to interfere with the workings of the executive.

A whole library of books has been written for the purpose of discrediting congressional investigations of one sort or another. Most of them concern the late Senator Joseph McCarthy of Wisconsin and the House Committee on Un-American Activities (later the House Committee on Internal Security), but all tend to some extent to minimize the legitimacy of investigations as such. Frequent charges against McCarthy, for example, were that he sought to undermine and subvert the executive branch by soliciting data from dissident employes, that he challenged executive supremacy in the conduct of foreign affairs, and that he disparaged the supposedly majestic doctrine of executive privilege.*

Even in less controversial and emotional cases, the liberal view has usually inclined against the congressional investigative power. A typical statement is provided by Harris, who claims that congressional investigations disrupt and demoralize executive departments, are inefficient in gathering data, are often spurred by pub-

---

* According to liberal spokesman Telford Taylor: "The essence of the constitutional crisis of 1954 . . . is the effort of some legislators, notably Senator McCarthy, to destroy the President's effective control of the executive branch and bring it under their own domination." (*Grand Inquest,* Simon & Schuster, 1955, p. 112.)

licity-seeking congressmen, involve enormous overlaps of responsibility, and are excessively time-consuming. A more appropriate method of conducting inquiries, he suggests, would be to establish special commissions of inquiry under *executive* control, to look into things in an orderly and responsible manner.*

The Fallacy of Reform

The antagonism toward Congress made manifest by such suggestions is equally clear in other projected "reforms." These include weakening the powers of the committees and their chairmen, consolidating committees to avoid "overlapping," and abolishing seniority. Other proposals that would have the effect of weakening Congress *vis à vis* the executive include providing four-year terms for congressmen, with elections conducted in presidential years; forming committees to parallel the structure of the executive bureaucracy; and giving the executive branch power to engage in various legislative functions. Additionally, liberal reformers have favored methods to eliminate procedures in Congress that enhance its pluralistic and deliberative character—abolishing the filibuster, packing the influential House Rules Committee (a successful project of President Kennedy), forming congressional districts on mathematical population bases, and so on.

The purpose of all these alleged reforms is evident on the face of it. What is demanded is a Congress in which actions can be taken swiftly, impediments and delays and parochial interests don't get in the way, and in general it becomes possible to "get things done." The object, in short, is to transform the legislature, as much

---

* "The President should be authorized, as is the governor of New York under the Moreland Act, to institute such inquiries when there are charges against public officials. . . . Provision should also be made for outside inquiries into administrative management of the government, another area in which congressional inquiries have not been effective. By authorizing the president to institute inquiries in these areas Congress would not give up its authority to look into any aspect of the work of the government, but would provide supplemental machinery which would in some types of investigation be more effective." (*Congressional Control of Administration,* Doubleday Anchor Books, 1965, pp. 326–27.)

as possible, from a pluralistic, diverse, and essentially political body into a handmaiden of the administrative, technical, and social-planning conception of our government.

To grasp the essential fallacy of such proposals, it is necessary to rethink the assumptions that underlie the planners' vision of the state. First off, we may consider the notion that the job of government is to "get things done," and that Congress should be judged according to its ability to meet this standard with efficiency and dispatch. While we may grant and even insist that certain things get done in government, we may also challenge the idea that the proper method of gauging official performance is simply to measure how much is done and how fast it happens.

On the founders' limited-government model, after all, it is just as important for government *not* to do certain things as it is to accomplish certain others. In some respects, indeed, *not* doing things is by far the more important consideration. Our Constitution-makers built restraints and barriers into the system for the explicit purpose of ensuring that certain things did not occur—to forestall precipitate actions that might be injurious to popular freedoms. To say the proper standard of government performance is one of "getting things done," period, and that therefore restraints and barriers must go, is to smuggle a directly contrary assumption into our political discourse.*

Moreover, even on the obvious supposition that *some* things should get done, the liberal way of approaching the matter has reversed the basic principles of the system. The planning model assumes that somebody or other (liberal theorists, the President, various "experts") has already determined *what* needs to be done, and that the performance of Congress is to be measured by its willingness or ability to accomplish these objectives. The point of our system is the reverse: *What* needs to be done is just the question that requires deciding, and with the provisos already noted is for Congress, and not the executive and its various outriders, to decide.†

* This does not mean, of course, that any particular restraint is justified— but simply that "getting things done" as a generic argument against restraints is fallacious.
† Confusion on this point is closely tied to the idea of government as the preserve of "experts" weighing technical issues in which the goals to be

From a libertarian perspective, then, it is desirable that Congress reassert its authority in the equation of governmental powers, that it defend its diverse and pluralistic attributes, and that it retain the various procedural filters and impediments that serve to prevent "getting things done" according to the planners' model. It is extremely doubtful that our constitutional system, our personal liberties, and our economic well-being can survive the continued absorption of power into the executive vortex, or the conversion of Congress into a planners' helper. Reforms are needed, but they are generally of the opposite tendency from those suggested by the usual spokesmen.

---

sought are already known and debate is reduced to a question of how best to achieve them. In this conception, Congress is thought to be in need of expert counsel, and the executive bureaucracy with its complement of experts is seen as the superior instrument of policy. The founders' view was of course quite different. The truly important questions, again, are not *technical* but *political*—not *how* we do something, but *what* we are to do.

In making such decisions, the common sense of the average citizen and of his representatives in Congress is supposed to be paramount, with technicians called in where needed to help achieve the *politically* determined objective. The repeated suggestion that the real issues are "technical" in nature bootlegs the idea that planning is the goal to be sought, and also, of course, enhances the power of the supposed experts in the executive branch to control and direct our national policies.

5

The Court
and
the Constitution

One of the prevailing myths about American liberalism is that it is more concerned with procedures than with objects. On the usual argument, the liberal outlook is one in which certain "democratic" or libertarian guidelines are the major topics of interest. The essence of the creed, before all else, is to live within the guidelines. Thus presented, the liberal view of politics is like a sportsman's view of an athletic contest. If the game is fairly played and the proper rules adhered to, the democratic liberal will acquiesce serenely in the result.

This attitude is phrased in various ways, depending on the issue up for consideration. In philosophical discourse it becomes commitment to the scientific method—to the process of investigation rather than the product of it. On the university campus, we know the doctrine as academic freedom—devotion to a method or condition of inquiry rather than a fixed conception of the truth. In explicit politics, it becomes commitment to the "democratic process," or, perhaps, to the open society. However phrased, the common assumption in all these cases is that, if the rules are followed out implicitly, the chief imperatives of liberal faith will be fulfilled.

It is widely assumed, by liberals and conservatives alike, that liberals really do believe such things. Americans for Democratic Action, for example, begins a typical manifesto by declaring: "ADA's most fundamental tenet is faith in the democratic process," [1] while conservatives such as editor William Buckley and academician Willmoore Kendall have repeatedly flayed the liberals for their announced allegiance to such fatuous notions. It makes for interesting and amusing debate, and has produced some first-rate polemics. The only difficulty with it is that the whole affray is based on a false assumption. For on the record before us, liberals really don't believe anything of the sort.

It is true, of course, that many American liberals are concerned with right procedure in specific cases, and some of the politest people in American politics are liberals. To that extent, the conventional utterance is correct. But the fact remains that liberalism, as a body of working political doctrine, is not really committed to any set of institutions; nor is it willing to forego specific objectives in deference to any identifiable "process." It may be plausibly argued that the actual situation is just the reverse: that American liberals, first and foremost, are interested in achieving certain results, and only secondarily in *how* those results are obtained. And that, if a given set of rules does not produce as expected, liberals will set about forthwith to change them. This is a mind-set profoundly hostile to American freedoms.

Granted that liberal attitudes toward rules-of-the-game will vary according to what the particular rules may happen to be—those that enjoy higher status than others being less readily abandoned. But the general thrust of liberal advocacy on most political issues is tolerably clear, and strongly in the other direction. It says that if a particular set of rules does what you want, then they should be treated with the utmost piety. If not, get rid of them and find some new ones.

This mentality emerges quite clearly in our discussion of the executive, where alleged commitment to a set of political arrangements dissolves abruptly when those arrangements no longer produce desired results. Such reversals have occurred with respect to other arrangements as well, which gain or lose procedural sanctity in keeping with their ideological yield. The most obvious case in point, beyond the presidency, is the liberal attitude toward the courts. In many ways, indeed, this is the more interesting topic, since it involves not only the liberal attitude toward a particular set of rules, but toward the idea of *having* any rules at all.

Liberals Against the Courts

In recent years, the liberal-left has been quite enamored of the courts, particularly the Supreme Court under Earl Warren. Liberals have been ecstatic with high court rulings on civil rights, criminal procedure, internal security, pornography (for a time), abortion, and numerous other matters. School integration rulings beginning with *Brown v. Board of Education* (1954), decrees on criminal procedure beginning with *Mallory v. U.S.* (1957), and reapportionment decisions such as *Baker v. Carr* (1962) have been particular favorites. Moreover, leftward activists have taken routinely to the courts to obtain objectives blocked in legislative chambers—bringing class action and "public interest" law suits respecting prayer in the schools, educational financing, civil rights, abortion, busing. It is fair to say that for the past two decades the courts have been the most effective of all the instruments of government in promoting liberal social policies.

It is hardly surprising, therefore, that liberals in this period have been smitten with the Federal judiciary. They have taken up the cudgels to defend the Warren court from the aspersions of its critics, and have stoutly argued the wisdom and finality of various Federal court decrees. Criticism of such rulings or efforts to alter them by amendment or legislation, they have argued, strike at the majesty of law and the sacred concept of judicial review (the power of the courts to pass judgment on the constitutionality of actions of the executive or the Congress).*

* As Professor Charles Black put the matter in the 1960s: "What we are being asked to do, by those who would have us give up or seriously weaken judicial review, is to change the essence of the structure of government under which our nation grew to what it is, to jettison the postulate of limitation on government that has from the first been one of our fundamental political assumptions, and to embark on the experiment of doing

As with the presidency, however, 'twas not always thus. In point of fact, the liberal position on such questions for many years was exactly the opposite—a stance of fierce *hostility* toward judicial review, the Federal courts, and judges in general who imposed their notions of constitutionality on the actions of the legislature or the President. The very idea that judges of the Supreme Court or any other could or should impartially measure constitutional issues was hotly contested, and the practice of judicial review disparaged as an intolerable breach of majority rule.

To illustrate the point, we need only flip back the pages of our history to an era in which the courts were doing not what the liberals wanted, but what they despised—the epoch of the early New Deal. In this period, the President and Congress were devising numerous schemes for the extension of Federal power such as the National Recovery Act, wage regulation, and farm quotas, creating bureaus, engendering programs, and issuing orders in great profusion, in a considerable departure from what the Supreme Court perceived to be the meaning of the Constitution. As a result, various programs were struck down, bureaus abolished, and orders canceled by judicial decree.

Anger against the court in liberal intellectual circles was unconfined. The "nine old men" were denounced in editorials and ridiculed in cartoons. Senators berated them as usurpers of legislative right, and learned scholars demonstrated their incompetence to stem the flow of democratic progress. In 1937 President Roosevelt climaxed the onslaught with his court-packing plan, which would have expanded the number of justices and permitted him to appoint a majority in favor of his programs. The plan was not enacted, but the threat of it was sufficient to turn the court around and open the way for Federal regulation of the economy.

All of which, by liberal standards, was very meet and proper. Consider the testimony of Robert Jackson, who was successively

---

without the practical effects on government of one of our chief elder institutions. . . . it must be a foolish generation indeed that would change radically the form of government under which it and its fathers have prospered [on less than conclusive grounds], whatever theoretical arguments might be put forward." (*The People and the Court,* Spectrum Books, 1960, p. 171.)

solicitor general and attorney general under Roosevelt, and thereafter was himself appointed to the high tribunal. Jackson spelled out the New Deal view of the court and its functions in a 1940 volume called *The Struggle for Judicial Supremacy.* Like other liberal statements from that era, it makes provocative reading nowadays.

"The basic grievance of the New Deal," Jackson wrote, "was that the court has seemed unduly to favor private economic power and always to find ways of circumventing the efforts of popular government to control or regulate it. . . . liberal-minded lawyers . . . recognized that constitutional law is not a fixed body of immutable doctrine. . . . What we demanded for our generation was the right consciously to influence the evolutionary process of constitutional law."

Thanks to the turnaround of the court, Jackson added, "my generation has won its fight to make its own impression on the court's constitutional doctrine. It has done it *by marshaling the force of public opinion against the old court through the court fight,* by trying to influence the choice of forward-looking personnel, and, most of all, by persuasion of the court itself." [2] (Italics added.) Not exactly a picture of dumbfounded awe before the majestic power of judicial review.

Nor were such opinions confined to partisans like Jackson. On the contrary, the New Deal packers were able (and retrospectively still are) to call on scholarly folk who thought that Roosevelt was perfectly justified in his position. Thus law professor Alpheus Mason informs us that the court's "obscurantist" and "reactionary" rulings made the packing plan "well-nigh inevitable." "It was quite clear," Mason says, "that the trouble lay not with the Constitution but with men, the nine justices of the Supreme Court. . . . Armed with this brand of realism, FDR girded for battle. Rather than resort to the long-drawn-out amending process . . . the President chose to effect a showdown by drawing on existing constitutional resources—congressional control of the court's size and the President's appointing power." [3]

In attacking the court and its rulings, the liberals did not omit attacks on the idea of judicial review as such. Liberal philosopher Morris Cohen observed that our liberties were much better off in the hands of Congress than in the hands of the judiciary,* and found his argument seconded by liberal historian Henry Steele Commager. Commager asserted that the American experience "justifies us . . . in believing that majority will does not imperil minority rights, either in theory or in operation." In proof of this contention he ran through a list of notable cases and concluded: "What is perhaps most impressive about this record is that it tends to support the Jeffersonian allegation that the court is neither more learned nor more objective than the political branches of the government. . . . The conclusion is almost inescapable that judicial review has been a drag upon democracy, and—what we may conceive to be the same thing—upon good government." [4]

Historian Irving Brant synthesized these various liberal attitudes toward the court in a 1936 volume called *Storm Over the Constitution*. The high tribunal, according to Brant, had substituted its judgment "of what serves the common defense and the general welfare for the judgment of the lawmaking body." Such legislative judgment, he contended, "is outside the legitimate bounds of judicial review," and the court had in consequence become "a veritable third chamber of the legislative branch, a superchamber of nine members chosen for life."

In Brant's conception, citizens and Congress were not powerless to change the results of Federal court rulings—even though he disparaged resort to the amendment process (which he thought excessively cumbersome) and opposed overt attempts at packing. The best and ultimate solution in his opinion was to elect Presidents who would appoint the right kind of justices, but short of this there were powers in Congress by which the courts could, and should, be brought under restraint.

---

* Cohen put it this way in a 1935 essay for *The Nation:* "Quite fallacious is the rhetorical argument that without this power vested in the courts we should be at the mercy of legislative majorities. This argument ignores the historic fact that in few, if any, actual cases have the majority of our people felt themselves saved from congressional oppression by judicial intervention. On the contrary, Congress being more responsive to popular demand, our people as a whole have felt more resentment at being at the mercy of a small judicial minority than at being at the mercy of very large legislative majorities. Besides, the mischief of congressional wrongs can be readily remedied at the next election, while the mischief of judicial decisions in the name of the Constitution requires the laborious consent of two-thirds of each house of Congress and three quarters of the state legislatures."

"Presumably," he wrote, "Congress could forbid inferior Federal courts to nullify Federal statutes, since the lower courts may be created or abolished by the will of Congress, and the statute creating them determines their jurisdiction." To this he added in a footnote that, "whatever is done about judicial review in general, the power of district and circuit courts to nullify Federal laws should be taken away. Intolerable confusion results when laws are operative in some districts, inoperative in others."

The Supreme Court was a tougher nut to crack, since it has original constitutional status, but Brant had suggestions for getting around this problem, too: "The Constitution in express terms permits Congress to restrict or take away the appellate jurisdiction of the Supreme Court, except in certain cases." Moreover, "Congress might require a two-thirds vote in the Supreme Court, or even a unanimous vote, to nullify a Federal law. Even without a constitutional amendment, therefore, the power of judicial review can be so circumscribed as to make it difficult indeed for the courts to set aside Federal law."

Brant did not favor totally eradicating judicial review, but made it plain that he approved the suggestion for limitation. "On balance," he wrote, "the record is overwhelmingly against judicial review of acts of Congress, measured by the actual use to which that power has been put. Limitation of the power to nullify acts of Congress, by requiring more than a simple majority in the court, would simply apply the principle of certitude used in ratification of treaties or the overriding by Congress of a presidential veto." [5] *

In considerable measure the liberal offensive of the 1930s was successful. It not only turned the nine old men around in their tracks, but it obliterated the notion of judicial review itself in matters of economic compulsion. The hallmark of the court after 1937 was, precisely, that it would avert its gaze from any sort of congressional action in the field of property rights, or contracts, or industrial regulation, and let the majority do as it pleased. Both

---

* In 1963 this volume was reissued, with a preface lauding the Supreme Court of that day. All the language quoted here, with the exception of the first and last paragraphs, was dropped from the text. In its place Brant inserted a statement that either abolishing judicial review or establishing a "rule of unanimity for invalidation of federal laws" would "create worse evils than it could cure"—on the latter point, a statement substantially opposite to his view when the court was in conservative hands.

in theory and in practice, judicial review in cases of this type was simply done away with—to the loud and continuing applause of liberal legalists.*

The Liberal Rationale: the Theory of Dominant Power

Again it appears the liberals have blandly changed the rules of the game, opposing the court when it hurt their cause, supporting it when their cause was helped. If that were all there was to the matter, we might chalk it up to human nature and the games people play when their interests are at stake.† The problem, however, goes considerably deeper than mere hypocrisy. For the liberal spokesmen have a rationale for such reversals, suggesting that the conversion from one opinion to the other is a natural result of their philosophy. And it is this rationale that is the most disturbing factor in the argument.

On the liberal analysis, the basic issue in discussion of the courts, as in discussion of politics in general, is the matter of *dominant power*. At any given time, liberal spokesmen have theorized,

---

* Thus liberal historian Leonard Levy says: "The only check now on Congress' exercise of the commerce power is Congress' own sense of self-restraint. . . . There are no longer any meaningful constitutional limitations on the national commerce power. Congress may do as it wishes; policy is politically determined, without constitutional restraints. . . . The commerce clause is Congress' authority to regulate every aspect of the nation's economy, should it wish to do so. . . . One cannot imagine a legitimate economic regulation by Congress which the court might void as a violation of the commerce clause. Whenever a case raises a question of the constitutionality of congressional exercise of this power, the only thing in doubt is the size of the court majority. No act of Congress, needless to remark, has been struck down on commerce grounds, since 1936. . . . In sum, the court has abdicated its power of judicial review when passing on the constitutionality of congressional exercise of the commerce power." Levy is of the opinion that this "comports with the framer's intent." (*American Constitutional Law,* Harper Torchbooks, 1966, pp. 188–90.)

† It is true that certain conservative spokesmen have executed the same maneuver in reverse—favoring judicial review in the 1930s, opposing it in the 1950s and 1960s. They are wrong, too. Such conservative reversals are considered further in Chapter 17.

the majority should be able to do what it wants, and should not have impediments placed in its way. In this conception, the role of the judiciary is seen as the essentially modest one of assisting in this process and making it work as smoothly as possible. Justice Oliver Wendell Holmes had expressed the position about as clearly as it could be stated:

> It has always seemed to us a singular anomaly that believers in the theory of evolution and in the natural development of institutions by successive adaptations to the environment should be found laying down a theory of government intended to establish its limits once for all by logical deduction from axioms. . . . All that can be expected from modern improvements is that legislation should easily and quickly, yet not too quickly, modify itself in accordance with the will of the *de facto* supreme power in the community, and that the spread of an educated sympathy should reduce the sacrifice of minorities to a minimum. . . .[6]

Holmes was to stress this idea repeatedly throughout a long career of defending government power against the rights of individuals * and it won him numerous hosannahs from the liberals. Reverence for dominant power was a leading motive in liberal speculations on the Constitution, the legal process, and judicial review throughout the 1920s and 1930s. It was, in essence, the obverse or flip-side of the liberal view examined in Chapter Two, wherein ideas of an unchanging higher law are dismissed as naive and foolish. Since values are always in flux, it follows that legal truth must move with the pulse of constant change—and thus with majority sentiments of the moment.†

---

* "The first requirement of a sound body of law is, that it should correspond with the actual feelings and demands of the community, whether right or wrong." (*The Common Law*, Little Brown, 1963, p. 36.) "The truth seems to me to be that, subject to compensation when compensation is due, the legislature may restrict or forbid any business when it has sufficient force of public opinion behind it." (*American Constitutional Law*, p. 166.)

† One especially influential version of this outlook was the testament of judicial realism published in 1930 by Judge Jerome Frank. According to Frank, the notion of unchanging axioms of law was a childish delusion;

Such conceptions are obviously hostile to judicial review—at least as that idea had been enunciated by Sir Edward Coke back in the seventeenth century and by others of his tradition. The basic theory was that judges should take the actions of the legislature or other branches of government and lay these alongside some sort of "higher law," which was supposed to direct and limit official activity. If the ordinary law was in conflict with the secular approximation of the higher law (in Coke's case the common law, in ours the Constitution) then the ordinary law, majority or no, was invalid.

Since the basic liberal position was, precisely, that there *wasn't* any "higher law," and that constitutions were simply human wishes like any others, the whole procedure as conducted at this level was at best a bit of a charade, at worst malicious interference with needed social action. And since their alleged function in applying the higher law was therefore either meaningless or anti-social, it was time for judges to stop pretending they were messengers from Olympus and let the majority have its way.*

The liberal spokesmen were prepared to grant that judges were necessary in society to arbitrate disputes that could not be

---

"adults" would realize that the dictates of the law must change as circumstances change. Law is but an approximate solution to human problems, and "the economic political and social problems are ever shifting. So that, in the very nature of the situation, the approximations must be revised frequently and can never be accepted as final in terms of satisfactory consequences. . . . [Legal] abstractions . . . are tools whose whole value is instrumental. They have been contrived to meet particular problems. As new problems arise, the old tools must be adapted to cope with them." (*Law and the Modern Mind*, Doubleday Anchor Books, 1963, p. 263.)

* The climactic argument to this effect was provided by President Roosevelt himself:

The courts have cast doubts on the ability of the elected Congress to protect us against catastrophe by meeting squarely our modern social and economic conditions. . . . Since the rise of the modern movement for social and economic progress through legislation, the court has more and more boldly asserted a power to veto laws passed by the Congress and by the state legislatures. . . . There is no basis for the claim made by some members of the Court that something in the Constitution has compelled them regretfully to thwart the will of the people. [Robert H. Jackson, *The Struggle for Judicial Supremacy,* Vintage Books, 1941, pp. 343–44.]

settled otherwise. But the liberals vigorously contended that judicial decisions were law-*making* decisions, that judges were simply human beings wielding political power. As part of the total process in which dominant power asserted itself, they were themselves to be judged accordingly—judged, as Brant and Commager suggest, according to *what* they decided, rather than by any abstract merit attaching to their station.*

Once broken to the bit, the mustang is a serviceable mount, and may be treated in kindlier fashion. Liberal attitudes toward the court reversed quite sharply after 1937, as the justices endorsed and ratified the work of democratic progress. By knuckling under to Roosevelt, the court had grown immensely in stature. "It took an agonizing rumpus," writes Professor Mason, "to force [Chief Justice] Charles Evans Hughes to realize that 'statesmanship in a democratic community consists in the use of public authority to make the necessary adaptation to the changing political and social demands of the time.' " [7] The court had received the liberal message and said "uncle" to the majority, so its "incidence upon American life" was generally to be approved.

If the story simply ended there, we would have a happy morality play in which the Supreme Court grew up and was accepted by the liberals. There are, however, some problems. Most of this theorizing about the "will of the people" had rather blandly assumed that what the majority of the people wanted would roughly correspond to what the liberals wanted. This was, after all, an era flushed with Rooseveltian landslides and shot through with assumptions about the inevitable leftward drift of everything. It was widely supposed that dominant power in the regular politi-

---

* Max Lerner also wrote that the Supreme Court was "a crucial agency for social control. As such it is part of our fabric of statesmanship and should be judged in terms of its incidence upon American life." (In Robert G. McCloskey, ed., *Essays in Constitutional Law*, Vintage Books, 1957, p. 139.) The view expressed by Brant was similar: "A Supreme Court so minded has but to interpret the implied powers of Congress as broadly as the framers saw them, to make them adequate to Federal responsibilities." That day would come, he thought, "should the people ever realize, as the feudalists have realized for generations, that the court is an agency for the expression of power, and not a force all-powerful in itself, impersonal and changeless." (*Storm Over the Constitution*, Bobbs-Merrill, 1936, pp. 247–48.)

cal process was going to favor the liberals; hence it followed that dominant power should be, well, dominant.

In recent years, however, these suppositions have been badly shattered. It turns out that the dominant force in the world of politics can be, and frequently is, quite contrary to what the liberals want—as, for example, in civil liberties cases involving Communists or other unpopular minority groups, prayer in the schools, racial integration. In instances like these, one's stand on judicial review can no longer be based on simple grounds of majority rule —the bad court of the 1930s opposing the majority, the good court of the post-packing era assisting it. For in these latter cases, the court is clearly *opposing* itself to majority sentiment, yet the liberals have praised its decisions and rallied eagerly to its defense.

This situation presents the liberals with a rather delicate dilemma. Having disparaged the higher law in favor of dominant force, and opposed judicial review in favor of the majority, they must suddenly wheel about and start marching off in the other direction: Now they must *oppose* the majority and *support* judicial review. But since they have pretty well disposed of the old restraints, a full-scale reversion is hardly possible, or seemly. They have therefore attempted to devise a halfway formula that blunts the implications of their earlier stance. In *some* cases, they now inform us, we must let the majority override the strictures of the courts; but in *other* cases, we must let the courts override the majority.

Exactly how this peculiar position is argued, and what its merits are, will be considered in Chapter 17. For the present, suffice it to observe that the rules are altered once again. On this analysis, the test of judicial policy is not whether the court agrees with the majority and lets it work its will, but whether it *agrees with the liberals*. If so, it is to be praised; if not, condemned. We arrive at a situation, quite simply, in which the will of the liberal intelligentsia is sovereign—and the actions of President, Congress, courts, and the people themselves, will be weighed accordingly.

What Is the Proper Judicial Role?

To criticize the liberal performance on judicial review is not, of course, to settle the question or establish the proper role of the judiciary. The problem is admittedly vexed, and scholars of considerable reputation have spoken out on either side of the matter, apart from ideological confusions. The silence of the Constitution has given rise to boundless speculation, and makes it possible to score points for either position. Nonetheless, for those who favor limited government, the case for judicial review is persuasive.

Indeed, it is difficult to see how a system of checks and balances could work without it. The American Constitution, as noted in Edward Corwin's famous essay on this subject, presupposes the existence of a higher law that constrains the actions of the government, and the written Constitution is the secular approximation of this law—or at least the best approximation fallible man has been able to come up with. Implicit in this view is the idea that the conduct of different elements of the government will be matched against the constitutional standard—and if found wanting, disallowed.

That the judges were meant to perform the role of matching ordinary laws to fundamental law is at least strongly suggested by the intellectual background of the founders and their experience living in the British colonies. Their fealty to Lord Coke was famous, and Coke was most celebrated for his articulation of judicial review as a method for measuring acts of government against the accumulated precedent of British law that wended back to Magna Carta. The thrust of Coke's position was that the Constitution, applied by judges, was binding on King and Parliament alike.*

When John Marshall asserted the right of judicial review in *Marbury v. Madison* (1803), he was performing a role correlative to Coke's, moving to make the Federal judiciary a balance-wheel against the other elements of the system. He was saying that acts

---

* America's founders studied Coke religiously in their battles with King and Parliament, and repeatedly invoked his authority and that of Magna Carta and the common law, along with their charter rights as colonists, in opposition to the arbitrary use of power. These precedents were all thrown into the fray over the writs of assistance in 1761 and the Stamp Act in 1765 and were explicitly linked to the concept of judicial review.

As John Adams put it in summarizing the colonial case against the writs: "An act against natural equity is void, and if an act of Parliament should be made, in the very words of the petition, it should be void. The executive courts must pass such acts into disuse."

of the executive and the legislature must be made to conform to the dictates of the Constitution, that where they did not they would be void, and that this determination fell by law and logic to the judiciary. While one may differ with the court's decision in any given case, it is hard to see how the restraints of the constitutional system can be made to function if this power is not invoked.*

Perhaps the best argument for judicial review is a consideration of the alternative systems suggested in its place. The most usual alternative is the later British model provided by William Blackstone, the famous legalist, and pressed so insistently in America during the epoch of the New Deal: the notion of unfettered legislative (or executive) sovereignty. In this conception, the legislature can do as it wishes because it is the embodiment of the popular will, and as such the epitome of "democratic" feeling. If the courts with their notions of constitutionality stand in the way, the legislature should be able to override them. The fount of this conception is Blackstone's assertion that Parliament is the seat of that "absolute despotism" which must reside somewhere in every political system.

Whatever else might be said about such attitudes, it should be clear that they are not compatible with the idea of limited government. The very idea of such a system is that nobody possesses "absolute despotism," and that "the people"—meaning a majority thereof at any given moment—may *not* do whatever they wish. The logic of checks and balances is that every form of political power must be subject to *some* constraint. It would seem to follow that judicial review is essential to hold the exercise of government power accountable to the dictates of the Constitution—although

---

* Marshall argued that this responsibility of the courts was at once made more imperative and more obvious by the fact that America had what Britain did not—a *written* Constitution defining the scope of governmental powers and the interrelationship of the various elements. Enactment of this Constitution and the debates surrounding it made it crystal clear that in the United States neither legislator, nor President, nor anyone else, possessed sovereign power to do whatever he wished, but rather was to conduct himself within the restraints provided by the Constitution. What Coke asserted for England was in America tolerably clear from the outset. Over there, the notion that king or Parliament was subject to higher constraint was a source of endless battling; over here, the corresponding notions were part and parcel of the original settlement.

other restraints may and should come into play as well (as when the executive and legislative branches check each other).

Having said all this, however, we must admit there are problems with the concept. The most obvious of these is the objection raised by Madison—the anomaly of giving one branch of a supposedly balanced system decisive power over the others.* The point is well taken. The object of checks and balances, as Madison also said, is not to seal off the branches in tripartite seclusion, but to provide each with a "partial agency," or check upon the others. That argues the need for judicial review; but it also argues against the notion of the court as more exalted than other members of the Federal triad. It is no more necessary to assume the court is higher than or better than the other branches to support the cause of judicial review than it is to assume the President is higher or better than the Congress because he possesses the veto. Both are aspects of "partial agency."

If all this be so, it implies an important corollary: The court itself, at some point along the way, is also subject to constraint. For if the logic of the constitutional system is that no person or group of people can exercise "absolute despotism" without running up against some kind of barrier, then the court itself must be subject to some restriction.

This point would be valid under any circumstances, but becomes especially so when the court assumes an activist and social engineering posture. Charles Black argues in behalf of the court that it has only a negative, restraining power rather than that of initiating constructive or affirmative action. "The very most the court ever has," he tells us, "is a veto." [8] Therefore, we need not

---

* In general, Madison said, the court should see to the normal adjudication of the law—but where the powers of the other branches were concerned the problem became much more difficult. ". . . I beg to know," he said, "upon what principles it can be contended that any one department draws from the Constitution greater powers than another in marking out the limits of the powers of the several departments. The Constitution is the charter of the people in the government; it specifies certain greater powers as absolutely granted, and marks out the departments to exercise them. If the constitutional boundary of either is brought into question I do not see that any one of these independent departments has more right than another to declare their sentiments on that point." (Debate in Congress, June 17, 1789.)

worry about the policy attitudes that prevail there or the willingness of the justices to inject their attitudes into the process of construing the laws.

If this were true the question of whether the court should be submitted to constraints could be kept comfortably abstract and theoretical. So long as that tribunal is essentially passive, preventing enactment or enforcement of certain legislation, the social costs may often seem objectionable, but at least we are left essentially where we were. In that event, the court cannot materially alter the contours of our system and cannot do irreparable damage to our freedoms.

The situation becomes quite different, however, when the courts decide to take on themselves the task of projecting affirmative policy, ordering that certain things be done, commanding actions and expenditures, assuming control of prisons and schools and asylums (all of which has happened recently), and do so in order to achieve legislative effects that have been rejected by the legislatures themselves. Obvious examples of this tendency include decisions on reapportionment, abortion, school finances, and racial balance busing, wherein the courts have actively commanded steps that legislatures have refused to take, or else demanded actions in contravention of legislative statement.

Our system of government dictates an equation of federal powers. The Supreme Court should, indeed, have the power to negate laws of Congress and actions of the executive, to apply a necessary restraint to their actions and ensure that they remain within their constitutional limits. By the same token, the Congress and the President should have at their disposal means for limiting the court if, *in extremis,* such limits are required.

6
The
Growth
of Government

In response to the ideas traversed in the preceding chapters, the past forty years have witnessed an exponential increase in the scope of Federal power. On a variety of pretexts, authority has been drained upward out of the states and into the central government, and within that government away from the Congress and into the hands of the executive. The result is that we have erected on the banks of the Potomac precisely the kind of concentrated, untethered system of political and economic authority that America's founders wanted to avoid.

As we have seen, there has been a revision of liberal thought concerning certain applications of this power. But the revision is only partial; it seems for the most part to consist of the view that the wrong kind of people are exercising power rather than the belief that the power itself is excessive. For most purposes, the liberal orthodoxy still favors concentration of political authority, and hardly a day goes by that some liberal spokesman or other does not propose still more of it.

Later sections of this volume will examine the various extenuations offered for such proposals and the assurances given us concerning them. First, however, it would be well to establish the nature of the transformation that has come over our political system. Despite a general awareness that we are living in an era of "big government," many of the facts concerning how big it is, why it got that way, and who exactly is responsible are not widely understood.

How Big Is It?

That the Federal government today is very big will be denied by no one. Evidence of its growth is apparent on every hand. There are, by actual count, upward of 1,000 different Federal programs being administered throughout our society, and it is the rare citizen who does not encounter a Federal functionary in some capacity or another—as tax gatherer, subsidy-dispenser, regulator, counselor, baby-sitter, or inspector. There is virtually no zone or echelon of American life that does not have its own set of Federal agents and monitors, who make it their ceaseless business to watch over, guide, assist, and rebuke the private citizen in his daily round of activities.

The process has extended so far that the figures documenting the Federal elephantiasis are almost meaningless. We know, for example, that there is an enormous Federal budget of $300 billion or so, and we can discover that this sum sustains some 6 million Federal employes (military and civilian) with an annual payroll of almost $60 billion; that the Federal government owns some 760 million acres of land—one third of all the land in the United States (up from 400 million in 1959); that it owns 406,428 buildings; and that its total property holdings as of 1972 were worth a cool $435.6 billion. And so on.[1]

But what, exactly, does it all mean? The figures are so large as to boggle the imagination. Their very hugeness, indeed, makes the whole affair so generally incomprehensible that the position of such as John Kenneth Galbraith is in a way enhanced. Since nobody understands it anyway, it is just as easy to argue that government should somehow be even *bigger* than to suggest it should be smaller. What's another $100 billion, or another 37 programs? To John Q. Public, it's all a bit of a fantasy, so the suggestion that we have somehow "starved" our public services and should be giving them even more goes down without rebuke.

Adding to the confusion is that besetting evil of our political discourse—an almost total lack of perspective. We have had big government for so long now that many people can't remember anything else. In particular, a couple of generations of us have been born and raised in a period when it has simply been assumed the Federal government should have extensive responsibility for our lives, and the idea that the situation might ever have been otherwise doesn't often suggest itself. The enormous Federal government is simply there, and always has been.

The size and scope of Federal authority, however, *haven't* always been there, and they do not exist as part of the natural order of things. They have been created in obedience to liberal doctrine, as a result of continuous striving to add new programs, enact new regulations, and above all spend more money. The governmental establishment that exists in America today has grown by steady and discernible stages, and if we set up a few reliable benchmarks, we can clock its progress with a fair degree of precision.

Perhaps the simplest method of proceeding is to examine the budgetary record for the past four decades, a record that is a matter of public information and accessible, presumably, even to Galbraith. The figures show that the growth of government since the epoch of the New Deal has been truly enormous.

To measure the enormity, we need only note that Federal expenditure in calendar 1929 came to less than $3 billion ($2.6 billion, to be exact), whereas the budget for fiscal 1975 is approximately $300 billion. That works out to a 10,000 percent increase over a span of 46 years. This has occurred at a time when America's population was growing from 120 million or so to approximately 210 million, a hike of 75 percent. Federal expenditures have thus been escalating 130 times as fast as population. And the problem is intensified by the fact that state and local expenditure has been growing simultaneously on its own. Such spending in 1971 amounted to $117.7 billion, compared to $7.6 billion in 1929—an increase of approximately 1,000 percent.[2]

These data show that government growth at every level has been colossal, but also that the Federal sector has far outstripped the state and local components. As a result there has been not merely a tremendous increase in the size of government, but a radical transformation of power relationships *within* the political system. In 1929, state and local governments together were spending three times as much as the Federal government; but in 1971, the Federal government was spending almost twice as much as the other two levels of authority combined. (In addition, much of the state and local spending is undertaken at the explicit order of the Federal government anyway.)

These are measures, of course, of gross enlargement. They do not account for such factors as the interposition of a world war and the Cold War, increase of the gross national product (GNP), or the impact of inflation—all of which affect our angle of vision. When these are considered, the total growth record is mitigated, but the remaining indices are still impressive. It is obvious, for example, that the national mobilization for the Second World War raised Federal spending levels to unprecedented heights. But if we focus our attention on the course of events succeeding that war, we find the growth of Federal power has continued upward at a steady pace.

During the war years, the Federal budget rose to $95.5 billion, while state and local budgets remained essentially static. But by 1947 the effects of war expenditure had subsided and the Federal budget for that year was only $29.8 billion. This means that in the 25-year period from Truman to Nixon the Federal budget soared from less than $30 billion to $300 billion or so, an increase of roughly 1,000 per cent—less appalling than 10,000 percent, but appalling nonetheless. (Huge percentage increases, of course, become less feasible as the base figure expands, but we must admit the Federal spenders have managed to sustain a handsome growth rate despite this handicap.)

During all this period GNP has also increased, a datum often cited by proponents of further spending. What counts, they say, is not the number of dollars disbursed, but the relation of these to the country's total product. And it is true that in terms of GNP the hike of government spending is slightly less astronomical than suggested by the dollar totals. But it is still awesome. Between 1929 and 1971, for example, GNP increased from $103 billion to $1 trillion—an impressive record of growth. But during the same span, total government spending increased from $10.3 billion to $339 billion. While GNP was increasing 10 times, that is, government outlays were increasing 33 times. In terms of aggregate burden, the progression in total government spending is clear: from 10 percent of GNP to 32.2 percent.[3] *

Another measure of official growth is the number of people on public payrolls, and again the long-range comparisons are instructive. In 1929, there were more than 28 million Americans in private jobs; by 1971 this figure had risen to better than 57 million, slightly more than double the earlier figure. The public sector has expanded much more rapidly. In 1929, there were just over 3 million people on government payrolls. In 1971 there were 14 million. Private employment had gone up 104 percent—government employment, 319 percent.

Sticking to the postwar years, we find the number of employes in private industry increased by about 40 percent—from 40 million to approximately 57 million. In the same span, the number of government employes increased by 100 percent—from 7.2 to 14.4 million. If we exclude the military component, the official increase is still more than 100 percent—from 5.6 to 11.6 million. This explosion of the bureaucratic population gives us one civilian government payroller for every five in private industry, compared to one for every seven back in 1949.[4]

Such calculations do not include the corresponding increase in the nation's welfare population, which grew from an estimated 6 million in 1950 to 15 million or so in April 1972. Between 1960 and 1971, U.S. population increased by roughly 13 percent, but the number of people on welfare increased by more than 100 percent. All told, therefore, we are talking about 30 million people who for whatever reason are directly supported by the taxpayer— and this does not count many millions more who are recipients of subsidies, direct or indirect, from various levels of government.[5]

---

* In 1929, Federal spending amounted to 2.5 percent of GNP, while state and local spending amounted to 7.4 percent. By 1971, the Federal share had gone to 21 percent, while state and local had moved up to 11.2 percent.

The Taxpayer's Burden

The impact of all this is felt by the average citizen in a number of ways, but the most obvious is the burden of taxation. Once more, if we review the long-term record, we see the growth rate is enormous. The per capita tax load to pay the costs of government at all levels increased from $65 in 1932 to $1,502 in 1972. And again we can see that the pace has continued in the period after the Second World War. In 1959, for example, the per capita tax burden was $630, compared to more than $1,500 in 1972. It almost tripled from the time of Eisenhower to that of Nixon.[6]

Expressed as a share of personal income, the present tax load comes to a cool 44 percent. More graphically, the U.S. Chamber of Commerce calculated in 1971 that the average American would work more than four months of the year—until May 10—just to pay his taxes. Put another way, on the Chamber's calculation, the average citizen would work 2 hours and 51 minutes out of every 8-hour day just to meet his tax bills.[7]

Over the years there has been considerable speculation about what percentage of taxation should be considered excessive—with some spokesmen suggesting 25 percent, others 33, others 40. By almost any standard it is possible to say the present tax burden in America is onerous, but such theoretical discussions ignore the essential point about taxation. *Any* level of taxation is too high if and when the voters think it is too high. Taxes are voted by politicians who are answerable to the voters; when the voters make it clear they have had enough, that becomes the definitive judgment.

How and why the voters reach determinations of this sort is somewhat elusive. All of us stand in two different relationships toward government spending: On the one hand we are, in some fashion or other, beneficiaries of what government is doing—if not in the form of subsidy, then in the enjoyment of some protection or service we consider essential. On the other hand, we are all in a sense victims of the system, in that we must pay the bills through taxes or inflation or submit to other social costs imposed by the enlargement of government powers.

Politically speaking, the crucial question is which of these capacities is uppermost in our minds. If most people view themselves as *beneficiaries* of what the government is doing, then it is reasonable to expect them to favor increased spending and official intervention. If most people view themselves as *victims* of what the government is doing, then it is reasonable to expect them to favor less spending and official intervention. The subjectively onerous tax level is that which causes the second perception to replace the first.

From the New Deal forward, the role of beneficiary has been predominant, as the American people were encouraged to look to government in general and Washington in particular as the font of social wisdom. Numerous devices have been employed, moreover, to keep the question of costs from becoming a major topic of discussion. Undoubtedly the most effective of these is the withholding tax, which anesthetizes the taxpayer because he never sees the money he is paying out. Another is the substitution of payroll "contributions" (for example, Social Security), with half the cost allegedly borne by employers, for conventional taxation. Yet another is the device of the hidden tax, imposed at various points along the line of production and ultimately absorbed by the customer. By employing devices of this kind, the spending interests have deadened the pain a bit and managed to push the total burden much higher than might otherwise have been the case.

Signs are, however, that the average taxpayer by now has had enough. He may not understand the various devices by which his money is being siphoned away, but he is acutely aware of the fact that there isn't enough left over when the process is completed. The total burden has become so large there is no possible way to conceal its aggregate size, and rumblings suggesting an incipient tax revolt have repeatedly manifested themselves. Since the level of taxation is ultimately a political issue, this statistical measure is the one that counts most of all.

In the spring of 1973, for example, both George Gallup and Louis Harris conducted opinion polls that found some 65 percent of those responding saying Federal income taxes were too high. This opinion was shared across the board by just about every group of taxpaying Americans—including a majority of those in the $3,000 to $5,000 annual income bracket. Especially noteworthy was the Gallup finding that complaints were highest among

Democrats and "the increasingly affluent 'blue collar' group." [8] *

American opinion as measured by Harris has long been trending in this direction. A 1971 Harris survey found 64 percent of his respondents saying taxes had reached the breaking point, 66 percent saying taxes were too high, and 69 percent who said they would sympathize with a tax revolt in which people refused to pay their taxes until the spending was brought under control. Harris concluded that "confidence in government has reached a low point over the past four or five years. The public no longer looks to government as a credible agent for generating solutions to the problems which beset them. The prevailing mood of New Deal days, when sizable majorities of the public believed that government could accomplish anything, has now reversed almost 180 degrees." [9]

All of which suggests that the magnitude of government spending has become so great as to constitute a decisive political issue, and this has presented liberal spokesmen with a painful dilemma. They are committed by doctrine and political interest to the growth of government and the extension of Federal powers—and have built constituencies responsive to such notions. Now, however, they confront a rising public protest against the costs of government and demands that the tax burden be eased. They are in danger of being caught between opposing forces. An expedient is needed that will permit them to negotiate between the subsidy-seekers on the one hand and the taxpayers on the other.

Where Does the Money Go?

In response to this necessity, advocates of liberal government have taken to offering up selected scapegoats—shadowy malefactors

---

* Manual workers polled by Gallup claimed their Federal income taxes were excessive by a thundering margin of 73 to 23 percent—a higher level of umbrage than that recorded by business and professional people (65 to 29 percent). A Gallup survey conducted a year earlier found middle-income respondents most vehement of all in demanding curtailment of Federal outlays in preference to a hike in taxes (59 to 35 percent). Harris discovered in April 1973 that 64 percent of his sample felt Federal income taxes were too high.

who can be rhetorically flayed for "causing" the burden of taxation. If only we socked it to these mysterious culprits, it is said, our problems would be solved, and there would be manna aplenty for domestic spenders and suffering taxpayers alike. Such arguments are doubly useful in that they divert attention from the question of aggregate government growth, and that in many cases they can be used as pretexts for promoting even further growth in areas with political sex appeal. (Most useful of all, of course, is the fact that they serve to keep the public generally baffled about who is doing what to whom.)

Undoubtedly the scapegoat belabored most heavily of late has been the "military-industrial complex." Since the latter 1960s we have been treated to a lurid scenario depicting our nation at the mercy of militant generals and profit-happy contractors. These sinister forces have assertedly drained the taxpayer dry while meritorious welfare, educational, and environmental projects have withered in neglect. If only we could curtail such extravagance, it is said, we could balance the budget, enjoy a tax cut, and still have plenty of dollars left over to care for "unmet social needs."

While this facile explanation of our budget woes has been pounded home in countless speeches, articles, books, and TV specials and is widely believed by considerable segments of the public, there is not a shred of truth to any of it. It *is* true that the Pentagon is enormous (more than a million civilian payrollers), that military spending has risen over the years, and that the military has its share of waste. But the obvious fact of record is that the continued growth of Federal outlays and the resulting increase in the burden of taxation owe little or nothing to the inputs of the Pentagon. Indeed, of all the categories of Federal spending, military expenditure has experienced the *slowest* growth rate, not the fastest, and has been dealt a steadily decreasing percentage of Federal outlays as a result.

Between 1952 and 1972, to be specific, the military budget rose from $46.6 billion to $78 billion, an increase of 67 percent. But total Federal expenditures burgeoned from $71 billion to $236.9 billion—an increase of 233 percent. As a result of these contrasting trends, the percentage of Federal outlays devoted to the military *declined* throughout the period—from 49 percent in

1952 to 33.8 percent in 1972—exactly the opposite of the statements we are accustomed to hearing on this subject.[10]

Of special interest is the history of the 1960s, when the costs of the Vietnam war were a major factor in military outlays, and Pentagon-baiting became a popular outdoor sport. Although Vietnam pushed hard on defense expenditure, that pressure could not keep pace with the growth of domestic spending. In 1963, the Federal budget stood at $111.4 billion, while military spending amounted to $52.2 billion—roughly half the total. By fiscal 1973, the budget stood at $246 billion, while military spending had risen to $73.3 billion. In sum, the share of Federal outlays consumed by the Pentagon, with occasional variations, diminished right through the period of the Vietnam war. The following table shows the trend:[11]

FISCAL YEAR	TOTAL OUTLAYS FOR DEFENSE (IN BILLIONS OF DOLLARS)	PERCENT OF TOTAL BUDGET DEVOTED TO DEFENSE
1963	52.257	46.9
1964	53.591	45.2
1965	49.578	41.9
1966	56.785	42.2
1967	70.081	44.3
1968	80.517	45.0
1969	81.232	44.0
1970	80.295	40.8
1971	77.661	36.7
1972	78.336	33.8
1973	73.300	30.8

If we adjust these figures to account for inflation, the result is even more enlightening. On a constant-dollar basis, defense expenditure in 20 years' time rose from $75.8 to $78 billion, a bare increase of 3 percent. And in the decade of the 1960s, there was no increase at all in the amount of spending available for basic defense needs: in adjusted dollars, this figured out to $75.2 billion as of 1961, and exactly the same as of 1972. The 1972 budget, moreover, represented a temporary upturn. From 1969 through 1973, *absolute* dollar amounts for defense were reduced as well—from $81 billion to $73 billion.[12] *

If the mysterious bloodsuckers at the Pentagon did not make off with the money, why did the Federal budget increase by 150 percent in the span of a single decade? The answer is quite simple. The decade in question happens to have been the era of triumphant liberalism, in which billions of dollars were flowing out of Washington for the favored nostrums of the left—education, health care, poverty, food stamps, public housing, training programs, welfare, model cities, and so on. While military spending increased by $24 billion, domestic Federal spending increased by $108 billion—and an enormous chunk of the domestic increase was for the very welfare programs liberal spokesmen said were being neglected.

In 1965 the total Federal expenditure for "social welfare" of various types came to $37 billion. In six short years this shot up to $92 billion. It is this development, *not* the spending of the military, that accounts for most of the increase in the Federal budget. The point is made quite clearly by the Brookings Institution, which notes that "the outstanding fact in budgetary growth in the past decade . . . is the introduction and growth of a host of new (or sharply modified) programs, the 'major Great Society programs.' They have grown from a modest $1.7 billion in 1963 to a sched-

---

* Economist Roger Freeman of the Hoover Institution gives this summary for spending trends over the two decades:

> Defense costs went up 57 per cent between 1952 and 1971, which is barely ahead of the simultaneous rise in prices; in relative terms, defense fell from 66 per cent of the total budget to 36 per cent, from 13.6 per cent of GNP to about 7.1 per cent. Spending for domestic purposes meanwhile multiplied 7.6 times (+662 per cent) and its share of the budget jumped from 17 per cent to 47 per cent. . . . Outlays for education, health, and welfare multiplied 12.4 times (+1,142 per cent), for all other domestic purposes combined, 3.2 times (+219 per cent). . . . Between 1952 and 1969, all government expenditures in the United States . . . for domestic purposes increased 420 per cent; for education 489 per cent; income maintenance, 694 per cent; health and hospitals 286 per cent; for all other domestic services 299 per cent. [*Intercollegiate Review*, Winter-Spring 1972, pp. 15, 16.]

uled $35.7 billion in 1973"—a tidy increase of 2,000 percent.[13] *

Viewed in the long term, the increase of spending for social welfare purposes is even more dramatic, and even more closely correlated to the overall growth of the tax burden. In 1929, total government outlays for social welfare purposes—health, education, social security, public housing—stood at a modest $3.9 billion for *all* levels of government. By 1950 the figure had grown to $23.5 billion, and by 1960 to $52.3 billion. In the 1960s, the spending really began to escalate, until by 1971 it stood at an almost incredible $171 billion. The major components of this outlay were social insurance ($66 billion), education ($55 billion), welfare ($21 billion), and government medical programs ($18.6 billion). "Social welfare" spending at all levels of government has increased by 2,000 percent since 1929, and by 250 percent since 1960.[14]

Symbolic of this process is the new supremacy of the Department of Health, Education, and Welfare (HEW). For many years, despite its declining percentage of total outlays, the hated Pentagon could at least be described as the largest single agency within the Federal establishment. That no longer is the case. For fiscal 1974, the Pentagon was scheduled for $81.1 billion, HEW for $93.8 billion. Twenty years before, Department of Defense spending had stood at $46.6 billion, while that for HEW stood at $1.9 billion. The budget for DOD increased 74 percent over the period; that for HEW, 4,837 percent.[15] Yet the McGoverns and Kennedys still tell us the military is "starving" our domestic services into penury.

One may assume if he wishes that all this social welfare spending is immensely beneficial and responsible for all manner of good

---

* Brookings explains that "of this total, some $20 billion is accounted for by programs that provide goods or services directly to the people, principally the poor or aged: housing subsidies to low- and/or moderate-income families; Medicare (for the aged); Medicaid (for the poor); food stamps and school lunches; loans and scholarships for higher education. . . . In 1950 Federal income-support payments were $13 billion and accounted for 29 per cent of Federal expenditures, or nearly 5 per cent of Gross National Product. By 1973 these payments will exceed $103 billion, account for 39 per cent of Federal expenditures (60 per cent of civilian outlays) and amount to nearly 9 per cent of GNP. . . ." (*Setting National Priorities: The 1973 Budget,* pp. 11, 175.)

works (although the facts of the case, as we shall see, are decidedly otherwise). The point is that it is *this* spending, good or bad, which is responsible for the steady upward push of Federal, state, and local budgets, for the corresponding bite that government takes from the GNP, and for the heavy burden being shouldered by the average taxpayer.

The foofaraw over the "military-industrial complex," in sum, is merely an effort to conceal this fact from the American people. The names have been changed to protect the guilty.

PART II
Policy and Planning: The Crisis Is in Washington

7
The Regressive State

It is widely assumed in our political debates that the functioning of our government has both progressive and regressive characteristics. Some aspects of official activity, that is, are punitive toward the wealthy, while others are punitive toward the poor. Thus far, for once, the conventional wisdom is on target. It is mistaken only in that it has the progressive and regressive components reversed.

On the standard analysis, the progressive functions of our government are its various spending, service, and social welfare programs—which supposedly redound to the benefit of the impoverished. We have, after all, a "welfare state" and an extensive "poverty program," and the going assumption is that the principal beneficiaries of these activities are the very poor.

Balanced against this, however, is the regressive part of the system—our unfair tax laws. Here, supposedly, malefactors of great wealth, oil zillionaires, and tricky businessmen with expense accounts are taking advantage of tax breaks and loopholes that poor people don't know how to use. Billions of dollars in revenue are thereby lost, to be made up by the little guy. To close the circle of our felicity, we obviously need some "tax reform" to separate these shysters from their money.

Taking a careful look at the economic record, we discover the actual situation is just the opposite. It is the *program* side of the government's activities that, by and large, is authentically regressive, while the taxing side is considerably less so. It develops, indeed, that to the extent the taxing situation *is* regressive, it has become so because of what is being done by the people running the programs.

There are some obvious reasons for this discrepancy. From the program side, the workings of the Federal government—or almost any other—are essentially an *influence* system. There is only so much pie to be carved up and passed around, and somebody has to get it in preference to somebody else. If you are fairly savvy about the way the process works, then you can get yours. If you aren't, then you can't. A premium is placed on comparative advantage in contacts, know-how, and political muscle; those who lack the necessary leverage will lose out.

From the taxing side, some considerations are the same, but the basic ones are not. Obviously, a degree of political know-how can be immensely helpful when it comes to writing tax laws, or taking advantage of them. But every such effort runs counter to the master impulse of the government—the lust for revenue. In dispensing favors, government must be selective. But in the matter of taxes the equation is different: The desire and need of government here is to be universal, to soak everybody for as much as possible.

There is nothing in which the Federal government is more proficient than collecting taxes. You may not yet have received the air mail letter sent to you last month from Seattle, and the government may have totally bollixed up a housing project in your city. But rest assured, when it is time to pay the bills for these alleged services, the tax collector will track you down with great efficiency. They couldn't nail Al Capone for bootlegging or murder, but they got him on a tax rap. You may be certain they can do the same for you.

It is because of this universal hunger for revenue that the alleged "loopholes" and tax breaks in our system are much less inequitable than we have been led to suppose, and that the taxing side of government is so much less regressive than the spending side. In this chapter and the next we shall examine some of the data that go to prove this curious fact of governmental life.

The Influence System

The principal argument for the increase of government programs and government spending is that such activities are necessary to help the poor and chastise the rich. Only a big and powerful government, it is said, can control the abuses of the corporations, provide security to the little man, and prevent the exploitation of helpless workers and consumers.

Such is the conceptual model on which the interventions of the past forty years have been based and which is repeatedly invoked to explain the need for still more interventions. We are continually informed that we need government action to regulate the big guys and protect the little ones. Thus are justified countless pieces of legislation and administrative action to regulate wages, extend subsidies, provide housing, fix prices, impose consumer controls, break up big business, regulate transit, and so on.

This conceptual model is derived from the theory of "countervailing power," popularized some years ago by our friend John Kenneth Galbraith. It seems to be almost universally believed in American society—especially on the nation's campuses. I have discussed questions of government intervention on literally hundreds of campuses in this country. Almost invariably at these sessions someone will remark: "You keep talking about the power of government; but what about the power of the large corporations? Don't you think we need big government to handle the problems presented by big business?"

At the worst, such questions assume with the liberal theorists that business or corporate power is a malign influence in our society, grinding down workers, exploiting consumers, and in general exerting an unhealthy impact on our economy; government power, in contrast, is assumed to be a beneficial factor, working for the good of the little fellow and against the rapacity of the corporations. At best, the questioner appears to believe the power of business and the power of government are roughly equivalent, the second supplying a necessary balance against the first.

Despite the widespread acceptance accorded to such notions, a little examination will show them to be mistaken. On theoretical grounds alone, it should be apparent that this bland equation of government with business misstates the nature of both institutions, while on empirical grounds it is demonstrable that programs of intervention supported on this basis do not in fact assist "the little guy," but do him considerable harm. It is statistically demonstrable that people of relatively high income are better off *with* the present system of government intervention, while people of relatively modest income would be better off *without* it.

The error in the theoretical model is readily apparent. The power of a government and the power of a corporation are very different things. A government can arrest you, take your money by compulsion, put you in jail, draft you into the armed services, send you off to fight a war; it can through the legal process deprive you of your liberty and even your life. A corporation can do none of these things. It can hire you or fire you, sell you its products or purchase your own, cajole you through its advertising, and if it is large enough affect your economic well-being by its impact on the economy. But it cannot in a free market *force* you to do anything.

A corporation or any other economic interest can coerce you into doing something only if its economic influence is *united* with the power of government. Where such economic interests are favored by the powers of government, they can obtain exclusive franchises, deny competitors the right of entry to the market, force consumers to pay artificially high prices, and in general exploit people along the lines suggested by the interventionist model. But it is precisely the intervention of the government in the first place that makes this exploitation possible.

When this occurs, as it frequently does, the result is the very opposite of "countervailing power." Rather than acting to check or constrain abusive economic interests, governmental power is joined to economic leverage and generates abuses of its own. To the extent that such intrusions permeate the economy, the voluntary exchange system is replaced with an influence system, in which economic rewards are distributed in proportion to one's official contacts and know-how and ability to manipulate the political process, irrespective of service to the consumer.

A system of this type is far more likely to produce a regressive distribution of economic goods than is a regime of unfettered exchange. Under such a system, whoever wields paramount political authority will *also* by definition wield paramount economic authority, since if you appoint the regulators you can decide who gets the rewards. This guarantees in turn that those who have economic influence and want to keep it will labor diligently to control the government.

An influence system will benefit in particular those who begin the struggle with better economic positions and more sophisticated knowledge of the political process—like business interests and labor leaders—and will be harmful to those who are poor and ignorant and baffled by the complexities of government—like the average taxpayer. And it will favor those who are cohesive and conscious of their interests and who will therefore be attentive to the regulatory system, and harm those who do not have concentrated and self-conscious interests and who are diffused and disorganized—which is a good description of the average citizen and consumer.

Principal Beneficiaries

These considerations suggest the principal beneficiaries of government programs are not in fact the impoverished and the downtrodden, but relatively affluent people who enjoy some sort of leverage in the governmental system. This favored segment of our population *does* include a number of corporations and other business interests, most especially in protected and regulated industries (transit, communications, energy) where political clout is essential to prosperity, and we shall examine some of these in subsequent chapters. But it also includes nonbusiness interests with political leverage—labor unions, members of the academic and foundation worlds, and, most notable of all, members of the governmental establishment itself.

Illustrative of the manner in which government moneys get allocated along the vectors of political influence is the history of the nation's burgeoning system of Federal aid. The premise of this system is that certain states are less well off than others in terms of personal income and resulting tax base, and that therefore the national government must step in to even up the balance. Given this rationale, one would suppose the net effect of Federal "aid" would be to redistribute money from the relatively wealthy states to those that are less wealthy. But if one supposed that, he would be very wrong indeed.

In general, the pattern of distribution of Federal-aid benefits tends to follow lines of political force. While there is some redistributionist effect, on the whole the money goes where influential politicians want it to go, not where a dispassionate view of economic necessity would suggest it should go. Thus we confront the anomaly that New York State, the richest state per capita in the union, is a net beneficiary of Federal aid programs, while less affluent states such as New Hampshire, Nebraska, or Indiana must pay more for every dollar of Federal aid than they are given in return.[1]

Instances of regressive distribution of our tax dollars abound in the archives of the Federal and other governments—including protections and benefits for certain industries, loans and special favors, and countless lucrative contracts. As a result of these procedures, many of the large corporations that are supposed to be chastised by government are in fact among its beneficiaries. Thus millions of dollars expended in the nation's "poverty," housing, and other programs have in fact gone to large corporations—Litton Industries, Westinghouse, National Homes, and so on. (We shall review some specific examples of this process in a selected field—transportation—in Chapter 10.)

Certain industries, indeed, have been kept afloat through government contracts, particularly in the field of defense contracting (General Dynamics is a good example). One does not have to subscribe to conspiracy theories of government to see that there is a natural, almost inevitable, interlock between people of influence in the business and financial communities and people of influence in government—the two quite comfortably go together. And while all this assistance to people on the outside is occurring, we may be certain the people on the inside, the government functionaries themselves, are doing rather nicely also.

For understandable reasons, this latter point is seldom stressed in liberal discussions of government spending, but it is in many

ways the most crucial consideration of all. The principal beneficiaries of the money absorbed and dispensed by government are
not poor blacks in ghettos or Appalachian whites or elderly pen-
sioners receiving Social Security checks—the usual figures con-
jured up when social welfare spending is discussed. The major
beneficiaries, instead, are the *employes of government itself*—people engaged in administering some real or imagined service to the
underprivileged or, as the case may be, the overprivileged.

That government employes should be the principal gainers
from government programs is not, on reflection, astonishing. If
anyone is "inside" the system and alert to its intricacies, it is the
people who actually work in government offices and administer
the programs. It is their job to know exactly how the government
process works, where the pressure points may be found, and how
to exert the maximum leverage on the legislative bodies that control the funds. And since their livelihood is directly dependent on
the outcome, they have the strongest possible motivation to use
their knowledge to the utmost in their own behalf.

It should hardly surprise us, then, that government employes in
general and Federal employes in particular are much better compensated than is the average American. This is most obviously true
in the case of congressmen, executive administrators, and other
high government officials, but it is true of rank and file employes
as well.

In 1971, for example, the average earnings of an employe in
private industry came to $7,924. Average earnings for a civilian
employe of the Federal government came to $10,972—better than
$3,000 higher. (For all civilian government employes, the aver-
age was $8,958—less opulent than the Federals by themselves but
still $1,000 better than the taxpayer.) This means the gross effect
of increased government spending is to transfer money away from
relatively low income people—average taxpayers who must pay
the bills—to relatively high income people—Federal functionaries
who are being paid out of the taxpayer's pocket.

To illustrate the point still further, one need only note that the
two richest counties in the United States are not Westchester in
New York or DuPage in Illinois, Fairfield in Connecticut or Marin
in California. They are, rather, Montgomery County, Maryland,
and Fairfax County, Virginia—principal bedroom counties for

Federal workers in Washington, D.C. In 1972, Montgomery had the highest median family income in the nation at $16,710, while Fairfax was a close second at $15,707. It is obvious that the sacrifices of government service are very great.[2]

The extent to which social welfare spending is a device for providing government functionaries a living at the expense of everyone else may be gauged by considering the enormous increase in this spending over the decade of the 1960s. As we have seen, social welfare outlays at all levels of government increased by $120 billion between 1960 and 1971—from $50 billion to $171 billion. This enormous expenditure went into creating poverty bureaucracies, increasing official salaries, building new schools, conducting studies of poverty problems, paying consultants, improving compensation for teachers and administrators, and so on. Some of the spending increase actually reached the poor people in the ghettos, but most of it perforce did not—as may be readily demonstrated.

Poverty estimates in this country vary widely, but the census figures tell us there are some 25 million people in America who are poor (officially defined as a household of four with less than $4,137 in annual income in 1971). If we accept that definition, we may calculate that the increase in social welfare spending over the decade of the 1960s (not the whole thing, just the *increase*) could have provided every single poor person in America with an outright gift of $4,800 annually—which means a yearly stipend of $19,200 for a family of four, or $28,800 for a welfare mother with five children.[3]

In other words, if we had simply *given* the poor people of America this increment in social welfare spending, we could have abolished poverty outright. In fact, we could have made every family of poor people about two-and-a-half times as wealthy as the family of the average wage-earner. Needless to remark, we have done nothing of the sort. The extra $120 billion, by and large, has not gone into the pockets of poverty families; it has gone instead into the pockets of government functionaries, consultants, and business entrepreneurs who are better off than the average American, and who promise to get more so as the scope of such activity increases.

Regressive Government Programs

In large measure, the regressive character of social welfare spending derives from the prominent role assumed by public education. This has been of course a sacrosanct cause in American politics, and the various levels of government have vied with each other to pump out dollars for the schools. Between 1950 and 1972, spending for public schools ballooned from $5.4 billion to $46 billion—an increase of 758 percent.[4] All of this has been done to help "the children," and since the children of the poor attend the schools it might be assumed the result would be to benefit the impoverished.

It doesn't work out that way. There is for one thing rather convincing evidence that the outlay of all these billions for public education has been ineffective in improving learning skills among the poor—a point we shall be examining in more detail. There is for another the fact that the major recipients of the money spent for schools are school administrators and teachers, who, contrary to general impression, are well *above* the average in levels of compensation. Every increase in school spending, whatever else it does or does not do, again takes money from relatively low income citizens, the taxpayers, and bestows it on relatively high income citizens—teachers, counselors, and school administrators.*

This anomaly has been examined at length by Daniel P. Moynihan, former counselor to Presidents Kennedy and Johnson. Moynihan notes that teachers receive about 68 percent of the

---

* In reviewing recent increases in educational spending, the Brookings Institution notes that "almost two-thirds of the increase in per pupil outlays was related to increases in the amount spent for teachers and other instructional personnel, such as librarians and guidance counselors. Teachers as a group have fared somewhat better as to salary than the average American worker during the past 12 years. While the average wage for full-time employes in all industries was rising by 74 per cent, teachers' salaries went up by 90 per cent, and the salaries of other instructional personnel grew by more than 100 per cent. Since 1966, average teacher salaries have increased at an annual rate of almost 8 per cent—about one-third faster than wages in general. Whatever the reasons, the relative rise in wages of teachers has played a crucial role in the growth of expenditures for education." (*Setting National Priorities: The 1973 Budget*, pp. 322–23.)

operating expenditures of elementary and secondary schools, and observes that "over the past two decades teachers' pay has increased at a rate roughly twice that of wages in the private economy." The result is that, in 1971, teachers had an average annual salary of $9,210—$1,300 higher than the average taxpayer.[5] When we reflect that more than two-thirds of these teachers are women for whom the money is a second family income, the disparity is even more obvious.*

Even more regressive is the practice of subsidizing colleges and universities and providing less-than-cost tuitions to university students. These institutions are overwhelmingly middle class in composition, including administrators, faculty, and scholars, while the tax revenues to support them are derived not only from average-income citizens but, in states where the sales tax is a major source of government revenue, from the poorest segment of the population as well. This presents us with the spectacle of poor black citizens in the inner cities paying taxes to subsidize college educations for the children of middle class families in the suburbs.

This paradox has been statistically developed by W. Lee Hansen and Burton Weisbrod in an examination of university costs in Wisconsin and California. In Wisconsin, they found, the average family income of those whose children attended the state university was $9,700—compared to $6,500 for those without children in the state universities. In California, the corresponding figures were $12,000 and $7,900.[6] †

It is noteworthy that spending for education is at once so regressive *and* so sacrosanct; one is tempted to infer a connection. On the one hand, the fact that the program is considered above criticism makes it easy to increase expenditure, without a great deal of careful scrutiny of what is being done with the money.‡

---

* Moynihan notes that "when the teacher is a married woman, family income is likely to be in the top quintile (fifth) of income distribution, even the top five percent." (*The Public Interest,* Fall 1972, p. 75.)

† These researchers conclude that "on the whole, the effect of these subsidies is to promote greater rather than less inequality . . . by making available substantial subsidies that lower income families are either not eligible for or cannot make use of because of other conditions and constraints associated with their income position."

‡ It is only very recently, for example, that anyone has thought to conduct careful studies of the *results* of educational expenditure. The disappointing results of all this spending are examined in detail in Chapter 11.

On the other hand, the fact of enormous spending creates a vested interest that labors to make sure the program *remains* sacrosanct. This syndrome is plainly visible when cutbacks in educational spending are suggested by local school boards or state legislatures. Nothing is more certain to bring out throngs of tax-paid educationists, demanding that spending be increased so that "the children" will not be shortchanged.

Perhaps this kind of relationship explains the fact that America's *most* sacrosanct government program is also, by all available indices, its most regressive. This is the Federal Social Security program, which in 1972 accounted for more than a third of that $170 billion-plus in social welfare payouts. The Social Security idea was criticized a bit when originally introduced, but as the number of beneficiaries increased it became a political untouchable. Senator Barry Goldwater, for one, felt the heat in his 1964 presidential race when he dared to drop some disparaging remarks about the program; his suggestion that participation be made voluntary was accounted a major factor in his defeat.

This sacred aspect of the program has led to a continual series of congressional votes to step up outlays for Social Security, with little or no attention to the costs. In 1972, for example, Congress voted a sizable increase in Social Security benefits to be delivered before election day. Nothing was said about the taxes needed to pay the bills, which did not go into effect until *after* election day. The benefits were ballyhooed up front while the added taxes were left to languish in the political shadows. The result of such procedures is that Social Security has "growed like Topsy"—the level of benefits exploding from $10 billion in 1960 to $66 billion in 1973. Social Security taxes now constitute a quarter of Federal revenues and will almost certainly increase their take still further.[7] *

What is especially remarkable about all this is that the Social Security revenue structure is harshly regressive. The system is financed by a flat tax on a given slice of income, with no exemp-

---

* This continual increase of the tax load is necessary because, contrary to assurances of its backers, the system is actuarially insolvent; every hike in benefits requires another hike in taxes, piling up still other obligations for the future, which now amount to at least $500 billion, and, by the estimate of the *Wall Street Journal,* as much as $2.1 trillion.

tions or deductions. Under amendments passed by Congress in 1973, the tax rate was 5.85 percent on the first $13,200 of income, with a similar sum paid by the employer. Since the employer's portion is in fact computed as wage costs, the true effective rate for the employe is 11.70 percent—an astronomical figure for low and middle income taxpayers.[8]

Because the Social Security levy is a flat tax, it is proportionately heavier for the low and moderate income citizen than it is for the wealthy. A worker making $13,200, for example, paid the effective rate of 11-plus percent of his income, but a business tycoon making $150,000 paid slightly over 1 percent of his. The system is therefore financed by a tax that becomes proportionately *lighter* as one ascends the income scale. The irony is deepened by the fact that many low income citizens are paying heavy Social Security taxes to finance benefits for retired people in comfortable circumstances.*

More serious still is the absolute weight of the Social Security tax on the low-to-average income citizen. For many of these, the Social Security levy is already steeper than the Federal income tax. Under rates prevailing through 1973, for example, a family man earning $5,000 a year might have paid $102 in Federal income taxes, but had to pay a total of $585 (counting the employer's portion) for Social Security. On this same basis, a worker making $10,800 a year had to pay $1,263. And under amendments passed in 1973, the worker receiving $13,200 had $1,544.40 subtracted from his annual paycheck.[9]

Because Social Security taxes are politically camouflaged, our lawmakers have voted year in and year out to increase these levies without the slightest hesitation. Federal income taxes, on the other hand, are more visible and therefore more objectionable, and Congress has been less willing to boost these—voting instead for a series of "cuts" in income levies throughout the decade of the 1960s. (For someone making $6,000, for example, Federal income taxes were $351 lower in 1973 than in 1963; for a citizen whose

* And deepened still further by the earnings limitation that cuts back on benefits for retired wage-earners who go out and make more than $2,400 a year, but permits a retired tycoon to receive his interest or dividends in full without imperiling his Social Security benefits.

gross income was $10,000, the reduction was $467; for the tax-payer in the $35,000 bracket, the saving was $1,591, and so on proportionately.) [10]

The result of these contrasting trends is that the silent increase of Social Security taxes has canceled the advertised decrease of Federal income levies, while shifting the Federal tax base as a whole onto a more regressive basis.* Since 1947, Social Security levies have increased by more than 4,000 percent (from $1.5 billion to $66.6 billion). As a share of national income, Social Security has grown from 0.8 to 6.1 percent, and as a share of Federal budget receipts from 3.4 percent to 24.7.[11]

The constant rise of Social Security levies is the most obviously regressive feature of our tax system, but it is far from the only one. As we shall see, the American tax system as a whole takes a larger percentage from the income received by poor people than it does from the income of the affluent. This occurs because the total spending burden and the multiplicity of levies required to pay the bills have saddled us with innumerable taxes that are *not* imposed proportional to income.

State and local sales taxes, Federal and state excise taxes, property taxes passed on as rent, and corporation taxes passed on to the consumer are paid in like amounts at the point of purchase, irrespective of income brackets. Studies by Joseph A. Pechman of the Brookings Institution show that total effective tax rates in this country are high for people of extremely low income, descending as income rises (although this statistical picture is somewhat overdrawn). It is not until income surpasses the $15,000 level that the "progressive" curve turns back up. In 1968, for example, taxes took 50 percent of the income of those who earned under $2,000 a year—compared to 30 percent for those in the $8,000–$10,000 bracket.[12]

According to a study published by the Conference Board, the

---

* "While the Federal tax load has been trimmed back substantially at most levels of earnings, drastic increases in the Social Security payroll tax have offset much of the tax relief. In fact, for the great middle-income group—between, say, $16,000 and $17,000 of annual income—the tax relief has been reduced to token levels or eliminated completely." (*U.S. News and World Report*, October 1, 1973.)

total incidence of taxation at all levels in the United States for
1968 looked like this:[13] *

INCOME BRACKET	PERCENT OF INCOME PAID AS TAXES
Under $2,000	50
$ 2,000–$ 4,000	35
$ 4,000–$ 6,000	31
$ 6,000–$ 8,000	30
$ 8,000–$10,000	29
$10,000–$15,000	30
$15,000–$25,000	30
$25,000–$50,000	33
$50,000 and over	45

These figures emphatically do not suggest that taxes on low-
income people are high because people of high income are getting
away with murder. People with really high incomes *are* paying a
steep effective rate, and even the low rate in this table, the 29 percent of income paid by people in the $8,000–$10,000 bracket, can
be considered "low" only by comparison. These people were paying nearly a third of their income in taxes in 1968, and the effective rate for everyone has increased since then. So there is little
justification for supposing that the tax burden on low-income citizens can somehow be eased by loading the burden onto somebody
else.

The problem is the burden itself—the total load of government spending. Government is simply spending so much and taking so much to pay the bills that it has saddled heavy tax loads on
everyone—including the poor people who are supposed to be the
beneficiaries.

All of this, moreover, considers only the income transfer
aspects of the problem. More important in many ways are the
regressive and counterproductive social costs imposed by the con-

* These percentages will vary among income groups according to the
assumptions made concerning the incidence of different taxes. See discussion of "tax reform" in the next chapter.

tinual interference of government functionaries in the workings of the economy. Again, the rationale for such interference is to help the poor and needy, but the results are almost invariably the opposite. In subsequent chapters we shall examine several government programs that have as their alleged purpose the alleviation of human distress and the uplifting of the downtrodden, and we shall see in case after case that the true effect is almost always the reverse.

The regressivity of the big-government system is an embarrassment to its sponsors, and from time to time they have tried to invent some explanations. We shall examine one of these—the theory of "tax reform"—before proceeding to a discussion of specific liberal programs.

8
The Road to Tax Reform

While the myth of the military-industrial complex discussed in Chapter 6 has demonstrable public-relations value, it is not entirely sufficient for liberal purposes. There have been occasional constraints imposed on military spending, after all, yet the Federal budget has not relented in the slightest from its steady upward course. The dilemma therefore remains: Recipients of government dollars continue to demand increased appropriations, while the taxpayer continues to cry out for relief. Simply belaboring the Pentagon will not resolve this awkward problem, however adroitly the facts of budgetary record may be obscured.

Further expedients are thus required to explain to taxpayers just why they should place the blame for increased spending on someone other than the people doing it. In response to this need, the liberal community has developed and deployed a battery of arguments to focus the taxpayers' anger on mysterious parties alleged to be responsible for their distress. These arguments revolve around the notion of "tax reform" of various kinds, the unifying theme being the suggestion that if only certain people paid more taxes and certain technical changes in the revenue structure were adopted, somehow the problem would go away.

The specific kind of "reform" that is sought will vary from case to case, depending on the level of government and the kind of tax that is up for consideration. At the Federal level, the principal topics of discussion are exemptions and/or deductions received by certain people and organizations. At the state and local level, the usual issue is "property tax relief," allegedly to be achieved by transferring a given tax burden from one plateau of government to another.

While these proposed reforms vary in their details, they have one notable feature in common: None discusses the general growth of government or the aggregate level of spending as a possible source of the problem. In every case it is assumed that we should have the spending we do have, if not a good deal more, and that the issue to be decided is simply *who* should pay for it. The total outlay of the government is taken as an uncontested axiom, with all our ingenuity and planning directed to the question of how to provide the necessary funding.

As a consequence, most of these alleged reforms not only succeed in diverting attention from the authentic problem, they often serve to make it worse. For each suggests that things will be set right if only we *raise* the taxes paid by somebody else, rather than lower them for anybody. The impulse toward reform is thus converted into a pretext for raising taxes even further, and for greater government spending, rather than less.

Federal "Tax Reform"

At the Federal level, the most popular of alleged reforms has to do with "loopholes" in the tax laws. It is argued that loopholes are the result of special privilege, and that by abolishing these we could bring in much revenue that is currently escaping. Favored targets of such demands are possessors of great wealth who pay no taxes, special rates for capital gains, and mineral depletion allowances. If only we socked it to these beneficiaries of special privilege, it is said, the rest of us would have fewer taxes to pay.

As intimated in the preceding chapter, there are many problems in the Federal revenue code that are the despair of the average citizen and anathema to conservative economists.* To argue this point, however, is not to suggest that the average citizen must pay in heavy taxes because the "special interests" are getting away with murder—the usual contention of the reformers. The record before us suggests a rather different picture.

Perhaps the most sophisticated study of the incidence of taxation undertaken to date is that authored by Joseph Pechman and Benjamin Okner for the Brookings Institution. In this survey, the authors employ several sets of assumptions concerning the burdens that particular taxes impose on different income groups. (The most notable variation concerns the corporation tax, which on one set of assumptions is considered a levy on capital, on another is thought to be passed along in appreciable measure to the consumer.) Throughout the study comparisons are drawn between the least progressive and most progressive interpretations.

While the results tend to vary with the assumptions, certain conclusions emerge quite clearly from this careful statistical approach. The first and most important is that the American tax system, taken as a whole, is neither grossly regressive nor sharply progressive, but is roughly proportional throughout all income groups. This occurs because the effects of different levies such as income taxes (progressive) and Social Security taxes (regressive) tend to balance out, and because the mix of taxes at all levels of government (income, sales and excise, business, property) tends to catch almost everybody in the revenue net one way or another.

Tax incidence charts provided by these authors display a consistent pattern: The tax bite appears to be very large at the lower end of the income scale, dips as income rises into the lower-middle income ranks, then rises again as one advances into the higher-

---

* Economist Milton Friedman, for one, has long advocated a program to cut through the thicket of tax-law complexities: eliminate all but the most essential exemptions and deductions, and establish a uniform basic rate of 16 percent or thereabouts Friedman argues that such a course would be fairer to the individual taxpayer and would yield about the same return as the present complicated system of high progressive rates punctuated with exceptions and special provisos.

middle and high income brackets. The differences among the readings are in the degree to which these variations occur, and in the movement of the graph line at the very highest level of the income scale. Under one set of assumptions, the tax rate for incomes of $100,000 and over ascends sharply; under another it rises slightly and then tapers off again at the million-dollar level.

Pechman and Okner observe that some of the regressivity at the lower end of the tax scale is misleading because this income bracket includes retired people and others who temporarily have high consumption levels relative to current income, a variation that would be flattened out if the computation included income levels over a period of years. Even this apparent regressivity, moreover, has little to do with the Federal income tax laws; it is principally the result of sales, excise, and passed-on corporation taxes paid at the point of consumption irrespective of income levels. The authors conclude:

> Regardless of incidence assumptions, the tax system is virtually proportional for the vast majority of families in the United States. . . . Effective tax rates are high at both the bottom and the top of the income scale. The high rates for those in the lowest income classes are probably not indicative of their tax burden over longer periods, because in these classes there is a heavy concentration of retired persons, as well as of individuals whose incomes are low temporarily. The very rich pay high taxes because a substantial portion of their income comes from property. . . . Federal taxes are progressive throughout the income scale (except for the lowest income classes) under all the incidence assumptions used in this study.[1]

This is, moreover, just the beginning of the story. The truth is that progressive tax rates on high-income citizens can do little or nothing to relieve the tax burden on the average American. There are simply too few high-income people for progressive rates to make much of a dent in the total enormous revenue burden, so that even if these citizens had *all* their income confiscated outright the rest of us would go on paying exorbitant taxes. The rationale for steeply progressive rates is punitive, and has little to do with aggregate revenue needs.* Representative Bob Wilson (R-Calif.), puts the matter this way: "If the Federal government confiscated all income earned by all the millionaires in the nation, it would pay the cost of government for only 39 hours." [2]

Thus if we abolished every "loophole" now enjoyed by wealthy citizens, whether justified or not, we would do little to affect the tax burden on the rest of us. Even this formulation, however, puts the matter in a misleading light. For the fact is that most of the so-called loopholes in our tax laws accrue not to the relatively rich, but to the relatively poor. Some three-quarters of the untaxed income in our country ($344 billion out of $465 billion in 1970) consists of personal exemptions, social benefits, mortgage interest, and the like—with the result that 97 percent of nontaxable returns belong to people with annual incomes of $5,000 or less.

Conversely, the number of wealthy taxpayers who escape the IRS is microscopic. A periodic hullaballoo goes up about people with enormous incomes who manage to avoid the payment of taxes. As noted by Roger Freeman of the Hoover Institution, the argument is erroneous: Of 15,323 individual returns filed in 1970 with adjusted gross incomes of $200,000 and up, 15,211 paid taxes. On the average, these citizens paid 60 percent of their taxable income to the Federal government—and 99.3 percent of them were doing the paying.[3]

For the 112 who did not pay, losses, deductions, and other mitigating circumstances converted a gross income of $200,000-plus into an absence of taxable income. Whatever the rights and wrongs of those specific cases, it is obvious that the revenue involved ($47 million in aggregate income) is a drop in the bucket compared to the total expenditures of the Federal government.

---

* As Walter Blum and Harry Kalven observed in their definitive study, *The Uneasy Case for Progressive Taxation:* "Something less than a quarter of the total revenue currently raised through the personal income tax is attributable to the graduated surtax rates, and there can be no doubt that it would be quite possible to obtain the same total through a personal income tax having a single basic rate." (University of Chicago Press, 1963, p. 5.)

Viewed as a percentage of all Federal revenues, the yield from progressive rates is even less significant—about 8½ percent according to F. A. Hayek, the 1974 Nobel laureate in economics.

Exactly the same is true respecting alleged revenue yield from reforms of capital gains or depletion allowances. It is widely believed, for example, that capital gains are a plaything of the rich, and that people of modest incomes obtain no benefit from these provisions. In 1970, however, more than two-thirds of those who realized capital gains on investments had adjusted gross incomes of less than $15,000. (Capital gains are income derived from the sale of long-term assets, held for more than six months. They are subjected to a tax rate one-half the income tax rate, on the grounds that such transactions convert assets from one form to another rather than representing true income.)

Equally to the point, the revenue to be derived from cracking down on capital gains is small and likely to get smaller. Liberal economist Irving Kristol estimates that complete abolition of the capital gains tax and taxation of investment yields as normal income would net $8 billion revenue on paper, but that in fact the yields would be much smaller. For under such a tax system the transactions in question would diminish to the disappearing point.[4]

Indeed, this process is already observable with the increases in capital gains taxes voted in 1969. The Securities Industries Association estimates that gains taken in 1970 might have been $3.5 billion higher had the rate remained at 25 percent—and, of course, such calculations do not measure the national economic loss incurred through discouragement of investment.

Considering the gravity of the recent energy crisis, proposals to abolish or reduce mineral depletion allowances are perhaps the strangest "reform" of all. Outright abolition of these allowances would bring in about $1.5 billion in revenue, again assuming that the operations to be taxed continued as before. Such added revenues would do little to pay for the bloated Federal budget, and the tax would surely discourage America's faltering efforts to locate and acquire petroleum supplies.*

---

* It is noteworthy in this respect that the Tax Reform Act of 1969 cut depletion allowances from 27.5 to 22 percent, even though the trend had been toward less exploration than needed rather than more. The number of new oil wells started in 1970 was only half the number started in 1956—and it is estimated that investment in petroleum exploration for the ensuing decade is far below the level needed to fulfill our energy requirements. (See Chapter 16.)

Put together, all these asserted "loopholes" would yield only a modest amount of revenue to the Federal government. This suggests that most deductions and exemptions in our tax laws affect the average citizen, not just some particular interest. To take an obvious instance, abolition of tax deductions for mortgage interest payments would bring in some $20 billion in added taxes —but it is doubtful that many of our tax-reforming politicians would seriously propose this step.

State and Local "Tax Reform"

The cry for "tax reform" at the Federal level has its analogy in a perennial demand for "property tax relief" in the legislatures of the several states. While the particulars are different, the object is the same: to convince the taxpayer his major problem is not the aggregate burden of government spending, but the technical minutiae of how the spending is financed. Again we witness a curious tableau in which the people who have been spending the taxpayers' money come forward with "reforms" that in many cases would actually make the spending burden bigger.

Wherever state lawmakers have assembled for the past decade they have been thronged by educationists, lobby groups, and government experts who informed them that the urgent need of the hour was to pass major increases in statewide taxes to provide the citizenry with "property tax relief." Almost invariably the major feature of such proposals has been the idea that funding of schools and certain other functions should be transferred in whole or major part from "inflexible" local property taxes to "broader based" and supposedly fairer state sales and income taxes.

To judge from this continual uproar, one could only suppose the property tax is the most oppressive levy Americans have to bear, and that it is increasing at a rate above and beyond that attained by other taxes. The truth, however, is exactly the opposite. While there are legitimate criticisms to be made of property levies (ask any property owner), the simple fact is that the total burden of the property tax is considerably *less* than the burden of the other taxes, and that compared to the rate at which non-property levies have been growing, the increase of the property tax is almost infinitesimal.

Thus in 1902, property taxes amounted to 3.3 percent of the gross national product; in 1971, they came to 3.4 percent. Although the increase in absolute dollar amounts has been great, the proportionate weight of property levies on the total wealth of the nation has hardly grown at all. By contrast, other forms of taxation have been going through the roof. In 1902, non-property taxes were comparable to property taxes in their total weight—amounting to 4.7 percent of GNP. But by 1970 their proportion had soared to 31.4 percent, a seven-fold increase in the share of national product consumed.[6]

These long-term data, moreover, conceal a fairly recent *decline* in the percentage of GNP absorbed by property taxes—albeit a decline with an upward curl at the end of it. The Brookings Institution notes that in 1927 property taxes accounted for 4.9 percent of GNP, and fell as a percentage until 1956, when they stood at only 2.6 percent. Thereafter, the curve turned upward, arriving at 3.4 percent in 1971. The percentage rise from 1956 to 1971 reflects in considerable measure an almost incredible binge of spending for public education. Since 1957, total spending on public schools has tripled, to a level of $46 billion a year—or an increase from $335 per pupil in 1957–58 to $867 per pupil in 1970–71.[7]

In tempo with this spending splurge, property taxes roughly doubled—from a national take of $19 billion in 1962 to more than $38 billion in 1971. Even so, the hike in property levies was *less* dramatic than the contemporaneous increase of other state and local taxes—whose take zoomed from $22.5 billion to more than $56 billion. So even in a period when property taxes were growing at perhaps their fastest rate in history, they were not increasing quite as fast as other levies.[8]

Why, then, the specific outcry over property taxes? The reason for this agitation is relatively plain. Property levies are visible, they are painful, and they are locally imposed. They are in many cases paid in a lump sum, by sitting down and writing a check, and the people who vote them are relatively accessible to public pressure. Some jurisdictions require a popular referendum to raise the rates for certain purposes. These factors serve to make the public acutely conscious of property taxes, stir resistance to precipitous hikes, and give the taxpayer means of doing something about them.

The net result is that there are limits to the amount of spending that can be financed from such taxation. Watching the proliferation of government at every level and feeling heavily overtaxed, people react by digging in their heels against the form of taxation most noticeable to them. The "inflexibility" complained of by the critics of the property levy is therefore not economic, but *political.* The property is there to be taxed *—people are simply refusing to accept increases in their rates. (It is noteworthy that in 1970, nationwide, about half the referendum requests for hikes in school taxes—mostly in the form of property levies—were defeated.)

Similar comment might be offered about the charge of "inequity" leveled against this tax—which generally means assessments in many cases are too *low,* and that they are kept this way for purposes of drawing industry to one location as opposed to another. One critic complains, for example, that many tax jurisdictions "have been created, and are perpetuated, precisely to provide preferentially low tax treatment of property within their boundaries." ° This is another way of saying that, because they are locally imposed, property taxes are subject to competitive downward pressure—which is bad if you are a government spender, not so bad if you are a taxpayer.

It is for this combination of reasons that property taxes have risen so much less than other taxes and appear to have reached their limit as a funding source for educationists and other political spenders. If schools and city functions continue to rely on property taxes, the spending splurge of the past fifteen years will have to be brought under some kind of control—and this, of course, the planners do not want. They have thousands of exciting things they want to do with our money, an army of civic counselors to be put to work, and countless social engineering diagrams on their drawing boards—if only the property tax with its built-in limits weren't standing in their path.

* As noted by the First National City Bank of New York, "the available evidence suggests that in the postwar period the market value of taxable property has grown at least as rapidly as the bases for most other major taxes, including excise and retail taxes and corporate profits tax."

The answer, clearly, is to get away from local property levies and shift the spending base to forms of taxation where the political factors don't get so squarely in the way. Sales and income taxes, for example, are relatively "painless" and "invisible." They are gradualist in nature, usually collected by withholding or by adding a few pennies to purchases. In addition, they are generally imposed by levels of government more removed from the taxpayer than localities, and they bear no discernible connection to specific projects desired by the spenders.

With taxes of this sort, it is possible to extract much more from the taxpayer than is feasible when he has to sit down and write a lump-sum check for the entire thing. Property levies ignite the taxpayer into resistance; nonproperty levies anesthetize the taxpayer and make it easier to separate him from the contents of his wallet.

Add the fact that when these taxes are imposed top-down by the state—or better yet, by the federal government—there is no distressing competition among different areas to keep the tax rates low. Such "inequities" as a locality's deliberately holding its taxes down to attract an industry can be eliminated; there can be one (high) rate for everybody. In this respect, of course, the issue is not so much the kind of tax, but by whom it is imposed—the state or Federal government as opposed to the city, the county, or the local school district.

Against this background, the seemingly paradoxical demand that finance of schools be transferred from the relatively modest property tax to booming state or federal taxes is more easily understood. Spending interests meeting resistance in the city council can finesse their opponents by conducting an end run to more lucrative taxes at a remoter level of government. As a pamphlet from the National Education Association (NEA) frankly put it some years ago: "Once public education has been made as much a federal responsibility as national defense or national highways, more money than was ever dreamed of will be spent on it." [10]

Legal challenges to the property tax dovetail with this larger design, but contain some wrinkles of their own. In a series of rulings that began with *Serrano v. Priest* (1972), the courts began gravitating toward the view that reliance on the property tax for finance of schools was "unconstitutional," since unequal valuations among districts imply unequal education. This was the boldest end run of them all. On the *Serrano* logic (somewhat ambiguously rejected by the Supreme Court in 1973), it didn't matter what local voters thought about higher taxes, or even what state legislatures or the Congress thought. The courts would simply order still more spending as a matter of "constitutional" right, presenting the spectacle, in Daniel Moynihan's words, of "big government ordering itself to become bigger." [11]

As noted by our friends at NEA, the move away from local property taxes is aimed at unleashing government and educationist forces for a burst of taxing and spending the likes of which we have seldom seen. And, in addition, it would centralize effective control over America's schools, first in the state education bureaucracies, and thereafter in the Federal authorities—whichever supplied the substitute money.

Control, after all, follows finance, and if local school boards lose financial leverage over education they will lose all hope of controlling it as well. This pattern is already discernible in states such as New York and Michigan where legislatures provide a large percentage of educational funding—and state authorities prescribe textbook standards and other particulars of the school regime as a result. It is also apparent in the standards and guidelines handed down by Federal planners to recipients of their "aid" in schools and elsewhere. Once the schools are financed in whole or in major part by the states or the Federal government, they will be controlled by whoever holds the purse strings.

In short: If finance of schools is kept chiefly on the property tax, the spending forces can be held in check, and local authorities can maintain some semblance of control over local education. If finance of schools is transferred chiefly to state or federal taxes, the spenders will be home free, with unbridled access to the public pocketbook and thoroughgoing control of the nation's schools.

Whether we are dealing with Federal "tax reform" or local "property tax relief," therefore, the basic point is essentially the same: The burden of taxation on the average citizen *cannot* be eased by soaking the rich, rearranging the load, or raising taxes in one sector in order to lower them somewhere else. No such expedient will accomplish the desired objective, for the simple reason that *exorbitant taxes are caused by exorbitant spending,* and nothing else. So long as the spending continues to soar, the social costs of spending will have to be paid.

9
There Is No Urban Crisis

The pattern of counterproductive activity that emerges from consideration of tax and spending issues becomes increasingly plain if we turn our attention to specific problem areas. Despite the tremendous diversity of government programs in existence today, one common feature manifests itself in any careful survey of results: in case after case, the programs in question have not only failed to assuage distress in our society, they have created it. Indeed, it is not too much to say the "problems" usually cited as reasons for further government intervention are themselves the product of earlier intervention. The result of this procedure is that we are continually being called on to enact new government programs to remedy the failure of previous ones.

This rule of thumb holds true, I believe, for just about every sector of American life—and we shall have occasion to note a considerable number of these as we proceed. In the present chapter, we may begin by reviewing some aspects of the much-lamented "crisis" of America's cities. Although it has in recent months yielded pride of place to ecology and energy, the "urban crisis" has been a steady theme of liberal exhortation for the past decade, and remains such today. Over the long pull, it is doubtful any issue has been hammered more relentlessly, or used more successfully as a pretext for programs of government intervention. And few issues reveal more clearly the utter bankruptcy of such programs.

The general burden of the urban crisis litany is well known. In essence, we are told that the aggregation of people in the cities, the closeness of urban living, and the shift of population patterns have created a knot of spontaneous vexation that cries out for official remedy. America's cities are congested and unhealthy, choked with traffic and pollution, and rapidly losing the resources to deal with their problems. Our urban centers are becoming progressively ghettoized, inhabited by poor blacks who cannot find work, or decent housing, or proper schools.

From all of which it is concluded that major Federal programs are required to provide the cities with additional revenue and expert counsel to deal with matters of employment, housing, education, transit, pollution, and so on. What has been created by the malfunctionings of an unplanned, haphazard system must be corrected by infusions of government expertise and dollars. Such are the general features of the "urban crisis" as it is generally presented in the halls of Congress, the legislatures of the states, and various city halls around the nation.

Not all these assertions are factually correct, but in a general way we can concede that each of the items listed is a "problem" in one degree or another, and as such requires analysis and correction. Stipulation of that fact, however, is something rather different from agreeing to the substance of the "urban crisis" plaint. For the problems in question have not sprung up through biogenesis from the city pavements, nor will they be cured by further interpositions of government. The situation, on the record, is clearly the other way around: rather than arising spontaneously and demanding coercive action by way of remedy, these problems have in the normal case arisen through the use of coercion and can best be corrected by policies that favor spontaneous action.

The Unemployment Problem

To demonstrate the point, let us consider the matter of employment, which is the principal historic reason for the growth of

America's cities and widely acknowledged to be a major subject of governmental concern. A goodly share of Federal policy since the 1930s has been aimed at eliminating unemployment, and joblessness remains a major topic of liberal oratory today. Nearly everyone is aware that unemployment in the central cities, particularly among young, impoverished, and restless blacks, is an acute problem for American society. There is less awareness of how and why this problem came into existence.

A typical statement on this subject was offered in the summer of 1973 by Herbert Hill, labor director for the National Association for the Advancement of Colored People. In an address before the national convention of that organization, Hill asserted that "rates of unemployment among black youth have reached disastrous levels." He added that if such rates continue, "and unfortunately there is every reason to believe they will, then it is necessary to conclude that virtually an entire generation of ghetto youth will never enter the labor force." [1]

In view of recent gains by blacks, these remarks may sound extreme, but the data back them up. According to the Labor Department's *Monthly Labor Review*, the jobless rate for nonwhite teen-agers in 1972 stood at the astronomical figure of 33.5 percent, meaning tens of thousands of adolescent blacks in search of jobs were unable to get them. Such enormous unemployment among the young and energetic is an obvious hardship not only to them, but to society: They are prevented from obtaining needed skills and thrust increasingly into dependence; society loses their potential talent, while a pervasive unrest among the jobless is hardly conducive to the public order.

What is the source of this appalling unemployment? Although the causes are seldom discussed with any clarity in our national debate, the economic record is tolerably clear. The problem so correctly complained of by Hill and so frequently cited as an urgent reason for government action is itself the *result* of government action—specifically, the statutory minimum wage. Adolescent Negro unemployment is demonstrably correlated to periodic increases in the minimum and extensions of its coverage—a correlation that is blandly ignored by Congress as it continues to press for ever-higher minima.

The record is as vivid as it is depressing. In 1951, when the federal minimum was 75 cents an hour, adolescent black unemployment stood at 14.8 percent. In 1956 the minimum went to $1 an hour and adolescent black unemployment went to 18.1 percent. By early 1968 the minimum had risen to $1.60 an hour and teenage joblessness among blacks stood at 26.3 percent. By 1971 this unemployment figure had broken 30 percent—and with the $2.20 minimum recently mandated by Congress it will almost certainly go higher still.

The reason for this process is simplicity itself. Labor costs are the largest single factor employers have to absorb (80 percent on the national average), which means they cannot afford to pay $1.60 (or $2.20) an hour to unskilled, marginal workers who can't produce an equivalent value for consumers. When minima go up, the unskilled are the last to be hired and the first to be laid off—which means countless disadvantaged workers, mostly young and thus untrained, are prevented from getting jobs and acquiring skills that would allow them to become productive citizens.

Extensive studies on this issue have been conducted by Marshall Colberg, Yale Brozen, Thomas Moore, John Peterson, Charles Stewart, and several others—including economists for the U.S. Labor Department, which in the past has aligned itself with forces urging bigger and better minima. The most comprehensive single survey is Peterson and Stewart's *Employment Effects of Minimum Wage Rates*. This volume analyzes innumerable studies on the impact of statutory wages on industries, regions, age groups, and occupational categories, and concludes that as a result of minimum wage hikes:

> Small firms tend to experience serious profit losses and a greater share of plant closures than large firms. Teen-agers, non-whites, and women (who suffer greater unemployment rates than workers in general) tend to lose their jobs, to be crowded into less remunerative noncovered industries, and to experience more adverse changes in employment than other workers. Depressed rural areas, and the South especially, tend to be blocked from opportunities for employment growth that might relieve their distress. . . . The evidence provides . . . basis for the claim that while [wage minima] help some workers they harm those who are the least well off.[2]

Although the total number of jobs lost because of such developments is hard to estimate, the authors pass along some sobering particulars. They cite findings by economists H. C. Barton, Jr., and Robert A. Solo that, while modest minima had small effect on employment growth between 1945 and 1954, "the rapid increase in these rates between 1955 and 1959 reduced employment growth to one-sixth its former rate." [3]

Studies by other scholars indicate that some 38,000 manufacturing jobs were lost as a result of minimum wage increases between 1949 and 1958, while an earlier doubling of factory wages in Puerto Rico proved "so disastrous that the minimum rate was unenforceable." A survey conducted by Peterson in conjunction with A. F. Hinrichs, assessing the impact of minimum wages in the garment industry, found that "the lowest-wage plants had the largest declines (or smallest increases) in man-hours following the imposition of the minimums, and that the highest-wage plants had the highest increases (lowest declines)." [4] *

One partial solution to this dilemma would be a youth wage—a differential between the minimum required for adults and that required for adolescents. This approach would have the advantage of permitting young people to obtain odd-job or part-time employment in soda fountains, department stores, hardware stores, and the like, in tasks that are not worth the adult minimum to an employer but that would provide young people with the dignity of earning and a start on development of skills. Such a differential has been endorsed by the Labor Department, which says "it would offset some of the hurdles that young people face in finding employment and would open up more job opportunities to young people." [5] To date, this notion has been rejected by Congress.

The liberal answer to all such documentation might easily have been lifted from the thought balloon of a Jules Feiffer comic strip.

---

* On that distasteful record, what may be expected of a $2.20 minimum, the next succeeding phase envisioned by Congress? Exact projections are difficult because of the many variables involved, but Thomas Moore of Michigan State University offers one arresting scenario. He calculates that with such a minimum, nonwhite teen-age unemployment would increase by approximately 20 percentage points a year up through 1979. If that analysis is anywhere near correct, Herbert Hill's lugubrious vision will very nearly be fulfilled.

According to Senators Harrison Williams of New Jersey and Jacob Javits of New York, the minimum must be raised because (1) to do otherwise is to go back to the nineteenth century, (2) human beings cannot be submitted to the laws of economics, and (3) we must respect the dignity of young people, domestics, and farm workers—ignoring the fact that these are the very people the minimum throws out of work.

The idea that wages should be dictated by congressional fiat is exploded by the empirical record, but it is more easily deflated perhaps by a little common sense. If it is authentically humanitarian to pass a $2.20 minimum wage, why stop there? That is, after all, a relatively puny figure. Why not a $10 minimum, or even $100? If Congress in its sovereign will can repeal the laws of economics it is obviously derelict in its duty by stopping off at $2.20 an hour. It should immediately resolve that all Americans of whatever age or condition, employed or not, will live forever on the Big Rock Candy Mountain.

Until that blissful consummation is achieved, however, we must all keep living in the material world where supply and demand continue to function and where—in obedience to the pieties of such as Senator Javits—a third of the black adolescents seeking jobs are unable to find them.

The Housing Problem

What is true in the matter of employment is equally true in another major sector of urban concern—the matter of housing. Here again we have repeatedly been told there is an enormous crisis in our cities, that the private sector cannot or will not do the job, and that the only alternative is to have the Federal government step in and provide the indigent with decent housing. George Romney, former Secretary of Housing and Urban Development, gave a representative statement of this view back in 1971 when he asserted that "we're pricing people out of the housing market faster than we can take them in," and that American homes "are dilapidating faster than building and rehabilitation" can keep pace.[6]

Such statements might be duplicated at length from the literature of exhortation about the housing crisis, and their constant

repetition has obviously convinced a lot of people the private construction industry has fallen on its face. The facts of record, again,
are somewhat different. Private builders have done not merely a
good job but a phenomenal one—better than the performance of
many other sectors of our economy and certainly better than the
government planners who are supposed to remedy the defects of
the market.

To begin with, government intrusion in the marketplace has
not assisted the low-income citizen in his quest for better housing.
If anything, governmental interventions and constraints such as
Federal Housing Administration mortgage insurance (a form of
subsidy through lowered interest rates), the construction of super-
highways, and the general drift of zoning regulations have skewed
the market more sharply toward suburban development than
would have been the case in an unhindered market, although this
diversion is partially compensated by the resulting speed-up in the
turnover or "trickle down" process, whereby "used" housing of constantly higher quality goes up for sale.

More grievous are the interventions through which the Federal
planners have actively proposed to help the disadvantaged—principally, urban renewal and public housing. In a 1967 survey Richard Cloward of the Columbia University School of Social Work
observed that "since the public housing program was legislated
in 1933, some 600,000 low-income housing units have been built,
but in the last 15 years urban renewal and highway construction
alone have demolished 700,000 low-rental units. . . . It is estimated that probably one million low-income units have been destroyed. . . . In this same period, urban renewal has built at the
most 100,000 units. So . . . the net loss in low-income housing
is probably about 250,000 units." [7]

A more recent update by economist John Weicher suggests an
even larger toll of destruction. As of 1965, some 444,000 dwelling units had been scheduled for demolition under urban renewal,
and only 166,000 had been scheduled to replace them. Since 1967
the basis of the figuring has been changed, but Weicher notes that
the record is just as bad: from 1967 through 1971, urban renewal
demolished 538,000 dwelling units and built 201,000—a net loss
of more than 300,000. [8]

Numerous other studies bear out these researches, showing

that Federal urban-renewal and housing policy has been a resounding failure. A comprehensive picture of housing trends was provided in 1972, for example, by Irving Welfeld, then associated with the Department of Housing and Urban Development. Writing in *The Public Interest,* Welfeld noted that from 1948 through 1967, public housing completions in America totaled fewer than 475,000 and that public housing starts amounted to less than 2 percent of the national total. The Federal government, according to Welfeld, destroyed more units of housing in this span than it managed to build—which makes the testimony on that score pretty unanimous.[9]

An especially valuable study of these issues has been conducted by economist Richard Craswell. The virtue of his survey is that it brings together in one connected narrative the various elements of the Federal tragicomedy: urban renewal, public housing, attempted rehabilitation, rent supplements—the whole shebang. Not a bit of it, on Craswell's assessment, has worked. He calculates that government programs have been responsible for the net destruction of at least *1 million* housing units, as illustrated in the following table:[10]

HOUSING UNITS DEMOLISHED	
Urban Renewal (through Jan. 1, 1968)	404,000
Urban Highway Clearance (1956–1968)	330,000
Public Housing Site Clearance (Dec., 1968)	177,000
Equivalent Eliminations (December, 1968)	143,000
Building Code Enforcement (1960–1968)	384,000
State Action (1960–1968)	208,000
Total Demolitions	1,646,000
PUBLIC HOUSING CONSTRUCTED	
(1950–1968)	559,000
Net Demolitions	1,087,000

In addition to the housing destroyed outright, there is the housing that government has kept from being built or caused to be abandoned. The University of Chicago's Yale Brozen calculates a quarter of a million units had been left standing vacant in New York City over a three-year span because of various government impediments. George Sternlieb of Rutgers points out that because of rent controls on older housing and other constraints, "the private new-housing market in New York City has ground to a near halt." Between 1963 and 1968, Sternlieb says, the number of new privately backed apartment buildings constructed per year in Manhattan fell from 93 to 5.[11]

Add to this the fact that the typical dwelling unit destroyed through urban renewal is occupied by people with relatively low income, while those constructed are occupied by people with relatively high income. This process is in keeping with the urban renewal notion of "upgrading" downtown neighborhoods, improving property values, and making the central cities more attractive to members of the upper and middle income brackets (which usually does not occur). The unstated result is to provide housing for the well-to-do at the expense of the poor—with turnover effects reversed or badly distorted.

Theoretically, people uprooted by urban renewal are to be taken care of by public housing and subsidy programs, but the record on these has been dismal indeed. The verdict on direct provision of public housing is uniformly bleak. Rare is the city that cannot display a public housing project converted into instant slum, with broken windows, mounting piles of refuse, and rampant criminality. The acknowledged failure of the Pruitt-Igoe project in St. Louis is the most famous recent example, but that fiasco can be readily duplicated in New York, Chicago, Washington, and countless other cities.*

Realization that public housing as such has failed led to the so-called turnkey approach in which private developers supply the housing and public subsidies are provided for mortgage payments, rehabilitation, and rentals. Housing expert Harrison G. Wehner has examined these programs in detail, and concludes they are comparable in many ways to the previous failures of urban renewal and public housing. He offers these observations:

---

* As noted by Craswell, public housing is also more expensive to build than private housing. In Washington, D.C., he observes, a one-bedroom public housing unit costs $32 more a month (in terms of real total cost) than a comparable private unit; in Pittsburgh the difference is $40, in Seattle $64.

. . . a recent congressional investigation found instances of fraud and exploitation, especially in the Section 235 rehabilitation program. In fact, the program is an open invitation to fraud. No matter what the price of the house (within certain limits), the purchaser's monthly payments are limited to 20 per cent of his adjusted income, and the government pays the balance. The purchaser, therefore, has little or no incentive to negotiate on price. . . .

Defaults on mortgages insured and subsidized under Section 235 (primarily rehabilitated housing) have made the Federal government the nation's largest slumlord, with over 50,000 homes in its possession. This consequence is hardly surprising since an eligible family may pay less each month for a house that it nominally purchases than it would pay in rent. With no stake to lose, the family will abandon its "purchase" as readily as it will move from a rented unit.[12]

There are many difficulties enfolded in the public housing muddle, but the fundamental flaw in all such programs is essentially the same: Incentives to maintain a property provided and paid for by somebody else range in typical instances from small to nonexistent. That flaw will not be corrected by switching from high-rise to low-rise or from direct provision to turnkey—but by getting government out of the housing business entirely and letting the private market do its job.

That the market is eminently capable of handling matters is more than demonstrated by the record of the housing industry. Housing starts over the past two decades have far exceeded the increase of America's population—averaging 1.5 new housing units for every added household. Up through the 1960s, approximately a million and a half units were being produced annually, resulting in a 50 percent expansion in the number of available units since the census count of 1950. Frank Kristof, former assistant chief of the Census Bureau's housing division, observes that "the nation's housing problem has little relationship to physical shortages of housing. If anything, the evidence suggests housing surplus rather than housing shortage. . . . Any talk of housing shortage in America constitutes one of the great mythologies of housing discussion." [13]

As for the claim that housing costs have priced the average-

and low-income American out of the market, B. Bruce-Biggs of the Hudson Institute shows that housing has gotten progressively cheaper as a percentage of income, rather than more expensive. Thus in the decade 1960–70, median income in the United States rose from $5,620 to $9,867—an increase of 75 percent. In the same span, the median value of houses rose from $11,900 to $17,000—an increase of only 43 percent. Obviously, income has been gaining on housing costs, rather than the other way around.[14]

All very well, it may be objected, but such aggregate figures are not responsive to the basic problem in our housing economy —provision of dwelling places for the very poor. Private industry spends all its time developing suburban ranch homes and exurban manses, and cannot or will not come up with housing for the disadvantaged. It is in this area, according to the usual complaint, that government action is sorely needed and that we have to step up our efforts to supply the nation with Federal housing.

It is true that private industry does not ordinarily construct new low-income housing, but the inference rising from this fact is different from that suggested by the fans of public housing. People in low-to-middle income brackets do not generally live in new housing and have no need or desire to. Most of us live in "used" housing, formerly occupied by someone else and made available when the previous occupant hied off to another address. Whether a house is new or not is nothing to the purpose. Some of the most elegant homes in America are quite old; some of the least elegant are of very recent vintage.

Housing turnover accounts, as noted, for the continual upgrading of the nation's dwelling units. Every time a developer builds a new house for somebody in exurbia, the owner vacates a generally less expensive house somewhere in the next interior ring of residences. When that vacant house is in turn occupied, still another house is opened up somewhere else, and so on down the line. (Bernard Frieden of MIT reports a New York study showing housing starts involving 64 new units "gave rise to a chain of turnovers involving 90 additional units.") [15] It is precisely the competition from these low-cost but livable "used" houses that makes it uneconomic for developers to pursue the business of constructing new low-income housing.

The net effect of all this building and housing turnover may

The Improvement in Housing Conditions, 1950-70

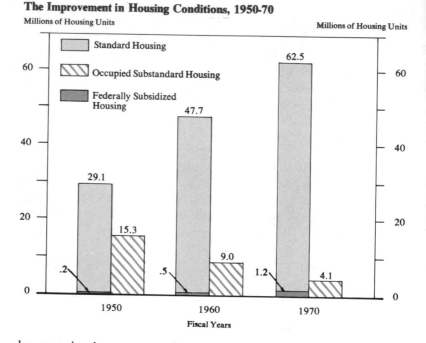

Millions of Housing Units

Millions of Housing Units

Standard Housing

Occupied Substandard Housing

Federally Subsidized Housing

Fiscal Years

be seen in the accompanying graph, adapted from the Federal budget summary for fiscal 1975. Closely analyzed, this chart tells an amazing story of American progress, comparing the condition of housing in 1970 with that prevailing in 1950. In this span of 20 years the number of "standard" housing units in our country has more than doubled, from 29.1 to 62.5 million. At the same time, the number of occupied "substandard" units has dramatically fallen—from 15.3 to 4.1 million.

Translated into percentages, this means the proportion of American houses rated "standard"—with indoor plumbing, not in need of major repair, not excessively crowded—has zoomed up from 66 percent or thereabouts to an almost incredible 94 percent. Which means in turn that the problem of inadequate housing has been virtually abolished in this country, surely one of the most astonishing records in the annals of private enterprise. And make no mistake about the fact that private enterprise, not government, is the responsible party.

The graph also shows the government contribution to the development of housing in this span, and it is meager indeed. For while the total stock of standard housing was growing by 33.4 million units, the number of federally subsidized units was increasing by exactly one million, and therefore constituted roughly 3 percent of the total expansion. Those figures provide an instant answer to the perennial cry of housing "crisis" sent up by liberal spokesmen in Congress and elsewhere who demand more Federal housing programs.

Moreover, these official statistics obviously *overstate* the Federal contribution to our housing stock—since the 1 million dwelling units credited here to government subsidy are in considerable measure canceled by the net destruction of 1 million other units by various Federal programs up through 1968. Nor does this include the economic costs of urban renewal programs that have destroyed or displaced some thousands of American businesses. All in all, it would appear the best thing government can do to improve American housing is to get out of the way so private enterprise can do its work. That observation, as we shall see, applies to almost all the other aspects of the "urban crisis" as well.

10
Sick Transit

Government planners of the liberal mold have one notable feature in common with the Bourbon monarchs as described by Talleyrand —they don't seem to learn very much from experience.

Despite the repeated failures of interventionist programs, the planners keep telling us we need to pile still other programs on top of those we already have—allegedly to cure the problems resulting from the existing level of intervention. Their attitude seems to be that expounded some years ago by former Kentucky Governor A. B. "Happy" Chandler: "The haystack's on fire; pour on more hay!"

A vivid example of this process appears in the recent agitation on the subject of mass transit. It is possible the transportation industry has been the subject of more controls, subsidies, and general distortions of the market than any other—replete with restricted entry, monopoly suppliers, protected routes, regulated rates, irrational discriminations, and outright punitive treatment of certain carriers in favor of certain others. The result has been a fairly egregious mess, which the government planners now propose to make still worse.

The nature of our transportation woes was summed up a few years back by John H. Frederick of the University of Maryland. Although a number of details have changed in the interim (mostly for the worse), his general analysis is as good today as it ever was. Reviewing the deterioration of transit services since the era of the Second World War, Frederick suggested these major difficulties:

(1) As an industry whose service standards and rates are controlled by national and state regulation, every mode of common carrier transportation has seen rising costs absorbing ever-increasing proportions of revenues, resulting in inadequate earnings and declining dividend-paying capability which have made it virtually impossible to obtain equity capital needed to benefit fully from technological progress.

(2) Subsidies have distorted the true economic cost of services for various kinds of transportation, resulting in many cases in the diversion of traffic from the more economic agencies.

(3) Outmoded labor rules have resulted in high costs and have imperiled the job security of many in the industry.

(4) Transportation policy, outmoded in many respects, combined with a regulatory system characterized by obsolete procedures, overlapping jurisdictions, and contradictory laws and decisions, served as serious impediments to the economical functioning of carriers.

(5) A greater transportation capacity than can be economically used in peacetime raises the question of how the excess capacity should be supported and to what extent this excess is justifiable on the ground of future civilian and defense needs.[1]

The remedy for all this now being proposed in Washington is to pour on more hay. Congress has moved to crack open the highway trust fund and divert a portion to government-sponsored transit systems, adopt a multibillion-dollar mass transit bill, and infuse some hundreds of millions into the decrepit railroads—where the head of the Interstate Commerce Commission sees "no alternative to a substantial level of federal government involvement."[2] In cities across America, local governments have taken over bus companies or are in process of doing so, and are promoting ambitious plans for tax-supported rapid transit.

The argument in all such cases is that private enterprise has failed, that transportation is a basic "right," and that the government must step in to make certain this right is freely available—through further regulation, subsidies, or outright ownership of the railroads, bus lines, or other transit systems. As in the case of employment and housing, this presentation is a substantial inversion of the truth. The fact is that, like most other urban problems, our transit woes have been created by government, not by private enterprise. And we may be certain that the recent deluge of proposals for more of the same will make the situation worse, not better.

Regulation of Rail Transportation

The railroads are perhaps the most notable example of what can happen under policies of excessive regulation. In their nineteenth-century heyday the rail companies were recipients of a number of governmental favors—subsidies, rights of way, and leases. In the twentieth century, however, and especially in the past fifty years, they have been subject to increasingly punitive and discriminatory regulation by the Federal government and on occasion by the several states. The effect has been to place the rails at a severe competitive disadvantage and to drive them to decrepitude.

Under the Transportation Act of 1920, the Interstate Commerce Commission (ICC) assumed authority over central managerial functions of the railroads, inducing a general rigidity of thought and practice for which the railroads have since become notorious. Under ICC regulation, for example, railroads had to acquire a certificate of convenience and necessity to build new track or otherwise enlarge services. Conversely, they could not *abandon* any service without ICC determination that the public could afford to be without it. Nor could the companies issue long-term securities unless the ICC vouchsafed permission. Both maximum and minimum rates were subject to control, as were determination of routes, disposition of rolling stock, and rates of return.*

---

* Historian Clarence Carson aptly summarizes matters when he states: "Rail executives could not, and cannot, buy, sell, build, abandon, or dispose of

It is hardly surprising that railroad managements, thus impeded, developed a semibureaucratic mentality that sought to limit potential losses instead of striking out aggressively in quest of profits. They were prevented from acting as entrepreneurs because the number of directions in which they could move was severely limited, a condition made still worse by explicit government patronage for other forms of travel. For while the rails were being hindered in their ability to operate, competitive modes of transportation were being encouraged by implicit and explicit government policy.

Most obvious of these was highway travel, which in the 1920s and thereafter became a favored object of government solicitude. Literally billions of tax dollars have been poured into the construction of public highways, culminating in the grandiose Interstate highway system with its 40,000 miles of road constructed at the cost of a $1 million a mile. The effect of this policy has been to encourage private and commercial transportation by highway as opposed to rail, and it is rather clear that such decisions have in considerable measure spurred our nation's reliance on the automobile.

Almost as notable has been official sponsorship of air travel, through provision of air mail contracts, maintenance of traffic control and safety systems, and government construction of landing facilities. It is not unusual in many American communities to find an expanding and busy airport constructed with tax dollars (slowly being amortized by landing fees), while a few miles distant stands a dingy and sepulchral train station that is entered on the books as private property and liable to a heavy tax. The appearance of both facilities is a direct and predictable result of government policy.

Whether user taxes pay sufficiently for upkeep of the highways or landing fees pay off the bonds on airports is an arguable subject, but a conclusion on that point is not essential to gauging the difference between the treatment given these modes of travel and

---

their facilities without commission approval. They could not sell stock to raise new funds nor consolidate with other lines without the authorization of the ruling government body. In most of the usual ways, railroad managers could not compete in price, in supplying certain kinds of service, or even, if the commission so determined, in the exclusive use of better located facilities." (*Throttling the Railroads,* Liberty Fund, 1971, p. 83.)

that accorded railroads. Highways and airports, in the usual case, are capital outlays made by government, while railway roadbeds and terminals are private property subject to substantial taxes. That differential in many cases would be sufficient by itself to establish the margin between success and failure—and it is not, of course, kept by itself.

Adding to the railroads' difficulties has been consistent government support for the demands of the railway unions, including a hefty retirement fund, rising pay scales, resistance to automation, "featherbedding," and, in some states, so-called full crew laws. The effect of these provisions is to increase the railways' sizable cost structure, and to constrict still further their narrow range of managerial freedom. Nothing has been left undone, it seems, to make sure the railroads are operated as uneconomically as possible.

Additionally, the ICC has displayed a considerable bias against, or perhaps an ignorance of, the well-being of the railroad consumer. It has frequently acted as if its job were to protect other carriers from the discipline of competition by the railways. This mentality has been expressed, for example, in refusals to permit rate *reductions* by the railroads in an effort to attract new or enlarged business. In one famous rate case of this type Southern Railway wanted to reduce its price for grain transportation by 60 percent, to take advantage of large-capacity freight cars. The barge lines and truckers protested this proposal, and the ICC accordingly denied it.

The agency has denied other rate reduction proposals as well —as when it turned down suggested reductions by railroads serving Portland (Maine), Boston, Albany, and New York City. (This denial, aimed at supporting preferential treatment for other ports, was subsequently overturned by a U.S. District Court.)

How the ICC views matters of this type has been quite frankly expressed. On one occasion, for example, the agency stated that when "carriers of competing modes of transportation propose reduction in their rates from levels not in excess of reasonable maximum rates for the sole purpose of attracting regulated traffic from one mode to another, and the only result thereof to respondent would be a net revenue loss for all the carriers concerned, the proposals constitute a destructive rate war which this commission is empowered to avert." Moreover:

> The parties [do not] contend that they would be better off
> from a net revenue standpoint if the rates of both modes were
> reduced as proposed. The evidence is convincing that the op-
> posite result would be inevitable. The rate relations between
> them would remain approximately as they are today, so that
> no material changes in the traffic flow or volume could be ex-
> pected, and the net result would be *a needless dissipation of
> revenue by both modes.* [Italics added.] [3]

This passage tells us quite a bit about the ICC mentality. Its
concern is to prevent "revenue loss" to carriers that are themselves
requesting rate reductions. What is described as revenue loss, of
course, is simply a lower price to the consumer. The ICC in this
instance perceived its role as one of holding prices high for carriers, as opposed to achieving optimum satisfaction for consumers.
This is all too often the logic of transit (and other) regulation, in
which the regulator assumes the role of guardian and spokesman
for protected segments of the industries being monitored.

The result of all this is that one of the simplest and most logical mass transit systems ever devised lies virtually unused across
the North American continent. U.S. railroads among them own
some 200,000 miles of track, which on a map of the United
States form a pattern of such extreme density as to blanket the
middle and eastern portions of the nation. Every major American
city has rail lines converging on it from every accessible direction,
and all are interconnected by trackage along which thousands of
people could be transported at once, pulled by a single engine,
in relative comfort and safety at high speeds. Yet for purposes of
passenger transportation, this system is either dead or dying, a
desolate monument to government regulation.

None of this is to suggest, however, that other types of transportation in America are especially sound, or that they have
escaped their share of counterproductive regulation. Competitive
modes have been favored relative to the railways, and, as measured against the railroads, have enjoyed a period of relative well-
being. Yet the regulatory net has tightened around them, too,
mandating uneconomic decisions, choking off competition, and
raising costs to travelers. Indeed, there is no segment of our

national transportation web that is exempt from this pervasive interference, whether Federal, state, or local.

Regulation of Air Transportation

An identical pattern is apparent, for example, in the case of the Civil Aeronautics Board (CAB). The principal activities of this agency have been to restrict entry into the field of commercial aviation, provide route monopolies, and prevent competitive pricing. It is noteworthy that since the CAB came into being in 1938, there has not been a single new major trunk line founded in the United States—in an industry field that has been marked by rapid technological advance and explosive growth.

In 1938, there were 19 major trunk lines. As of 1973, there were 11—the number having been shrunk by mergers and the refusal of the CAB to permit competitors to enter the field. Thus the airlines have been run on a cartel basis, with results that can be expected from such arrangements. Little consideration has been given the well-being of the consumer; routes have been handed out on a monopoly basis, and fares have been held well above the levels that would obtain under competitive conditions.

The CAB provided a classic statement of its anti-competitive bias in a 1949 decision concerning the relationship of smaller feeder lines to the major carriers. "We would like to emphasize again," said the agency, "that we have neither the disposition nor the intention to permit local air carriers to metamorphose into trunk lines in competition with the permanently certificated trunk lines." And in case there was any doubt about the matter, the CAB expounded further on the subject of competition in terms that might have been lifted from a clinical discussion of the bubonic plague: "We recognize that some competition between local service carriers and trunk lines is inevitable, but we intend not only to minimize such competition but to prevent its development to the greatest feasible extent." [4]

Not content with sealing the airline business off from normal market forces, the CAB of late has moved to eliminate the little competition that remains in discounts, frills, and service convenience. In 1973, for example, the CAB outlawed special discounts for youth fares, family units traveling together, and tourist excursions. The board originally suggested that this would be countered by a reduction in regular fares, but later decided otherwise. Also in 1973, the CAB blocked efforts of certain European carriers to offer reductions in trans-Atlantic rates.

In 1974, the CAB made its price-raising proclivities even more explicit—along with a drive to obtain a cutback in service. Sizable domestic and overseas fare increases were voted, and airlines were encouraged to put a minimum floor under charter rates to overseas destinations, on pain of having the floor made mandatory by the agency. Simultaneously the CAB reduced the number of flights by about 6 percent from the preceding year in order to force fuller planes and get bigger airlines profits. As one CAB official put it, "we've had too much emphasis on passenger convenience in the past." [5]

Justification for this anti-consumer policy is that the financially ailing airlines need larger returns on equity, through which they can attract capital. That the airlines need to be financially sound is apparent enough—and it would be incredibly short-sighted to *force* a rate structure below prevailing market levels and thus to drive the carriers into insolvency. But the evidence before us is of an entirely different character. What is clearly happening is that the CAB is *preventing* lower rates that would result from competition, while the ailing condition of the carriers is itself a product of their regulated status.

What would the situation be in the absence of such regulation? An answer is suggested by experience in the state of California, which is large enough geographically to support intrastate airlines not subject to the CAB's attentions. As a result, California has a competitive airline market and has developed carriers, most notably Pacific Southwest Airways, that charge rates half those of the CAB trunks. Leonard Ross of Columbia University Law School observes that a ticket from Los Angeles to San Francisco costs about 4.8 cents a mile, compared to the 9.9 cents a mile it costs to fly from Boston to Washington, D.C.[6]

Economist Theodore Keeler of the University of California at Berkeley has conducted studies comparing CAB's national rates with those prevailing in intrastate, and therefore competitive, conditions. The conclusion of this analysis is that the Federal regulators have imposed an average fare increase of roughly 74 percent on passengers who fly on an interstate basis. The following table reflects the differences, as of 1972, as they emerge from Keeler's studies:[7]

	CAB FARE	INTRASTATE FARE FOR COMPARABLE DISTANCE	INCREASE
New York–Washington	$ 24.07	$14.96	50.8%
Chicago–Washington	$ 47.22	$30.97	52.5%
Los Angeles–New York	$150.93	$90.21	67.3%
Miami–New York	$ 76.22	$41.76	84.0%
Los Angeles–Reno	$ 39.63	$15.28	116.0%

Regulation of Highway Transportation

The record in highway transportation is not appreciably better. Competition in the motor truck business is strictly regulated and limited; anyone who wishes to go into the trucking business will find himself before the ICC or a state public service commission in quest of a certificate of "convenience and necessity." If he cannot prove beforehand that customers are lined up and clamoring for his as-yet non-existent truck service, he will very likely be denied the certificate and prevented from operating. This method of licensing protects the suppliers already in the field, effectively cutting out the little guy who could otherwise start up a trucking business of his own.

The ICC, once more, is rather frank in its collusive, anti-consumer attitude. In matters of commercial trucking, the agency asserts that "from the beginning of federal motor carrier regulation, restrictions generally have been imposed to protect already authorized carriers from unintended or unwarranted competition." [8] It would be hard to state the case more clearly than that. And, in general, the ICC has been as good as its word, enforcing rate, route, and entry policies that protect existing carriers and hurt everyone else.

Ralph Nader's report on the ICC observes that "gateway restrictions, restricted use of interstate highways, and circuitous regular routes increase mileage unnecessarily. For instance, a carrier providing service between Eastern Pennsylvania and eastern Virginia is forced to travel a circuitous route, through western Virginia, in observance of a gateway restriction. A trip down the Atlantic coast would save up to 60 percent in mileage and a comparable amount in time. The inefficiency of this practice is patent; its justification is to prevent that carrier from luring traffic from carriers who already hold direct route authority." [9]

Because the motor transportation of certain agricultural commodities has been exempted from restrictions of this type, it is possible to make some cost comparisons between regulated and unregulated trucking—which redound entirely to the benefit of the latter. A study by economist Walter Miklius (cited in Nader's report) discloses, for example, that the unregulated service is faster, more personalized, and cheaper than the regulated one—a conclusion consistent with the results recorded by nonregulated airlines.

To make sure that we are lacking nothing by way of transit regulation, most urban communities maintain strict limitations on common carriers—including licensed entry, monopoly franchises, a ceiling on the number of taxicab medallions, union requirements for deadhead runs, regulation of routes and rates. The net effect has been not only to protect existing carriers from competition, but also to lock those carriers in as "public service" agencies whose management decisions are swayed by political factors as much as or more than business factors, with consequent irrationalities in the deployment of resources.

Such favoritism by regulatory bodies is frequently denounced by the liberals who promoted the regulation in the first place. The object of the system, they say, has been perverted, and it is essential to get better people to administer it. The empirical base for this objection is sound, but the proposed solution is not. Such "perversions" are built into the regulatory process and cannot be eliminated except by getting rid of the regulation itself. The liberal quest for better-quality regulators is simply another refusal to face the facts of government intervention.

Alternatives for Consumers

That the producer interest should prevail above consumer interest in transit or other regulation is not mysterious. By comparison to the potential consumers of their product, producers are relatively few (and regulation keeps them fewer than would otherwise be the case). Their stake in any given regulatory decision is often astronomically high, while that for any given consumer is comparatively low. The question of an air-fare hike before the CAB, for example, is of the most absorbing interest to the major airlines, but of marginal importance to any one consumer who may pay a few dollars more for a ticket. This equation ensures that the producer interests will be extremely attentive to the regulatory process; the average consumer, by way of contrast, will hardly know the process is occurring, and would have neither time nor incentive to do very much about it if he did.

It was in response to these considerations that the Naderite "consumer" movement took form and that demands have been heard for different and more public-spirited regulators. But this agitation misses the point. However the personnel are chosen, the interests involved are not commensurate. In a controlled situation, those whose stakes are high will always be more avidly interested than those whose stakes are low.

Nor is the situation helped appreciably when business interests are displaced by anti-business reformers whose motivation is political power or collectivist planning. This changes personnel and outlook, but does not change the asymmetry of the equation. One type of interested decision is simply substituted for another. What is needed, in the transit field or elsewhere, is to prevent *any* such decision from impeding the free choice of consumers as to which mode of supply they prefer, and to permit the market to offer them its full diversity of services.

It is hardly an accident in the midst of all the constrictions and rigidities existing in the transit field that consumer preference (with an assist from the highway program) has trended strongly to the one form of transport that is least regulated and most flexible—the private automobile. Although it requires high capital outlay, the private auto gives the consumer what other existing transit systems cannot: a vehicle that will take him exactly where he wants to go when he wants to go there, and that is therefore responsive to his demands rather than to the convenience of the regulators.

One possible answer to this consumer preference might be the development of "public auto" or jitney services, employing small buses, limousines, or modified taxicabs—vehicles that would be demand-responsive, economic for short hauls, and capable of carrying more than one passenger at a time. Unfortunately, this development has also been impeded in many major communities by various types of government interference. In most large cities, municipal limitations on the number of taxicabs and rate-setting by government tend to favor the companies in the field and to block out entry by competitors. Nonetheless, some of these communities have seen the rise of "gypsy cabs" (unlicensed taxis) and experiments with a jitney service on a limited basis, which appear to be responsive to consumer needs and indeed would not exist under such onerous legal conditions if there were not a vigorous demand.

Under conditions of competitive entry, it is entirely likely a number of small-bus or jitney companies would enter the mass transit field, serving local or specialized markets as needed and thus permitting fixed-route systems to limit service to periods of use (morning and evening) when employment of larger carriers is economic. Where such services are in demand the market will supply them, just as it supplies the far more complicated need for the vehicles themselves, or television sets, or shoes, or clothing— none of which requires the intercession of planners or the outlay of tax dollars.

The notion of jitney service for urban transportation is not, it should be added, blue-sky or theoretical. Once upon a time, back around 1915, the country had a flourishing jitney business from coast to coast. In this industry, private automobile owners would work on a full-time or part-time basis as they pleased, on their way to other jobs, at peak traffic periods, or when they were otherwise unemployed. They would simply post a general direction or destination on their windshields, then stop and pick up passengers at trolley stations or elsewhere along their routes and carry them where they wanted to go—charging what the market would bear (at that time about 5 cents a ride).

As described by economists Ross Eckert and George Hilton, the system functioned in approximately the same fashion as present-day airport limousine services—except that the vehicles moved in every direction, not simply over a fixed route. The advantages were many. The jitneys provided service to any and all points. The supply was enormously flexible, since anyone who had an automobile and wanted to make some extra money could participate. The service could be expanded at peak periods and would contract when demand was slight. Its free market pricing also meant it was available at higher costs in late hours or bad weather when ordinary public transportation was not available.[10]

So long as the market forces of supply and demand were permitted to function, the jitneys flourished. This was not to last very long, however, since street car companies didn't like the competition and moved to have some regulations enacted. This effort was generally successful, and it is noteworthy that the regulations imposed were exactly of the type to remove the flexibility, convenience, and demand-responsiveness of the system.

While the requirements varied from place to place, their most common features were demands for expensive licensing and bonding procedures; fixed route scheduling, which removed a major advantage over the linear street car systems; and requirements for long work days, which prevented the entry of carriers oriented to peak periods. The combined effect was to kill the jitney industry dead.

The effect was also to make public transportation fixed, linear, and increasingly uneconomic by requiring service at low traffic periods and discouraging it at peak periods. Again, it is hardly surprising that people turned increasingly to the private automobile, thus further accentuating the uneconomic status of the public transportation industry.

What, then, is the indicated answer to our transit problems? The general answer is clear enough. As in matters of employment and housing, we need above all to start removing government restrictions rather than to continue imposing them. Some specific steps that need to be taken:

(1) Abolish the ICC, or at least remove its power to regulate the essential decisions of railroad management. Above all, this agency should be deprived of its power to restrict entry of compet-

itors and control rates. Under competitive conditions, *if* demand exists, some hardy entrepreneurs attuned to the profit motive will devise brands of rail service and commuter amenities that could revive the railroads.

(2) Abolish the CAB, and transfer its safety functions to the Federal Aviation Authority (FAA). The California experience clearly shows that, in the absence of the CAB's interference, air travel would be accessible to a far greater number of people at far lower cost than is presently the case.

(3) Abolish Federal, state, and local restrictions on entry into the transit field generally—trucking, bus lines, and taxicabs. This proposal will stir the cry from the affected industries that there are too many people in the field already, but this is only the old producer-guild mentality speaking. If such producers are rendering good service to consumers, they deserve to stay in business and under market conditions will do so. If not, then not.

(4) Bring back the jitney.

11

Some Myths of Liberal Education

No subject of political debate is closer to the American people than the education of their children, and up until recently few causes were politically more sacrosanct. Public education has historically been viewed as one of our finest institutions, occupying a place of honor only slightly behind the revered positions of church and family. Of late, however, this perception has begun to change, and it is widely acknowledged that the public schools are in deep and serious trouble.

Principal symbol of this distress is that most explosive of political issues—the busing of school children for purposes of racial balance. For the past few years, the subject of busing has stirred enormous emotional upheaval, bitterly divided many American communities, and in several cases brought the process of public schooling to a virtual halt. In certain areas of the nation, the issue has totally blotted out other questions, and it is the rare American politician who has not felt constrained to address himself to the subject in one fashion or another.

Yet despite the turmoil and the talk, it is probable that busing is the *least* widely understood of all our major topics of controversy. Most political statements concerning it, whether from critics or proponents, have little to do with the substance of the issue, and it is safe to say the average American has only the slightest notion of what, exactly, the furor is about. Such confusion is understandable. It is impossible to grasp the significance of busing unless we first appreciate the recent history of education in this country—which is a story not widely known. For busing is a final, desperate effort to salvage something from the debris of a colossal failure.

Input vs. Output: Some Surprising Conclusions

For the past few decades, the dominant view on public schooling in America has equated proper education with increasing outlays of money. We have been told that "quality" is chiefly a matter of money for teachers, facilities, counselors, special aids, smaller pupil-teacher ratios, and the like, and it is for this reason that the traditional system of locally funded schools is alleged to be improper. Under this system, it is said, we have rich schools and poor ones, with suburban whites enjoying luxurious diggings in the rich schools and ghetto blacks being downtrodden in the poor ones.

In obedience to such notions there has been a steady campaign to enlarge school expenditures, cut down on pupil-teacher ratios, project compensatory programs for inner-city children, and more recently to convert the funding of schools from local property taxes to higher and more equalizing jurisdictions. All this activity has proceeded on the assumption that educational output could be improved by better funding of disadvantaged schools.

In the past few years, however, a considerable body of evidence has emerged suggesting these conventional notions of educational progress are badly in error. The net conclusion arising from this evidence is that larger infusions of money haven't upgraded the quality of education, and in particular haven't conferred appreciable benefit on Negro children of the inner city. In many jurisdictions, indeed, the trend is clearly in the other direction. The story begins with the so-called Coleman Report of 1966, a survey commissioned by the Department of Health, Education, and Welfare under the Civil Rights Act of 1964 and directed by James S. Coleman of Johns Hopkins University. Stated purpose of this

analysis was to measure "equality of educational opportunity" in
the United States, and one supposes, given the auspices, that the
sponsors expected the normal run of liberal assumptions about the
schools to receive empirical verification. If so, the sponsors must
have been astonished at what they had wrought.

Instead of finding huge inequalities of educational product
deriving from inequalities of inputs, the Coleman analysts discovered, pretty generally, the reverse: To the surprise of all and sun-
dry, their researches suggested that differences in expenditure,
pupil-teacher ratios, and physical facilities had almost *no* correlation to the quality of educational achievement. In particular,
there seemed to be no observable nexus between physical measures of "quality" schooling and the classroom performance of
black pupils who entered school with educational deficits and got
further behind in succeeding years.

The authors did their best to find some confirmation for liberal educationist views, but the results were marginal indeed. When
all was said and done, the major findings were that the nation's
schools "are remarkably similar in the effect they have on the
achievement of their pupils when the socioeconomic background
of the students is taken into account. . . . When these factors are
statistically controlled . . . it appears that differences between
schools account for only a small fraction of differences in pupil
achievement. . . . It appears that variations in the facilities and
curriculums of the schools account for relatively little variation in
pupil achievement insofar as this is measured by standard tests." [1]

For those who had been promoting increased-and-equalized
expenditure as the path to quality education, such statements came
as an embarrassing bombshell, and for a considerable period the
Coleman findings were allowed to lie there, quietly unattended. By
the early 1970s, however, a number of somewhat puzzled liberal
scholars had decided to pursue the matter further—and as a result
produced some additional studies that turned out to be minor
bombshells in their own right. These documents made the point
so clearly and explicitly that it could no longer be ignored.

First of these was a compilation of papers derived from a
Harvard seminar on the Coleman Report, edited by Frederick
Mosteller and Daniel P. Moynihan, in which a group of sixteen
scholars reexamined the record on inputs (per pupil expenditure,

school facilities, textbooks, and so on) and their relation to outputs (achievement skills of the students). The net result was to
confirm the Coleman findings on essentials and to lay waste in
every direction to liberal notions about the schools.

On the question of spending differentials, for example, the
study revealed the conventional wisdom has the situation backward. It is usually assumed that schools attended chiefly by Negroes
are less adequately funded than those attended by whites, and
that this disparity is most acute in the states of the Old Confed-
eracy. Our scholars found, however, that in many respects the
level of spending on Negro schools is *higher* than that for schools
that are chiefly white, and that where discrepancies exist in favor
of whites they are less discernible in the South, not more.

Mosteller and Moynihan observe that "there did not turn out
to be differences of such magnitude between the schools of Negroes
and whites, within regions," and that "the tabulated data do not
support the presumption of gross discrimination in the provision
of school facilities in the South." Contributor Christopher Jencks
puts it that "despite popular impressions to the contrary, the
physical facilities, the formal curriculums, and most of the meas-
urable characteristics of teachers in black and white schools were
quite similar." [2]

These scholars confirmed as well the general finding of the
Coleman Report that variation in school facilities has little to do
with variation in achievement. Mosteller and Moynihan endorse
the Coleman view that there was "so little relation as to make it
almost possible to say there was none. . . . The variation in these
facilities seemed to have astonishingly little effect on educational
achievement. One example is the importance to educational achievement of the pupil-teacher ratio"—which the Coleman Report dismissed entirely because "it showed a consistent lack of relation to
achievement among all groups under all conditions." [3]

While the emphasis of the sixteen scholars varied on numerous
points, the overwhelming conclusion was that paying out money
for the schools has no appreciable effect, beyond a certain threshold, on educational quality. A similar view was expounded by
Jencks in a second study out of Harvard, conducted with the aid
of a team of research associates. This volume, entitled *Inequality,*
was written from a liberal-left perspective with a bias toward
egalitarian formulas. Nonetheless, Jencks and Co. were relentlessly

honest in assessing the results of those formulas and found the record immensely discouraging.

Their survey encompassed a vast amount of materials gauging just about everything connected to the schools, and reached the finding that little of what is done by different schools makes much of a difference in educational product. In particular, they discovered, there is no demonstrable connection between attendance at one sort of public school as opposed to another and results computed in terms of cognitive skill, further educational advance, or adult economic status. Among their conclusions on this score:

> . . . no specific school resource has a consistent effect on students' test scores or on students' eventual educational attainment. . . . We can see no evidence that either school administrators or educational experts know how to raise test scores, even when they have vast resources at their disposal. . . . Achievement differences between schools are . . . relatively small compared to achievement differences within the same school. . . . Additional school expenditures are unlikely to increase achievement, and redistributing resources will not reduce test score inequality. . . .
>
> Our research suggests . . . that the character of a school's output depends largely on a single input, namely the characteristics of the entering children. Everything else—the school budget, its policies, the characteristics of the teachers—is either secondary or completely irrelevant.[4]

This is not the final word on the subject, since research on "outputs" is continuing, and the programs that Jencks and others would premise on such findings are often more distressing than the system they criticize—but that is a topic for another sermon. The relevant point for here and now is that spending millions for "quality" schools, according to these researches, is a complete delusion.

The Rationale for Busing

From the perspective offered by these studies we may understand the phenomenon of "racial balance" busing—which in recent years has stirred such bitter political controversy across the nation.

If there were ever an issue on which the American people have spoken as one, busing would appear to be it. Polls have shown that 70 to 80 percent of the public is opposed to busing and wants to maintain the neighborhood school. Presidents Nixon and Ford have said they are opposed to busing, as have countless members of Congress. All across the land state officials and school boards have vowed their hostility to the practice, and those who waffle may find themselves removed from office. Just about everyone, it seems, is opposed to busing. So the question is this: Why do we have busing?

The standard answer of Federal functionaries and liberal interest groups who have promoted busing is that the practice is required to overcome the effects of historic discrimination and to bring about authentic "integration," allegedly mandated by the Constitution and the nation's civil rights laws. It is in supposed service to these legal requirements that the courts keep ordering "racial balance" mixes, cross-county transfers, and avoidance of racial tipping-points (the percentage of black enrollment that supposedly generates an exodus of whites).

Yet in point of fact such racial balance busing is directly *contrary* to the law of the land as stated by Congress. The Civil Rights Act of 1964, which allegedly gives Federal judges jurisdiction in such cases, says that " 'de-segregation' shall not mean the assignment of students to public schools in order to overcome racial imbalance." And it further states that ". . . nothing herein shall empower an official or court of the United States to issue any order seeking to achieve a racial balance in any school by requiring the transportation of pupils or students from one school to another or one school district to another in order to achieve such racial balance."

Busing forces prefer to ignore this language if possible, but when called on to recognize it they say it was meant to forestall busing only in cases of *de facto* segregation, not in cases where segregation has been accomplished by law (*de jure*). In the latter instance, it is argued, the courts may order busing or any other remedy to correct the discriminatory evil. This explanation explains little, however, since the author of the language in question, former

Representative William Cramer of Florida, explicitly noted that its goal was to prevent "*any* balancing of school attendance by moving students across school district lines to level off percentages where one race outweighs the other." [5] To prevent, in sum, exactly what has been ordered by Federal courts all over America.*

If "the law of the land" does not compel busing, what does? The answer may be discovered, once more, by going back to the Coleman Report—and to a companion study issued by the U.S. Civil Rights Commission, entitled *Racial Isolation in the Public Schools* (1967). Between them, these documents provide the official rationale for busing—which has almost nothing to do with the legal arguments propounded in its behalf.

The Coleman study, as we have seen, found little relationship between the amount of money spent for schools and the educational product that issued from those schools. In the case of black pupils, in particular, it found no consistent correlation between the measure of educational inputs and the performance of children who, in contrast to the standard expectation, "fall farther behind the white majority" as they proceed through the school system. Whatever the source of black educational deficits, the study found, "the fact is the schools have not overcome it." [6]

Conventional integration apparently had minimal impact on the problem, but it suggested, the authors thought, a possible solution. They believed, on the one hand, that educational deficits were probably owing to a "combination of nonschool factors— poverty, community attitudes, low educational level of parents." They noted, on the other hand, that it "appears" pupil achievement is "strongly related to the educational background of the other students in the school." From these two factors the conclusion seemed to follow that "if a minority pupil from a home without much educational strength is put with schoolmates with strong educational backgrounds, his achievement is likely to increase." [7]

Coleman explained the matter further in a subsequent article,

---

* Nor is the 1964 Civil Rights Act the only such manifestation of congressional intent. Over the past decade Congress has expressed its wish that the busing cease and desist, that Federal funds not be used to promote busing, and that a moratorium be imposed on court-ordered busing plans. The judicial busers have treated these enactments with indifference and gone right ahead to force the practice on an unwilling nation.

opining that what we needed was "a more intense reconstruction of the child's social environment," that goes beyond the matter of nondiscriminatory school assignment. In particular: "For those children whose family and neighborhood are educationally disadvantaged, it is important to replace this family environment as much as possible by an educational environment—by starting school at an early age, and by having a school which begins very early in the day and ends very late." [8]

The Civil Rights Commission report, for its part, stresses that legal segregation is *not* the issue—that separation of the races by reason of circumstance is just as objectionable as separation created by law. The commission asserted that both should be eliminated because "Negro children suffer serious harm when their education takes place in public schools which are racially segregated, whatever the source of such segregation may be." [9] The commission recommended that no school have higher than 50 percent black enrollment—so that the children would not be reimmersed in the black environment that was the supposed source of their trouble.

In sum, the educationists became convinced and apparently convinced a number of our Federal judges that Negro children must be taken out of their homes and neighborhoods and placed in an "artificial environment" created by government, where they will be immersed as fully as possible in an altogether different culture. The object is to break into the Negro family and culture pattern and remold black children according to guidelines preferred by middle-class (and predominantly white) social planners who think they have a commission to tinker around with the psychic makeup of the human species.

Busing is essential to this enterprise. It involves long periods of transportation that maximize the amount of time a child is away from his home and parents, and it takes him to a distant school where his parents in many cases can have little knowledge of what is occurring, can exert zero influence on the school's official performance, and would feel constrained from doing so even if they could physically reach the school.

At the same time, busing is required to shuttle the students around so that no school will ever become predominantly black —which would return the student to the very culture he is supposed to be escaping. Against that background it is apparent that nearly all the discussion that surrounds this issue is off the point. All that argument about *de jure* and *de facto* segregation is essentially phony, since the object of busing is to prevent the schools from becoming black in character for whatever reason.

The Effects of Busing

Unfortunately, busing has been no more successful than the other enthusiasms that preceded it. A dozen surveys have weighed the effects of busing in diverse communities across the nation, and the net of the evidence is that busing has not only failed to achieve its stated goals of improving educational skills and racial feeling, but in many instances has actually served to make the situation worse.

A major study on this issue was made by David Armor, an associate professor of sociology at Harvard and a former researcher for the Civil Rights Commission. Armor brought together a series of studies, involving some 5,000 school children in grades one through twelve, which tested educational results of those who were bused against a control group of children who were not. Covered in this analysis were schools in Boston; Ann Arbor, Michigan; Hartford and New Haven, Connecticut; Riverside, California; and White Plains, New York.

Armor found no consistent evidence of educational improvement as a result of busing, but considerable proof of adverse effects on the students who were bused. In some instances there were slight gains for bused students, but in other instances the control group showed the greater degree of improvement. Moreover, the pupils who were bused developed lower educational aspirations and a higher degree of racial antagonism than did those who weren't—directly contrary to the theory.

"None of the studies," Armor concludes, "were able to demonstrate conclusively that integration has had an effect on academic achievement as measured by standardized tests. . . . [In Boston] there was a significant decline for the bused students, from 74 per cent wanting a college degree in 1968 to 60 per cent by May 1970. . . . the bused students were 15 percentage points more in favor of attending non-white schools than the controls. . . . 80 percent of the bused group said they were 'very favorable' to the program in 1968, compared to 50 per cent by 1970."

Also in the Boston study, bused pupils in grades three and four showed slight gains in reading achievement over the control group, but in grades five and six students who were *not* bused did better than those who were. "The results for reading achievement are substantially repeated in a test of arithmetic skills," Armor says. "The bused students showed no significant gains in arithmetic skills, compared to the control group, and there were no particular patterns in evidence."

Halfway across the nation, in Ann Arbor, Michigan, the results were much the same. Bused students did not make significant gains when compared to the control group, nor did the bused students cut into the black-white gap on achievement tests: "On the contrary, a followup done three years later showed that the integrated black students were even further behind the white students than before the integration project began." [10]

These findings have been updated in an extensive survey of the busing question by Jeffrey Leech of the Indiana University Law School. To the results of the Armor study, Leech added more recent data concerning busing experiments in Berkeley and Sacramento, California; Buffalo and Rochester, New York; and Evanston, Illinois. On every major point at issue, the findings produced by Leech confirm the lugubrious reading of the Armor report.

Leech observes that "of the 10 cities which have systematically studied the effects of busing on the achievement levels of school children, one shows moderate gains (Sacramento), two show mixed results (Hartford-New Haven, Rochester), three are inconclusive (Buffalo, Evanston, White Plains), and four show either losses or no significant gains (Ann Arbor, Berkeley, Boston, Riverside). In every city studied, busing failed to reduce the gap between black and white achievement."

"In fact," Leech goes on to report, "most cities reported that the achievement gap had grown even larger after busing. Scholars who have reviewed the evidence . . . have concluded that busing has little if any effect on the academic achievement of either black or white children. Thus the most recent sociological evidence fails to confirm a basic premise underlying the rationale for court-ordered busing; i.e., that it will positively affect the academic performance of minority children."

This author also examined data concerning self-esteem, achievement goals, and racial harmony, and came to similar negative conclusions. He found the result of busing to be psychologically harmful rather than beneficial, and in particular to be a source of racial friction rather than amity. He notes several cases where antagonisms were directly traceable to busing and adds that "in no city did busing appear to increase interracial contact or better interracial understanding."

Leech urges a searching reappraisal of the whole busing enterprise, concluding that "in the light of the tremendous social, political and economic costs being paid for busing, the absence of any consistent educational gains, the deleterious psychological impact of busing upon black children, and the increasing polarization of the races, such a re-examination is long overdue." [11]

Researches of this type will continue, of course, and it may be that sooner or later they will come up with a liberal program that actually works. For the moment, however, we are left with the impression of total shipwreck: the original formulas having failed, the remedies for those formulas turn out to be failing also. After the expenditure of billions on billions of dollars for "quality" education and the instigation of massive upheaval in American communities through busing, the Federal educationists have little to show in terms of educational advancement.

They do, however, have a powerful headlock on America's schools, and plenary powers over American school children. And, as Chapter 23 discloses, that is a chilling story in itself.

12

The Cause and Cure of Inflation

Few issues in American politics are at once so crucial to our national well-being and so thoroughly confusing to the public as the topic of inflation.

In part the confusion is a natural one, arising from the complexities of the subject and the necessity of distinguishing between an immediate problem on the one hand and hidden causes on the other. But in substantial part it is also contrived. There are elements in our society who are busily creating inflation and benefiting from it, and it is to their advantage to keep the matter as obscure as possible. An inherent difficulty is thus compounded by a determined effort to generate misinformation.

The subtleties of the matter were colorfully and correctly noted by that most sophisticated of economists, John Maynard Keynes. According to Keynes's early volume, *The Economic Consequences of the Peace,* Communist leader V. I. Lenin was supposed to have said "the best way to destroy the capitalist system was to debauch the currency." In this malign opinion, Keynes averred, Lenin was unquestionably correct, since "the process engages all the hidden forces of economic law on the side of destruction, and does it in a manner which not one man in a million is able to diagnose." [1]

These observations have been fully and rather sadly validated by the recent history of the United States. For the past few decades, and especially in the 1960s and 1970s, our economy has been ravaged by inflation, and the effects are everywhere apparent. The purchasing power of our currency has been debauched, with attendant impact on savings, fixed incomes, interest rates, and the workings of the price system. The toll of economic destruction has been immense, and popular understanding of how and why it has occurred is almost nonexistent.

As bad as the inflation itself have been alleged efforts by government to combat it. Beginning in August 1971, the American nation struggled fitfully under the burden of wage and price controls supposedly required to halt the upward push of prices. Visible results of this experiment were discouragement of investment and production, dislocation of supply and demand, and critical shortages of commodities from food to fuel supplies. (See Chapter 16, "The Energy Crisis.") These painful effects were justified to the American public as part of the "sacrifice" it had to make in the battle against inflation.

The absurdity of that sacrifice becomes especially vivid when we reflect that the controls did *not* in fact curtail inflation or impede the general advance of prices. Nor had they any prospect of doing so from the outset, for the simple reason that wage and price controls deal not with the causes of inflation but with the effects. Attempts to stop the upward trend of prices through the imposition of controls are the equivalent of trying to stop a fever by breaking your thermometer, or cure a case of measles by painting over the spots. It is to attack the symptoms of the problem, rather than the causes.

The Cause of Inflation

Inflation is not created by cost push, administered prices, excessive profits, or any of the other usual phrases of the political marketplace. It is created instead by government, through continual expansion of the money supply. By definition, in fact, inflation *is* expansion of the money supply, which is generally identified by economists as currency in circulation plus demand deposits—those deposits withdrawable without a waiting period. Prices are a ratio between this money supply (M1) and the available stock of goods and services; so many dollars in the marketplace bidding for so many offered commodities determine the general price level. It follows that if the money supply is increased relative to the stock of goods and services, the general price level will rise; if the money supply is decreased, the general price level will fall.

The notion that "rising prices" are the cause of inflation, rather than the reverse, is of course widespread, and difficult to combat. From the standpoint of each individual, the source of the problem always seems to be the other fellow's prices. The average business-man, for example, finds the costs of his materials, labor, and con-tributory services constantly rising and must raise his prices in turn to cover his costs. The obvious solution appears to be to hold down the prices he himself must pay. This kind of argument is frequently used by businessmen who suppose the "cause" of infla-tion is militant wage demands. But while such demands can *con-tribute* to inflation, they emphatically are not the cause of it.

A little reflection will serve to demonstrate that no individual price increase or wage demand can possibly cause a general infla-tion. Let us assume, for purposes of argument, that the stock of money is fixed and then consider what would happen in the case of heavy wage demands by the United Auto Workers or a sudden hike in prices by General Motors. If the money supply is not en-larged to accommodate these factors, there transparently can be no general inflationary effect. For in that event a dollar *more* to pay the wages of a UAW worker, or buy a Chevrolet, becomes a dollar that *cannot* be spent for something else. Any extra money spent in one place must be subtracted from some other place. *Total* demand therefore remains the same, and while individual prices will fluctuate the *general* price level, other factors being equal, will continue as before.

Expand the money supply, however, and all these considera-tions change. Now it is possible to spend more money *both* for the Chevrolet and for something else, and for all prices to rise simul-taneously. That, indeed, is one reason for monetary expansion— the fact that, for a time at least, the generally rising level of prices and wages permitted by it gives the illusion of augmented prosperity for everyone. It is the monetary expansion rather than the wage and price demands, in sum, that is the source of the difficulty.

Because these processes take time to make themselves apparent, there is often a lag between a given expansion of the money supply and a given inflationary effect. Nevertheless, the record over the long pull is tolerably plain, and the accompanying tables reveal the truth with considerable clarity. They indicate that the rise in prices that has marked our economy in recent years is a

HOW PRICES FOLLOW MONEY SUPPLY

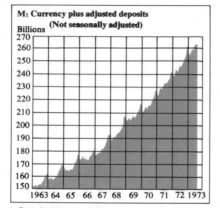

1. Growth of M_1: charts prepared from data published in Federal Reserve Bulletins.

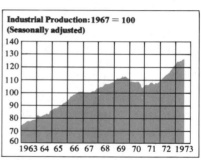

2. Industrial Production: charts prepared from data published in *Survey of Current Business* and Federal Reserve Bulletins.

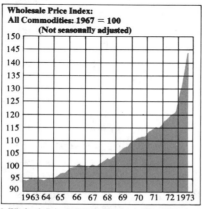

3. Wholesale Price Index: charts prepared from information published in *Survey of Current Business* and Federal Reserve Bulletins.

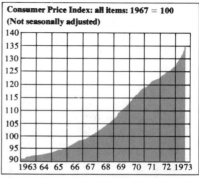

4. Consumer Price Index: charts prepared from information published in *Survey of Current Business* and Federal Reserve Bulletins.

direct result of monetary expansion, and that wage and price controls had not the slightest influence in restraining it.

In the latter part of the 1960s and in the early 1970s, for example, the stock of money increased at rates sometimes exceeding 8 percent a year. From 1967 through 1973, the money supply quite literally exploded—and consumer prices followed faithfully in its wake.

In September 1967 currency plus demand deposits stood at $183.7 billion. In the six years through August 1973, the money supply grew to $260 billion—an increase of roughly 44 percent. In the same span, the index of industrial production rose from 100 to 126.2—an increase of 26 percent. The predictable result of increased numbers of dollars chasing a lesser increase in the available stock of goods is an upward push of the price level, and this is exactly what occurred. In this six-year period, consumer prices jumped by 35 percent—more or less the order of magnitude one would expect from the discrepancy between money and production.[2]

What was the impact on all this of the various phases of wage and price controls? Examination of the relevant tables shows that, for all intents and purposes, there was none. Throughout the control period the Federal Reserve Board (which regulates the nation's monetary policy) continued to expand the money supply along the general curve that had prevailed for the preceding decade —with a couple of dips in early 1972 and another in 1973, but with a stratospheric increase toward the end of 1972 that more than compensated for these periods of curtailment.

Wholesale and consumer prices continued to soar, taking off in an especially giddy climb in 1973. There were occasional dips here and there, but the steady upward thrust right through the period of controls is apparent on the face of it.

Inflation and Unemployment

Although working economists are aware of all this monetary expansion, a number of them have been willing to play the inflationary game for what they consider good and sufficient reason. As formulated by the Keynesians, the problem before us is one of choosing between inflation on the one hand and unemployment on the other. If we do not inflate, it is said, we will have rising job-lessness, and in the Keynesian scheme of things inflation is the preferable option—an opinion generally shared, for the political reasons we have noted, by Federal officeholders.

Exactly why we should be confronted with this unpleasant dilemma is never made quite clear, and one would suppose from much of what is said about it that the Hobson's choice of inflation or unemployment is built into the structure of the universe. There is, however, a very specific reason for this conundrum that was understood quite well by Keynes and by his more candid disciples.

Under normal conditions of supply and demand, of course, there would in theory be no such thing as chronic high unemployment because falling demand would set wage levels at a lower rate, and that would clear the market—all offered services being accepted at some diminished price. The basic argument of the Keynesians, however, is that wages are "sticky" in a downward direction [3] (Paul Samuelson's phrase) and thus cannot be adjusted to meet conditions of falling demand. Services are offered at a fixed rate for which there are no takers, the market is not cleared, and unemployment results. Inflation is the Keynesian solution—a method of lowering real wages through dilution of purchasing power while leaving more visible money wages intact.

Viewed in that light, the Keynesian economists ask, what's wrong with a little inflation? If in fact the process can cure the problem of unemployment, why not resort to it? As long as people keep on making more money they can pay the higher prices and aren't really harmed by the process. We translate everything into higher numbers, with prices going up but with purchasing power going up as well. And what's wrong with that?

The answer, unfortunately, is that just about everything is wrong with it. To begin with, it doesn't work. Labor unions have long since caught on to what is happening to the purchasing power of wages and have countered by including cost-of-living clauses in their contracts. This defeats the original object of reducing real wages, which was to restore the equilibrium between supply and demand. Thus the effort to cure unemployment through inflation simply veils and postpones the effects of the disequilibrium rather than resolving it: whenever inflation starts to ease up, the disequilibrium will reappear in the form of rising unemployment.

This race between the unions and the government printing presses ensures that our economy will continue to vibrate between unemployment on the one hand and inflation on the other, and that we shall eventually wind up, not with a "little inflation," but with a lot of it. Only a fundamental adjustment of supply and demand can right the imbalance. Unfortunately, government intervention in the marketplace through minimum wages, backing for militant union demands, and subsidy arrangements to pacify the unemployed ($4.9 billion in unemployment compensation in 1972) are all designed to prevent that readjustment from occurring. In the familiar pattern, one species of intervention becomes the pretext for another.

Inflation would be objectionable even if it "worked" as the Keynesians originally wanted it to. Deliberate inflation of the money supply is wrong on a number of grounds besides the technical ones—including the fact that its effects are not distributed equally, and that it does *not* simply convert the economic process into higher figures. On the contrary, some elements and classes in the economy are helped by inflation, while others are hurt by it. And invariably the people hurt are those who lack the political or economic muscle required to keep abreast of the Federal printing presses.

Why Government Creates Inflation

As noted by economist David Levy, the fundamental impulse behind inflation is a simple one. the age-old desire of people in government and elsewhere to secure something for nothing—to acquire some portion of other people's earnings without the formality of asking for it, or overtly imposing a tax. Inflation is an admirable method of doing this because it is so silent and circuitous that the victims are seldom conscious of what is happening to them or who is doing it. In the realm of economics, it is close to being the perfect crime.[4]

The dollars we possess represent our proportionate claims on the stock of goods and services available in our economy. To the extent that someone else can simply *manufacture* dollars, he can carry off some portion of the things we have worked to earn. In effect, a fraction of our earning power is transferred to whoever is able to create and deploy money in this fashion. It is for this reason that counterfeiting is a crime and that one can go to jail for printing up false stock certificates.

The stockholder comparison may be used to illustrate the point. If there are 10 shareowners in a company, each holding 10 shares, these shareholders are each entitled to 10 percent of the company's earnings. But if someone else can simply print up stock certificates in his own behalf, he can diminish the earnings of the original owners as he pleases. If he prints 100 shares for himself, he can co-opt half the property of the original shareholders without doing any work or putting up any capital beyond the ink and paper necessary to produce his certificates. In practical effect this is what government does when it inflates the money supply. It prints up titles to a share in the national output.

The ability to transfer wealth in this manner is particularly appealing to politicians and to client groups who get some portion of what is transferred—an appeal enhanced by the factors mentioned in the preceding chapters. As noted, the conflicting demands of spending blocs and taxpayers call for expedients that will permit the payouts to continue while the anger of the taxpayers is diverted into irrelevant by-ways. By far the easiest and most venerable of these expedients is inflation, which permits the spending to continue without stint, gives the appearance of keeping taxes low, and spreads the social costs in a way that is difficult for the average citizen to fathom.

The binge of welfare spending discussed in Chapter 6 has been heavily financed on the cuff—to the tune of $110 billion in deficits from 1965 to 1972. While this enormous indebtedness does not directly create inflation, it has been and continues to be a major pretext for inflationist policies. Up until a few years ago, indeed, the need to inflate the money supply as a method of "supporting" the Federal debt was openly acknowledged by the Federal Reserve. In lending such support, the Fed simply "buys" treasury paper and becomes a "creditor" of the Treasury Department, printing currency as need be to facilitate the transaction. In consideration of Treasury bills, deposits are created in Federal Reserve Banks against which the government can draw. This procedure means the government is borrowing from itself—which is simply a complicated way of creating new money. It's called "monetizing the debt," and the money created is called "high-powered money" because its status as a fractional reserve generates credit in multiples of the created deposit.*

Indirectly, the Fed's support is just as important. When the Treasury goes into normal money markets to finance deficits, it places pressure on the supply of credit, which under normal conditions forces interest rates up. The Federal Reserve's Open Market Committee is under continual ideological and political stress to combat this tendency with "easy money"—that is, inflation. This has the desired result of keeping rates low for the government itself, and keeping them low for other borrowers who otherwise would be incensed about the impact of government policy on money markets.

The effect of it all is a steady increase of the money supply. The Fed has "purchased" more and more Treasury bills and paid for them with created money, and the Open Market Committee has kept an attentive eye on interest rates and attempted to "lean against the wind" whenever they seemed to be getting too high.† It has only been since 1970 that the Fed has begun placing analytical emphasis on the factor that *really* needs watching—the total growth of the money supply. Unfortunately, what they have been watching, with few exceptions, has been a continuous record of expansion.‡

---

* The banking system in effect creates credit through the practice of maintaining only a fraction of its deposits—historically about 20 percent—to cover possible runs (heavy withdrawals). Four out of five deposited dollars are thus recirculated, and when they are deposited elsewhere generate additional credit in similar fashion. If all banks are "loaned up" under such a fractional reserve system, one dollar in deposits can generate five in credit.

† It is noteworthy that, over the decade of the 1960s, the ownership of Federal securities by commercial banks held fairly steady at around $60 billion ($61.5 billion in 1959, $59.5 billion in 1972) while the value of securities held by Federal Reserve banks almost tripled—moving up from $26 billion in 1959 to $71.4 billion in 1972.

‡ The Federal Reserve System is a prime example of the manner in which political action generates economic problems—and supposed reforms lead on to grief. Establishment of the system was a major accomplishment of Woodrow Wilson's administration, and was widely accounted as an important liberal reform. The Fed was to function as a bank of last resort, control reserves of member banks, and stabilize the fluctuations of the econ-

The Social Effects of Inflation

There are a number of losers in this complex transaction, but by far the most seriously injured are people on fixed incomes or pensions, which for the most part means the elderly. Between 1940 and 1972 the purchasing power of the dollar was cut to 34 cents in constant dollar terms.[5] Two-thirds of its value was silently subtracted by the process of inflation. For those who are still in the active working force, it is possible to keep pace with this erosion by running faster and earning more—as the labor unions have demonstrated. But if one is not in the active labor force and is required to lived on a fixed income, the effects are ruinous.

Imagine a couple who saved their money and in 1940 began investing in a retirement annuity that would bring them $3,000 a year. In 1940 that would have been a sizable amount of money. But now it is the early 1970s and retirement arrives, and that

omy. It was, and is, widely assumed that the Fed's performance has helped improve our economic fortunes.

The facts of record are rather different. Economist Milton Friedman of the University of Chicago has compared the monetary history of the nation in the half-century preceding establishment of the Fed with the half-century following. In a 1958 analysis he concluded that "the 44 years since 1914 have been characterized by considerably more instability in the stock of money than the 47 years before that date. . . . [And] what is true of the stock of money is also true of economic conditions in general. The 33 peacetime years after World War I were among the most economically unstable in our history. The instability is concentrated in the period between the wars. Those two decades encompass three severe contractions: 1920–21, 1929–33, and 1937–38. There is no other 20-year period in American history containing comparably severe contractions." (*A Program For Monetary Stability,* Fordham University Press, 1959, p. 14.)

The problem with the Fed, as Friedman demonstrates, is that it reacts to surface phenomena rather than underlying problems, and often launches counter-measures that are totally ineffective in meeting immediate difficulties but set off long-term movements creating problems for the future. Most notably, the Fed has tended to concentrate on interest rates rather than monetary aggregates, and in an effort to affect these rates has repeatedly embarked on monetary expansions (contractions, too, though expansions are the rule). The result is an erratic roll effect, but with continual pressure toward inflation.

$3,000 is worth only $1,000 in purchasing power. There is no conceivable way this couple can live on this amount of money. They have been robbed by the Federal government and its clients.

After a while, of course, the people being hurt by all this begin to protest. They demand that something be done to stop the constant upward push of prices, whereupon the inflationists are prompt to send the injured parties hallooing off in search of scapegoats. A case in point is the recurring attack on food chain stores, replete with picket lines of angry housewives, organized boycotts, and indignant statements by politicians. This perennial uproar is a prime example of inflationist demagogy, particularly ironic in view of the fact that retail supermarkets happen to be one of the lowest-profit and most intensively competitive of all American industries.

A glance at the figures is instructive. Between 1965 and 1972, per capita disposable income rose by 62 percent. In the same span, food prices rose from an index level of 94.4 to an index level of 126—an increase of 32 percent.[6] Quite clearly, food prices had been *following* the inflation rather than leading it. The problem confronted by the food chains was that they were from the consumers' standpoint out in front where fluctuations in price were visible and acutely felt, while the forces creating the inflation were dimly noticed, if at all.

In many respects this social effect is the ultimate evil of inflation—the manner in which it sets producers and consumers to squabbling with each other about who is to blame for the constant upward push of prices. We have seen much of this recrimination recently: housewives picketing hapless grocers, labor and management blaming each other for the inflationary spiral, motorists angry at gas station dealers, dealers denouncing petroleum companies, truckers demanding a rollback in the price of gasoline, and so on.

Such unpleasantness and social discord are inevitable by-products of the inflationary process, and they illustrate all too well the fact that inflation is hardly an innocuous or neutral business. All these people have been injured by inflation, are seeking redress, and are looking for somebody to blame. The politicians and planners who are the authentic culprits are more than happy, of course, to serve up such private scapegoats in abundance—railing against the supermarkets, the oil producers, the doctors, or anyone else who appears to be a handy and visible target.

Viewed in this way, inflation is a question in ethics before it becomes a problem in economics. Implicitly by their actions, and often explicitly by their words, many of our spending politicians are fomenting a class-struggle mentality where none has previously existed, playing groups and classes off against each other. The resulting strife has its political uses, but we are entitled to question the moral standing of those who engage in such divisive practices to enhance their own political interests.

Indeed, perhaps the most obvious comment one can make about the whole inflationary procedure is that it is just plain dishonest. It attempts to sustain the illusion of something for nothing, divest people of their purchasing power by stealth, and then pin responsibility for the resulting anguish on innocent parties who are generally victims of the process themselves.

In extenuation it may be said that such behavior has been characteristic of governments down through the centuries, a result of the all-too-human political impulse to be all things to all people. In that homely light, our government is doing what countless of its predecessors have done before it. What is radically wrong about the present situation, however, is the degree to which supposed intellectuals who should be pointing out the cruelty and dishonesty of such tactics have instead been striving to make the situation worse, giving sanction to the most vulgar forms of popular error. Rather than warning against inflation and explaining what it is, far too many academic economists have been urging more of it and helping to obscure the mechanisms that produce it.

Inflation, in sum, is the creation of government itself—a method of financing continued spending programs while diffusing the costs so widely that taxpayers have trouble assessing blame for the resultant discomfort. Because the process is generated by government expansion of the money supply, it cannot be halted by controls or exhortations to consumers to change their buying habits. The cure for inflation, and the only cure, is to make certain that the national pool of money and credit is not expanded more rapidly than the annual increase in the volume of production.

Inflation is a perfect example of the manner in which political intervention becomes the source of economic problems, and the fashion in which one kind of intervention becomes the pretext for

another. Nowhere is this sequence more apparent than in the matter of medical care and the recent outcry concerning rising medical
costs. Here the scapegoating has run rampant, and promises to
get worse. How and why this gambit has been worked on the
American people will be considered next.

13
Government Can Be Hazardous to Your Health

The secret of winning a debate is to define the grounds on which it is conducted. Liberals in Washington and in the various state assemblies have long been conscious of this simple precept, and as a result have been winning debates—and legislative roll calls —from time out of mind. Non-liberals seem to have trouble grasping it, and in consequence find themselves repeatedly debating *which* projected liberal remedy must be applied to "problems" obligingly formulated for them by their opponents.

A textbook example of this procedure may be discovered in recent discussions of the so-called health care crisis in America. Among others, Senator Edward Kennedy, organized labor, and various elements in the media have argued that private medical care is a shame and disgrace that should be corrected by some kind of Federal health care scheme. The Republican administration, the American Medical Association, and a variety of Republican legislators have hopped directly into this rhetorical bear trap, saying yes, there is a health care crisis, but *our* solutions are infinitely preferable to Senator Kennedy's. The major point at issue—the alleged defects of the private system and the need for

Federal action—was thus conceded at the outset and further government intrusion all but assured.

This result becomes the more ironic when we reflect that the "health care crisis" cried up by Kennedy and confessed by the Republicans is almost totally devoid of factual content. The truth of the matter is that the quality of health care in our country has been getting better and better, that the benefits of such care have been made increasingly available to ever larger numbers of people, and that most of the asserted shortages and deficiencies complained of are imaginary in nature. Equally important, it develops that where our health care problems are real and not illusory, they are demonstrably the result of government intervention.

The Quality of America's Health Care

In his major speech on this question in the summer of 1970, Senator Kennedy alleged that health care services in our country were progressively deteriorating and that decent care was not available to most Americans. "In spite of the broad agreement that our population has a right to health care," he asserted, "the evidence is overwhelming that this right cannot be adequately exercised by most of our people. . . . If we are to avoid the collapse of our health services and the disastrous consequences that would ensue for tens of millions of our citizens, we must take action. . . . the cost is increasing, but the quality is declining." [1] *

A glance at the relevant statistics will show this picture to be completely erroneous. The quality of medical care in the United States has in fact improved continuously across the decades, conquering such once-dreaded diseases as polio, tuberculosis, typhoid fever. Because of these achievements, average life expectancies have increased dramatically—from 49 years in 1900 to more than 70 years today. Among the more impoverished members of our society, particularly Negroes, the average life expectancy is

---

* The Kennedy health plan, as originally introduced, was a comprehensive program, compulsory on all Americans, providing for unlimited payment for physician services and most kinds of hospital care. It would have eliminated private health insurance plans. First-year cost of the program, as estimated by the Department of Health, Education, and Welfare, would have been $77 billion.

lower than that for the population at large—64.6 for blacks as opposed to 71.3 for whites. But the gap has narrowed, and in the later
years of life, when medical care is a crucial factor, there is virtually
no difference at all. (At age 65 the average white American male
can expect another 13 years of life; the average black American
male another 12.7 years.) [2]

Among the major allegations against the present system is
the "doctor shortage." In fact, the ratio of physicians to general
population is better in the United States than in the major European nations to which we are so frequently and unfavorably compared. And it is continually improving—from one physician for
every 712 Americans in 1960 to one for every 600 in 1972. (In
France the 1972 ratio was one physician for every 750 people,
in Britain one for every 1,150.) There are problems of physician
availability in America created by the proliferation of government
medical programs (28,000 MD's in government service), but the
fact remains that physicians and health care personnel have been
produced in impressive quantities.[3] *

Since 1965 the number of doctors in America has increased
three times as fast as population growth, the number of auxiliary
medical personnel almost four times as fast. As of 1970, there
were some 323,000 physicians in the United States and an enormous army of four million health workers all told. Also in 1970
the nation had about 7,000 hospitals containing 1.6 million beds,
and these institutions employed more than 2.5 million people. (In
1960 the corresponding figure was about 1.5 million employes.)
These data compare to an average daily patient population in
American hospitals of about 1.3 million people in 1970—which
means almost two employes per patient.[4] †

* Concerning the complaint that there is a "maldistribution" of medical
services, the 1967 comment of the presidential Commission on Health
Manpower is to the point: ". . . physical distance from available care
is not a major barrier for either urban or rural residents. Even in rural
areas, hospital facilities of 25 beds or more are within a 25-mile distance
of all but 2 per cent of the population, and only one-tenth of one per
cent have to travel more than 50 miles." (Marvin Edwards, *Hazardous
to Your Health*, Arlington House, 1972, pp. 104–05.)

† "For the entire year," notes Harry Schwartz of the *New York Times*,
"there were almost 32 million hospital admissions. Between 1960 and
1970 the number of persons in the United States rose only about 13 per
cent but the number of hospital admissions jumped by almost 27 per

Private health care insurance has been one of the major growth industries in America. Long before adoption of Federal health care programs the vast majority of Americans carried such insurance. In 1940, 12 million Americans were covered by medical policies; by 1959 some 127 million people, about 72 percent of the civilian population, had some form of health insurance. By 1972 the number had reached 182 million—roughly 90 percent of the American population. These figures do not suggest that coverage has been denied to most Americans or that they are too dumb to apply for it. Yet despite these facts the Federal planners insist on inventing universal schemes of subsidy and compulsion to cover people already covered.[5]

Arguments for Federal health care make much of statistics for infant mortality—usually played off against the corresponding figures for Sweden and other Scandinavian countries and used as a reproach against the American system. Since these statistics are kept on totally different bases in other countries (the Swedish practice of not requiring a report of birth until five years after the event providing one notable example) such comparisons are completely invalid—and have been so designated by the World Health Organization, which compiles them.

Infant mortality statistics do, however, provide a convenient test of Senator Kennedy's charge of progressive deterioration in medical care—which they refute in toto. The figures for America show that in 1950, 29.2 babies out of every 1,000 died within the first year of life; by 1970, this figure had been reduced to less than 20 per 1,000—a drop of 33 percent. The record is one of obvious improvement, not progressive breakdown.[6]

On the total record, indeed, it seems the Federal health care proponents would be a little wary of invoking foreign comparisons—particularly with Sweden. The availability of medical services is a much greater problem in Scandinavia and Europe than it is in America. Author Allan Brownfeld reported in 1970 that "there is hardly a single hospital in Sweden where there are not

cent. . . . In 1970, these data suggest there were 20 million or more patient-doctor contacts and about 2 million people spent at least one night in a hospital. In the United States in the 1970s medical care is available to the great bulk of the population; it is not limited to a small clique of the rich and powerful." (*The Case for American Medicine*, McKay, 1972, p. 10.)

long waiting lists for all kinds of hospital care. It is estimated that in Stockholm alone there are more than 4,000 persons waiting to enter hospitals, 1,800 for surgery. In some cases, waiting periods for minor operations may be more than half a year." [7] The reason for the crowding is that, under Swedish health insurance, people tend to use their "free" care to the fullest.

As noted by the *New York Times,* Swedish medicine is plagued with numerous other problems, including rising costs that have pushed the tax burden to stratospheric levels. An average Swedish family with about $12,000 in annual income pays 55 percent of that in tax, compared to less than 30 percent for an American family similarly situated. Since Sweden converted from a system of voluntary health insurance to government-provided coverage, medical costs have gone through the roof. Within twelve years costs increased ninefold—from $305 million in 1960 to $2.77 billion in 1972. [8]

This expansion is readily understandable. Since nobody has any incentives to control costs, patients come to hospitals for the most minor or imaginary ills and hospital stays are protracted. Private practice of medicine on an outpatient basis has been discouraged, although steps are afoot to alter this. In addition, the Swedish system has discouraged entry into medicine by new physicians, and it is noteworthy that the doctor-patient ratio is considerably lower than in the much more populous United States. In America there are 172 doctors for every 100,000 of population—in Sweden approximately 135.

A similar story has been written in England, where the crush of national health insurance has brought a marked deterioration of medical services. Medical writer Marvin Edwards notes that more than 40 percent of the hospitals in England are 100 years old or more, and most of the others are more than 80 years old. Between 1948, when socialized medicine was instituted, and 1962, there were no new hospitals built. Only three were built between 1962 and 1970. There is a tremendous overcrowding of British hospitals, and only 30 percent of them, according to a committee of British physicians, have adequate emergency facilities.* The

* These problems are accentuated by the fact that length of confinement in British hospitals is considerably greater than in America—a usage encouraged, again, by the availability of so-called free medical care. Government figures in August 1966 disclosed that more than 100,000

situation prevailing in the United States seems almost idyllic by comparison.

Wherein, therefore, lies the American crisis? The answer appears to consist of one factor only—the rising cost of health care services. As President Nixon put it in his 1974 health care message: "The overall cost of health care has . . . risen by more than 20 percent in the last two and a half years, so that more and more Americans face staggering bills when they receive medical help today." [9] And this, we may grant, is indeed a problem. But what is the source of it? The answer, as in so many other species of national distress, is that the Federal government itself is directly responsible for the evil complained of.

The Cost of Health Care

It is rather plain that over the long pull the medical price index has been moving in synchronization with prices generally—in response to the inflation that has ravaged our economy. As we have seen in the preceding chapter, that inflation is the work of the Federal government through its continued expansion of the money supply. Like the more general effort to scapegoat private industry for inflation, the outcry over medical prices is a case of the Federal culprit crying "thief."

It is noteworthy that elements of our medical system have experienced slower price hikes than have numerous nonmedical items. Department of Labor statistics as of 1970 showed medical costs in the previous two years had risen less than meat, poultry, and fish, home ownership, transportation, and so on. Between August 1971 and August 1972, the medical price index rose only 2.2 percent, less than the general cost of living. And between 1965 and 1970, physicians' fees rose less than the average hourly compensation in the private economy. So in some particulars the price of medical care was moving upward in less vertiginous fashion than other elements of the economy.

Yet it would be foolish to deny there has been, on the whole, a continuous and often precipitate hike in medical costs—most

elderly and chronically ill Britons were on waiting lists to get into hospitals.

notably hospital room rates, which approximately tripled in the decade of the 1960s. In general, both doctors' fees and hospital costs were increasing more rapidly in the early 1970s than they had in the early 1960s, and these factors have frequently been cited by proponents of further Federal intervention. So it is here, apparently, that we find the bedrock proof of privately generated crisis.

Yet in point of fact this hike in medical costs above and beyond the general inflation is *also* the consequence of Federal intervention in the medical marketplace—through the Medicare and Medicaid subsidy programs enacted in 1965 to provide medical care to the aged and the indigent. As a result of these programs, millions of extra dollars have been poured into the medical system, putting enormous pressure on facilities and boosting prices skyward—results that could have been predicted by anyone who had bothered beforehand to weigh the relevant economic factors.

Indeed, in viewing this procedure, one may plausibly reverse the usual complaint and contend the problem with American medicine, to the extent there is one, is that for many people it is much too cheap. If that statement seems outrageous in view of rising outlays for health and hospitals, it is because the people who incur the bills are often different from the people who pay them. This is, in fact, the essence of the problem. When people using medical facilities see the service as being "free" or extremely inexpensive, rising frequency of use will push the total cost up through the roof.

Consider what would happen, for example, if people were told they had a right to "free" gasoline, food, automobile repairs, clothing, airline tickets, or anything else, with the bills for whatever they consumed to be forwarded to someone else for payment. The crush of demand would be unmanageable, and the "someone else" who had to pick up the tab would be headed for the poorhouse. This is in essence what has been happening in the matter of subsidized health care.

The fact is that the free market pricing system is the only rational method of apportioning available resources. Among other benefits, that mechanism enables us to sort out demand intensities—providing service where it is seriously required but discouraging frivolous or excessive use. If airline tickets were free, you might fly to San Francisco or New York every weekend. If you had to pay your own way, you would be a bit more cautious in your traveling. Where price considerations are obscured, demand and resulting costs will skyrocket.

This pattern has been repeatedly shown in studies of health insurance programs, and has become especially acute in the decade since the Federal government got into the health care business. Our medical economy has steadily shifted away from direct payment by the patient to third-party systems in which someone else picks up the tab. The result has been skyrocketing use of services and facilities.

Between 1965 and 1971, for example, direct payment for medical care increased only from 18.9 to $24.2 billion. Third-party payment, however, leaped up from $22 billion to approximately $50 billion—with government outlays almost tripling from $10.8 billion to 28.5. As recently as 1965, more than half our medical outlays were for direct payment; by the early 1970s the proportion was down to slightly more than a third.[10]

As that sequence suggests, the decisive factor was the arrival of Medicare and Medicaid, entitling millions of people to medical care at someone else's expense. An enormous surge of monetary demand was unleashed, crowding in on doctors' time and health facilities. The double effect was to saddle taxpayers with a staggering bill (up to $25 billion annually) and to push up prices as demand outstripped supply. Between 1960 and 1965, the physician component of the Consumer Price Index rose by about 3 percent annually—but between 1966 and 1970 it rose by an average of 7 percent. The unit cost of hospital care increased more rapidly still: In the early 1960s it was rising by about 6 percent a year. Since the advent of Medicare and Medicaid, it has gone up by an eye-popping 13 to 14 percent annually.[11] *

---

* Other data on the medical trend of the 1960s are also instructive. For one thing, while the population of America increased by only 13 percent, the number of hospital admissions went up by 27 percent. For another, low-income Americans received more hospital care and physicians' services per capita than did those in high and middle income brackets. In the latter 1960s, the poor averaged 114.5 hospital admissions per 1,000 of population and 4.6 physician visits per capita. The corresponding figures for middle income Americans were 95.4 and 4.0.

Economist Herbert Klarman suggests, in this connection, two principal explanations of our rising medical costs:

> Medicare increased the flow of funds to hospitals. Along with other forms of health insurance or prepayment, Medicare also perpetuates a dual set of prices—a gross price received by the provider and a much lower net price paid by the consumer out of pocket at the time of illness. The dual price distorts reality for the consumer and encourages the provider to enhance and elaborate the quality of care, even at a higher cost.
>
> The other explanation, which I tend to stress, focuses on cost reimbursement, which was widely adopted under Medicare (and Medicaid). Under this method of payment a hospital is paid a daily rate related to its own cost of operation. The hospital administrator can no longer deny requests for higher wages or more supplies on the ground that money is lacking; to get money, he need only spend more.[12]

It is precisely in the latter category that the most phenomenal increases in medical prices have been occurring. Hospital rates that stood at roughly $45 a day in 1965 had shot up to an estimated $115 a day in 1973, with further increases on the way. By far the vast majority of these expenditures—roughly 70 percent—have gone to pay the wages of hospital personnel, as wages pushed steadily higher by employe demands have connected up with public funds. (Ironically enough, the very union leaders who have helped to organize these demands are in the forefront of lamentation about the excessive costs of hospital care.)

All these trends have been evident in the rocky course of the Medicaid program, which has provoked a deluge of medical claims and placed a number of states under severe financial stress. In California, the "Medi-Cal" program wound up in 1970 with two-and-a-half million people on the rolls and annual costs of $1.2 billion. Per capita medical costs in California were driven up to $517 a year, compared to $312 per capita for the rest of the nation. A similar story was written in New York, Texas, and numerous other states. In Indiana, a supposedly "minimal" Medicaid program that was to have cost some $300,000 a year soared in cost to $115 million in fiscal 1975.[13]

Nationally, Medicaid costs increased from $1.3 billion in 1967 to $5.5 billion in January 1970—in keeping with a similar explosion of costs for Medicare. Robert J. Myers, former chief actuary of the Social Security administration, observes that cost overruns for Medicare during the first three years of operation amounted to $11 billion—41 percent above the original estimates.[14] For the hospital insurance portion of the program, costs were approximately double the original estimates. These results, of course, are in complete conformity with the experience of other nations that have adopted government "health insurance" programs.

As ever, a government-sponsored problem calls forth a government-sponsored solution, and legislators concerned about the rising cost of Medicare and Medicaid decided to pile another intervention on top of those already noted. In an effort to get the situation under some kind of control, Congress in 1972 passed a little-noticed amendment establishing so-called Professional Standards Review Organizations to determine the propriety of doctors' fees and the treatments being prescribed.

Through the device of PSROs, functionaries at the Department of Health, Education, and Welfare are able to sit in judgment on physicians; they are also able to examine medical records in doctors' offices. While the asserted purpose is to find out if doctors are making proper charges under Medicare and Medicaid, it is noteworthy that the right to snoop in medical files extends to private patients as well.

Since the regional review boards involved in the program are staffed chiefly with doctors, PSRO has been advertised as a way of letting the medical profession police itself. Close examination of the law, however, makes it plain that the real policing is to be done by the Secretary of HEW and his subordinates. The law repeatedly states that PSRO procedures shall be conducted "in accordance with the regulations of the secretary . . . ." Under this direction, the network of PSROs is to establish national norms of treatment of illnesses that are or "may be" paid for by Federal programs.

The law says "each PSRO shall apply professionally developed norms of care, diagnosis and treatment" for specific ills and also maintain computerized profiles of individual physicians to see that they are behaving properly. If not, sanctions may be imposed, up to and including fines of $5,000. The offending physician would also be subjected to orchestrated professional opprobrium under the provisions of the law. Thus does one act of government intervention beget another, and another.

Federal Drug Regulation

Similar lessons may be gleaned from another crucial aspect of American health care—the production and marketing of beneficial drugs. The longterm record of the American drug industry is phenomenally good; the production of such beneficial substances as sulfa drugs, penicillin, and the Salk vaccine has contributed enormously to the conquest of disease and improvement of life expectancies. Yet in recent years these advances have slowed perceptibly, as a direct result of Federal interference.

The principal villain in this scenario is a set of drug law amendments passed by Congress in 1962. In response to drug scares of that epoch, our legislators decreed that no new drug could be licensed for sale until it had been proved "safe and effective" by laborious procedures. Before that time, the standard had been "safe," which is hard enough to determine by itself. But "safe and effective" has proved to be a formula for bureaucratic seventh heaven.

To establish compliance with these criteria, the Food and Drug Administration (FDA) has taken to pawing through thousands of pages of data covering tests and re-tests of proposed new drugs. The nature of the change may be judged from the fact that in 1948 one well-known pharmaceutical company (Parke Davis) had to submit 73 pages of evidence to secure the licensing of a drug. In 1968, this same company had to submit 72,200 pages of data, transported by truck, in an effort to have an anesthetic licensed.[15]

As a result of this drawn-out procedure, it takes an inordinate amount of time for a new drug to be cleared, and the number of beneficial drugs arriving on the market has been reduced accordingly. Prior to 1962 it took about six months for a new drug application to be processed. A decade later the time lag was 27.5 months. More ominous still is the sharp decline in the total number of "new chemical entities" coming on the market. Prior to 1962, it was 41.5 a year; by 1970 it had dropped to 16.1.[16] *

What these figures suggest but cannot tell us explicitly is the number of Americans who are suffering in pain, or dying, because drugs that could have saved them are not being marketed in their country. We do know that dimethyl sulfoxide (DMSO), an effective pain killer developed in the United States and used around the globe, has been arbitrarily banned from use in America. We also know, on the testimony of Dr. John Laragh of Columbia University, that the FDA held up the marketing of diazocide—"a lifesaving drug for patients with serious high blood pressure"—for 10 years of "clinical trial and administrative debate." [17]

Indeed, it is altogether possible that Americans could become a "have not" people in their access to medication—with the fruits of chemical and technological improvement created here exported to others but denied us. *Medical Economics* observes that three-quarters of the new drugs being developed by American pharmaceutical firms are going exclusively to people in other lands and are barred from use in America.[18]

In similar vein, seven new asthma medications have been introduced in Europe in the past decade, but only two of these have made it to the United States. Forty-seven new medications to treat heart and circulatory problems came on the world market between 1967 and 1971, but only six were made available in this country. Five new drugs for the treatment of hypertension have recently appeared in Europe, but no new general-purpose hypertension medicine emerged in America between 1963 and 1972.

It is noteworthy that penicillin, if discovered today, probably

---

* In the five years 1957 through 1961, before the new drug law amendments took effect, a total of 261 new drug entities were produced in America; in the ten years 1962 through 1971, the total was 167. In 1961 America was the world leader in production of new drugs, with a total of 31, compared to 9 for France. Over the next eight years, the United States introduced only 35 new drugs all told, while France produced a total of 156.

could not pass the relevant tests of the bureaucracy. After all, the drug does cause unfavorable reactions in some people, and it is less effective in certain cases than in others—considerations that could flunk it on FDA's "safe and effective" meter. Yet penicillin has saved thousands of people from pain and death, and only a fanatic or perhaps a bureaucrat would contend that humanity would be better off without it.

The point of these reflections is we can't know for sure how many penicillins are nowadays being blocked from the market or interminably delayed by the procedures of the FDA. We know simply that an enormous number of beneficial drugs have been denied to Americans by the self-same Federal government that is supposedly bending every effort to upgrade the quality of their health care.

We confront, in sum, a round-robin of government-generated answers to government-created problems—answers that are, or very shortly will become, considerable problems in themselves. Where private medicine has been allowed to do its work, the American record has been one of steady and often miraculous improvement; where evils in the system are complained of, we may almost invariably trace them back to one or another species of intervention. The indicated answer is not to get the government further into medicine, but to get it out—as rapidly as possible.

14
The Population Scare

For the greater part of human history, the subject of population has been treated in opposite fashion from that of the weather: Everybody did something about it, but hardly anybody talked about it.

Of late all that has changed, and the subject of population has very nearly been talked to death. For the past decade or so the American nation and the Western world in general have been terrorizing themselves with the specter of massive population growth.* Would-be futurologists have had a field day multiplying demographic ratios into infinity, and political activists have used the issue as an asserted reason for everything from crash-building mass transit systems to transforming our Western value system in its entirety.

* In the early 1960s, for example, *Newsweek* asserted that "the current rate of growth, continued in 600 years, would leave every inhabitant of the world with only 1 square yard to live on. By the year 3500, the weight of human bodies on the earth's surface would equal the weight of the earth itself. By the year 6000, the solid mass of humanity would be expanding outward into space at the speed of light. 'The world has

217

218

Warnings of this type have issued with systematic fervor from many alleged authorities. A typically horrific view was provided in 1972 by a liberal group called the Club of Rome, in a widely publicized volume, *The Limits to Growth*. This document informed us that America and the world were caught up in a cycle of "exponential growth" that could issue only in disaster, and that we must aim by way of remedy at a zero-everything status in which the number of people and volume of production in the world would be stabilized—a goal that would concededly require "a fundamental revision of human behavior and, by implication, of the entire fabric of present-day society." [1]

Such statements, which might be duplicated at endless length, provide us with a revealing insight into the twentieth century malaise and on that account deserve the most exacting scrutiny. The population issue is crucial not merely because it involves so many areas of contemporary political and social dispute, but because it so compactly illustrates the condition of the modern intellect. It might be described, indeed, as the most typical of modern confusions, arising as it does at the vector point of liberal assump-

---

cancer,' a top Rockefeller Foundation official has said, 'and that cancer cell is man.' "

In the middle of the decade, *Life* reported that "a British scientist recently calculated that with the population of the world now about 3 billion and doubling every 37 years, we will reach the ultimate terrestrial limit of 60 million billion humans in somewhat less than 1,000 years. At that stage, people will be jammed together so tightly that the earth itself will glow orange-red from the heat." Not to be outdone, another scientist proclaimed that "if world population growth continues its ever-increasing pace, the time will come when 'men will have to kill and eat one another.' "

As these quotations suggest, much of the population rhetoric has had a kind of competitive quality about it—as various experts have vied among themselves to project the most appalling visions of disaster. A possible winner in this competition is a scientist named Robert White-Stevens, who not only predicted the impending catastrophe but nailed it down to a specific day: November 13, 2026. On that date, UPI reported White-Stevens as saying, "the world's population will have reached 50 billion—a point where there are more mouths to feed than food available, and more bodies to house than land. He said there would be 10,000 persons in every square mile of land, including Antarctica and the Sahara Desert." (All quotes cited in *The Myth of Overpopulation*, by R. J. Rushdoory, Craig Press, 1969, p. 13.)

tions about the nature of man and liberal error concerning the nature of politico-economic activity.

The litany of alleged population dangers faced by the United States is familiar enough to anyone who has been following discussion in the academy or the communications media. Our imagined peril has ignited presidential panels into action, called forth the Zero Population Growth brigade, and engendered numerous proposals to put a check on demographic expansion. Burgeoning population is thought to be a major contributor to the congestion of our cities, the breakdown of our transit systems, and the groaning burden of our welfare caseload. Spiraling numbers are also said to be fouling up the air and waterways and consuming our resources.

In political terms, it is assumed that steady population growth and a declining median age will have enormous consequences for the elections of the future. A constantly younger population will presumably be more liberal and more innovative than its elders, so that as the boom continues we may expect a "greening" of our politics. Aspirants to public office will themselves be younger and more liberal, and will perhaps take lessons on the sitar.

Finally, our population phobia has powerfully spurred the recent movement toward demographic controls. The crusade for elective abortion has been greatly aided by population fear, while a national campaign for euthanasia, or mercy-killing, is also taking form and drawing strength from similar apprehensions. Also being bruited about are programs for controlling births generally, more active steps toward contraception, and proposals for compulsory sterilization. (See Chapter 24.)

These themes have been repeated so often in recent years that numerous Americans have become convinced of the reality and urgency of the population crisis, and persuaded of the need for drastic measures. Yet examination of the relevant data suggests that little if any of this continued agitation is based on fact, and that by far the greater part of it is pure mythology.

Fallacies of Population Phobia

In its most common form, extending back to Thomas Malthus, population phobia has its roots in economic innocence. The

Malthusian formula is as well known as it is mistaken: It assumes that human population increases geometrically ("exponentially") at a compounded rate of growth, while food and other resources essential to life increase arithmetically. Thus as the number of people doubles and redoubles, the food supply can increase only by slow and painful increments. In relatively short order population outruns food, and the only correctives are famine, pestilence, war, and resulting death.

That explanation is conceivably true for some societies under some conditions. But such notions are inapplicable to modern societies since the era of the industrial revolution—and in this respect one should recall that Malthus wrote his book in 1798, before the full effects of industrialization became apparent. And it is precisely this neglected factor that makes all the difference.

For thousands of years of human history and in many contemporary societies as well, people have lived at levels of bare subsistence, able to scratch out a living by the use of their hands and a few rude implements for tilling the soil or taming the wilder reaches of nature. This situation can be altered only as mankind is able to deploy natural and mechanical sources of energy to multiply its muscle-power and accomplish more through a given input of human effort. This is what has occurred in the United States and other industrially advanced societies, enabling them to reverse the Malthusian forecast in dramatic fashion. In our society particularly, the ability to produce essential foodstuffs has far outstripped the growth of population.

Consider, for example, the record compiled in the two decades from 1950 through 1970. In this span, American population grew from 150 to 203 million, while the number of acres farmed fell by 48 million, and the number of hours worked was cut in half. Yet the American people were fed and clothed much better than ever before. In these two decades, vegetable productivity rose by 82 percent; cotton by 60 percent, milk by 251 percent, poultry by 471 percent, and beef by 127 percent. In 1950 the farmer got 37 bushels of corn per acre; in 1970 the figure was 87 bushels. Wheat yields were increased by 83 percent per acre. In 1950, the efforts of one farmer fed and clothed some 15 city dwellers. By 1970, one farmer fed and clothed more than 47.[2]

What is true in agriculture is true of economic life in general.

The key to economic progress is productivity, not numbers of people. If productivity is high, a relatively large population can exist at an increasingly comfortable standard of living, since it will be able to generate economic satisfactions far beyond the needs of subsistence. If productivity is low, a relatively small population can live in terrible poverty, since it will be unable to do much more than scratch together what it needs for daily survival. To approach the problem from the standpoint of numbers *per se* is to get the whole thing almost hopelessly backward.

If there is not an *economic* problem, what about the other problem? What about the aesthetic and cultural impact of being crowded and crushed together, even if we do have enough to eat? And what about the ethical and social readjustment required to deal with constant population growth and a declining median age? Aren't these factors sufficient to justify a national population policy, abortion and sterilization, zero population growth (ZPG), and the rest of it? Again the answer is "no"—since all the phenomena complained of are either illusions or else have nothing to do with population growth as such.

To begin with, the idea that the United States is becoming intolerably crowded by its 200-plus million population is erroneous. As it happens, America is one of the most sparsely populated nations in the world—and shows no promise of being anything else. Our population density as of the last census was a very thin 55 people per square mile—compared to 607 in West Germany, 436 in Italy, and 374 in India.[3] * The notion that our

---

* Demographer Ben Wattenberg put the matter in perspective in a 1970 article: "The current population of the United States is 205 million. That population is distributed over 3,615,123 square miles of land, for a density of about 55 persons per square mile. In terms of density, this makes the United States one of the most sparsely populated nations in the world. As measured by density, Holland is about 18 times as crowded (at 975 persons per square mile), England is 10 times as dense (588 persons per square mile), scenic Switzerland seven times as dense (382), tropical Nigeria three times as dense (174), and even neighboring Mexico beats us out with 60 persons per square mile." (*The New Republic*, April 4 & 11, 1970.)

Notre Dame's Charles Rice provides another angle of vision when he observes that if you took "every person now alive—we presume 3½ billion—and gave each person six square feet of ground to stand on, you could fit them all in the Eastern end of Suffolk County in New

country is in danger of being carpeted with people from coast to coast may easily be disproved by journeying through the vast and largely empty American interior.

It is significant, indeed, that so much of the uproar about population comes from government, media, and academic types who live in Washington, New York, and other areas around the nation's seaboards. These places *are* congested, of course—in considerable measure by the people who complain about their congested status. That the complainants reside in these areas is, in most cases, a matter of personal choice rather than of any inexorable fate, and has nothing to do with absolute population growth. While these particular areas have become crowded, numerous other areas of the country have become progressively *less* crowded, and the complainants (uniformly members of our most mobile class), could take up residence in these uncrowded places if they so desired.

The point was made in a 1970 address by Conrad Taeuber of the Census Bureau. During the preceding decade, Taeuber noted, "about half our counties lost population—the number not much different from the number which also lost during the 1950s, and to a large extent they were the same areas in both periods. *There are approximately 1,000 of our 3,000 counties which have lost population for at least three consecutive decades.* Many of them have had losses ever since 1900 or even before. There is a great band of counties in the Plains States from the Canadian to the Mexican borders, and reaching from there across much of the rural South, which includes most of the counties which have continuing losses." [4] (Italics added.)

While these counties and in some cases whole states (North and South Dakota) have been losing population, people have been locating heavily around the two ocean shores, the Gulf of Mexico, and the Great Lakes. Taeuber noted that "in 1970, we have a little more than half of all our people living within 50 miles of the seacoasts." [5] Advocates of ZPG could, therefore, easily get what they want by moving to one of the counties or states that have been losing people. It is doubtful they will do so,

---

York and have 168 square miles left over." (*The Manion Forum,* radio broadcast, January 17, 1971.)

however, since their present choice of residence suggests they enjoy the services and amenities available in the metropolitan centers. They want the things other people supply, but not the people themselves.

Even these considerations, however, don't reach the fundamental error of the populationist analysis. For the fact of the matter is that American demographic trends in general are totally different from what the populationists have led us to believe—and have been so for a considerable period.

In the years succeeding the Second World War, of course, there *was* a notable increase in American birth and fertility rates, and it was this phenomenon that provoked the anxiety of the populationists. They assumed that what was happening in the postwar era would keep on happening indefinitely. This apprehension was unfounded. For better than a decade now, the American birth rate has been falling steadily, with no apparent let-up in sight. In 1960, for example, the "crude birth rate"—births per 1,000 of population—stood at 23.7. By 1965 it had descended to 19.4, and for 1972 it was 15.6. The result of this continual decline is that the decade of the sixties saw America's infant population (under five years of age) decrease by 15.5 percent—which means three million fewer of these youngsters in 1970 than in 1960.[6]

An even more important population indicator than the crude birth rate is the fertility rate of American women of childbearing age. In assessing population growth, this is the key to everything else. Simply to *replace* the existing population in America there must be an average of 2.1 children born for every woman in the country, to supplant the preceding generation plus a small margin to allow for early deaths. It is for this reason that 2.1 is the ZPG figure—the rate at which the number of children entering the society will balance the number of adults who must eventually leave it.

What is so curious about the population uproar is that during all this recent period of panic and despair, the fertility rate for American women has been consistently and unmistakably in a *downward* direction. This has been so since 1957, when the rate hit its postwar high of approximately 3.75. Throughout the sixties the rate steadily descended, falling to 3.5 in 1962, 2.9 in 1965, and 2.5 in 1968. It was as this decline in fertility rates occurred that the population bombers sent up their full-throated cry of massive overpopulation.[7]

A few of the populationists, of course, were following these developments. They took some solace from the fact that, between 1968 and 1970, the fertility rate had apparently bottomed out and was holding steady at 2.5 But even this has proved to be a temporary respite. For 1973, the estimated rate was 1.9—*below* the figure for ZPG and in fact the lowest rate in American history.[8] If this rate should hold, much less continue getting lower, we could very rapidly enter a period of population decline. For a variety of reasons, including simple economics, this would be a much greater calamity for our nation than all those futuristic projections of explosive growth.

The Effects of a Shrinking Population

The demographic trends, in sum, are directly contrary to the population scare and its imagined implications. From the birth rates that have prevailed since the latter 1950s, we can expect political and economic results exactly the reverse of those that have been so insistently projected in the popular media. On the political front, to take one prominent example, the figures suggest the fatuity of all those speeches, magazine articles, and motion pictures that sketch a political future directed by the young. Far from facing a future in which young people will increasingly dominate the rest of us, we face exactly the opposite—and, despite the recent confusion, we always have.

The constant tendency since the founding of our republic has been for the median age to rise, not drop, and the recent shrinkage in the birth rate will accelerate the trend still further. In 1820, for example, the median age was 16.7 years; in 1900 it was 22.9; and in 1970 it was 28.0. There was a slight downturn in the sixties owing to the postwar baby boom, but now the curve is back on its steady upward march.[9]

What this implies for the future of our politics may be seen from the projections of the Census Bureau, which has generally been high in its estimates of population growth. On the high population projection of the bureau (about 300 million people), the

median age by the year 2000 will be up to 29.1; on the low projection (about 250 million people), the median age will be 35.8.
In either event, since a generally older population in some respects
means a more conservative one, the political effects will be quite
different from those we have been led to anticipate.[10]

In economic matters, the outlook is also directly contrary to
the conventional wisdom. A homely hint of the problems we confront may be gleaned from recent television commercials in which
a masculine-looking chap proclaims the virtues of using baby
shampoo. This otherwise puzzling advertisement is in tacit
acknowledgement of the fact that we have come up with a shortage of babies, and as a result some product lines once geared to
use by infants must be converted to use by adults. Among those
affected are the toy industry, children's furniture and clothing,
and products for young people generally. Also affected are hospital maternity wards and other institutions geared to expectations
of a rising or at least stable birthrate.

But these problems are minor compared with those that confront American taxpayers. On the one hand these citizens will
soon be discovering, if they have not already, that they have invested billions in surplus classrooms and training for teachers and
may wonder why such expenditures keep rising when enrollments
have begun to decline. On the other hand, these taxpayers will
face enormous difficulties in funding other obligations. Most
notable of these is the Social Security program, which operates
on the assumption of an expanding work force in which younger
people entering the job market pay taxes to furnish benefits for
the retired. In a population of constantly rising average age and
a shrinking number of working young people, the due bills of this
system must force a constantly bigger tax rate, or eventually out-
strip ability to pay, or both.*

All this is implicit in the present state of affairs, which finds
our total population continuing to grow despite the declining
birthrate. It could get worse. If the *below* zero population fertility

---

* This fact finally pushed its way through to general recognition in the
summer of 1974, as a number of publications, including *Harper's, The
Wall Street Journal,* and *Chicago Today,* focused attention on Social
Security's looming insolvency.

rates that prevailed in 1972 and 1973 continue to decline we could actually suffer a decrease of population in the foreseeable future. The number of births still exceeds the number of deaths, but since the former is declining while the latter inexorably rises a continuation of the trend lines 'would put us into population retrograde.

Should that occur, the effects would be felt not only by industries and institutions oriented to the young *per se,* but by our whole society. Most of our economic and other calculations are based on the idea of at least a minimally expanding economy and the rising availability of jobs and concomitant demand. Should we enter a phase of ZPG or declining population, the wrench of adjustment could injure almost everybody.

In this event it is likely the people now troubling deaf heaven with their cries of excessive population will run off in the other direction with shouts of alarm about the dwindling of our population—and demand government programs to do something about *that.* It is therefore worth entering the caveat that these projections, too, are merely possibilities, and may not pan out in population loss. Demographic trends, far from being steady and certain, are immensely variable. The point is simply that, if the experts had correctly read the data, their projections would have been for nearly certain ZPG, rather than for an exploding population.

Nor should it be supposed the advocates of ZPG, abortion, and demographic panic can take credit for the reversal of our population trends. Fertility rates have been in steady decline since the latter 1950s, falling from more than 120 children born to every 1,000 women of childbearing age in 1957, to 88 in 1967, to 66.6 in 1973. (The last-named figure is below the hitherto historic low of 75.8 recorded in depression year 1936.) [11] The reduction got going before the population-bombers set up their threnody of fear, and in its major dimensions quite clearly owes nothing to the recent outcry. To the extent that the recent scare has affected the matter at all, it appears simply to have intensified an already severe decline, thereby making a troublesome situation worse.

Exactly why birth and fertility rates fluctuate as they do is an unanswered question. The conventional view is that the recent downturn results from the availability of "the pill," but this does not explain the continued decline of birth and fertility rates from the turn of the century through the 1930s. Another thesis is that people curtail family sizes in response to economic hardship. Yet birth rates declined throughout the economically expansive twenties and started on an upward trend in the trough of the depression—only to go into sharp decline throughout the prosperous 1960s. There is the additional fact that affluent industrial societies have lower birth rates than do more impoverished ones —which runs directly counter to the idea that economic hardship is the key constraint.

The only conclusion which emerges with any degree of clarity is that trends in population have a way of correcting themselves, so that "expert" panic concerning them is almost always wrong. In the 1930s some demographers believed that we were headed for national extinction because of our declining birth rate; in the 1960s, the fear was just the opposite. In both cases the panic was totally needless, and the lesson to be derived is one of skepticism about the self-anointed population authorities. As in most other categories of public policy, the unfettered decision of the people is generally more sensible than the agitations of the planners.

The Global Food Crisis

It would appear, therefore, that population is not a menace to America and its industrial society—a point that certain of the populationists, when pressed, will be constrained to grant. But this, they say, is not the problem they are worried about. While America and other industrial nations may have beaten the Malthusian equation, the same cannot be said of other countries. It is in the underdeveloped nations that population is running ahead of productivity, people are starving, and drastic measures must be taken by way of remedy.

The classic example cited in many populationist pamphlets is the case of India. Looking at India's teeming millions, crowded cities, and relative poverty, it is easy to conclude that the trouble is simply that there are too many people. The situation seems dramatically different from that prevailing in the United States. Control the growth of population, and the standard of living will rise. It all seems perfectly simple.

In fact, the problem in India is exactly the same as the problem in the United States. The difference is in the *solution*. What is perceived as a crisis of "too many people" is in fact a crisis of too little productivity—which exists entirely apart from the number of people, which would not be solved by cutting back on population, and which could conceivably be made worse by a reduction in the number of people entering the society.

Routinely omitted from populationist oratory is the fact that every human being born into this world is a potential *producer* as well as consumer—in non-developed societies as well as our own. Indeed, since production in the former countries so often rests on human muscle power, this producing status is more acutely significant than it is in the industrial West. Such nations cannot afford to have whole groups of consumers such as children, welfare cases, or recipients of unemployment benefits sequestered from the working population. All, including the youngest children, must do their work in the rice paddies or potato fields.

In non-developed societies large families are often considered an economic benefit—as a work force or defense against attack. Each child has one mouth to feed, but two hands with which to do useful work, and our casual assumption of a class of growing children who consume but do not produce is a choice example of American ethnocentrism. The higher yield each new family member can produce may only slightly exceed the amount consumed, of course, and long-term advance can happen only through the introduction of machinery. These considerations indicate the problem is *not* the presence of the people, but the absence of the machines.*

---

* The point is made by Pakistani scholar Wajihuddin Ahmed, a consultant to the International Planned Parenthood Federation. "A poor peasant," Ahmed observes, "cannot hire laborers, invest in farm machinery, or in good plough animals. Since bare hands produce very little, he must have many. Even a small holding consumes a great deal of human energy when human brawn substitutes for the costlier power of animals or machines. High fertility of the peasant is therefore an intelligent response to his low productivity . . . an expanding family is not only a source

That absolute numbers have nothing to do with economic well-being may be illustrated if we compare the United States today with India *ca*. 1900. As of the early 1970s, the United States had a population of approximately 210 million people—and was of course the richest society known to history. India at the turn of the century had roughly the same population (supposedly about 235 million people) and yet was miserably poor —considerably poorer than it is today. If *numbers of people* were the determining factor, there should have been little economic difference between the two societies.

India and the United States today have about the same amount of available crop land. Yet from that acreage, we are able to harvest some 250 million tons of grain to their 100 million—a direct result of our superior productivity. Another way of looking at the same phenomenon is supplied by demographer Roger Revelle: If farmers throughout the world could get the same yields as do corn farmers in Iowa (about 100 bushels per acre) it would be possible to feed the world's present population on about one-tenth of the land now under cultivation. And the cultivable acreage of the earth could feed as many as 50 billion people.

The difference, to reiterate, is not in population as such, but in the productive system. Nations that have effective productive systems will have high standards of living, irrespective of population totals. A nation may have a large population, like the United States, or high population density, like Japan, and enjoy a high standard of living; another nation may have a small population, like Rwanda, or a low population density, like Brazil, and have a very low material standard of living. Population as such is essentially beside the point.

(Such comparisons, indeed, might be multiplied indefinitely. The United States at its founding had three million people; today it has upward of 210 million. Why isn't it poorer now than it was then? Canada and Australia are each much less densely populated than the United States. If sparseness of population were a key to prosperity, why aren't these countries richer than we?

of cheap labor but it is also the firmest source of supply." (*Bulletin of the Atomic Scientists,* June 1974, p. 32.)

Conversely, the six most densely populated countries in the world —Holland, Taiwan, England, Belgium, Japan, and West Germany—are all relatively prosperous. Some of the least densely populated—Red China, Paraguay, Bolivia—are quite poor. And so on.[12])

A further contrast may be drawn between the United States and the Soviet Union, which enjoys, like India, a collectivized economy and the benefits of successive five-year plans. The USSR today has roughly the same population as the United States (an estimated 220 million) and of course occupies an immense land area with abundant natural resources. Its population density is considerably lower than our own (29 people per square mile). Yet it has experienced severe problems of agricultural production and has had to go to the outside world—particularly the United States—to secure sufficient wheat to feed its people.

This latter necessity is particularly ironic in view of the fact that pre-Communist Russia was the world's largest exporter of wheat. After a half century of Communist planning, it has become a chronically troubled net importer. In terms of its ability to produce basic foodstuffs, the USSR has an obvious "population" problem—too little food to go around. But, again, it is apparent the real problem is in the lack of production, stemming from the Soviets' penchant for top-down planning and resultant hindrance to incentive and rational allocation of capital.*

---

* Commenting on the general record of agricultural improvement throughout the world, economist Peter Drucker says:

> Of all the industrially developed areas, only European Russia and Russia's European satellites are exceptions. There the farm population is still almost as large as it was around the time of World War II, with low productivity, even of the best 'commercial farmers' and a large reservoir of able-bodied, intelligent, and motivated people. But to tap this reservoir would require political changes that no Communist regime is likely to risk. At the least, the country would first have to pump tremendous investment into the farm economy—into housing, credit, education, health, and so on—before it could modernize agriculture and sharply reduce the farm population. . . . Politically it would demand a complete reversal of policies that are the foundation of the Soviet regime and essential to its staying in power. [*The Age of Discontinuity,* Harper & Row, 1969, p. 16.]

The idea that population increase is the cause of global starvation has been examined at enlightening length by Oxford economist Colin Clark. He marshals data showing that living standards around the globe have been increasing, rather than decreasing, as a result of improved technology and the "green revolution" that has turned such nations as Mexico and the Philippines into exporters of foodstuffs. Along the way, Clark also thoroughly deflates the idea that two-thirds or half of the world is suffering from malnutrition owing to the pressure of numbers.

Agricultural production per capita, he notes, has been increasing the world over, wherever technology and productive advance have been permitted to do their work. The exceptions are countries where per capita agricultural increase is no longer considered especially urgent, and nations whose internal political and economic arrangements inhibit production. In some of the latter, there has in fact been a noticeable *de*crease in agricultural productivity since the arrival of revolutionary governments designed to transport these nations to Utopia.

"Cuba and Algeria," Clark observes, "are sad examples of a decline of formerly productive countries, due to internal political disorder; and Ceylon of very slow improvement. . . . Tunisia and Morocco are also examples of decline, although not so serious as Algeria. . . . For most of the world, agricultural production is advancing faster than population, and is likely to continue to do so. . . . Countries in which agricultural production has not advanced as rapidly as population over the past decade . . . also include Latin American countries where the growth of productivity has been checked by economic disorder—Argentina, Chile, Uruguay." [13]

In these cases, as in the Soviet Union and India, the difficulty is one of economic organization, which will be solved only when the productive power of the market system is introduced into the equation. Where market forces are able to function and capital accumulation is allowed to occur, one finds a high and rising level of prosperity. Where Socialist "planning" is imposed, one finds the opposite. The difficulties put down to pressures of population are the outgrowth of collectivist economics, and like most of the other problems examined in this volume can best be solved by removing controls, not by adding to them.

This is not to say, however, that the population issue is *solely* economic. As in most of the other matters we have considered, a moral and philosophical dimension also needs discussion. Indeed, underlying the uproar over population, demands for ZPG, and the campaign for permissive abortion, there is a pulse of sentiment profoundly hostile to *people* as such, and a somber transformation of attitudes toward human life itself. All of which is immensely suggestive, and shall be examined a bit more fully later.

15

Friends of Earth, Enemies to Man

If any issue has been treated with as much fervor as the question of population growth, it is undoubtedly the subject of environmental pollution. This is not especially surprising, since the issues are closely linked both philosophically and politically, and the people who brought us the population scare have been working hard to do the same with respect to pollution. Fouling up the environment, after all, is one of the supposed evil consequences of having too many people.

By far the most striking resemblance between this pair of issues is the manner in which their proponents have managed to generate a considerable agitation on the basis of slender or non-existent data. The result of this success in both instances has been to stampede the nation toward adoption of measures that in many instances are needless and in others downright harmful. In some respects, the record of ill-considered action is worse in the case of environmental agitation than in the manner of demographics.

Before I attempt to document these statements, some preliminary observations are in order. First of all, it should be apparent on the limited-government framework already affirmed that anti-

233

pollution regulations as such are *not* an improper form of official activity. No one has a "right" either constitutional or otherwise to befoul the atmosphere or common waterways used by other people; such actions are clearly more than self-regarding, and involve obvious neighborhood effects. What is at stake, therefore, is not usually a matter of philosophical or constitutional propriety (though in extreme cases it has been pushed to that), but of practical dangers and remedies.

To this should be added, however, a countervailing observation. Contrary to assertions that the problem is one created by our system of private business, reflection suggests the trouble is just the other way around. That is, pollution is characteristically a feature of *communal* ownership. The things that get polluted, for the most part, are things that do not belong to anybody in particular: rivers, lakes, the oceans, the atmosphere, public highways, public parks and beaches. The reasons for this are fairly obvious. When someone owns something, he has an incentive to keep it cleaned up. When "everybody" owns it, this is the same as no one owning it, and nobody has such an incentive.

From these considerations it follows that we will have fewer problems with pollution under a general system of private ownership and control than under a system of public ownership and control. Where, for example, parks are maintained by private individuals and run on an admission basis, we may be fairly certain the proprietors will arrange to keep them clean and pass the costs along to the users.* If pollution were our only social concern, this would strongly suggest privatization of beaches, parks, and other public facilities as rapidly as possible. Of course, there are other social considerations involved in maintaining public parks and beaches, and many public goods—highways, waterways, the atmosphere—would be difficult or impossible to privatize. But this in no way alters the fact that pollution is distinctively a problem pertaining to *public* facilities, not private ones.

Finally, it should be understood that a totally spotless environment is both impossible and undesirable. All manufacturing activ-

---

* In addition, a private owner has existing remedy at law against those who pollute or otherwise damage his property, plus incentive to see that the remedy is invoked.

ity, locomotion, indeed all human or other life, involves, by definition, *some* disturbance of the environment. Every breath we draw, fire we build, or morsel of food we eat requires some rearrangement of the elemental order in which we find ourselves. The relevant question in every such discussion, therefore, is what balance we wish to achieve between the imperatives of existence on the one hand and the purity of the environment on the other. As we shall see, this is a consideration all too frequently omitted in environmental debate.

The Pollution Scare

The basic problem with recent discussion and legislation concerning the environment is considerably less esoteric than the foregoing considerations suggest. That problem, quite simply, is that much of what is asserted and widely believed about pollution is not correct.

Over the past few years, scare statements about pollution have issued in a steady stream from various supposed authorities, including agencies of the United States government. We have been told, for example, that automobile pollutants were choking our cities; that the world was in danger of running out of oxygen; that DDT and industrial mercury were poisoning fish and animals; that phosphate detergents were killing our lakes; and that, in general, we were in increasing danger of burying or choking ourselves to death in poisonous filth.

In response to these horrendous conceptions, we have seen anxiety levels about pollution rise dramatically—and politicians rushing to assuage this outcropping of imagined distress. In a relatively short span of time, the Federal government has passed the Environmental Protection Act and the Clean Air Act, created the Environmental Protection Agency and the Council on Environmental Quality, slapped stiff controls on auto and industrial emissions, banned the use of DDT, and encouraged the banning of phosphate detergents—among other things. It now develops that nearly all this activity has been counterproductive in one fashion or another, and that some of it has been demonstrably dangerous.

At the root of this excited activity has been a failure in perspective. Many of the people, particularly young people, who have become convinced the environment is getting progressively dirtier have been operating in an historical vacuum—without temporal benchmarks to measure what has in fact been happening. Anyone who lived through the 1930s, for example, can recall the clouds of soot that hung over many American cities—created by the burning of wood or soft coal. People who remember that phenomenon would be hard-pressed, on grounds of simple common sense, to conclude that atmospheric pollution in America has gotten *worse* in the interim. In fact, it has gotten considerably better—in appreciable measure because of technological and industrial advance.

A fairly decent accumulation of data on this subject shows that the prevailing levels of atmospheric pollution have been steadily falling and were doing so before the recent push for ecological legislation. Consider in this respect official measures of particulate matter in the urban atmosphere. Public Health Service tests conducted in 14 cities in the early 1930s showed an average concentration of 510 micrograms per cubic meter of air. By 1957, Federal measurements revealed an average urban concentration of 120. And by 1969, air monitoring in 64 cities showed average concentration down to 92—less than a fifth of the prevailing readings 40 years ago.[1]

What is true of particulates is also true of pollutants generally. The Council on Environmental Quality observed in its Second Annual Report that "ambient levels of carbon monoxide and sulfur dioxide have actually decreased in urban areas." As Matthew Crenson of Johns Hopkins University puts it: "The available evidence indicates that there has been a general decline in sulfur dioxide pollution during the past 30 or 40 years. In some cities, the sulfur dioxide content of the air today is only one-third or one-fourth of what it was before World War II. In some ways, at least, city air is probably cleaner today than it was 30 or 40 years ago." [2]

This record of improvement is apparent even in the largest and by general agreement most polluted of our major cities. Since 1966, New York has conducted a monitoring program reflecting the extent of atmospheric pollution. It shows that the level of all atmospheric pollutants progressively diminished between 1966 and 1970. Levels of sulfur dioxide, carbon monoxide, nitric oxide, suspended particulates, and other pollutants were all cut approximately in half—before the Federal Clean Air Act went into effect. Improvements in the same direction, and in some cases of similar magnitude, were recorded in Philadelphia, Chicago, and Los Angeles.[3]

If assertions of increasing pollution levels are false, the fright-wig notion of disappearing oxygen is preposterous. The oxygen content of the air has not changed an iota in this century. That content was 20.946 by volume in 1910, and it was 20.946 by volume in 1970.[4] A variant of this fear, the notion that we would eventually overload the atmosphere with carbon monoxide (CO), is equally unfounded. Despite the considerable increase in the use of internal combustion fuels in this century, the CO content of the atmosphere has remained constant—the excess apparently being absorbed quite handily by micro-organisms in the soil.

The environmental demonology gives considerable emphasis to pollutants generated by the automobile, which is the reason for the stringent standards imposed on automobiles by the Clean Air Act. And when the numbers are tossed around, they do sound impressive. We are told, for example, that automobiles emitted 400,000 tons of particulate matter in 1969. This seems immense, and frightening—until we get some data by which to orient our judgment.

Thus if we check the total record, we find the level of man-made pollutants is as nothing compared to the level pumped out unaided by nature. Carbon monoxide, for instance, is considered to be one of the most lethal by-products of the automobile. Yet CO is also produced by forest fires, plants, and the oceans. A team of researchers from Harvard has suggested that the natural chemical reaction of the hydrocarbon methane in the atmosphere could produce a quantity of CO equal to all the emissions from all the motor vehicles in the world.[5] Similar comparisons are possible for most of the other pollutants.

In a typical year, more than 50 million tons of dust are stirred into the atmosphere of the Northern Hemisphere, and between 10 and 20 *billion* tons of sea salts are thrown up by the oceans. Likewise, some 1.6 *billion* tons of methane gas are generated by swampy areas of the earth. Compared to all this, total man-made particulate matter in this hemisphere amounts to only 35.2 million tons, of which automobiles account for that relatively meager 400,000.[6] Even if we abolished the automobile entirely, this would hardly make a dent in the total problem.

Dr. William T. Pecora of the U.S. Geological Survey puts the matter into scale by observing that the volcanic eruptions of Krakatoa, Katmai, and Hekla volcanoes released more gases and particulate matter into the atmosphere than have been emitted by all of mankind's varied activities during the entire course of human history. "Add to the known volcanic activity the normal action of winds, forest fires, and evaporation from the sea," Pecora says, "and we can readily conclude that man is an insignificant agent in the total air quality picture. . . ."[7] From all of which it may reasonably be concluded that the problem of man-made atmospheric pollution has been, well, overstated.

Nonetheless, it may be and has been argued that the specific pollutants created by man, and most notably by the automobile, are uniquely harmful, and that *any* increment of these should be avoided. The best that may be said of this argument is that it deserves a Scotch verdict—not proved. Despite assertions concerning the danger of carbon monoxide from autos, for example, there is no evidence that this source of CO has harmed human health. The same may be said for that other supposed menace, leaded gasoline, as we shall note in a moment.

Like observations apply to most of the menaces that have excited so much recent wrath—automotive and industrial emissions, DDT, phosphate detergents, and so on. At most, researchers have observed toxic reactions from extremely heavy dosages to laboratory animals—administered in vastly greater volume than anything that would ever be experienced by a human being, under conditions light years removed from daily human existence. The regulators, however, have taken the attitude that, whatever the exact state of the scientific evidence, they are required to adopt a "safe" position, rigidly banning pollutants on the merest possibility that they *might* be harmful.

The Environmental Protection Agency assumed this posture, for example, toward phosphates and DDT, and in imposing air quality standards for automobiles and industry. The official view was expressed by regulator Delbert Barth as follows: "EPA has to protect public health and welfare. . . . Our only concern is health. We are required by law to provide an adequate safety factor. . . . *There are not a lot of good studies on health effects* . . . we do not even know what effect a pollutant might have in combination with other factors: age, other pollutants, genetics, and so on. Further studies might show we are not being tough enough. We have to act because of *potential* health risks." [8] (Italics added.) Especially intriguing is Barth's statement that EPA must play it "safe" where human health is concerned. As we shall see, the performance of the agency, in case after case has been exactly the reverse.

The Ominous Results of Regulation

Consider leaded gasoline. There has been a fervent crusade to "get the lead out," and a hasty effort to market nonleaded substitutes, on the premise that lead is hazardous to human health. Yet as Dr. Robert Kehoe of the University of Cincinnati College of Medicine observes, "in the entire literature on this subject there is not one whit of evidence that anyone has ever suffered any illness or impairment of health or well-being as a consequence of the occurrence of lead in the general human environment." The National Academy of Sciences confirms this in a 1972 report, asserting that "lead attributable to emission and dispersion into general ambient air has no known harmful effects." [9] *

In view of such data, EPA was constrained to back off a bit. It announced that when reductions in lead were first proposed, "it was thought that more than 2 micrograms of lead per cubic meter of air, averaged over a three month period, could cause adverse

---

* It also appears that "getting the lead out" has been counterproductive. As noted by *Barron's* (September 27, 1971), the danger of leaded gasoline is largely illusory, but that of nonleaded gasoline prototypes has proved to be quite real. Thus a test by the Bureau of Mines revealed that "leaded and the comparable quality prototype unleaded fuels yielded about equal amounts of emissions . . . [but] the fuel alterations from the leaded to the unleaded changed emission characteristics so that the pollution effect was increased as much as 25 per cent."

health effects. Subsequent information and a re-evaluation of the entire matter, however, show that it is difficult if not impossible to define a level of lead-in-air that is completely protective of health." EPA Administrator William Ruckelshaus noted that "if we removed all lead tomorrow, we would have to be very careful that what they [oil refineries] substituted for lead is not more hazardous than lead." [10]

Despite these admissions, EPA continued to insist on a (somewhat slower) phaseout of lead, on the altered grounds that the substance is uncongenial to catalytic converters required on new automobiles to meet the stringent air quality standards set by the Clean Air Act. It develops, however, that these catalytic converters are none too healthy themselves. While they neutralize some of the pollutants that concern EPA, they also have the characteristic of changing sulfur into sulfates. Sulfates are potentially quite dangerous to people with respiratory ailments—as lead, for example, is not. We must therefore get rid of a safe emission—lead—in order to make way for an unsafe one—sulfates.

Although this possibility was raised by EPA's own researchers, Ruckelshaus' successor Russell Train did not feel inspired to change the agency's policy. Train said the indications of danger were merely "preliminary," and that to be deterred by them would be to "throw off the entire momentum of the present auto emissions control strategy." [11] In other words, where existing auto mechanisms are concerned we must play it "safe," even though we have no proof those mechanisms are harmful; but where the EPA's own policies are concerned, we cannot play it "safe," because *that* would upset the line of conduct being pursued by the bureaucracy.

That journey through the looking glass is not atypical. Other areas of our economy have also witnessed enactment of stringent, single-objective regulations aimed at getting zero pollution in one area, thereby creating augmented pollution or health hazards in another. A case in point is provided by the celebrated instance of phosphate detergents, dreaded source of algae in lakes. That phosphates were a bad thing, to be eliminated as rapidly as possible, was one of the items that was supposedly "known" about pollution, and it was on the basis of this asserted knowledge that a crusade was mounted against them. In 1970, Federal officials called in the detergent manufacturers and recommended they substitute for phosphates an experimental substance known as NTA. By the end of the year the manufacturers had used more than 100 million pounds of NTA in their detergents.

This proved to be most unwise. It developed that laboratory tests with NTA caused birth defects in rats, and according to former Surgeon General Jesse L. Steinfeld NTA might be a cancer-causing agent (Steinfeld is presently head of cancer research at the Mayo Clinic). It also developed that caustic substances marketed in place of phosphates in many cases could cause damage if splashed in the eyes or swallowed. Certain of the nonphosphates also destroyed the flame-retardant qualities of infants' clothes—another obvious health hazard. Over against all this stood the rather wholesome record of the phosphates, which have never been known to harm anybody and show no promise of doing so.

All of which induced another reversal. Examining the total record, the EPA, the Council on Environmental Quality, and the Department of Health, Education, and Welfare turned on the retro-rockets and issued a statement warning against the *substitutes* for phosphates and suggesting that phosphates *not* be banned after all. They observed that "certain of the nonphosphate detergents now on the market contain ingredients that, if accidentally ingested, aspirated, or introduced into the eyes, may be extremely injurious to humans, particularly to children."

The Federal agencies added that nonphosphate products "utilize materials as a substitute for phosphates that are highly caustic and that clearly constitute a health hazard," which phosphates do not. And they concluded that antiphosphate laws enacted in haste to placate the antipollutionists could be affirmatively harmful: "In view of the unacceptable health risks of many phosphate substitutes and the plan for reducing phosphates in municipal wastes, states and their political subdivisions should reconsider policies that unduly restrict the use of phosphates in laundry detergents." [12]

Add to this the long-running vendetta against DDT, which has led to a sharp reduction and finally to the wholesale banning of this insecticide. The phaseout has had the most alarming consequences for agriculture and human life, including widespread infestations of destructive insects in Europe and America and a rise in the incidence of disease in certain parts of Asia. Of most immediate concern to Americans has been the destruction of literally millions of acres of forest land in the states of Washington, Oregon, Maine, Pennsylvania, New York, and New Jersey by tussock moths, spring budworms, gypsy moths, and other insects.

The banning of DDT has been based on assertions from the Friends of Earth, the National Audubon Society, and others that this substance is a persistent "poison" that retards the reproduction of fish and makes birds' egg shells thin. Other authorities, including the United States Forestry Service, contest these assertions, but even if they be granted one fact is perfectly clear: DDT is not harmful to human beings. This datum was brought forth strongly in the hearing record compiled by EPA itself, and was elaborated by hearing examiner Edmund Sweeney in his official findings on the subject. These include the following:

> DDT is extremely low in acute toxicity to man. DDT is not a safety hazard to man when used as directed. . . . DDT is not a carcinogenic hazard to man. . . . DDT is not a mutagenic or teratogenic hazard to man. The uses of DDT under the registration involved here do not have a deleterious effect on freshwater fish, estuarine organisms, wild birds or other wildlife. The adverse effect on beneficial animals from the use of DDT under the registrations involved here is not unreasonable on balance with its benefit. The use of DDT in the United States has declined sharply since 1959. . . . There is a present need for the continued use of DDT for the essential uses defined in this case.[13]

In the spring of 1973, officials in the states of Washington and Oregon petitioned EPA for permission to use DDT to combat the tussock moth epidemic. Ruckelshaus denied the request on the grounds that the epidemic would run its course and come to a natural end. This did not occur, however, and as a result evergreen trees were defoliated over a 1,400 square mile area of Oregon, Washington, and Idaho.*

Faced with mounting evidence of ecological damage, EPA again reversed itself and permitted use of DDT in the Northwestern states. This did not, of course, undo the damage already inflicted, nor did it extend to the Eastern states, which were trying to control their own pests while being denied permission to resort to mankind's most effective pesticide.

Denial of DDT in other countries has had even more ominous effects. In many nations, DDT is essential to control insects that threaten the very life of man—such as malaria-carrying mosquitos. In Ceylon, for example, the incidence of malaria has risen alarmingly. In 1961 there were only 110 cases of malaria in that nation, and no malaria deaths. By 1968, there were two and a half million cases, and over 10,000 deaths.

How many human lives have been saved by DDT is hard to estimate, but the World Health Organization (WHO) has made the attempt. This agency calculates that DDT saved five million lives in its first eight years of use, and that some 100 million illnesses were prevented by insect control. WHO asserts that in all a billion people have been freed from serious disease by the use of DDT, and warned that "even temporary lack of DDT for malaria control can seriously jeopardize the gains achieved at such great cost." [14]

---

* This drab scenario prompted Idaho Congressman Steve Symms to comment in October 1973:

> All states taken into consideration, we can estimate at this point that close to a million acres of timber are standing dead or so seriously debilitated that regeneration is unlikely. . . . I cannot resist the temptation to take a dig at the EPA for denying use of DDT in part because of its effect on wildlife. If there is an all-time loser in the tussock moth battle, it's our wildlife. Big game cover in Oregon and Washington is nonexistent for miles and miles in some areas. Fish suffer the increased water temperature levels that occur with cover loss. Our birds found nests exposed almost overnight to the elements as the tussock caterpillar eliminated needles. It has been charged—and I believe erroneously—that DDT thins egg shells. I have seen interesting photographs of eggs baked in their shells where denial of DDT has allowed substantial defoliation.

Equally vehement in opposing the ban is Nobel laureate Norman Borlaug, whose researches in high-yield grains are chiefly responsible for the "green revolution" increasing agricultural production in underdeveloped countries—which, as we have seen, has been essential to the improvement of living standards in those nations. By banning DDT, the environmentalists would undo this work and thereby intensify the very "population" problem they profess to worry about.

Borlaug sees the anti-DDT crusade as a threat to his prize-winning work. He asserts that "the safety record of DDT is remarkable," and that "conservationists and environmentalists . . . embarked on a crusade to deny the use of agricultural chemicals . . . give no thought to the end result of such actions: the eventual starvation and political chaos that will plague the world." [15]

Such looking-glass results are in the all too obvious pattern: action to clean up the environment that results in the marketing of substances more lethal than those prohibited; defense of our natural resources that ends up defoliating millions of acres of forest land; efforts to improve the level of health and safety that cause a resurgence of dreaded diseases and potential famine. So consistent a record of counterproductive action suggests a deeper cause at work, consistent with our earlier comment about the derangement of the times.

In a purely structural sense, of course, we can expect mistaken conclusions to follow from mistaken premises. More deeply, the readiness of so many people to believe they are being subtly poisoned and to rush around in panic is philosophically suggestive. As historian Stephen Tonsor has observed, many people in our country are ready to respond with eagerness to such initiatives because in some way they "feel sick," and this is a method of objectifying and thus of remedying a situation rooted in metaphysics rather than the earth.   *

* Also suggestive is a palpable feeling that nature is somehow more important than man—that nature is, indeed, a kind of deity to be served by humankind. This is a virtually pagan attitude, directly contrasting with the Judaic and Christian view that de-sacralized nature and declared humanity's dominion over it. This reversion is manifest in counterculture hostility to material progress and advanced technology and associated yearnings for "zero growth" in industrial matters as well as in population.

In addition, the environmental crusade has incorporated all the conventional antagonisms toward American business, a naive belief in regulatory wisdom, and the one-eyed notion that it is possible to achieve desirable goals through compulsion without considering side-effects or secondary consequences. Pragmatically considered, its most obvious failing is an unwillingness to realize that decisions concerning the environment always involve trade-offs, and that other factors in the equation of existence do not hold still while we obsessively pursue a single goal with blinders on. The consequences of this mentality will be examined next.

16

The
Energy
Crisis

The energy crisis of the 1970s has thrown into bold relief a number of issues considered in this book. Indeed, it would be hard to imagine any single series of events that could demonstrate more clearly the interconnection of all the economic factors reviewed here, and the manner in which an intrusive government can serve to create our problems rather than to cure them. Moreover, the national trauma over energy illustrates quite plainly the relationship of our economic woes to deeper causes in the realm of social and philosophical confusion.

The Case for Consumption

One fact that has been repeatedly driven home in recent debate is that the United States is a nation that uses enormous quantities of energy. It is frequently stressed that, while America has only 6 percent of the earth's population, it consumes some 33 percent of the world's energy—which is close enough to the facts of the case to serve as a working description. In 1973, the average

American family spent $743 on energy (about 7 percent of its annual income) and Americans used about 60 barrels of oil per capita—compared to 20 barrels per capita in Europe. Most usually, these data are cited as a reproach, as though there were something shameful about our national lust for energy. But in fact there is nothing shameful about it.

Consumption of energy, as it happens, is an accurate measure of an advanced industrial civilization, closely correlated to the standard of material life available to its inhabitants. America consumes a lot of energy because it is an industrial nation that has spread the material benefits of life quite widely throughout its society. To say America should not absorb high levels of energy is, in effect, to say it should not be such a nation and that its citizens should not enjoy secure shelter, abundant food supplies, efficient heating and lighting, machines to do useful work, advanced communications and means of travel, improvements of health and sanitation, or economic surpluses for education and research and leisure.

Now there are a number of people who more or less accept this correlation, and who profess themselves willing to take the consequences of declining energy consumption. Such views are held, for example, by some romantic conservatives, some Luddite opponents of machinery, and a number of back-to-nature environmentalists. We have, they say, gone too far in our pursuit of industrialization, and committed countless vulgarities in its name. We should therefore call a halt to the process, or at least slow it down, which means in essence that we should curtail our use of energy. Thus stated, the position is at least theoretically coherent. But certain problems enter in.

First, if one adopts such a position, he should fully acknowledge its implications—one of which is, precisely, the energy crisis. All efforts at acquiring external energy sources involve some disturbance of the environment, and efforts to halt such disturbance according to absolutist standards will *ipso facto* prevent the acquisition of energy. It is perfectly consistent to say we should stop despoliation of the environment by all conceivable means and therefore should have less energy production. But it is perfectly *in*consistent to demand a widespread network of environmental controls while simultaneously deploring the existence of an "energy crisis." The second is a predictable consequence of the first.

Opposition to industrial advance and jeremiads about energy pigs are also inconsistent when they proceed—as they often do—from those who complain about the plight of the impoverished and the need to distribute economic benefits more widely. One can argue this way or that about the workings of our economic system and the alternative methods of carving up its product. But it is tolerably clear that without *an* industrial system, consumption of energy, and related environmental disturbance, there would be no economic product in the first place. It is impossible to distribute the result of productivity and technological advance if the production and technology do not at first exist.

How to Create a Shortage

Beyond these considerations, the energy shortfall has demonstrated certain other facts of economic life. Most important of these is that our energy problem, in almost all its dimensions, is the result of governmental policy—and not, as sometimes suggested, of private malfeasance or natural shortage. The fossil fuels that constitute our present energy supply are finite, of course, and will eventually be used up. But that point of disappearance is far off in the future, and we have sufficient quantities of coal, oil, and natural gas to last us longer than the history of the United States to date.

Our coal supply alone, for example, is sufficient to power our economy for anywhere from 300 to 900 years—depending on the uses to which it is put—while gas and oil and coal together are obviously good for many centuries. The uses of nuclear power, meanwhile, have hardly been tapped at all. So whatever the *long-term* outlook for these energy sources, it is obvious natural shortage cannot account for a *present* energy crunch. The resources are out there waiting for us, but we have for other than natural reasons experienced difficulty getting at them.[1]

For purposes of illustration, let us examine a case that far predates the energy-conscious seventies—that of natural gas. This fuel is American industry's most important source of energy, supplying 49 percent of our industrial needs. It also provides 60 percent of the requirements of commercial enterprise, 52 percent of residential needs, and 24 percent of power requirements in the generation of electricity (figures as of 1971). Yet despite its enormous significance to our economy, supplies of this major energy source in certain areas are nearing total depletion—as a number of "interruptible" customers have learned to their chagrin. Of all the shortages we face, that of natural gas has been the most critical.

The reasons for this calamity are not far to seek. Since the middle 1950s the Federal Power Commission (FPC) in its wisdom has regulated the price of natural gas at the wellhead, as an allegedly humane piece of political business. The artificially low price has encouraged widespread consumption while depriving developers of capital and incentives to explore for new reserves. The result is that demand has far outstripped supply and chances for appreciable enlargement of our natural gas resources, absent de-regulation, are virtually nil.*

The explosion of demand may be seen from the fact that in 1954, when the Supreme Court conferred authority on the FPC to regulate gas prices, demand was 23 million cubic feet a day. By 1973 it had nearly tripled, to 63 million. Without incentives to explore, much of this production has been taken out of our reserves. When the regulation began, proved reserves were equal to 23 times annual production. In 1972 they were equal to 11 times annual production. Project the trend lines and depletion of our natural gas reserves is inescapable.[2]

Investment for exploration is a function of expected yield on that investment, and the yield from regulated natural gas has been

---

* Such an outcome could have been predicted by any competent economist who understood the working of the price system, since it is precisely the function of rising or falling prices to clear the market and any effort to hold a price below its natural level will create a tendency toward shortage. Paul Mac Avoy of the Massachusetts Institute of Technology has traced the workings of this process in the case of natural gas in detail. In a meticulous analysis for *The Journal of Law and Economics* (Vol. XIX, 1971), Mac Avoy demonstrated that ceiling prices for natural gas "have added to demand and reduced supplies of new reserves. . . ." He estimated that in the absence of controls new reserve findings would have been 40 percent higher.

so small that capital has been diverted elsewhere. As a 1972 marketing analysis prepared by Chase Manhattan observes, "the natural gas sold by the nation's largest oil companies represented an enormous amount of petroleum energy," but only 3.6 percent of total operating revenue was received from this source because "governmental price regulation prevented a more realistic yield." [3] Under such conditions, it is difficult to attract the capital outlay required to open up reserves.

This particular exercise in regulation has also contributed to the depression of the coal business, since the artificially low price of natural gas made it a more economical source of energy than coal. "The coal industry," says Chase, "was dealt a devastating blow by the rapidly expanding invasion of its . . . markets by exceedingly low priced natural gas. . . . Unable to compete in terms of price, the coal industry experienced a large-scale loss of markets. With declining markets, and a very low price received for the coal it was still able to sell, the industry had neither the financial means nor the incentive to develop additional productive capacity. Indeed, it was not even able to maintain existing capacity, as it continued to encounter rising costs of operation." [4]

More recently, the shortfall of natural gas has accelerated our dependence on oil, and will eventually raise our need for oil by an additional four million barrels a day. That extra usage is more than double the anticipated output from the North Shore of Alaska when we finally start receiving it. Thus the regulation of natural gas has managed to bollix up not one resource, but three. And note that we have been here examining only *one* example of such regulation; when we add in and multiply a score of others, the dimensions of the problem are apparent.

One obvious energy resource, for example, is offshore oil. The U.S. Geological Survey estimates there may be as much as 190 billion barrels of crude oil and 1,100 trillion cubic feet of natural gas on America's continental shelf—twice as much of both commodities as has been produced in America since the petroleum industry got started. At present, however, these resources are largely inaccessible as a result of environmental regulation. Because of an oil spill in the Santa Barbara Channel in 1969, oil leases there were cancelled and others not issued. Paul Wollstadt of the American Petroleum Institute reports that "of the 72 tracts leased in the area, only two are currently in production. Of the remaining 70 leases, one was surrendered, 17 are being reviewed for production, and 52 are dormant except for some small exploratory activity. At the time the moratorium was imposed, there were an estimated four billion barrels of recoverable crude oil beneath the channel and surrounding area." [5]

The story has been much the same for Alaskan oil, which could bring us some 2 to 3 million barrels daily but which was delayed by the environmentalist desire to preserve the tundra from the necessary pipeline. As Lawrence Rocks and Richard Runyon point out in their book, *The Energy Crisis,* an oil spill from such a pipeline (an unlikely event) would damage approximately .01 percent of the tundra and Alaskan forest. [6] The dictionary definition of "tundra," incidentally, is a "treeless plain" that "consists of black mucky soil with a permanently frozen subsoil, but supports a dense growth of moss and lichens" (a lichen is a combination fungus and alga, the latter being bad in lakes but good in tundra).

The Alaskan reserves, discovered in 1968, constitute the largest oil field ever found in the Western hemisphere. It is estimated Prudhoe Bay contains nearly 10 billion barrels of oil and 26 trillion cubic feet of natural gas. Yet six years after the discovery, not the first barrel of oil or cubic foot of natural gas had made its way to the American consumer. Lawsuits were repeatedly filed on the grounds that the pipeline needed to transport this oil would deface the Alaskan landscape (the Alaskans themselves did not agree), and then on the grounds that the right of way did not conform to the Mineral Leasing Act of 1920. It was not until November 1973, in the midst of the energy crunch, that an act of Congress finally pushed the project forward.

Not content just to close down new sources of oil, the regulators have also contrived to use up the existing supply more rapidly, chiefly through the Clean Air Act of 1970. Under its impossible standards, the auto industry has produced a breed of gas-hungry vehicles precisely at the time the oil companies were feeling the pinch of shortage, and restrictions on power plants had caused them to turn from coal to fuel oil. As in the case of natural gas, therefore, the regulators ingeniously managed to pump up demand while diminishing supply—a pretty good formula for shortage.

As we have seen, the emission standards imposed on auto-mobiles were often unnecessary and counterproductive from an environmental standpoint. For the moment, however, the relevant aspect is their bearing on the question of energy, which is con-siderable. According to *Fortune,* the emission-control equipment mandated by the Environmental Protection Agency for 1973 mod-els reduced gas mileage by about 7 percent—just when the need of the hour was more mileage, not less. Add to this the demand to "get the lead out," which meant that fuel for efficient high-compression engines became appreciably more expensive.

The effect of it all was estimated in 1973 by the Office of Emergency Preparedness as an increased gasoline consumption of 300,000 barrels a day—which works out to 4.5 billion gallons of gas a year.[7] As bad as this was, however, it was nowhere near as bad as the effect of emission standards on industry, which reacted indirectly but massively on the nation's petroleum supply.

Back in 1967 demand for distillate fuel oil by the nation's electric utilities was only 8,000 barrels a day, and declining. By 1970 the demand was up to 68,000 barrels a day, and by 1972 the daily demand leaped up to 186,000 barrels—an increase of 2,300 percent in five years' time. Environmental standards for automobiles and industry thus account for an increased demand of roughly half-a-million barrels of oil a day. Increased usage by electric utilities alone is equal to 75 percent of the requirements of America's railroads in 1972 and 36 percent of the diesel fuel used by U.S. trucking.[8]

What is true in the case of natural gas and oil is doubly true in the case of coal. This resource is available in abundance and can be obtained quite cheaply by surface mining. It can be burned directly or converted into synthetic oil and gas or used for the generation of electricity. But the regulators have moved to stop its production by cracking down on "strip mining," contesting the lease of government lands for mining even low sulfur coal, and imposing the ever-popular emission standards. As an official of the Ford Foundation put the matter: "There are only two things wrong with coal: We can't mine it and we can't burn it." [9]

One of the big deals emerging from our recent siege of en-thusiasm for ecology is the requirement that everyone be cogni-zant of "environmental impact." The Environmental Protection

Act of 1969 requires that Federal agencies with licensing powers over public works file "environmental impact" statements concerning the effect of such proposals on the earth, including its atmosphere and waterways. The concept has spread to other layers of government, and findings of bad "environmental impact" have recently stalled all sorts of projects, including improvement of electrical facilities, construction of refineries, and nuclear power plants.* Consolidated Edison for example, has been hung up for a decade in its effort to build a storage plant to improve electric service in New York. One state, Delaware, has forbidden by statute the construction of any new oil refineries on its territory.

Stampeding forward in the quest for a spotless environment, the regulators have been largely indifferent to the effect on the economy. They inform us that their statutory duty is to stop the pollution, period, and if this means having people riding bicycles to work, or unable to get heating oil, or facing sudden unemployment, that's tough.

This mentality is sketched quite lucidly in a staff report on Federal energy organization released by Senator Henry Jackson. The Jackson report zeroes in on the effect of environmental regulations on the energy situation, and gives particular notice to the role of the Environmental Protection Agency:

> In effect, the EPA encouraged the states individually to take actions which cumulatively resulted in a critical impairment of the nation's fuel supply. The EPA, of course, has not been given authority to qualify its environmental standards to accommodate other social objectives. . . . [But] the establishment of environmental goals inevitably involves sacrifices in the achievement of other social objectives. . . .
>
> The EPA is a single-purpose agency by definition. It serves a very special clientele and looks to it for support. Its "missionary" role has attracted personnel who have internal-

---

* Needless to remark, the very mention of the (quite safe) expedient of nuclear energy sends the regulators into paroxysms of fear. Although the safety record of the civilian nuclear reactors already on stream is exemplary, a cultivated campaign of terror against anything "atomic" in the nation has brought a flurry of suits against development of nuclear energy and slowed this program to a crawl.

ized the values of the environmentalist community it serves. It is not equipped to make tradeoff decisions between environmental and other objectives.[10] *

On top of all this regulation, the Federal government beginning in 1971 laid yet another layer of force—President Nixon's program of price controls. The workings of this program were often and obviously in contradiction to the need for intelligent deployment of energy resources, but the contradiction seemed to escape the planners. In the fall of 1973, for example, the nation's energy czars were urging everyone to turn down thermostats, pondering the pros and cons of rationing, weighing national speed limits, and considering enormous taxes on motor fuel to tide us over the shortage. We were on a crisis footing, supposedly, to curtail the consumption of gasoline.

But while all this was going on still *other* departments of the Federal government, administering the price controls, were doing their bit to *encourage* consumption of gasoline, by holding its price below the market level. The same dispatches that brought us news of all that feverish planning to conserve the use of motor

---

* Further insight into the economic impact of environmental regulation is provided by a 1972 report of the Office of Science and Technology. This document estimated that between 1976 and 1985 the nation would pay out some $64 billion above and beyond the benefits it might be expected to receive, and about $3.8 billion annually thereafter, for environmental protection equipment that in numerous areas of the country might be totally unnecessary. According to the report "analysis shows an excess cost to the nation over the expected benefits both during and after the decade required to change to cars complying with the Clean Air Act specifications. . . . About three out of every ten purchasers of new automobiles of 1976 vintage will be paying a large extra initial cost and a higher operating expense for stringent emission control features which may be unnecessary in their areas. Not only would this constitute a major economic penalty for a significant fraction of the population, but it would also represent a serious waste of the nation's resources."

The report concluded that "establishing standards beyond the known state of the art on the theory that industry can do anything if enough pressure is put on it is not likely to result in wise governmental decision making or to provide the greatest net benefits to society. . . . Furthermore crash efforts to meet fixed time limits can delay the development of alternative and perhaps better technology."

fuel also informed us of ceiling prices on gasoline that had to be posted by retailers, adjusted only to allow for their increased costs.

The Quest for Scapegoats

As the energy crisis became progressively more painful to the public, the regulatory types who had done so much to bring us to this unhappy impasse became concerned about the possibility of a "backlash." * They therefore set to work to find some convenient patsy who could be blamed for the nation's anguish. As ever, they were aided in their efforts by a considerable reservoir of confusion on basic economics, the timidity of the relevant industries, and the ideological leanings of the national media.

The convergence of these factors made it possible to hammer home the idea that the energy problem had somehow been created by the energy industries themselves—that big oil, in particular, had somehow connived to create the looming shortages of petroleum and natural gas. Exactly how or why this connivance had occurred was never made quite clear. The point was "they"—meaning big business in general, big oil in particular—had created the problem, and "they" should be punished accordingly.

The alleged answer to the malfeasance of the companies was, of course, added controls, mandated rollback of prices, and a healthy dose of antitrust. All of which could be counted on to make the problem worse, not better, and was vaguely reminiscent of the parson who berates his congregation for the lethargy of those not in attendance. Of the several parties mentioned, after all, it was the oil industry, and only the oil industry, that had been supplying us with any petroleum whatsoever.

---

* Although it is widely believed that curtailment of supplies from the Arab countries in the fall of 1973 "caused" the petroleum shortage, that interruption might more accurately be described as the occasion for glimpsing the problem rather than the source of it. "Official figures show that the U.S. is now producing almost 75 percent of its petroleum needs here at home, relying on Middle East and North African imports for 8.1 percent. Of the Arab-country imports, a 5 percent cut would reduce America's supply of crude oil by only 0.4 percent." (*U.S. News and World Report,* October 29, 1973.)

On logical grounds alone, the idea that the oil companies deliberately cut back on production and thereby provoked the energy crisis was an evident fantasy. For a period of years, the companies had been trying to open the Alaska pipeline, secure permission for offshore drilling, and obtain more leases for exploration. The thrust of their policy had been to develop new and bigger supplies of oil—which is natural enough since they are in the business of selling it. All these initiatives had been forestalled, of course, by the regulators and environmentalists.*

What about the other charges tossed at the companies—such as shipping oil to foreign nations, or holding back supplies to wait for better prices? Although the facts of record were in a bit of a muddle, these accusations were probably true. But the conclusion to be drawn is rather different from that preferred by critics of the industry. The diversion of petroleum from American consumers was an indictment, not of oil producers, but of the Federal regulators.

Consider the price situation in petroleum. Under Federal controls, the price of "old" oil (from existing wells) in America in early 1974 was $5.25 a barrel compared to $10.35 for "new" (from newly opened wells) or stripper well production, and up to $20 in world markets. Who among us would sell his wares at a controlled price one-fourth or one-half the going rate? Quite obviously, any individual or corporation—particularly one confronted with rising costs and capital needs—will sell in the dearest market, not the cheapest. Such is the basic law of economics.

Were petroleum companies also holding out supplies and betting on a higher price at home? Many companies deny it, but it would be astonishing if they were not. The situation was exactly comparable to that confronted by livestock growers in the summer of 1973 when the Federal government imposed a "freeze"

---

* The oil companies do have a major failing on this front, and it is one they share with other members of the U.S. business community—their partiality for protectionist quotas, which have existed since Eisenhower imposed mandatory import controls in 1959. But while this policy has unquestionably curtailed the influx of foreign oil to America, it has just as clearly *increased* the production and sale of domestic petroleum— which, indeed, was its major economic purpose. So on the count of holding back domestic production, the industry stands acquitted.

on meat prices, with special severity on beef, as an alleged means of helping consumers. The result of this decisive stroke was that growers refused to bring their stock to market and meat of all varieties vanished as though by magic from the stores. When the meat controls were lifted, the result was an enormous surge to markets and a decline—not rise—in prices. The shortage, in sum, was the result of government interference, and the cure for the shortage was to lift the controls. The fuel crisis was in every key respect identical.[11] *

Numerous politicians who took up the cry that somehow the petroleum industries were to blame for the problem focused particular attention on the "windfall profits" allegedly being harvested by the industry. Much was made of the fact that oil profits in the third quarter of 1973 were up by 63 percent, or 79 percent, or some other enormous figure, over the corresponding period a year before. The impression conveyed was that oil companies were rolling in profits while gouging the public and that their behavior was the source of the discomfort experienced by everyone else.

Newsweek magazine, a typical exponent of such opinions, reported that "profits are at record levels this year, and many consumers are concluding that the industry is profiteering from the shortages." *Newsweek* found industry assertions of insufficient earnings "astounding in light of oil profits this year: up a total 79 percent in the third quarter over last year and an average 59 percent for the first eleven months. . . ." The magazine concluded that if the shortages were drawn out, "some kind of legislation directed against the industry—perhaps a lower depletion allowance, or even a specific antitrust law mandating breakup— seems all but inevitable."[12]

---

* Under controlled prices, as noted by Professors Philip Gramm and Richard Davison (in an analysis for the *Wall Street Journal*), there is little incentive to go out and get new reserves or invest in the technology required to recover oil that is presently considered unrecoverable. At market prices, it would be economically feasible to develop these and other sources currently dormant. Gramm and Davison noted that between 1947 and 1952 each 1 percent increase in prices was on the average associated with a 4 percent increase in gasoline production. They estimate that removal of price controls on oil could have the effect of tripling U.S. oil reserves.

Fact A in such discussion is that oil profits, far from being enormous, are and have been comparatively modest. In the third quarter of 1972, for example, oil industry profits on sales amounted to 6.7 percent—compared to 9.7 percent for the office equipment industry, 8.5 for chemicals, 11.1 for instruments, and so on. In the third quarter of 1973, in the face of surging demand, oil's percentage margin improved to 8.3 percent. It is this rather moderate improvement that works out to the 63 and/or 79 percent increase that scandalized the critics of the industry.[13] *

The truth is that oil profits for the past ten years have lagged behind the profits of manufacturing industry in general (11.8 percent as opposed to 12.2 percent). In 1972, the petroleum industry retained only 6.5 percent of its gross revenue as net earnings, down from 7.4 percent a year before and 9.5 percent four years earlier. By contrast, 14.5 percent of oil's gross revenues were taken by government in the form of taxes. Indeed, for those who like exploding statistics, it is noteworthy that taxes on the oil industry had increased 112 percent in four years' time, while dividends fell to 3.5 percent of revenues, an all-time low.[14]

As a result of these contrasting trends, oil companies had less capital for exploration and potential investors could do better by putting their money elsewhere. And since *Newsweek* quotes Chase Manhattan Bank as an authority on the size of oil profits, it may be well to see what that authority has to say on the whole question of the energy crisis, the performance of the industry, and the profitability of oil investments. Here is a more full-bodied statement from Chase:

The United States does not lack basic energy resources —an enormous additional supply of energy could be made

---

* Anyone can play such percentage games, of course, depending on the point you want to make. For example, by the same misleading standard, the profit hike of *Newsweek*'s own parent company, the *Washington Post*, was a cool 249 percent. That sounds like an astonishing increase, but the figures backing it up show an average profit on sales inching up from a paper-thin 1.1 percent in 1972 to 3.3 percent in 1973—quite a different impression. It is the second set of figures, not the first, that provides real insight into the profitability of the firm or industry in question. The same applies to oil.

available if only the necessary expenditures were possible. But faulty policies of government have operated for more than three decades to prevent the required expenditures. And the current energy shortage is the harvest those policies have reaped. . . .

Even in the face of a progressively worsening shortage of petroleum, government continues to exhibit little evidence of understanding the industry's essential need for adequate financial resources. . . . The lack of concern is made abundantly clear when government prevents the generation of the capital funds needed to provide additional petroleum supplies by imposing artificial restraints on petroleum prices.[15] *

This analysis concluded that the problem confronting the industry and the nation is a lack of public awareness of the facts concerning slack earnings and lack of capital, and suggested energetic efforts were needed to get these points over to the American people. When we read articles in *Newsweek* quoting selectively from Chase Manhattan to argue for still more punitive treatment of the industry, there is nothing very mysterious about the confusion of the public.

---

* "Over the past four years," Chase added, "the taxes paid by the major petroleum companies increased by as much as 112 percent. But the combined net earnings of the companies increased by only 2.9 percent— an average growth of not even 1 percent a year. Because of its inability to obtain from earnings enough money to satisfy growing capital needs, the industry was forced to borrow much more heavily. . . . over the four year period capital expenditures rose by no more than 16.6 percent —far less than the amount necessary to keep pace with the expanding need for petroleum. No wonder petroleum is in short supply."

PART III
Freedom Is As Freedom Does

17

Liberalism
and
Civil Liberties

It would thus appear that the concentration of power alleged as an economic necessity under modern conditions is in fact an economic misfortune. The obvious conclusion to be derived from this skein of woe is that the imagined "economic and social knowledge" imported into our constitutional law by Justice Louis Brandeis and his cohorts back there in the 1930s is no knowledge at all, but a species of ideological voodoo. It is passably clear that the maestroes of big government don't have the faintest notion of what they are doing, and that central planning from a single power center in Washington is a hapless method of seeking economic satisfactions.

If liberalism's first assurance on economic matters is thus mistaken, what of the second? What of the promise that, despite this enormous concentration of political and economic power, and despite the general effort to elasticize the constitutional limits, we shall somehow maintain our essential liberties? On inspection, it develops that this assurance, too, is mistaken: The concentrated power that has failed to solve our economic problems and in fact created many of them has also become a serious menace to our freedoms.

The extinction of freedom in certain matters, of course, was the motive of liberal planning to begin with. The very object of turning the Constitution on its head, declaring the irrelevance of the founders, and exercising compulsion over the American economy is to substitute the judgment of the planners for that of American citizens acting freely according to their own desires. Free decision, after all, is supposed to lead to "chaos," and a proper economic order can be obtained only when the crucial choices are made by government experts instead of farmers, businessmen, and workers going about their own affairs.

Despite this tireless emphasis on the need for compulsion, liberalism through the years has cherished a seeming ambiguity on the subject of freedom. The philosophic leading strings going back to Mill have not been entirely broken, and the average Western liberal still likes to think of himself as something of a libertarian. Depending on the issue, liberal spokesmen will frequently contend that they and not their conservative foes are the authentic spokesmen for individual freedom. This stance is especially notable in internal security cases, matters pertaining to the Communist Party, revolutionary political activity in general, the legal rights of criminal defendants and prisoners, rights of certain minorities, abortion, censorship, student protests, drug indulgence, and so on. In all these matters and some others, liberals characteristically urge a relaxation of government powers rather than their extension.

The Liberal Doctrine of Preferred Rights

Given the statements reviewed in Chapter 3, how are these two positions to be reconciled? The answer given by the liberal spokesmen runs roughly as follows: Yes, they say, we are in favor of compulsion and planning in certain cases, and we acknowledge that if our programs are going to take effect, various rights and liberties will have to be abridged. But the matters to be treated in this fashion have only to do with *property* rights, which occupy a relatively modest and indeed in many cases a disreputable position in our society's scale of values. "Freedom" in this realm, they concede, is not a major liberal concern.

The liberal interest in freedom, we are told, is found on a different level—in concern for "human rights." Such human rights take many forms, but they include most obviously the essential liberties set forward in the Bill of Rights—such as freedom of speech, religion, press, and assembly. Freedoms of this type, according to the liberal view, are essential to a "scheme of ordered liberty" (Justice Benjamin Cardozo's phrase), and we must battle to maintain them, even though the limited meaning of our Constitution otherwise has had to yield to the familiar imperatives of modernity.

This outlook, rendered explicit by Chief Justice Harlan Fiske Stone in *Jones v. Opelika* (1942), is known as the doctrine of "preferred position." In essence, it argues that certain freedoms protected by the Bill of Rights are so essential to the well-being of our society that they must be jealously protected, and that when considering them we should reverse the usual rule of loose construction and interpret the relevant language strictly, minimizing rather than extending the reach of governmental power.

In particular, it is argued, First Amendment rights are more important than other rights because they are the vital substructure of a free society. So long as they remain intact, it is always possible to protest, agitate for change, or throw out the people who are in charge of things. So if we hold fast to these particular guarantees, we need not fear for the general survival of our freedoms or worry much about the government's intrusion elsewhere. As Alpheus Mason puts it, through these rights the majority "must leave open the political process by which it can be replaced when no longer able to command majority support." [1]

This outlook is widely accepted in scholarly and juristic circles nowadays, and is more or less the basis on which a number of Supreme Court decisions have been rendered. Yet on reflection it raises far more questions than it answers—spanning the contradictions in the liberal outlook but hardly resolving them. It tells us *what* the liberals are doing, but explains imperfectly why they are doing it, and gives us very little reason to suppose that what they are doing is correct. The unanswered questions that come to mind are chiefly of three types.

First, as a matter of constitutional probity, how does it happen that some phrases in our basic law have gotten themselves into "preferred position"? By what constitutional standard is such a determination made, and who is entitled to make it? Second, as a practical matter, how valid is the notion that rights of speech and press are more essential than, say, the right to own and dispose of property? And, third, presuming such distinctions are possible, is it really true that liberal jurisprudence construes the Bill of Rights in general and the First Amendment in particular in strict-constructionist fashion?

At all three levels, the indicated answers are hostile to the liberal argument. In the matter of constitutional interpretation, it should be apparent that any rule of "preferred position" in the application of the fundamental law is a self-created license to pick and choose among our constitutional guarantees. If we are to be ruled by the Constitution, then *all* the guarantees contained in it should be enforced impartially, whatever one's subjective opinion of them. If only those that suit somebody's particular theory of "rights" are to be enforced, then it should be apparent we are being ruled not by the Constitution but by the people making the selection. Either we have a Constitution or we don't.

It is true, of course, that all constitutions have to be interpreted, and that in the act of interpretation subjective readings will enter in. This is the normal problem of human frailty, which will always exist under any system of government. What is being argued in the case for "preferred position," however, is something entirely different—not a statement that human beings will necessarily differ in their reading of the basic law, but that certain human beings have assumed the privilege of dispensing with various precepts of this law while retaining others.

From the standpoint of practical wisdom, "preferred position" is equally dubious. We may grant that rights of speech, press, assembly, and so on are important to our society; but why are other rights any less so? Some of us make our livings by writing and speaking; others by laying bricks, manufacturing pumps, or driving cabs. Who has commissioned liberal jurists or anyone else to decide that one profession is sacrosanct, while another may be regimented at will? That notion smacks of philosophical arrogance of a particularly self-serving kind, since the people drawing the imagined distinction are all professional verbalizers. So long as the peaceful pursuit of any one of these endeavors does not endanger human life or abridge the rights of someone else, why shouldn't it be just as exempt from interference as the others?

As for the notion that rights of speech and press are logically prior to rights of property, this is not in the least self-evident. Indeed, it may be plausibly argued that the true relationship is all the other way: Only to the extent that one enjoys property rights and some sort of economic base of operations can First Amendment rights become effective. As Hamilton put it, a power over a man's subsistence is a power over his will—and therefore over his voice. If I can control the economic aspects of your life, then I can control whether you live or die, or what you say or print. (The workings of this relationship will be examined in the next chapter.)

Beyond these considerations, it is patently clear that liberal scholars and jurists do *not* in fact interpret First Amendment and other guarantees in the Bill of Rights in strict-constructionist or "absolutist" fashion. The more general rule is one of interpreting away those rights that clash with liberal doctrine, while wildly extending others that happen to agree with it. In neither case do we encounter "strict construction" or even a minimal consistency. What we confront, instead, is the unhindered sway of liberal ideology.

How Liberals Construe the Bill of Rights

The liberal stance becomes quite clear when we examine specific provisions in the Bill of Rights, and the characteristic liberal view concerning them. Most obvious case in point is the Tenth Amendment, which asserts that "the powers not delegated to the United States by the Constitution, nor prohibited by it to the states, are reserved to the states respectively, or to the people." As we have seen, this language expressed the rule of "enumerated powers" that afforded constitutional preference to the states: As the original seats of authority, their powers were "numerous and indefinite," those of the Federal government "few and defined." This language sums up the limited, federal character of the system, and was demanded in one fashion or another by a majority of the original states.

What has been the liberals' attitude toward this particular constitutional safeguard? The answer, of course, is that they have worked by every stratagem conceivable to demolish it entirely—an enterprise in which they have handily succeeded. Their basic argument has been, quite simply, that the language should be construed as meaningless. This became the accepted view in a 1941 Supreme Court ruling, wherein it was declared that "the amendment states but a truism that all is retained which has not been surrendered," and therefore is not a barrier to the Federal government's taking power wherever it pleases.[2] As Mason observes: "In the face of this unequivocal ruling it could no longer be maintained that the Tenth Amendment reserves to the states any inviolable sovereignty whatsoever."[3]

While this is perhaps the classic instance of the liberal yen to contract protections afforded by the Bill of Rights, it is far from isolated. Consider, for example, the fate of the Fifth Amendment provision (duplicated in the Fourteenth Amendment respecting the states) that no citizen of the United States shall be "deprived of life, liberty, or property, without due process of law." This phraseology has a long history of variant interpretation—some judges reading it to give the maximum scope to individual freedom, others reading it to afford maximum latitude to Federal regulation. The former approach is generally known as "substantive due process" (i.e., limiting incursions by government), the latter as "procedural due process" (i.e., concerning merely the way in which the incursion happens).

It is unnecessary for present purposes to enter into the merits of these opposing views. We need only note that we are here confronted with two basic approaches to a provision of our Bill of Rights—one enlarging the scope of liberty in relation to the Federal government, another diminishing that scope. Were we to take at face value conventional statements about the sanctity of the Bill of Rights, we would naturally assume the liberal view would favor "substantive due process." And we would be entirely wrong.

In actual fact, it was the conservative justices of the Supreme Court such as Van DeVanter and Sutherland who favored "substantive due process" as a method of protecting rights and liberties, and the liberal justices such as Black and Douglas who fought, successfully, against it. The normative liberal view is precisely that the "due process" clause affords little protection if any against the compulsory exercise of power, including the most arbitrary employment of eminent domain, occupational licensure, seizure of property, price fixing, permitting workers to be forced by law to pay homage to labor unions, and other species of regulatory compulsion.*

A further elasticization of the Bill of Rights occurs in discussions of the Second Amendment. It is hardly a secret to anyone who has followed the recent course of political debate that many American liberals are passionately interested in the cause of gun control. One difficulty with this crusade, however, is that the Bill of Rights contains a very explicit provision that guarantees the right of American citizens to keep and bear arms. The Second Amendment asserts that, "a well regulated militia being necessary to the security of a free state, the right of the people to keep and bear arms shall not be infringed." All the various gun control bills that are constantly being proposed and demanded by the liberals would, of course, infringe that right in very short order.†

How can people who claim to defend the Bill of Rights countenance this obvious violation of the Second Amendment? We confront again a necessary distinction. In many cases, of course,

---

* The point is well made by legal authority Carl Brent Swisher, who observes: ". . . in connection with the exercise of both state and federal power, the Supreme Court seems quietly to have devitalized the due process clauses as far as what is known as substantive due process is concerned. That barrier to governmental interference with the rights of property, elusive of definition as it was, had stood squarely in the way of recognition of the changes in the character of private property which the changes in the essential character of our economy were forcing upon us. In the hands of Justice Sutherland and others who accepted his point of view, it was a potent weapon. His successors, regarding it as an over-used weapon for the achievement of undesirable ends, seem to have thrown it into the discard." (*The Growth of Constitutional Power in the United States*, Phoenix Books, 1963, pp. 228–29.)

† And no bones about it: "What paralysis of feeling, what failure of will and understanding allow this kind of human sacrifice to be continued without an effort to prevent it? All of us—Congress and country alike —have sat apathetic and bemused by the perverted logic of the gun lobby about the right to keep and bear arms." (*Washington Post*, October 22, 1965.)

the gun controllers simply ignore the language of the Second Amendment entirely. When called on to notice it, they argue that the phrase "well regulated militia" means the amendment pertains only to groups like the national guard and not to individual citizens (a view accepted by the Supreme Court). Alternatively, they suggest that since a "militia" is no longer an essential part of America's defensive alignment, the guarantee about the right to keep and bear arms is no longer pertinent.

Whatever happened to "strict construction"? The amendment, after all, does not say that "so long as a militia is needed," there *may* be a right to keep and bear arms. It says that right "*shall* not be infringed," period. The language is mandatory, not permissive. And even if one were to suppose that the militia concept and the right to bear arms were an inseparable unit, this still would not justify restrictive gun laws. It would simply mean, by the terms of the amendment, that the American people have a right to bear arms *and* to maintain a militia if such is their wish, and no one has been commissioned to abolish one of these rights by asserting the irrelevance of the other.

Again, however, we need not determine the abstract merits of these arguments concerning gun control and the Second Amendment. The point at issue, rather, is the total dissimilarity between liberal arguments on the Second Amendment rights at stake in this dispute and other rights, such as those guaranteed by portions of the First Amendment. Liberals don't like private ownership of guns; their approach to the Second Amendment, therefore, is one that talks away restraints on government and justifies limits on private behavior. Liberals *do* like certain species of ideological dissent; their approach to the First Amendment, therefore, is one that seeks to impose restraints on government action and abolish limits on private behavior.*

---

* Examples of supposed strict construction that are in fact the opposite might be multiplied still further. One added instance, taken from the legal crusade against capital punishment (see Chapter 20), may be useful. In this dispute liberal legalists have argued that the death penalty is "cruel and unusual punishment," and hence a violation of the Eighth Amendment. Yet it is obvious that the founders who devised the Eighth Amendment did *not* intend to outlaw capital punishment, since the selfsame Bill of Rights containing it specifically sets forth guidelines and

As it happens, it is unnecessary to consider the Second, Fifth, or Tenth Amendments to show the liberal view of the Bill of Rights is not authentically strict-constructionist. The point emerges with reasonable clarity if we confine our discussion to the First Amendment itself. Take, for example, the "right of privacy." There has been a great deal of talk about this right in recent years; Supreme Court decisions in matters of criminal search, contraception, and abortion have turned on it; and numerous liberals have spoken out in its favor. There are countless good things that might be said about the "right of privacy" (although, as we shall see, some bad things too). One thing that emphatically *cannot* be said about the "right of privacy," however, is that it derives from a strict-constructionist reading of the Constitution.

To be sure, specific guarantees in the Constitution do protect certain *aspects* of our privacy—most notably the Fourth Amendment restriction on searches and seizures by agents of the Federal government—and to insist on observance of these safeguards is in fact an exercise in strict construction. But to assert a generalized "right of privacy" in the Constitution and Bill of Rights, and to make this right superior to other constitutional considerations, is the very opposite of strict construction. For no such right is asserted in the Constitution or in the Bill of Rights.

On this account, we have the candid admission of none other than Justice William O. Douglas, who tells us "there is no mention of privacy in our Bill of Rights, but *our decisions have recognized it* as one of the fundamental values those amendments were designed to protect." And again: "There is nothing specific in the Bill of Rights that covers that item. Nor is there anything in the Bill of Rights that in terms protects the right of association or the privacy in one's association. . . . Yet *we found those rights* in the periphery of the First Amendment." [4] (Italics added.)

Now one may conclude if he wishes that Justice Douglas and his brother judges have done a good and noble thing in finding

---

conditions under which the penalty is to be imposed. The Fifth Amendment states that "no person shall be held to answer for a capital or otherwise infamous crime, unless on a presentment or indictment of a grand jury . . . nor be deprived of life, liberty, or property without due process of law."

certain rights in the "periphery" of the First Amendment and seeking to protect them. One may even argue that in doing so they have realized the unavowed intentions of the founders and that if the latter were alive today they would smile their benevolent approval. But what one obviously cannot argue is that the liberal jurists have taken the words of the First Amendment as they come and followed them out in strict-constructionist fashion.

While examples of this type abound, one other may perhaps suffice to make the point—that of government encouragement of religious practices in general, and of prayer in the public schools specifically. As it happens, the words of the First Amendment on this subject are relatively few. The amendment says: "Congress shall make no law respecting an establishment of religion, or prohibiting the free exercise thereof." And while it takes a bit of analysis to determine what the "establishment" clause refers to and what constitutes interference with "free exercise," the language is totally unambiguous in stating the branch of government toward which its strictures are directed: The agency laid under restraint is Congress, simply and unequivocally named.

This clear prohibition against the *Congress* has been used by our liberal jurists to impose restraints on *the states,* to prevent them from authorizing the conduct of nondenominational prayer in the classrooms of the public schools. When we consider that this is an exact reversal of the original intent to prevent Federal interference with state practice, the outcome is especially ironic, but for present purposes it is sufficient to note that a proviso directly aimed at the Federal Congress has been converted into a weapon against the states.* Far from simply taking the words of the amendment as they come, the liberal jurists have been at

* How the liberal jurists arrived at this conclusion is a matter of some interest. In essence, they have argued that the passage of the fourteenth amendment applied the strictures of the Bill of Rights to the several states—and under this interpretation a whole raft of rulings in matters of criminal law, obscenity, and apportionment, as well as prayer, have been handed down imposing various regulatory restrictions on the actions of state governments. The "establishment" clause has in turn been interpreted to mean any and all support of, or official countenance of, religious sentiment, rather than the practice of having an "established" church. From these interpretations it is concluded that the several states

pains to import into these words particular meanings that did not reside there originally, in order to suit their own particular purposes.

It is rather apparent, in fact, that the liberal jurists do not in *any* sense hold an absolutist view of the First Amendment, or of any other part of the Constitution. Their view of the matter is altogether otherwise, and the "preferred position" they profess to extend to certain First Amendment rights rests ultimately on nothing more than their own subjective feeling that it is a *good thing* to have certain kinds of freedom, just as it is not a good thing to have certain others.

This is an attitude that extends back to Mill's original argument in *On Liberty*. His contention was that freedom of speech and expression generally are helpful to society, and that a nation in which these rights were fully exercised was in most cases better off than a nation in which they were not. It was *useful* to have ideas tested in the marketplace, to play one concept off against another, to settle issues by open debate rather than unilateral decree. The justification of free speech and publication, therefore, was not that some absolute criterion of right demanded them, but that from the standpoint of society's general health and vigor they had utilitarian value. Certain liberal writers today present essentially the same argument in more modern dress.*

---

cannot give official countenance to any form of religious sentiment under the First Amendment.

As Justice Felix Frankfurter and others have pointed out at considerable length, the notion that the Fourteenth Amendment incorporates the Bill of Rights and applies it to the states under the stewardship of Federal judges is highly problematical. Once more, however, we need not pursue that particular argument to its limit. We need only note that the liberal interpretation of the First Amendment in the prayer cases (and numerous others) is not remotely strict-constructionist.

* According to liberal Professor Thomas I. Emerson, for example, "maintenance of a system of free expression is necessary (1) as a method of assuring individual self-fulfilment, (2) as a means of attaining the truth, (3) as a method of securing participation by the members of the society in social, including political, decision-making, and (4) as a means of maintaining the balance between stability and change in the society." (*Toward a General Theory of the First Amendment*, Vintage Books, 1967, p. 3.) He goes on to argue at considerable length that the First Amend-

What we are being told is that, as a matter of *social calculation,* freedom of speech is valuable and should therefore be protected. And that is quite different from saying that free speech is a good thing and should be protected *because it is guaranteed to us by the Constitution*—the position liberals appear to be taking on the subject but which, in the light of their general view of constitutional issues, they could not in fact adopt with any semblance of consistency.

This point is of the utmost importance in any consideration of constitutional rights, since it marks the difference between a revocable guarantee and a certain one. If we enjoy a freedom because it is assured us by the Bill of Rights, then we shall enjoy it in season and out, not subject to anybody's discretion. But if we enjoy it because someone in authority finds it socially useful for us to do so, then the guarantee is secure *only* as long as that someone doesn't change his mind or isn't replaced by somebody else with a different opinion in the matter.

This latter point is illustrated by a number of more conservative spokesmen who believe that freedom of speech, press, and assembly *should* be limited by majority sentiment. These theoreticians have argued that the guarantees of the First Amendment must be subject to some constraint—and the battling of such spokesmen with various liberals has served to reinforce the notion that the latter are authentic civil libertarians. But if we examine the question carefully it appears the debate is one between two different factions that have, down deep, a similar view of the way in which our Constitution ought to be construed.

Thus if we peruse the writings of the late Willmoore Kendall, a respected conservative political scientist, we discover arguments about the First Amendment almost identical to those of the liberals on constitutional questions generally. Kendall told us, for example, that conditions have changed, that the founders could not have envisioned the challenges we face today, and that the guarantees of the First Amendment must be construed against an expansive reading of the "necessary and proper" clause. This conservative, in short, simply took the general liberal rule of

---

ment should be construed in an expansive fashion because it has a good effect on our society. He does *not* argue that it should be construed in this fashion simply because it *is* the First Amendment.

constitutional construction and applied it directly to the First Amendment.[5]

Even with respect to the First Amendment itself, this species of argument affirms the liberal premises—although it reaches different conclusions. Conservatives of this school in general accept the view that the proper test of First Amendment rights is whether they are socially useful; they simply differ with the liberals in their reading of the relevant utilities—concluding that, on balance, free speech *isn't* all that useful, that in certain cases it is positively harmful. Thus, there is no barrier whatever to having it done away with. All of which, on the liberals' own beginning premises, is perfectly consistent.

Wallace Mendelson of the University of Texas makes the same point in slightly different fashion. Using arguments that liberals apply to the rest of the Constitution, Mendelson suggests that the meaning of the First Amendment is indefinite, and that it must be invested with new meaning for the times on a case by case basis —in other words, a "living first Amendment." To clinch the case, he makes an analogy directly to the New Deal cases. "Surely," he says, "a judicial veto of anti-Communist legislation limits the range of popular choice just as effectively as a judicial veto of minimum wage legislation. Both say to the people these are choices you may not make." [6]

There is no effective liberal answer to this argument, except to assert that the First Amendment is more important than the other constitutional provisions and therefore should not be set aside so easily. But this is merely to restate the position under attack, rather than rebut the attack itself. And it is not, of course, a *constitutional* standard at all, but a matter of philosophical preference. So Professor Mendelson wins the constitutional argument hands down—*if* the original liberal premise be accepted.*

Freedom—at the Discretion of the Powerful

In contests of this sort it becomes apparent that what is being debated is not a matter of constitutional interpretation, or the

---

* A typical liberal "explanation" of this discrepancy is the following: ". . . judicial review may be less a check upon democracy than would a violation of the commerce clause; with the result that judicial review

legitimate scope of government power, or even the rule of law in general. The common assumption that government should do whatever the majority wants has settled all such questions at the outset. The only issue remaining is *who* will make the determination as to what the majority really wants, or needs. If liberals have the power, then X will be permitted but Y suppressed; but if certain conservatives have the power, then Y will be allowed and X suppressed. The same politico-economic machinery will simply be put to work for different purposes. In a sense that was what occurred when the Nixon administration came into office and started applying loose construction to such things as wiretapping, suppression of leaks, and shutting down domestic disorder.

This is the natural result of any doctrine that says government officials are entitled to pick and choose among our constitutional guarantees. That doctrine asserts quite plainly that all our freedoms should depend, not on the known rule of the Constitution, but on the discretion of those with power. And until we know the identity of those who rule and what their pleasure is, we have no assurance whatever as to the nature of our rights and privileges. Which is the very opposite of what we mean by the rule of law— is, indeed, according to Madison, the very definition of arbitrary and tyrannical government.*

---

in protection of a First Amendment freedom, or any provision of the Bill of Rights, may be counter majoritarian, but not undemocratic." (Leonard Levy, *Judicial Review and the Supreme Court,* Harper Torchbooks, 1967, p. 17.) Has everybody got that?

* A single standard on judicial review vs. majority opinion has been proposed by a number of learned scholars and jurists. Herbert Wechsler of Columbia and Robert McCloskey and Paul Freund, both of Harvard, have questioned the double standard on such matters, as have such judges as the late Learned Hand. Supreme Court Justices Robert Jackson and Felix Frankfurter both favored a single standard approach—suggesting judicial quiescence in civil liberties as well as in matters of property right. The proper single standard from a libertarian perspective, of course, would be to *protect* both kinds of freedom, rather than subject both to a common indifference.

McCloskey notes the illogic of trying to tuck the First Amendment into a "majoritarian" stance on the grounds that one thereby protects a potential future majority. If this is the justification, McCloskey wonders, does it extend to minorities that manifestly have no chance of becoming a majority (e.g., the Flat Earth Society)? If the purpose is

The interchangeability of the power components in our political system and the divergent uses to which they may be put will be examined in the next chapter. Here let us conclude by noting that this phenomenon contributes strongly to the impassioned and intensely personal character of contemporary politics. For if it is assumed that the Federal government is to deploy an enormous power over everything in our society, limited only by the discretion of the people wielding that power, then it becomes a matter of desperate concern to ensure that one's own faction has the power and that one's enemies never, ever get their hands on it. This perhaps accounts for much of the bitter intolerance that liberals display toward political contenders of the right. It is good and proper for John F. Kennedy to have all that power, but awful for Nixon to have it. By their own doctrine and practice, the liberals have turned the struggle for political supremacy into an apocalyptic battle where literally every freedom and every social value is at hazard.

---

simply to keep a pathway open for future majorities, why extend the privilege to those who don't possess the requisite potential? The logical answer to this very sensible question, of course, would be to confer rights of dissent on strong minorities but not on weak ones.

This is the very opposite of what the civil liberties types are up to. They would contend that weak minorities should be protected just as zealously as strong minorities, if not more so. That contention seems perfectly correct, but it also makes intellectual mincemeat of the notion that what is being done has anything to do with majoritarianism. It is, quite clearly, the *opposite* of majoritarianism—which means it is the opposite of what the selfsame liberals were telling us back in the days of the bad old conservative court.

18

How to Silence Dissent

Examples of the manner in which the machinery of economic control has impinged on our personal freedoms might be cited at considerable length. There are numerous cases in the record book of farmers who have lost their land for refusal to abide by Federal regulations, workers forced into labor unions as a condition of employment, businessmen subject to bureaucratic harassment. It would be possible to marshal countless horror stories of abuse through OSHA, the FDA, the CAB, the NLRB, the Labor Department, HEW, the EEOC, the FTC, the environmental agencies, the consumer agencies, and so on.

Yet all these matters, in one fashion or another, involve infringement of *property* rights, which as we have seen are not so highly esteemed by liberal planners. Such practices, supposedly, are the unavoidable by-product of the top-down planning required to keep our economy running. Although in fact the planning doesn't work, and the rights involved are of the first importance, this refusal to offer battle makes it hard to land on common arguing ground. The liberal spokesmen have simply consigned these

279

280

rights and privileges to secondary status, and have nothing further to say on the subject.

Rather than dwell on such matters, therefore, let us turn our attention to that zone of personal freedom that, according to the liberal scenario, is to be kept immune from government intrusion —those "preferred" rights of personal and political expression protected by the First Amendment and alleged to be a special object of liberal solicitude. If we focus in on these rights for a moment, we may discover the degree to which they are *really* protected in the liberal scheme of things.

To begin with, there is an obvious contradiction in the view examined in the preceding chapters. It is a logical and practical impossibility to construct a system of controls whereby government has total authority over the material elements of life but is somehow prevented from interfering with rights of expression. The planners may vehemently state their intention of avoiding the latter consequence, and doubtless mean it. They may even bend over backward in the interpretation of their powers to give considerable latitude to dissent. But the fact remains the job cannot be done. For any government that can control the material elements of life can control everything about us—including what we say and write, our movements in society, where we live and worship.

Hamilton's previously noted statement that "a power over a man's subsistence is a power over his will," puts the argument in a nutshell.[1] He who can deny me the wherewithal of life can deny me life itself. And if he can deny me life, then *a fortiori* he has the leverage with which to deny me the right of expression. That is the stark reality of concentrated economic power. And the subsidiary controls the economic regulators have fastened on at every juncture of our society give ample pressure points by which that leverage may be brought to bear.

Control of the Mass Media

The manner in which economic controls can lead on to control of political expression is demonstrated in the case of our mass communications media—which liberal spokesmen profess to defend from every sort of government intrusion. As a journalist, I have always found it astonishing that so many of my colleagues are eager to slap the stiffest possible regulations on that anonymous malefactor, "business," and yet speak out so zealously against controls upon the communications media. For every medium of mass communications in this country *is* a business, and controls that affect the economic aspect of our lives impinge upon communications as well.

Indeed, the closest this nation has come to seeing a wholesale shutdown of its newspapers occurred in the fall and winter of 1973 when labor troubles in Canada threatened to close off the supply of newsprint to a substantial number of dailies. The lesson of this episode was fairly obvious: Anyone who can control the supply of newsprint can also, if he wills, control the press. The same applies to anyone who can control access to presses, ink, transportation facilities, or the work force that puts a newspaper out.* Control any *one* of these things—much less the whole shebang— and you have in your hands the power to control America's newspapers.

The effect of such economic power is seen most readily, perhaps, in the electronic media. Here the Federal government has a stranglehold on the basic economic resource—the broadcasting frequency. Nobody can legally operate a commercial radio or TV station in this country unless he is granted a frequency and license by the Federal Communications Commission (FCC). And by law this license must be renewed by the government every three years. The equivalent arrangement in the newspaper field would be a situation in which the government owned all the presses in the nation and granted newspapers leases to use them, continually subject to renewal or cancellation.

That set-up in itself is sufficiently inhibiting to account for the incredible blandness of a great deal of television programming,

---

* It is likely more American newspapers have been shut down by labor union troubles than by any other single cause. In the past decade alone, New York City has lost four daily newspapers, principally as a result of strikes (the *Mirror*, the *Herald-Tribune*, the *World-Telegram*, and the *Journal-American*).

particularly in controversial areas by local licensees. If you have ever wondered about the general ineffectuality of television reporting of or editorializing on hotly disputed items by your local TV station, or why its stands on public issues are so often on-the-one-hand-this-and-on-the-other-hand-that, try to put yourself in the place of the owner or manager of that station.

Here he is holding a property worth hundreds of thousands of dollars, into which he has in all likelihood ploughed many thousands more—all held at the pleasure of government. He knows licenses are renewed except in unusual circumstances, and if he runs a businesslike ship and doesn't stir up a lot of fuss and feathers he should be able to get a renewal himself. But he also knows any citizen or group of citizens can challenge the renewal if they take a mind to, and just possibly put his property, investment, and livelihood in danger.

Under the circumstances, the station owner has every motive in the world *not* to make anybody mad at him, which he is certain to do if he throws the resources of his station into controversial issues. His safest course, therefore, is to avoid excessive controversy, be nice to everybody, and strive for the lowest common denominator of public opinion. Under the same set of circumstances what, exactly, would *you* do?

Right off the bat, therefore, it is obvious that economic control of media resources exerts a prior restraint on expression. But there is more. Beyond this generic inhibition, the Federal government has superadded still other controls, not only through the FCC but also through the Federal Trade Commission (FTC), which has as one of its appointed tasks the regulation of advertising that appears on radio and television. In typical fashion, these controls are said to be principally or even solely economic, but their effect on political expression has been profound.

A major source of difficulty for broadcasters—and for all Americans interested in free discussion—is a policy ruling of the FCC handed down in 1949 and occasionally refurbished since. This policy is known as the "fairness doctrine." Under its strictures, licensees are supposed to provide substantially balanced treatment of controversial issues, and they can lose their licenses if they don't. Here is the way the FCC explains the matter:

> . . . the fairness doctrine, embodied in section 315(a)
> of the Communications Act . . . imposes on all licensees
> the obligation to afford a reasonable opportunity for the pres-
> entation of contrasting viewpoints on any controversial issue
> of public importance which he chooses to cover. In discharg-
> ing this obligation, the licensee must play a "conscious and
> positive role"—that is, he must seek affirmatively to encour-
> age and implement the presentation of contrasting view-
> points. . . . Under the fairness doctrine, while a licensee
> may, of course, editorialize or in other ways present program-
> ming reflecting his own point of view, he cannot then block
> the presentation of contrasting viewpoints.[2]

This perhaps sounds very well, but it has had appalling implications for free expression—by the broadcasters themselves and
by others who have tried to gain access to the airwaves. For one
thing, the FCC has pursued this doctrine and other parts of its
regulatory mission in a curiously selective manner, showing a
particular partiality for regulation of conservative broadcasters.
Its general (though not exclusive) history on such questions has
been one of harassing conservative spokesmen, denying license
renewals to conservative stations, and ordering free time for various liberal interest groups to answer statements by their conservative opponents.

For instance, the FCC has subjected broadcasters such as
Dean Clarence Manion and the Rev. Carl McIntire, both spokesmen for the political right, to stringent "balancing" requirements
—which has had the effect in numerous cases of causing stations
to drop their programs. The nature of the problem is suggested
by the following letter to McIntire, from a station owner under
"fairness" pressure from the FCC:

> The tremendous additional work of pre-listening, dub-
> bing copies for persons attacked, and the correspondence
> involved with the present implementation of the "fairness
> doctrine" by the FCC may force us to discontinue many of
> our pro-American, conservative programs. It would take ad-
> ditional time for your office to make a transcript and dis-
> tribute it to each station carrying your broadcast. However,

without the extra effort on your part, the stations will *each* have to do the same work—or give up your broadcast.[3]

For many station owners, obviously, it is cheaper to get rid of the program that carries with it all this grief—plus the ever-present possibility of having to air *another* program in response and thus provide two political broadcasts for the price of one. This situation would be bad enough if the sanctions were applied impartially, but there is copious evidence that they have been deployed along a fault-line of ideological bias. It is noteworthy, for example, that while denial of license renewals on grounds of "balance" is relatively rare, the most prominent cases have all involved right-of-center stations.

One of these was McIntire's radio station WXUR in Pennsylvania, which was taken away from him upon petition from various liberal interest groups, including the Council of Churches, the UAW, the Civil Liberties Union, and the Urban League. A second instance was that of television station WLBT in Jackson, Mississippi, stripped of its license because of allegedly unfair handling of racial news in that city. These were both "fairness doctrine" cases. A third instance, that of WHDH-TV in Boston, although not based directly on the fairness doctrine, is in some ways even more bizarre.

The case of WHDH suggests not only the impact of economics on expression, but also the manner in which the Federal regulators curtail our freedom even while professing to expand it. The charge against this station was not that it had failed to live up to its obligations, or that there was anything in particular wrong with its operations. Its problem was simply that it was owned by a parent company which also owned the *Boston Herald-Traveller,* a right-of-center newspaper. The FCC removed the license on the grounds that this would encourage greater "diversity of opinion" in Boston. The immediate effect was that the *Herald-Traveller,* one of the few voices of conservative opinion in the Boston area, was stripped of needed television revenue and promptly went out of business.

It is not alleged that the FCC conducted this divestiture with the intent of killing off the *Herald-Traveller,* or that the commission members who approved the switch in ownership had any malign intent at all. We may assume, for purposes of argument, that the regulators thought they actually were going to increase the interplay of free opinion in Boston. That they succeeded in doing just the opposite is further testimony, perhaps, to the ineffectuality of Federal regulation as a method of achieving desirable social goals. It is also testimony, of course, to the power of economic control to stifle the communications media to the point of suffocation.

Not content with applying "fairness doctrine" requirements to the program offerings of the stations, the FCC has been heavily involved in promoting application of these restraints to commercial advertising. The regulatory fever has given rise to something called the "anti-commercial," in which groups who don't like the message of a commercial advertiser obtain free time in which to blast the product promoted or ideas expressed in the original commercial. The result has been a mare's nest of confusion, and a further inhibition of the rights of free discussion.

This particular snafu got started with cigarette commercials, which the FCC decided should be answered free of charge by *anti*-cigarette commercials. This proved so successful a tactic that other interest groups began to file their own demands for rebuttal time. In one such case, the Court of Appeals in Washington decided advertisers who promoted the sale of large automobiles should be answered (again for free) by people who didn't like large automobiles. Then the same court determined that an advertisement promoting completion of the Alaska pipeline should be answered by material that opposed the pipeline. All of which has sent tremors of horror through the networks—and has led directly to the stifling of political viewpoints on the nation's airwaves.

The clearest example of suppression resulting from this regulatory pressure occurred in early 1974 in the battle for public opinion generated by the energy crisis. This was a period in which numerous television news and documentary shows were socking it to the oil companies for allegedly causing the nation's shortage of petroleum. For those accustomed to the liberal tilt of national television, this one-sided commentary was not astonishing. It came as something of a shock, however, to learn that the petroleum companies could not even *buy* commercial advertising time with which to tell their side of the story.

Oh, the companies got commercial time, all right—we all saw the rather bland institutional ads they ran about the need for discovering more petroleum. But what we didn't see were the commercials the companies attempted to place setting forth the facts about their profits and capital needs, and the importance of offshore drilling. These the networks, in numerous cases, would not accept.

Exhibit A in this respect was ABC-TV's refusal to run a Mobil Oil company commercial in which a scuba diver talked about petroleum costs and profits and drilling requirements. According to the *Wall Street Journal,* the network explained the commercial was an effort "to evoke public sympathy for oil company financial practices which are under congressional investigation." [4] Hence the ad was excessively controversial. *Not* too controversial, however, was an ABC documentary called "Oil: The Policy Crisis" that zapped the oil companies and that Mobil for one protested as a flagrant misrepresentation. So TV "news" programs that socked it to the companies were acceptable; but paid commercials in which the companies defended themselves were verboten.*

The culprit in all this is not really the networks, but our old friend the "fairness doctrine." The electronic media are so swaddled in "fairness" they are in many cases terrified of controversy. Since licensees might have to make free time available to answer disputed commercials, and since there are many leftward groups just waiting to pounce on the oil companies, any sale of disputed commercials could thus turn out to be a package deal—two ads for the price of one. Hence the general rule: No controversial advertising.

For those who think it proper that the oil companies not be allowed to tell their side of things, it is worth remembering that this sword of regulatory power cuts both ways. While victims of this policy to date have generally been on the conservative or business side of things, the general inhibition against controversy

* The result of this blockage was that the companies sought to make their case chiefly through newspaper ads—where there is still, thank goodness, a bit of freedom left for diversity of expression. The pencil press is not subject to such regulation, although, as we shall see, there are some eager souls at work to change that for the worse. The importance of the distinction is becoming ever more obvious.

has affected nonconservative groups as well. Thus anti–Vietnam war ads were turned down by CBS, and the networks have imposed a general freeze on controversial advertising of all types (for example, all the networks refused a commercial for air bags in automobiles desired by Allstate insurance). So the networks' policy of refusing controversial commercials has clearly been induced by regulatory pressure, rather than by network bias, and it affects the left as well as the right.

The FCC's actions are bad enough, but to make the situation worse the bureaucrats at the Federal Trade Commission have also gotten into the act. Among its other duties, the FTC is empowered to police the "truthfulness" of commercial advertising on television, and it has not hesitated to use this power with vigor and enthusiasm. In 1971, for example, the agency charged that a TV commercial for Zerex anti-freeze falsely claimed its products would stop radiator leaks. After having made this statement, and undoubtedly having hurt the sales of the company, the FTC admitted the commercials were not deceptive after all.

In another case, the commission said the manufacturers of Wonder Bread made claims for their product that were concededly true but that did not point out that the attributes touted also applied to certain other varieties of bread. The lesson appeared to be that Wonder Bread should have devoted at least part of its commercial time to promoting competitors' products. Since the point of advertising Wonder Bread is to sell Wonder Bread and not some other brand, a stringent application of this peculiar logic would result in nobody running any commercials at all.

Some other proposals in this regulatory vein sound like George Orwell's *1984*. Former FCC commissioner Nicholas Johnson, for one, has suggested the media incur "legal liability" for alleged harmful effects of commercials and programs they air. "To state the extreme case," he says, "suppose a psychiatrist would testify that a child's mental illness was directly traceable to a particular show watched regularly. And suppose, further, that numerous other children were affected in this way—and that the network knew the program would produce that result? Is legal liability out of the question?" [5] The inhibiting effect of such a doctrine on broadcasters and advertisers should be apparent.

Again, for those who don't like commercials, this may seem

fine, but the effect is demonstrably harmful to the communications industry. When commercials are driven from the air or advertisers browbeaten into withdrawing ads, the public is doubly damaged. Advertising permits lower competitive pricing of products through mass merchandising, easy comparisons, and reduced search costs for buyers, so the anti-commercial drive in the first instance will mean higher consumer prices. And since commercials and advertising are the economic lifeblood of the communications industry, this drive also weakens the media and threatens to close down vital communications outlets. Thus economic regulation can, and does, have multiple impact on freedom of expression.

As a footnote to this subject, it is worth asking how television broadcasting might be financed in the absence of commercial advertising. One option, and potentially a good one, is through pay TV, transmitted over the cable. If this system were allowed to develop, there would quite possibly be much greater diversity of television fare, with less dependence on commercials. Why, then, don't we have it? The answer is that *this* option, too, has been forestalled by government regulation. True to form as a regulatory agency, the FCC has sought to freeze the existing set-up in place; in 1966 it decreed that cable TV was to be blocked out of the 100 largest markets in the United States.*

So while the government has slowed the development of an alternative TV system, it has moved to swaddle the system we do have in ever-tighter controls. The combined effect of these two tendencies, if we project them far enough, will be to ensure that there is only one source of financing and support for television—the government itself. Indeed, a government-run or at least a government-controlled system is the explicit demand of many so-called reformers in this area—a demand that would guarantee a minimum of free expression in the electronic media.

---

* This decision was questionable on a number of counts, notable among them the fact that there is no good reason for the FCC to regulate cable television at all. The rationale for regulating radio and TV is that somebody needs to divide up the frequencies to prevent jamming. Since cable TV does not operate through the atmosphere, this housekeeping chore becomes entirely irrelevant. Undaunted, the FCC staked out its jurisdiction in the matter anyway, and used its regulatory power to impede development of a system competitive with the existing arrangement.

Nor are the regulators content to stop with radio and television. Though they have run into some sizable and one may hope impenetrable roadblocks, the regulatory types have been casting an acquisitive eye on newspapers, too. A few years back FCC commissioner Kenneth Cox proposed that "fairness doctrine" restraints be applied to newspapers, on the all-encompassing grounds that they are items in interstate commerce. Former commissioner Johnson wanted a "public right of access to the mass media"—aimed mainly at television but also hinting at inclusion of newspapers.[6] Similar proposals have issued from selected congressmen, presidential commissioners, and state legislators.

In 1974 this particular issue came to a head when the Supreme Court reviewed a state legislative effort to apply "balancing" requirements to print media. A political candidate in Florida had brought an action against the *Miami Herald* under that state's "right of reply" law, which said that an aspirant for public office attacked by a newspaper was entitled to space for an answer. The court ruled against the Florida law, declaring that "the choice of material to go into a newspaper, and the decision made as to limitation on the size of the paper, and content, and treatment of public issues and public officials—whether fair or unfair—constitute the exercise of editorial control and judgment."[7]

Not unnaturally, the nation's newspaper editors greeted this verdict with enthusiasm, and certainly the logic of the court in assessing the effects of print media regulation conforms to the argument being made in this chapter. Yet it is disturbing to reflect that the same kind of control prevented here in the state of Florida by Federal authority is being exercised on a daily basis by the Federal government itself with respect to radio and television. If the state of Florida's law was in violation of the First Amendment, what can we say about the Federal government's own continued interference, on exactly the same basis, with the broadcast freedom of *all* the nation's television and radio stations?

Control of Political Expression

The Watergate scandal illustrated in a general way the dangers of having excessive power concentrated in the government, and especially in the executive branch. It also illustrated the manner in which this power may be used to silence dissent in the political arena, again through economic controls. One fact revealed in the hearings of the House Judiciary Committee, for example, was that Nixon officials had discussed using · the Internal Revenue Service as a means of exerting political leverage on political adversaries, including the brother of Alabama governor George Wallace and Democratic national chairman Lawrence O'Brien.

Senator Lowell Weicker, the maverick Republican from Connecticut, provided a more comprehensive view of such activities in the fall of 1973. Weicker announced he had uncovered a series of memos written by White House staffers concerning ways and means of getting more favorable treatment in the media. Most provocative of these missives was an *aide-mémoire* from former presidential assistant Jeb Magruder, which according to Weicker suggested the power of the government be mobilized against unfriendly commentators in the media.

Among the points in Magruder's memo were proposals that the Nixon regime:

> Begin an official monitoring system through the FCC as soon as Dean Burch is officially on the board as chairman. If the monitoring system proves our point, we have then legitimate and legal rights to go to the networks, etc., and make official complaints from the FCC. . . .
>
> Utilize the antitrust division [of the Justice Department] to investigate various media relating to antitrust violations. Even the possible threat of antitrust action I think would be effective in changing their views. . . .
>
> Utilize the Internal Revenue Service as a method to look into the various organizations that we are most concerned about. Just a threat of an IRS investigation will probably turn their approach.[8]

It is not clear how seriously this memo was received or whether the actions suggested were actually taken. The IRS discussions, on slightly different grounds, we know about. At one point the FCC did nibble a bit at the networks, and an antitrust suit was filed in April 1972 concerning the networks' practice of producing their own entertainment programs. Much of the administration's thrust against the media was rhetorical battle against bias, and by 1973, of course, the administration was far too busy backpedaling to mount much of an offensive against anybody.

Whatever the score on that account, the lesson of the Magruder memo is fairly obvious: Here was a member of the governmental establishment who disliked what was being said about the administration, and who urged deployment of Federal power to intimidate its critics. And there is little doubt, when one examines the actions suggested, that plenty of power is there to get the job done.

This is not, as it happens, the first time such a proposal has come to light. Back in 1961, Victor Reuther of the United Auto Workers addressed an even tougher memorandum to then Attorney General Robert Kennedy, urging the use of Federal resources to head off and dry up conservative critics of the administration. The Reuther memorandum is similar in specific proposals, general tone, and intended effect to the document unearthed by Weicker.

The Reuther memo started off by noting that President John Kennedy had recently delivered some speeches attacking "the radical right," but observed that speeches would not do much good unless accompanied by governmental action. It named a host of right-wing organizations and individuals as its targets, including the John Birch Society, Dr. Fred Schwarz's Christian Anti-Communism Crusade, anti-Communist generals and admirals, the William Volker Fund, Barry Goldwater, Strom Thurmond, and Billy James Hargis.

Concerning such people, the memo stated: "What are needed are deliberate administration policies and programs to contain the radical right from further expansion and in the long run to reduce it to its historic role of the impotent lunatic fringe. . . . they must never be permitted to become so strong as to obstruct action needed for democratic survival and success." To this end, the memo suggested a series of punitive actions against the rightwingers, including having them put on the attorney general's list of subversive organizations.

"There would . . . appear to be adequate grounds for holding a hearing on one or more of these organizations to determine whether they should be listed," it said. "The mere act of indicating that an investigation will be made will certainly bring home to many people something they have never considered—the subversive character of these organizations and their similarity to the listed groups on the left" (that is, Communist and Communist-front organizations).

Reuther went on to assert that "the flow of big money to the radical right should be dammed to the extent possible." The memo noted that Dr. George Benson's National Education Program, the Christian Anti-Communism Crusade, Hargis, and the William Volker Fund enjoyed tax exemptions, and said they should be deprived of that status. "Prompt revocation in a few cases," it said, "might scare off a substantial part of the big money now flowing into these tax exempt organizations."

Of particular concern to Reuther was the appearance of conservative groups in the broadcast media; the memo suggested the IRS look into the practice of business sponsorship for their programs. Reuther felt there were sufficient data to justify "the most complete check on these various means of financing the radical right." He added that there was also "the big question whether Schwarz, Hargis, etc., are themselves complying with the tax laws."

Broadcasting was treated again in a passage concerning the Federal Communications Commission. Noting that right-wing radio programs were lambasting President Kennedy and his policies, the memo suggested the FCC "might consider examining into the extent of the practice of giving free time to the radical right and could take measures to encourage stations to assign comparable time for an opposing point of view on a free basis." [9]

Again it is not altogether clear how these advices were received, although certain steps occurred in keeping with the Reuther recommendations. From 1963 on, as was noted above, the FCC began aggressively enforcing the "fairness doctrine" against conservative broadcasters such as Manion and eventually yanked that radio license from Dr. McIntire. On the IRS front, an effort was also made to put the heat on right wing groups. In May of 1963, Senator Maureen Neuberger (D-Ore.) addressed the AFL-CIO's Committee on Political Education (COPE) on the need to yank tax exemptions from any and all conservative organizations, including the most scholarly outfits imaginable. "It is painfully clear," she said, "that the tax service has simply not done the job

Congress gave it, to rout out the propagandists from the *bona fide* educators." Mrs. Neuberger's blast was part of a general effort spearheaded by COPE to indict conservatives for "political activity" in the guise of "education" (a curious charge considering the fact that COPE's own educational effort consists of pouring millions of dollars into political campaigns).*

The point of these reflections is not simply to suggest the hypocrisy of people horrified by such proposals under Nixon but indifferent to their counterparts under Kennedy—although, again, the hypocrisy is obviously there. It is rather that the urge to muzzle one's critics is fairly common in human nature, and that the existing machinery of Federal economic and political power is provably sufficient under appropriate circumstances to get the job done.

Indeed, what is especially striking about the two memoranda is that neither suggests the creation of *new* Federal powers as a means of discouraging dissent, or even considers that such an action is necessary. Both are content to rely on the existing panoply of Federal might to accomplish the desired objectives and simply urge that it be brought into play against political dissenters.

Also notable is the fact that both memoranda rely so heavily on economic controls. With the exception of Reuther's proposal that conservative groups be put on the attorney general's list, the sanctions are drawn from the realm of "property rights": action against sponsors, pressures from the IRS, use of the FCC, antitrust actions—all striking at the economic base from which the hostile commentators conducted their operations.

The lesson is an important one. A power over a man's subsistence is, indeed, a power over his will, and a government that can control the materials of economic life can therefore control the means of expression. The Magruder and Reuther memoranda between them clearly suggest the present level of government controls in our society is quite as hostile to political freedoms as it is to freedom of the marketplace.

---

* In terms of action, tax exempt status was removed from Billy James Hargis' Christian Crusade.

19
Freedom
and
Foreign Policy

To this point we have examined cases in which the exercise of political power exceeds the legitimate scope of government according to American constitutional principles. We have seen that, far from being necessary to correct the wrongs of our society and keep our economy perking, this extension of authority has all too often done the reverse. And we have seen as well that this excess of power violates the second key assurance provided by its sponsors—that it is somehow possible to heap up so much authority, break down the old restraints, and yet maintain our freedoms.

Findings of this sort are sufficiently grave to suggest that something is amiss in the liberal approach to public issues and start us casting about for an alternative. Unhappily, however, this is not the whole of the story. For it develops that beyond the enormous damage done to our society by the urge to pile up power in areas where freedom should be the rule, liberalism has displayed a countervailing yen to forego those functions of government that are not only legitimate but essential to the cause of liberty.

Government established on its proper foundation, as we have

seen, *is* supposed to perform a number of tasks, having chiefly to do with neutralizing the aggressive use of force. Foremost among these are provision of the national defense and suppression of internal crime. Both these functions are necessary in a *libertarian* sense, for if they are defaulted then the citizen is subjected to the incursions of foreign enemies or the reign of criminal violence. On the reasonings of the most eminent libertarian philosophers, these particular government duties must be performed consistently and well.*

It is therefore curious to observe—or maybe not so curious— that it is precisely on issues of this type that American liberalism has chosen to manifest its most active concern for civil liberties, and attempted to prevent the vigorous exercise of public author- ity. While voicing indifference to individual freedom in matters of everyday pursuit by peaceful farmers, workers, and businessmen, liberal spokesmen become impressively energized when the liber- ties up for discussion are those of criminals, purveyors of revolu- tion, or agents of a hostile foreign power. It is almost as if, having assigned to government all those powers that on libertarian prin- ciples it shouldn't have, the liberals have decided to divest it of all those powers it should.

The nature of this problem is most plainly illustrated, perhaps, in the conduct of our defense and foreign policies. Quite clearly, foreign defense is the first and pre-eminent function of our govern- ment, or almost any other. Unless this basic task is handled prop- erly, the rest of our discussion becomes a bit irrelevant. Debate about domestic issues will make very little difference if, in the extreme case, we are subjugated by a foreign enemy who can

---

* There is a species of anarcho-libertarian thought which contends that even these functions should be privatized—performed by independent contractors. Some such arrangements do exist, of course (private police and security forces), and there have been periods in which they were a principal form of social organization (feudalism being the most promi- nent example). It is worth noting, however, that nearly all forms of libertarian thought, including this one, stress that aggressive force must be neutralized if there is to be a regime of personal liberty. The *functions* in question, that is, must be performed by some agency if personal free- dom is to survive.

impose his view of all these questions on us willy-nilly, irrespective of our wishes.

As good logicians and practical statesmen, America's founders saw the matter in exactly this light. In their view, the principal object of our government in its foreign dealings, and its first object anywhere, was to protect the legitimate interests of the American people. It was in the area of national defense that they were most desirous, in contrast to their usual anxieties, to ensure that there was power *enough* for full and energetic performance. There had to be adequate provision for an army and navy; the President as commander in chief had to have sufficient authority to deploy these forces when required; and the national government had to have assurance that it could muster revenues to pay the bills. The Confederation, as the founders saw it, was woefully weak in all these departments.

The nature of the problem was stated with considerable candor in the *Federalist,* No. 15. "We may with propriety," wrote Hamilton, "be said to have reached the last stage of national humiliation. There is scarcely anything that can wound the pride or degrade the character of an independent nation which we do not experience. . . . Are we in a conditon to resent or repel [an] aggression? We have neither troops, nor treasury, nor government. Are we even in a position to remonstrate with dignity? . . . Is respectability in the eyes of foreign powers a safeguard against foreign encroachments? The imbecility of our government even forbids them to treat with us. Our ambassadors abroad are the mere pageants of mimic sovereignty." [1]

In the constitutional convention, according to Madison's *Notes,* Roger Sherman of Connecticut had spelled out the goals of the embryonic Federal government. "The objects of the Union, he thought, were few: 1. defense against foreign danger. 2. against internal disputes and resort to force. 3. treaties with foreign nations. 4. regulating foreign commerce and drawing revenues from it. These and perhaps a few lesser objects alone rendered a confederation of the states necessary." [2] Quite similar, again, to the view expounded in the *Federalist:* "The principal purposes to be answered by the union are the common defence of the members; the preservation of the public peace, as well against internal convulsions as external attacks; the regulation of commerce with other nations and between the states; the superintendence of our intercourse, political and commercial, with foreign countries." [3]

As Jefferson said and Lord Bryce reiterated, the major purpose of the Federal government as originally conceived was to function as the foreign office to the nation, with domestic matters left, essentially, to the states. It was for purposes of foreign security, above all else, that the new government was brought into being, and invested with powers greater than those enjoyed by the Confederation. So it is no hyperbole to suggest that, if our Federal government has any reason for being, it is precisely to perform the functions of national defense.

Liberal Foreign Policy: Supranationalism

Against this backdrop, it is possible to identify the anti-libertarian consequences of the liberal foreign policy outlook with some precision. The characteristic features of this outlook are well known, since they have been the dominant themes of American foreign policy for the past generation. The liberal view, most typically, is "internationalist," interventionist, and given to environmentalist panaceas. It has placed great emphasis on such ideas as "making the world safe for democracy," "reform" of allied governments, deployment of economic aid, support for supranational agencies, and—where the Soviet Union and other Communist powers are concerned—the virtues of negotiation, trade, disarmament, and détente.

Especially notable in the liberal foreign policy view is its persistent effort to submerge American sovereignty beneath the waves of internationalism. This has been manifest in numerous ways—Woodrow Wilson's devotion to the League of Nations, Roosevelt's enthusiasm for the United Nations, liberal commitment to the U.N. since then, the "one world" syndrome in general. This program follows from the liberal mind set, which is inclined toward leveling out distinctions and homogenizing people generally, and which, other things being equal, will prefer the larger unit of government to the smaller. Liberals tend to prefer the U.N. and its agencies to the merely "national" doings of the American government, on essentially the same principles that cause them to prefer the Federal government to the states.*

All these motives and some others of a psychological character that would lead us far afield from the present discussion make liberals deeply hostile to the idea of "nationalism," most particularly American nationalism. The *locus classicus* on this subject is Walt W. Rostow's candid statement that "it is a legitimate American national objective to see removed from all nations—including the United States—the right to use substantial military force to pursue their own interests. Since this residual right is the root of national sovereignty and the basis for an existence of an international arena of power, it is, therefore, an American interest to see an end to nationhood as it has historically been defined." [4]

Intertwined with all these supranational yearnings is the liberal stress on environmentalism, which plays as crucial a role in foreign policy matters as it does in issues of political economy. The liberal wishes to set the world aright, and believes that such of its troubles as cannot be traced to nationalism are owing to economic deprivation. Principal stress is therefore laid on material measures as the basic instruments of foreign policy, especially foreign economic aid. By extension of such aid, Americans simultaneously share a portion of their wealth with others, thereby rebuking nationalism and leveling things out a bit, and get at the "causes" of various global problems that the liberals perceive as being essentially economic.

Liberal spokesmen have held that economic measures are especially significant in the Cold War competition with the Communists. People "turn Communist," it is believed, because of economic backwardness, and foreign aid can overcome such difficulties. Thus, according to former Defense Secretary Robert McNamara: "There can be no question that there is an irrefutable relationship between violence and economic backwardness. . . . Our role must be precisely this: To provide security to those developing

---

* Max Lerner, for one, asserts that "there is plenty of room for doubt about the wisdom of the U.N.'s action, but no room for hesitancy in backing it up in an open-eyed way, doubts and all. Once the U.N. has decided, wrongly or rightly, that a certain political solution is necessary for peace, it seems to me it must be imposed." (*National Review Bulletin*, November 13, 1961.)

nations which genuinely need and request our help. . . . Development means economic, social, and political progress. . . . As development progresses . . . their resistance to disorder and violence will be enormously increased." [5]

Liberals tend to believe that economic measures not only prevent people from turning Communist, but can persuade them to act reasonably once they have turned. Communist regimes, it is thought, are hostile and suspicious toward the rest of the world during the early phase of their development, when they are hungry and therefore belligerent. But once they settle down and start becoming prosperous, they grow increasingly mellow. Hence our policies of economic aid and global commerce should be directed at Communist nations as well as at others considered likely to become so.*

As Rostow's utterance suggests, the supranational theme is also closely wedded to the ultimate "moral" imperative in the liberal hornbook—the idea of disarmament. This is a continuing preoccupation also following naturally from the liberal's environmentalist world-view. If material factors are the source of political difficulties, the liberal reasons, it follows that we can approach the goal of global amity by manipulating those material factors—including, most specifically, the material implements of aggression. In this conspectus, arms, not aggressors, are seen as the "cause" of war, so that if only we would dispose of the arms we could enjoy the blessings of peace.

The constant pursuit of disarmament is sometimes justified as well in abstract, moralizing terms. We are advised that it would

---

* A single chapter in a book devoted chiefly to domestic issues is not the place to answer all these doctrines. I have canvassed some of their errors in another volume, and in the present one must be content with three notes in passing. First, the idea that other nations should have a better standard of living is an admirable objective, but unless it has some demonstrable connection to the security of the American people, the propriety of pursuing it with their tax money may be questioned. Second, foreign economic aid as usually deployed does not alleviate global poverty, since it is administered by governments, sometimes in a fraudulent manner but almost always in a counterproductive manner through inefficient collectivist planning. Third, there is little evidence, as we shall see from the historical record, that this or other aspects of the liberal foreign policy approach have done much to stop the advance of Communism.

be highly moral of us to get rid of certain weapons, "take risks for peace," or even promote an overtly pacifist attitude on the part of our government. After all, we are enjoined by the greatest ethical teacher in history to "turn the other cheek." Why not, therefore, lay down our arms, and thereby choose the path of morality over that of narrow self-interest? (Such views are usually advanced by academic liberals rather than official ones—although, as we shall see, a heavy leavening of such thought has gotten into our official counsels as well.)

The National Interest Standard

This amalgam of liberal foreign policy views is usually presented in vivid contrast to the myopic opinions of various right wingers. Adversaries of the liberal outlook such as the late Senator Robert Taft, former President Herbert Hoover, or General Douglas MacArthur, are characteristically portrayed as foreign policy curmudgeons, distinguished by an outmoded faith in national sovereignty, hostility to global agencies, reliance on American strength, and disregard for the world's downtrodden masses. Their view was said to be selfish and "isolationist," as opposed to the enlightened, philanthropic, and highly moral view that is distinctive to the liberals.

This stereotypical picture of foreign policy functions has been and continues to be widely accepted (subject to some rather complicated revisions since the debacle in Vietnam). Yet the errors enfolded in it are fairly obvious. For one thing, there is nothing immoral about a foreign policy that takes as its central objective a stout defense of America's interests and refuses to subordinate these interests to globalist ambitions. As the founders construed the matter, the Federal government was *obliged* to protect the American nation from its enemies, and those who assumed positions of authority in its ranks were required to take (and still do take) a solemn oath to fulfill this function, foremost among all others.

Officials of our Federal government, that is, are *morally obligated* to pursue a *national interest* foreign policy, just as any agent contractually engaged to perform a service is morally constrained to fulfill the terms of his contract. That conceptual antithesis between "moral" and "self-interest" foreign policies is therefore spurious. The American government is bound by its covenant with the people to provide for the national defense and protect the interests of its citizens. What would be authentically immoral would be the deliberate failure to perform this obligation once accepted—an obvious truth that liberal foreign policy spokesmen have a distressing tendency to forget.*

It is in this context that the dispute about "isolationism" and "interventionism" must be examined. In and of themselves, it should be apparent, such terms mean relatively little. They become intelligible only if they are related to the legitimate purposes of our government. If our proper interests are vitally engaged, our government should act. If not, then not. Making such determinations is of course complex, and a decision to do one thing and not another can be argued, and has been, to the point of bitter controversy. But the principle is, or should be, fairly clear: America's national interest, not intervention or isolation as such, should be the deciding factor.†

Insistence on just that point has itself been described as "isolationism" by liberal spokesmen. Using the national interest standard, such conservatives as Senator Taft and former President Hoover argued that America should stay out of the Second World

---

* Thus the late Adlai Stevenson urged an increase of American foreign aid outlays, irrespective of national interest considerations, on the grounds that "unselfishness and magnanimity are also part of the American record." Such statements confound confusion. Unselfishness and magnanimity are indeed part of the American record, and one may hope they will continue to be. But American *officials* have no warrant for being magnanimous with the substance of the American *people,* any more than Mr. Stevenson as a lawyer would have had a warrant to play Lord Bountiful with the resources of a client. The moral obligation of the agent is to defend the well-being of his principal, or else resign his commission.

† This national interest criterion, it should be noted, does not mean that nations may do anything and everything. In addition to the restraint imposed by the defensive order-keeping conception, our foreign and defense policies should be conducted in keeping with international law: we should stand by treaty obligations, should avoid warfare when this can honorably be done, should abide by the articles of war when it cannot. The controversy here concerns the goals to be sought, rather than the methods of seeking them.

War on the grounds that Europe's troubles were none of our affair—and they were roundly attacked as "isolationists" for having done so. The premier example of so-called isolationism during this period was the "America First" committee, considered by many liberals to be the epitome of Neanderthal stupidity in foreign affairs. In point of fact, "America first" is a pretty good statement of what our foreign policy objectives ought to be, and "isolationism" in this sense is a proper goal of our diplomacy.

There is another sense, however, in which "isolationism" would be not merely wrong, but potentially fatal. If the term is taken to mean insistence that America should never look beyond the three-mile limit, on the assumption that other parts of the world have no relevance to our safety, then it is obviously illegitimate. Refusal to recognize the existence of authentic dangers to the American people would also default the basic function of our government. "Isolationism" thus construed would be just as clearly in violation of the proper criteria of national defense as would a reckless interventionism.

This kind of "isolationist" charge was laid against conservatives who opposed our entry into the Second World War—the contention being that Hitler was in fact a serious threat to us but that these particular isolationists refused to recognize the fact. The point is arguable. Much more apparent is the fact that isolationism of this type has become increasingly characteristic of American liberalism itself. The creed that was formerly marked by an intense desire to intervene in trouble spots around the world and that disparaged foes of such diplomacy as "isolationists" has itself become an "isolationist" movement in the worst interpretation of the word.

The Communist Movement

On the premises sketched above, the principal questions that need answering in deployment of our foreign and defense policies are fairly obvious: How and by whom is American security threatened? From what source may the American people anticipate danger? Against whom do they need to be defended? In today's world, answers to these questions suggest themselves quite readily. If there is any foreign foe against whom Americans nowadays need defending, that adversary can only be the Communist apparatus with its principal headquarters in Moscow and Peking. There are no other plausible candidates for the position, nor have there been for the span of decades since the Second World War.*

This being so, it is instructive to examine the factual record of the Communist movement in the world, and the liberal performance in assessing and responding to it. In this inquiry, we are favored with an abundance of facts—all of lugubrious implication. The Communist movement has exhibited a consistent behavior pattern wherever it has come to power. Two characteristics, in particular, have persisted without appreciable change: a grinding despotism on the home front, and an aggressive hostility toward non-Communist powers in the international arena.

The first of these is somewhat tangential to this discussion, but casts considerable light on the nature of Communism, and on the liberal response thereto. For years the bleakness and terror of the Communist regime in Russia (and also in China) have been ignored or minimized by Western liberals. But with the publication of Aleksandr Solzhenitsyn's epochal work, *The Gulag Archipelago,* the essential facts of the matter can no longer be dismissed so easily. Solzhenitsyn has published for all the world to see the brutal reality of life as it is lived in "the worker's paradise" of the Soviets, and the vision is a chilling one.

As Solzhenitsyn describes it, the Communist internal record has been one of horrifying violence, torture, murder, and enslave-

---

* It may be and frequently is argued that "international Communism," whether in Moscow, Peking, or anywhere else is not, or should not be, our enemy—the grounds for this non-adversary status being variously defined as polycentrism, the falseness of Cold War mythology, or the mellowing of the men in the Kremlin. Whatever the validity of these arguments (in my opinion not much) it is tolerably clear that there is now and for the foreseeable future no *other* such enemy, no nation or group of nations that combines the military power required to take on the United States with a demonstrable desire to do so. There is simply no alternative source from which a security danger may reasonably be apprehended, so we are justified in saying that *if* there is an enemy that requires the activation of our defenses, then the Soviet Union, and to a lesser extent Red China, are the obvious nominees.

ment. He recounts the blood purges that racked the Communist movement from the beginning, the brutal compulsions, the internal passport system, the deliberate starving of millions in a man-made famine, the subhuman existence of those condemned to the concentration camps, and the deployment of massive slave labor contingents to build canals and highways at an appalling cost in human life.*

The Bolsheviks came to power in Russia through acts of betrayal and aggression, and have continued in that manner ever since. Lenin & Co. got control of the Russian government in October 1917 by overthrowing the democratic regime of Alexander Kerensky and closing down the constituent assembly in which they held a minority of the seats (175 out of 707). That initial act of violence has been succeeded by numerous others—the most notable in the realm of foreign policy occurring in implacable sequence since the latter 1930s.†

Most stunning of the Kremlin's aggressions was that presaged by the Hitler-Stalin pact of August 1939. To the intense embarrassment of Western liberals and fellow travellers who had depicted the USSR as a bastion of "anti-fascist" sentiment, Moscow

---

* Similar conclusions have emerged from the researches of British scholar Robert Conquest, who estimates the death toll from the camps, enforced starvation, and repeated purges as at least 20 million human beings. Conquest documents the carnage at length, as do such eye-witness reporters of the Soviet debacle as Eugene Lyons and William Henry Chamberlin. In all of human history there is no record of horror to equal or surpass it—save one. The single exception is Communist China, where we have less systematic information but where the death toll has been authoritatively estimated to be as high as 60 million human beings.

† Lenin stated the basic doctrine in such matters with his usual brutal clarity: "The existence of the Soviet Republic side by side with the imperialist states for a long time is unthinkable. In the end one or the other will conquer, and until that time comes, a series of most terrible collisions between the Soviet republics and the bourgeois states is inevitable." Stalin was equally vehement, asserting that "the victory of Socialism in one country is not an end in itself; it must be looked upon as a support, as a means for hastening the proletarian victory in every other land." Khrushchev put it that "we must realize that we cannot coexist externally, for a long time. . . . We must push them to their grave." (Quoted in M. Stanton Evans, *The Politics of Surrender,* Devin Adair, 1966, pp. 26, 29.)

and Berlin signed an agreement of mutual assistance, which became the springboard for a joint invasion of Poland. (It was this invasion that touched off the global war, since Britain's agreement with Poland made the United Kingdom a participant in the hostilities.) This was followed by Moscow's attack on the Baltic states and by an invasion of Finland, whch incurred the Soviets' expulsion from the League of Nations.

The German blitzkrieg on Russia in June of 1941 threw the Soviets, against their will, into the camp of "the democracies." At the end of the war, however, the Bolshevik penchant for expansion asserted itself as strongly as before. In rapid order the Soviets colonized central Europe, began to assist in the communization of China, imposed the blockade of Berlin, and in general sought to "export revolution" around the globe.*

In keeping with Soviet international needs, these actions have been punctuated by occasional shifts of rhetoric, oscillating between a crude belligerence and a softer "coexistence" theme. These changes have occurred with metronomic regularity, "coexistence" attaining dominance in the middle 1930s, the desperate interval of the war, the latter 1950s and early 1960s, and again in the early 1970s. In all these periods the West has manifested hope that the Communists, at last, have mellowed. That hope has been as regularly shattered—by the Hitler-Stalin pact, the gobbling up of central Europe, the extermination of Hungary, construction of the Berlin wall, the Cuban missile crisis, the bloodbath in Czechoslovakia.

In view of this performance, there is little reason to suppose the Soviets have authentically reformed during any one of their repetitive coexistence drives. We have, indeed, the statement of Communist leaders revealing the ulterior if slightly obvious motive of such stratagems. Nikita Khrushchev, for one, declared in 1959 that "the policies of peaceful coexistence" were justified because they "facilitate the victory of the Communist Party and other progressive organizations of the working class in capitalist coun-

---

* Among the nations brought under Soviet domination in the post-war era were Latvia, Estonia, Lithuania, and parts of Finland and Japan (all absorbed directly into the USSR), Poland, Hungary, Romania, Bulgaria, Czechoslovakia, Albania, Yugoslavia, and East Germany.

tries, make it easier for the peoples to combat war blocs and contribute to the national liberation movements." [6] *

This is a thoroughly representative statement of Communist intent, sufficient to forestall surprise when "coexistence" doesn't stop the Soviets from crushing Hungary or Czechoslovakia, or engendering warfare in the Middle East. Soviet theoreticians have made it abundantly clear that "coexistence" is a one-way street— a relationship in which the Western nations are immobilized by hopes of global amity, while Communist forces continue to advance. The point of the strategy, according to one official Soviet spokesman, is to facilitate "an active and intense struggle, in the course of which socialism irresistibly attacks, while capitalism suffers one defeat after another." [7] Hence the Communist record, and *modus operandi.*

The Liberal Response

What has been the liberal response to all of this? There are, of course, variations in the liberal view of Communism as of any thing else. Some individual spokesmen (Sidney Hook, George Meany) have been inveterately hostile, and others (John Dewey) have converted from a stance of relative friendship to one of hard-line disapproval. Yet the predominant tendency of liberal views on dealing with the Communists is fairly clear. Subject to the prevailing atmospherics, the American liberal community has been congenitally eager to believe the Communists have changed,

---

* Khrushchev's successor, Leonid Brezhnev, has stressed identical themes. "It goes without saying," Brezhnev stated in 1966, "that there can be no peaceful coexistence where matters concern the internal process of the class and national liberation struggle in the capitalist countries or in the colonies. Peaceful coexistence is not applicable to the relations between oppressors and oppressed, between colonialists and the victims of colonial oppression." In 1972, in the midst of ballyhooed negotiations for *détente,* Brezhnev updated this by saying the USSR is determined to support "all revolutionary forces of our time." *Détente,* he said, "in no way signifies a possibility of weakening the ideological struggle. . . . On the contrary, we should be prepared for an intensification of this struggle." (Quoted in Richard V. Allen, *Peaceful Coexistence,* American Bar Association, 1966, p. 37; John Barron, *KGB,* Reader's Digest Press, 1974, p. 28.)

and to predicate our national strategy on that belief. In certain liberal circles, every breath of "coexistence" rhetoric from the East is received with joyful expectation and made the basis for new departures in foreign policy. At each recurrence we are informed that the Cold War at last has gone away—exactly as if we had not been given the identical message on a dozen previous occasions.

Thus in the early 1930s when Stalin was seeking recognition and trade concessions from the United States, the Soviets pledged to suspend their subversive-revolutionary activities against non-Communist governments, and they were believed by American officials. When Moscow sought assistance against the Nazis and received our billions in Lend Lease aid, it was argued that the USSR had become an amiable democracy. In the postwar era, the Soviets and their allies were given positions of leverage in Europe and Asia on the assumption they had abandoned their expansionist goals and could be trusted to abide by their commitments.*

Since it has developed in each of these cases that the Communists have in fact *not* changed in any appreciable manner, the result of our credulity has been to place the United States in a thoroughly weak position. Exactly according to the Soviet scenario, peaceful coexistence becomes a species of struggle in which socialism "irresistibly attacks, while capitalism suffers one defeat after another." The liberal inability to see the adversary for what he is, and willingness to be beguiled by hopes that the Cold War has somehow ended, have been steadily yielding the globe to the enemy.†

---

* Thus President Roosevelt: "I have just a hunch that Stalin doesn't want anything but security for his country, and I think that if I give him everything I possibly can and ask for nothing from him in return, he won't try to annex anything and will work for a world democracy and peace." (Quoted in Evans, p. 41.)

† A variation of this liberal failing has been the notion of the non-Communist Communist—the Bolshevik who isn't really a Communist but a nationalist or agrarian reformer, and therefore deserving of our friendship and not our opposition. This was the liberal argument concerning Mao Tse-tung in China and Fidel Castro in Cuba, prompting a withdrawal of American aid from their opponents. The two approaches, of course, can be combined, as in Vietnam: Here we have the non-Communist Communists of Hanoi, backed up by the mellow men of Moscow, from which it

The net effect of this procedure may be observed in the record of Communist expansion in the years since the Second World War. In 1944, Communism controlled one nation in the world, some 170 million people, and some 8 million square miles of the earth's surface. As of 1970, it controlled 18 nations in full and parts of four others, close to a billion human beings, and some 16 million square miles of the earth's surface. And it was encouraging and supplying further acts of warfare and aggression in a dozen different nations—Cambodia and Vietnam, Chile, Ghana, Nigeria, the Middle East—while continuing to promote aggression by espionage and subversion through the KGB and its enormous network of contacts in every quarter of the globe.

A useful survey by the AFL-CIO cites chapter and verse to show that the authentic "imperialists" in the world today are situated in Moscow and Peking. The union study notes that the two major Communist powers between them have directly annexed more than 825,000 square miles of territory from 11 other nations, embracing a population of more than 25 million people. They have also secured control over 13 dependencies with over 1 million square miles of territory and more than 146 million people. The total empire thus created—not counting the USSR and Red China themselves—amounts to 1.9 million square miles of the earth's surface and 172 million human beings.

While all this has been going on, the Western world has granted independence at a pell-mell rate to its former colonial holdings. No less than 68 newly independent nations were created in this fashion between the close of the Second World War and 1970. Independence was thus bestowed on 1.15 billion people inhabiting some 13.2 million square miles of territory. While the colonial empires of the nineteenth century European powers have been almost totally liquidated, conferring independence on more than a billion people, the Communist empire has steadily advanced until it embraces more than a billion people. So who, the AFL-CIO inquires, is the imperialist? [8]

Such simple arithmetic is sufficient to suggest the fallacy of believing the Soviets have changed when in fact they haven't, but

---

follows that we can sign agreements with the Communists in Vietnam and expect to have them honored.

there is more. For not only have liberal policymakers been willing to yield, conciliate, or give the Soviets the benefit of the doubt at crucial Cold War junctures, they have also constructed elaborate theories of Soviet "mellowing" that, in their further permutations, actually require us to *strengthen* the Communists while simultaneously *weakening* ourselves. The full extent to which these inverted notions have suffused our official policies is not generally understood by the American people. It is, indeed, so strange a reversal of the normal imperatives of foreign policy and simple common sense that many Americans would find it difficult to believe that such conceptions could possibly represent the thinking of our global strategists.

It can be shown, however, that the American government over the past decade has embarked on a policy of self-enfeeblement that has as its major objectives the piecemeal disarmament of the United States and the simultaneous build-up of our adversaries. Both these peculiar ideas grow directly from the idea of Soviet mellowing. The supposed logic is that by aiding the Communists we will encourage them to come out of their shell, and that by cutting back our military strength we give impressive notice of our good intentions.

The curious notion of beefing up the enemy and weakening ourselves got started back in the days of John F. Kennedy and Defense Secretary Robert McNamara, when a group of liberal-left intellectuals began cranking out studies arguing the need for "structure" in our relationship with the Communists—to be achieved by trade, economic aid, cultural exchanges, and disarmament. These ideas were spelled out in *The Liberal Papers,* "Study Phoenix," Study FAIR," and other such documents, many of which (including the last two) emerged from a government-supported think tank called the Institute for Defense Analyses. "Phoenix" author Vincent Rock suggested, for example, that it was in our interest to see the Soviet Union become stronger and that it could be "of great material importance if the United States were willing to help and the Soviet Union were willing to accept help." [9]

This doctrine was accepted by the Kennedy and Johnson administrations, and has been continued and expanded by their Republican successors. The amount of supposedly "peaceful" trade flowing from the United States to the Soviet Union has in-

The Soviet cargo ship Michurin, a product of American technology, on its way to North Vietnam, carrying cargo trucks that are also products of our technology. (Department of Defense photo)

creased exponentially (jumping from $200 million to $1.5 billion in 1971–73 alone) but has had considerably less than peaceful consequences. Rather than deploying our technology in behalf of peace, the Soviets, surprising us once more, have used it to strengthen their war machine. The result has been that American officials have found themselves calling on the American nation to "stand firm" against Communist offensives that our own diplomacy has helped equip and fortify.

In May of 1972, for example, President Nixon announced the blockade of Haiphong Harbor in North Vietnam, explaining that this step was necessary to protect American lives in Southeast Asia. "There is," he said, "only one way to stop the killing. That is to keep the weapons of war out of the hands of the international outlaws of Vietnam." In support of Nixon's action, the Department of Defense released a series of photographs portraying the influx of Soviet supplies into North Vietnam. One photo shows the Soviet cargo ship *Michurin* steaming toward Haiphong, with Soviet ZIL 130 cargo trucks and ZIL 555 dump trucks on deck. Others show Soviet T-34 and T-54 tanks, Soviet MIG 17s, and

312

Soviet 122 mm field guns—items that also turned up in the Middle East in the fall of 1973.

All these instruments of aggression, as it happens, originated in the United States and other Western nations. The cargo ship *Michurin* so graphically exposed by the Department of Defense photo is powered by a diesel engine designed and built in the United States and features a hull constructed in the United Kingdom. (Common enough for Soviet cargo runs to Haiphong, since 84 of the 96 ships identified making such runs are powered by Western engines.)

In like fashion, the GAZ trucks used on the Ho Chi Minh trail come from the Ford-built Gorki plant, the ZIL trucks from yet another American-built factory. The T-54 and T-34 tanks have modified Christie suspensions (Christie was an American designer). The MIG 17 is powered by a British Rolls Royce engine. The 122 mm field gun and other Soviet weapons use a propellant technology provided the Communists by American chemical firms.

The United States, in short, was sounding the alarm about an influx of Soviet weapons and support technology provided by, among others, the United States. And even as that unusual scenario unfolded, the Nixon administration was promoting still *other* transfers of our technology to the Soviets. Nothing symbolizes this irony better than the Kama River truck deal, in which a consortium of American firms were engaged in building for Moscow the largest truck factory in the world—while our government was deploring the use of Soviet trucks to smooth the flow of Communist forces in Vietnam.*

All of this would seem to be sufficiently bad, but even more distressing is the other side of our "structure"-building activity— the deliberate weakening of our own defenses. Here, according to the liberal intellectuals, we could best serve the cause of peace by pulling back on our forward weapons at overseas bases and approach the goal of global disarmament by sustaining a "balance of terror" in which pervasive fear of nuclear holocaust would

* The full details of how American trade and aid have built the Soviet economy and war machine are set forward by Antony Sutton in his massive study, *Western Technology and Soviet Economic Development* (Hoover Institution, 1973) and a more popular rendering entitled *National Suicide* (Arlington House, 1973).

make the idea of scrapping military hardware seem attractive by comparison.

These theories converged in a bizarre doctrine called "mutual assured destruction" in which it is considered desirable that the Soviet Union be able to obliterate our cities, just as we are capable of obliterating theirs. As *Liberal Papers* author Walter Millis put it, the end-product of such reasonings was the notion that "a genuinely deterrent policy would require the United States to cooperate with the Soviet Union in insuring that their retaliatory force was as invulnerable as ours and that our population was equally exposed to attack with theirs." [10]

Although the idea was considered far-out at the time by Millis himself, it rapidly became converted into official policy through the efforts of McNamara and Kennedy's disarmament adviser Jerome B. Wiesner. In relatively short order the Kennedy strategists set about to reassure the Communists by signing the Moscow test ban treaty, pulling back manned bombers ("provocative" to the Soviets), and holding up on anti-missile defenses. The thrust of our policy became to ensure that our defenses were downgraded to signal our pacific intentions to the Kremlin. It led to such exotic furbelows as that reported by defense expert Donald Brennan, in which McNamara ordered that the Sentinel ABM have "some specific weaknesses introduced to make the system more easily penetrable by the Soviets." [11]

Opposition to anti-missile defenses is the most characteristic gambit of the disarmament lobby, and as may be seen from the above has little to do with the various technical and economic objections usually stressed in public debate. The real reason for combatting ABMs is that by defending Americans from nuclear evaporation they would "destabilize" the strategic balance and interfere with imagined progress toward disarmament. The goal is a "stable balance of terror," with the American people perpetually exposed as nuclear hostages.

President Nixon came to office pledging to reverse the defense policies of his Democratic predecessors. A fairly steady stream of hard-line verbiage, in seeming contrast to the "doves" who populate the Senate, created the impression that a change had in fact transpired. In the more esoteric realms of arms discussion, however, it is apparent nothing changed at all. All that McNamara-

Wiesner fantasizing about the "balance of terror," the need to keep our civilian population naked to the enemy, and the desirability of reassuring Moscow was adopted outright by Henry Kissinger, and is the controlling factor in America's disarmament strategy at this writing.

The degree to which the Republican administration endorsed the principles of the *Liberal Papers* Democrats was made quite plain by Kissinger in a dissertation on the SALT accords banning ABMs before a group of congressmen and senators. In this briefing Kissinger stated that America and the Soviet Union each had "just come into possession of power single-handedly capable of exterminating the human race," and added that, "paradoxically, this very fact, and the global interests of both sides, create a certain commonality of outlook, a sort of interdependence for survival between the two of us."

Kissinger went on to say that "although we compete, the conflict will not admit of victory in the classical sense. We are compelled to coexist. We have an inescapable obligation to build jointly a structure for peace." He further suggested that "security requires a measure of equilibrium" and that "each increment of power does not necessarily represent an increment of usable political strength. . . . marginal additions of power cannot be decisive. Potentially decisive additions are extremely dangerous, and the quest for them is destabilizing." [12] This statement *in toto* might easily have been lifted from the think-tank productions of the Institute for Defense Analyses.

Indeed, the Republican administration had been taking steps to downgrade U.S. weapons technology even before the SALT accords were signed. As far back as July 1971, then Deputy Defense Secretary David Packard reassured a Senate Foreign Relations subcommittee about American ABM development, pointing out that "those Safeguard sites planned for initial deployment in ICBM fields defend some of the *most sparsely populated* portions of the United States" (italics added)—and therefore could not be misconstrued as, horror of horrors, attempts to protect our civilian population.

Packard also told the senators the administration had performed in proper fashion in the matter of multiple warheads for our missiles (MIRVing) because "this administration made a deliberate decision *not* to improve the accuracy of our MIRV . . . to what was and is technically feasible." [13] In other words, the administration had behaved acceptably because it had on the one hand left much of America's civilian population devoid of ABM defenses, and had on the other hand degraded the quality of our weapons so as to be less capable of attacking the Communist enemy. This is what is euphemistically known as our "national defense policy."

We emerge, therefore, on the nether side of the looking glass: By liberal lights, the objective of our defense and foreign policies should be to contrive an "end to nationhood," including our own, strengthen the Communist enemy that is pledged to our destruction, and leave our civilian population exposed to possible destruction. It is not inaccurate, I think, to say that we here confront a total inversion of the most essential functions of our government— and thus a final and potentially catastrophic default of the libertarian purposes of Western statecraft.

What could lead our theoreticians—and public officials under three different administrations—to such unlikely conclusions? One obvious answer is that a history of prior mistakes creates a hunger for eventual vindication. Having been so wrong before, you have a vested interest in hoping that something will turn up to prove you weren't so wrong at all. If, today, a brand-new hope arises that the Soviets *have* actually mellowed, the liberal theorist who accepted nonexistent changes in 1933, or 1945, or 1956, or whenever is powerfully tempted to believe just one more time. If *this* time he turns out to be right, all the earlier blunders will be retrieved.

But this, of course, merely transfers the problem to another level. Why have so many liberals been willing to trust the Communists in the first place? Part of the answer, I think, is the very hopelessness of the Cold War struggle as it appears from the liberal vantage point. As George F. Kennan has put it, the idea of total Soviet intransigence coupled with enormous Soviet might leaves us "no hope." [14] And since we cannot live without hope, we must somehow keep on trying to figure out a method of trusting the Soviets. (We could also stop building them up with transfusions of our technology, but this option doesn't readily suggest itself to the liberal intellect.)

Even deeper than these considerations, however, is the constant, if subterranean, pressure of ideological kinship: the fact that the collectivist liberal has seen in the "Soviet experiment" something of himself, and therefore cannot believe that the USSR could really be that bad. The liberal, for example, believes in "planning," and the Soviet Union obviously has plenty of that. A system that is "planned" must have *something* good about it— and certainly cannot be the embodiment of heinous evil. Thus the willingness to ignore the atrocities of the 1930s, to overestimate Soviet achievements, and even today to contend that the Soviets are doing better than we in various economic categories (as John Kenneth Galbraith does quite straightfacedly in his most recent volume).

"Planning" is suggested as the point of connection because it is specific and tangible, but it is only one of several linkages between the mentality of the Western left and that of the Soviet commissars. In their secularism, their materialist-environmentalist metaphysic, their desire to use the power of the state to make over human beings, the collectivist "isms," East and West, have numerous things in common. As noted, liberalism is in fact but a subdivision of the larger twentieth-century movement toward collectivism, and because the liberal must convince himself this movement is humane, he cannot accept the bleak reality of its chief exemplar.

20
Crime
Without
Punishment

If national defense is the first requirement of effective government, then suppression of crime must be the second. On the domestic front, this is obviously the bedrock function of civil authority. If peaceful citizens cannot be protected from the incursions of criminals, then other things that government may or may not accomplish are of dubious comfort. It does no good to receive a subsidy check today if it will be stolen from us tomorrow, to have handsome thoroughfares if we are afraid to venture out on them, or to be told we shall be transported to utopia five years from now if we are in daily fear for our lives, our families, and our property.

We come back, in short, to that minimal definition of the state —neutralizing the aggressive use of force. At bottom this is what government is about, and the state that fails to perform this elementary task has bungled its reason for existence. It is therefore troubling to observe that our liberal theoreticians and liberal statesmen have defaulted *this* particular function, too. As in the matter of foreign policy and defense, a process of inversion seems to be at work: The same people who would have our government do the things it shouldn't would also prevent it from doing the things it should.

The Liberal View of Crime

For the past few decades the administration of the criminal law in most jurisdictions in the United States has been guided by a cluster of assumptions derived from liberal metaphysics and liberal notions about the manner in which human beings function. With few exceptions, these assumptions reveal the essential worldview that has governed our domestic policies in matters of economic concern—and the results have been just as dismal.

It has been contended, first and foremost, that crime, like other types of human behavior, is the product of material circumstance rather than of ethical volition. Fashionable theoreticians such as Dr. Karl Menninger and former Attorney General Ramsey Clark have argued that people commit crimes because they come from impoverished backgrounds, or because they haven't had sufficient education, or because they have otherwise been subject to social deprivation. In certain cases, such as urban or campus rioting, this is amended to read that the actions occur because the perpetrators feel frustrated or rejected by "the system." In any event, responsibility is lodged with social and material circumstances rather than with the individual offender.

From these assumptions there has followed a fateful chain of imagined conclusions. Most notably, it has been supposed that if people are turned into criminals by poverty or other aversive aspects of the world around them, then the obvious way of correcting the problem is to focus our energies on the environment rather than the criminals. Above all, it is argued, we need programs to combat poverty, build decent housing, clean up the ghettos, give people job training, remedy defects in the home, and so forth. We must, that is, eliminate the "conditions" that give rise to criminal tendencies in the first place.

It also follows from this outlook that the criminal is not really to blame for his actions. Harsh or punitive measures are thus unjustified and will only serve to embitter him further, make him harder to rehabilitate, and do no good in preventing a recurrence of criminal behavior. We should therefore treat him with compassion and understanding, and by example show him the error of his deviant ways.*

Attitudes of this type have been dominant in the conduct of American criminal law and penal practices for the past several decades, and have raised up a whole host of environmental-treatment strategies for dealing with criminal offenders. In obedience to such notions, our police have been progressively restrained, our courts made more punctilious in the observance of defendants' rights, sentences shorter, probations and paroles more frequent. We have poured out billions in efforts to combat poverty, converted our prisons into treatment facilities, and otherwise deployed our energies according to the liberal analysis.

If the analysis were more or less correct, we should by now be seeing some observable diminution of the crime rate. What we have actually been observing is just the opposite. As we have concentrated on environmental strategies and become more lenient in the handling of criminal defendants, we have seen the indices of violent crime move rapidly up, not down.

Exactly how we have come to this alarming state of affairs may be discovered if we examine the liberals' favored theorems about crime and criminals and see how these have worked in practice. If it were true, for example, that poverty is a major cause of crime and that curing poverty can put a stop to crime, then some general economic relationships ought to be discernible. In particular, it should follow that a period in which large numbers of the American people were impoverished should have been a time of high and rising criminality, and that periods in which increasing numbers of people have been affluent should be periods of diminishing crime. In fact, the observable relationships are exactly the reverse of this.

One of the *least* crime-prone periods in recent American his-

---

* Menninger asserts that "we commit the crime of damning some of our fellow citizens with the label 'criminal.' . . . We commit this crime every day that we retain our present, stupid, futile, abominable practices against detected 'offenders.'" (*The Crime of Punishment*, Viking, 1968, p. 113.) Clark tells us that "rehabilitation must be the goal of modern corrections. Every other consideration must be subordinated to it." (*Crime in America*, Simon & Schuster, 1970, p. 21.)

tory was precisely that epoch in which millions of Americans were jobless and impoverished—the period of the Great Depression. With certain exceptions, which we shall have occasion to notice, the depression was marked by far less serious crime than the relatively prosperous decades that succeeded it. In 1933, for example, total recorded crimes against the person in the United States stood at about 150 per 100,000 of population. This figure dropped steadily throughout the continuing years of the depression and the enforced scarcity of the war. As prosperity returned after the war, the rate moved sharply upward and has continued to climb ever since. In 1970, the figure stood at 361—more than double the rate of 1933.

The record on property crime is even more dramatically opposed to the poverty argument. In 1933, total index crimes against property stood at slightly over 600 per 100,000 of population. Like crime against the person, this species of lawlessness declined as the depression continued and war supervened, reversing itself only as the war drew to a close. From that point on the rate went into a vertiginous climb—until in 1970 it stood at 2,386, almost four times the rate that prevailed in depression year 1933.[1]

An equally obvious refutation of the poverty thesis is the experience of the 1960s. This was by every measure a period of unparalleled affluence in American life. Substandard housing was virtually eliminated, the number of jobs in the economy was increased from 66 million to 79 million, the gross national product went from $500 million to $1 trillion, and median family income rose from $5,600 to $9,900.[2] It was also in this period that expanding affluence permitted the government to expand its outlays for social welfare spending from about $50 billion to $171 billion annually. If there were any correlation between economic deprivation and crime, the booming 1960s should have seen our crime problems dwindle away to almost nothing. The actual result was less encouraging.

In the years 1960 through 1970, the number of major crimes in the United States almost tripled—from 2.02 million to 5.9 million—a growth rate of 176 percent. Violent crime against the person grew from 286,000 to 816,000—an increase of 156 percent. Even more important in terms of victimization, the per capita rate of criminality also increased, as the growth of crime outstripped the growth of population. In 1960, the rate for all crimes per 100,000 inhabitants was 1,126. By 1970, this had ballooned to 2,907—a 144 percent increase. The rate of violent crimes per 100,000 of population had gone up from 160 to 361—or 126 percent.[3]

In other words, the general crime rate in America was *descending* throughout a period of widespread and spectacular poverty, and *rising* in a period of rapidly escalating prosperity. On these data there is no reason whatever to conclude that poverty as such is the cause of our recent upsurge of criminality. Whatever quantum of crime may be traceable to penury would have manifested itself in the depression and would be diminished by the access of prosperity. That enormous surplus of crime in a period of relative boom must obviously derive from other, nonmaterial sources.

Also instructive is the fact that during the 1960s crime experienced its most notable increase not in the inner cities, but in the affluent suburbs. Although the increase in both suburban and inner city crime rates slowed down a bit in the early 1970s, it is noteworthy that the decade past witnessed a rapid rise in suburban offenses.* If poverty were indeed the cause of crime, the comfortable suburbs would be the last place we might expect to look for it. While a great deal of crime has economic motives of one sort or another, it is obvious that the massive burst of crime experienced in the 1960s and the rise of crime in the suburbs cannot be put down to impoverishment.

Recent efforts to explain these discrepancies—when the data are noted at all—hold that in a time of prosperity it is more intolerable to be poor, or that a taste of comfort whets the economic appetite, both considerations contributing, supposedly, to the upward thrust of crime. Whatever degree of truth there may be in such explanations, it is sufficient to note they radically change the nature of the discussion. The argument for expanded welfarism is perhaps temporarily retrieved (this seems to be a

---

* As FBI Chief J. Edgar Hoover put it in a sample year in that decade's burst of prosperity (1964), "suburban crime has the sharpest trend, up 17 percent. . . ." (Federal Bureau of Investigation, *Uniform Crime Report, 1964*, p. 1.)

principal concern of the discussants), but the basis for the argument is altered. For now we are weighing questions of psychology, motivation, and character, rather than material measures of environmental poverty.

The Liberal Cure: Leniency and Rehabilitation

If conventional efforts to isolate the causes of crime have proved deficient, attempts to effect a cure have been downright calamitous. There is not space in this discussion to examine the liberal ethic's many contributions to the contemporary crime wave,* but we may focus for a moment on its central theme: the elaboration of newfound "rights" for criminal defendants and the general practice of leniency in the application of punishments to those convicted.

The relevant truism in consideration of this subject is that the vast majority of crimes in our society are committed by a small percentage of the population—which in theory should make the problem easier to control. The trouble is that this small percentage keeps committing crimes over and over again, so that in many instances a given individual may be responsible for three, four, a dozen, or even hundreds of criminal actions—and therefore for victimizing an equivalent number of law-abiding citizens. Indeed, the figures reflecting this "recidivist" tendency are somewhat astonishing.

The FBI's uniform crime report for 1972 informs us that some 228,032 offenders were arrested in that year for major offenses. These individuals accounted for a documented total of 867,000 crimes, and approximately 65 percent of these offenders (148,809) had been arrested two or more times. In other words, two-thirds of our criminals in 1972 had previously been in the clutches of the law not once but twice, and were out on the streets again. In particular, says the FBI report, "the predatory crime offenders had high repeat rates with 77 percent of the robbers, 73 percent of the auto thieves, and 71 percent of the burglars

---

* For a more extensive discussion, see M. Stanton Evans and Margaret Moore, *The Lawbreakers,* Arlington House, 1968.

arrested between 1970 and 1972 being repeat offenders. Likewise, 60 percent of the narcotics offenders were repeaters." [4] *

This means, in brief, that our national crime and victimization rates might be dramatically reduced if we could simply do something about the problem of recidivism—and it is this problem that liberal jurisprudence and penology profess to cure. It is sadly apparent, however, that they have done nothing to cure the problem and a great deal to create it. For it develops that the recidivist criminals who keep on victimizing our society have been returned to the streets, again and again, by those very jurists and corrections officials who insist that leniency and rehabilitation are the answer to our problems.

This tendency has been most visible, of course, in the courts. In a series of decisions beginning in the late 1950s, the Supreme Court has elaborated a system of federally defined rights and privileges for criminal defendants and imposed these on the courts of the several states. In 1957, the high tribunal stunned the nation with its ruling in the Andrew Mallory case, decreeing that a convicted rapist be freed because he had been held for seven-and-one-half hours prior to arraignment. His detention, said the court, violated his constitutional right to be brought before a magistrate "without unnecessary delay." Mallory, and a number of other criminal defendants, went free, and the likelihood that District of Columbia police could obtain confessions from defendants cooling their heels and thinking it over was thereby reduced.

In succeeding years, the court produced a sequence of decisions that weighted the scales of justice heavily in favor of criminal defendants. In *Mapp* (1961) the court severely restricted the

---

* Although the FBI report does not give the data, the same holds true, apparently, for the most serious crime of all, that of criminal homicide. In a study of murders committed in Philadelphia, Marvin Wolfgang observes that "contrary to many past impressions, analysis of offenders in criminal homicide reveals a relatively high proportion who have a previous police or arrest record. . . . The Philadelphia data have shown that 64 percent of offenders have a previous arrest record, that of these 66 percent have a record of offenses against the person, and that of these 73 percent have a record of aggravated assault. . . . The facts suggest that homicide is the apex crime—a crescendo built upon previous assault crimes." (*Patterns in Criminal Homicide,* John Wiley & Sons, 1966, pp. 323, 336.)

power of local police to conduct searches for incriminating evidence. In *Gideon* (1963) it ruled that indigent defendants had to be provided counsel by the state. In *Escobedo* (1964), that a man convicted of murder should be turned loose because he had not been permitted to see his counsel at the stationhouse. And in *Miranda* (1966), that police could not question a suspect who demurred, and that the services of counsel must not only be made available but be energetically pressed on him.

These and related decisions by the court have been widely hailed as "gains" in the battle for civil liberties. That verdict is extremely questionable. To the extent that the court's decrees authentically protected the innocent from being pressured into confession, the decisions may of course be construed as services to individual freedom. But to the extent they simply deployed a procedural mine-field that hindered proper law enforcement and permitted larger numbers of the guilty to get free again, they were the reverse, allowing criminals to strike repeatedly at law-abiding individuals.

What has been the actual effect of these decisions? In the development of our national criminality, it is difficult to assign percentages. One must consider the influence of home and school, the functioning of the corrections system, and numerous other influences, so that in the total conspectus it is hard to apportion cause and effect to individual factors. By examining some relevant statistics, however, it is possible to get a general idea of what the Federal judiciary has wrought.

Because Washington, D.C., is the only jurisdiction in which ordinary justice is dispensed directly by the Federal government, this city provides the clearest test of the impact achieved by our Federal jurists. And it is noteworthy that the trend of crime in our national capital has closely followed judicial shifts in attitude. When the courts have been relatively firm, the crime rate there has been correspondingly low. When the courts began to practice leniency, the trend reversed and the crime rate moved rapidly upward.

Throughout the early 1950s, for instance, the trend of crime in Washington was steadily downward. In 1950, there were 20,163 criminal offenses in the District of Columbia, and police recorded a clearance (or solution) rate of 48.5 percent. In 1957, the number of offenses had fallen to 15,544, with a clearance rate of 49.5 percent. Then came *Mallory* and the ensuing string of Federal prohibitions against the securing of confessions, and the D.C. crime rate began to soar out of sight. By 1966, the number of offenses had gone up to 34,765, while the rate of clearance had fallen to 26.3 percent.[5] In other words, the number of crimes committed more than doubled, at the same time that the number being solved remained approximately as before. The total picture is one of unhampered criminality, conducted with relative immunity from the efforts of the police.

If the courts have played a crucial role in releasing recidivist criminals into society, it is probable the corrections system, so-called, has been an even more important factor. The courts, at least, deal with a situation in which a doubt exists as to the guilt of the defendant. In the case of the prisons the situation is otherwise. Here we are dealing with people who have already been tried and convicted, and about whose criminal status there is no legal uncertainty. It is therefore the more disturbing to note that the prison system has been disgorging repeater criminals into society quite as enthusiastically as have the courts.

The vocabulary employed is indicative of the prevailing approach. The penal system is no longer described as such but as a "corrections" system. Prisons are "reformatories" or "facilities." Prisoners have become "inmates" and more recently "residents," and no doubt we shall soon be hearing them described as clients, patients, or students. The whole idea is that these are people who are in some fashion sick, in need of "treatment." Corrections experts, psychologists, social workers, counselors, and the like will step in and provide it.

Sad to say, there is not the slightest evidence these people know how to "treat" the clients-patients-students submitted to their care, or that the increasingly lenient probation and parole practices being followed as part of the "treatment" have any effect whatever in reducing the crime rate—as even the rehabilitationists themselves have admitted.

A few years back a liberal sociologist in New York City reviewed all the available studies on the effects of rehabilitation—and came to some astonishing conclusions. The scholar in question,

Robert Martinson,* drew together the available data on rehabilitation—some 231 studies of corrections procedures compiled around the country—and analyzed the various "treatments" that had been provided by them. His conclusion was that, "on the whole, the evidence from the survey indicated that the present array of correction treatments has no appreciable effect—positive or negative—on the rates of recidivism of convicted offenders." In essence, he found about the same perçentage of criminals will commit new crimes when they get out of prison, irrespective of the "treatment" services available inside.

In support of these observations, Martinson cited some curious individual cases—such as a supposedly successful experiment in which it was found that recipients of treatment actually committed *more* offenses than those who did not receive it, but were simply returned to prison less often by the authorities. The alibi that rehabilitation will work if we simply do more of it, Martinson notes, "begins to wear thin, since treatment has been the official ideology of corrections for over half a century." He concludes that "the myth of treatment is no longer consistent with liberal views or the 'passion for justice.' . . . If corrections does not correct, we should stop assuring inmates that it does or soon will." [6]

This point is seldom made, of course, in public discussion of the matter. Numerous interest groups (for example, the National Council on Crime and Delinquency) contend that we haven't done *enough* by way of "rehabilitation" and that our prison system is a failure because it is excessively punitive and custodial, rather than truly oriented to effective "treatment." If pressed hard enough, to be sure, some corrections officials will concede they really don't know how to achieve "rehabilitation." In its latest version, however, even *this* is developed as a reason for augmented leniency.

We have, for instance, the statement of one Norman Holt of the California Department of Corrections, at a correctional asso-

---

* Martinson's interest in penology developed when he himself was arrested as a freedom rider in Mississippi back in 1961. From that background it is apparent he is neither a conservative nor a presumptive hard-liner on penology.

ciation conference in the spring of 1974. Holt recounted the results of an experiment in which one group of inmates was paroled six months early while another was released at the normal time. On the record one year later, he noted, "the performance of the early releases was not significantly better or worse than the control group." He observed that "we can say with some confidence and degree of certainty, both *that the programs don't rehabilitate* and nor do longer sentences deter the offender." (Italics added.) These results more or less confirm the findings reached by Martinson.

But what is the conclusion drawn by Holt? It is that "the most rational correctional policy is not only the most humane but the cheapest, and that policy is *to get people out of correctional systems as soon as possible and keep them out.*" [7] In other words, the failure of lenient penology is a good reason for being still *more* lenient and letting prisoners out at a much earlier date than is the practice even now. Holt's idea is that at the end of 24 months, say, the inmate is just as "rehabilitated" as he is ever going to be, and that he will not be any more rehabilitated at the end of 36 months or 48. The rehabilitationists have done everything for him they can, so they might as well turn him loose.

These conclusions are inherent in the liberal way of looking at the criminal as a patient and viewing his incarceration as a "treatment." That outlook focuses on the psychology, well-being, and progress of the criminal, and examines his behavior pattern as it reflects or does not reflect his rehabilitated status. Thus viewed, his "recidivism rate" is a kind of psychological thermometer reading, and when it has been reduced as much as it is going to be, then his release is indicated.

The fallacy of this approach is readily apparent. For the "recidivism rate" that the correctionists view as a measure of rehabilitation is, from society's standpoint, a *victimization* rate; the longer the span of time in which that rate is operative, the greater the number of victims it is going to claim. It therefore follows, if the criminals are not in fact rehabilitated, that the proper conclusion is *not* to let them out, but to keep them in. The sooner they are released, the greater the total number of crimes they will be able to commit.

It also follows that, from the victim's standpoint, old-fashioned custodial justice is *more* libertarian than the practice of "rehabilitation." For under the custodial system, the criminals with their recidivist tendencies are kept under lock and key for their appointed terms, and therefore sequestered from potential victims. Under rehabilitationist or lenient justice, criminals with exactly the same tendencies are released back into society after only a half or a third of their sentences have run.

To this may be added the fact that punishment, after all, does deter crime, while lack of punishment encourages it. We have recent researches by Isaac Ehrlich and Arleen Leibowitz of Columbia University showing that in crime as in other things there is a correlation between the costs and benefits of any given course of action and the frequency with which that action occurs. If crime is severely punished, it happens with less frequency. But if potential lawbreakers believe their actions will be punished lightly, if at all, they are likely to indulge themselves accordingly.

The Leibowitz researches compared crime rates for different jurisdictions as these were affected by the probability and severity of punishment, controlling for other variables. Her findings were that "when other factors were held constant, the states which had the higher level of punishment [both in terms of length of sentence and likelihood of its being imposed] showed fewer crimes. Such crimes as rape and murder were deterred by punishment just as well as (indeed, perhaps better than) burglary and robbery." [8]

Ehrlich's study embraced fourteen different variables, three of which concerned punishment, and dealt with national crime statistics for the 1940s and 1950s. It concluded that the "rate of specific felonies . . . is positively related to estimates of relative gains and negatively related to estimates of costs associated with criminal activity. . . . The rate of specific crime categories, with virtually no exceptions, varies inversely with estimates of the probability of apprehension and punishment by imprisonment . . . and with the average length of time served in state prisons. . . ." [9]

Economist Gordon Tullock observes that in balancing costs and benefits, criminals can be quite as rational as anyone else. He recounts, for example, an analysis of the motivations and outlook of professional burglars suggesting that "most people who took up the profession of burglary had made a sensible career choice." They did not, he notes, make very much from burglary, "but they were not very high-quality laborers and would have done as badly (or worse) if they had elected honest employment. . . . At least some criminals make fairly rational decisions with respect to their careers, and hence raising the price of crime would presumably reduce the frequency with which it is committed." [10]

Under rehabilitationist notions of criminal justice, of course, the calculations are the other way around. Criminals may properly figure the chance of their ever being arrested is small, of being convicted even smaller, and of serving a long or onerous sentence smaller still. Against these considerations are weighed potential gain from a highjacking or hold-up, elimination of a rival, or whatever. Costs go down, benefits go up, and the likelihood of criminal action is increased.

So much is only normal common sense, but it is common sense that has been thoroughly obscured by the mumbo-jumbo of "corrections." Thanks to all this lenient obfuscation, we are encouraging the criminal impulse toward expression, and ensuring that the criminals are at liberty to express it. Our continuing rampage of criminality, in short, is exactly what we ought to expect from the policies we are pursuing.

The net effect of all this leniency may be glimpsed, once more, in the figures for recidivism. The FBI report for 1972 shows that those 228,032 people who committed all the major offenses in that year had an aggregate record of 244,399 convictions, but only 87,358 imprisonments of six months or more. In other words, roughly two-thirds of the convictions did *not* result in putting the offenders behind bars for any appreciable period, but left them on the streets where they could continue to commit crimes—which they proceeded to do. Similarly, in the decade 1963–72, 1084 offenders were identified in connection with the killing of policemen; of these no less than 59 percent had previously been convicted of criminal charges, and 61 percent of these had been granted parole or probation. [11]

FBI Director Hoover put the problem into perspective a decade ago when he observed that "for the 92,869 offenders processed in 1963 and 1964, 76 percent were repeaters; that is, they had a prior arrest on some charge. . . . Leniency in the form of probation, suspended sentence, parole and conditional release had

been afforded to 51 percent of the offenders. After the first leniency this group averaged more than three new arrests." [12] Translated, this means that three-quarters of the crimes committed in
these two years were committed by people who had already been
arrested and got free; and more than one-half were committed by
people who had been let off from their appointed sentence. *Our
crime rate for these years could have been cut in half merely by
requiring criminals already convicted to serve out their time.*

The Capital Punishment Debate

The ultimate expression of leniency in dealing with convicted
criminals is reserved for the ultimate penalty, capital punishment.
Opposition to this punishment has been perhaps the most successful of all the liberal campaigns affecting the criminal justice system. It combines within itself several leading features of the liberal
outlook, including hostility toward punitive measures, absorption
in the well-being of the criminal rather than the victim, and a belief that offenders are sick and in need of treatment.

The principal argument against capital punishment, repeatedly
stated as though it were self-evident fact, is that the penalty does
not deter—and that in view of this there can be no justification for
anything so horrible as the judicial taking of human life. The
horror is intensified, moreover, by the fact that the punishment is
unevenly applied, affecting the poor much more than the rich. It
is therefore on all counts a species of "cruel and unusual punishment" and should be rejected by any society that presumes to
describe itself as civilized.

There are reasons, however, to question these conclusions.
Consider, first of all, the inherent logic of the situation. On the one
hand we are told that capital punishment is ghastly and horrible,
a standing disgrace to our society. It is a barbaric act so dreadful
in its implications that we can hardly bear to contemplate its terrible character. On the other hand we are invited to believe this
self-same penalty gives not the slightest pause to people contem-
plating criminal homicide. The sanction that is considered a universal trauma for the human race is said to have no effect what-

ever in restraining those who may themselves be submitted directly to its terrors.

That proposition is, of course, absurd on the face of it. If capital punishment is as awful as the abolitionists contend, then we may be certain the prospect of having to face it personally has exerted a restraining influence on an unknown number of would-be killers and other violent criminals across a span of years, and has been responsible therefore for a sizable number of murders not committed. While a negative phenomenon of this sort is difficult to prove, we have persuasive evidence that this is precisely the nature of the case.

Not so long ago in our society capital punishment was used with considerable frequency. During the decade of the 1930s, for example, more than 1,600 prisoners were executed in the United States. Almost 1,300 were executed in the forties, while 717 were executed in the fifties. Toward the end of the fifties, the crusade against the death penalty got going in earnest, along with a more permissive attitude toward criminals in general. As a result of this campaign, capital punishment was abolished *de facto* long before the courts got around to overturning it in 1972. By 1960 the number of executions annually had fallen to 51, by 1964 it was down to 15, and by 1968 down to zero. There has not, in fact, been a legal execution in the United States since 1967. All of which is accounted by the abolitionists as a major victory for the cause of human dignity and justice.

What is generally ignored in all of this is the corresponding alteration in the crime rate. Although it seems somewhat incredible now, there was a time in America when the number of murders annually was moving in a downward rather than an upward direction. That downward trend, as it happens, coincided exactly with the period in which the death penalty was used with some degree of regularity—from the 1930s to the mid-1950s.

From 1935 to 1940, for example, the annual number of homicides in America fell from 10,587 to 8,329. That decline continued through the next two decades, bottoming out at 7,418 for 1955. An upturn occurred in the latter part of the decade, although the number of homicides in 1960 was still only 8,464—fewer than the number committed a generation before. Then came the 1960s and the steady abandonment of the death penalty. And exactly in tempo with this phase-out, the number of homicides each year has been going through the roof.

By 1968, the year of *de facto* abolition, there were no fewer than 12,000 murders in America; by 1971 there were 16,183; and by 1972, on the estimates of the FBI, there were a staggering 18,520. The enlightened sixties which saw the abolition of capital punishment also saw our annual quota of homicides more than doubled.[13]

It hardly seems a coincidence that the time of maximum use of the death penalty was a time of minimal homicide, and vice versa. Quite obviously, when a criminal knows his life will not be forfeit for an act of murder, the restraints against that act are considerably diminished. So, thanks to the abolitionists, we are now saving the 50 or so guilty lives that were being extinguished annually in the early 1960s. But we are also *losing* an additional 10,000 innocent ones as a result. All in all, not much of a victory for human life.

Taken together, the above considerations suggest that the so-called civil liberties view of the liberal community on matters of criminal justice is the opposite of libertarian. Because of increasingly lenient procedures, innocent people are being submitted to the rule of private violence. The criminals have more freedom, but the law-abiding have a great deal less. And the point of the system, we may recall, is supposed to be the other way around.

21
The Victims of Victimless Crime

Questions of economic policy and straightforward matters of "civil liberties" may admit of no definitive solution, but they do permit us to sort out the opposing factions. In both cases there is a "libertarian" side and an "authoritarian" one, and while the same people may not always show up on the same side of every issue, one side is at least clearly distinguishable from the other. There is another class of issues, however, for which these lines of demarcation are decidedly less clear.

Issues of this type are usually identified under the rubric of "victimless crimes." The exact designation of something as a victimless crime will vary from case to case, but contemporary debate typically includes such matters as drug use, pornography and obscenity, sexual conduct among consenting adults, and (a special case though it is generally lumped into the discussion) abortion. It is contended that a proper libertarian and limited-government view about such things would favor the weakening or abolition of restrictive measures concerning all of them, and that Supreme Court decisions which overturn state laws in such areas are to be welcomed on civil liberties grounds.

These issues differ from one another in several ways, and no single set of observations could provide an accurate summary of them all. There are, however, a number of considerations that generally apply to the "victimless crimes" debate, and that in one degree or another suggest a skeptical view of the conventional presentation.

To begin with, there is the *way* in which the debate is usually conducted. The characteristic mode of arguing, say, legalization of marijuana or homosexuality is to present the activity being restricted as a legitimate "alternative life style" that is perfectly good in its fashion or at least no worse than other activities already legal, but that is being suppressed through ignorance or bigotry. There is nothing wrong, it is said, with drug consumption, or homosexuality, or obscenity, except that you, the average citizen, don't happen to like or understand it.

It is precisely this aspect of the victimless crime crusade that is most troublesome. We are not being told, by and large, that these are immoral or mistaken practices that ought nonetheless to be tolerated in a pluralistic society (although, of course, some of the arguments are couched this way). We are instead invited to conclude that the practice in question should be licit because it is harmless or beneficial or as good as anything else—and thus to equate the notion of legalization with at least a tacit approval of the thing that is promoted.

This approach has two objectionable consequences—one at the level of philosophy, the other at the level of practical information. In philosophical terms, much of the victimless crime crusade appears to be a manifestation of the relativist notions examined in the Introduction, suggesting that one sort of practice is just about as good as another, and that nobody can really say that homosexuality or drug use or anything else is "wrong," so anything should go. If carried to its logical conclusion, that intellectual view would be the opposite of libertarian.

The cause of liberty must ultimately depend on certain axioms of belief about the nature of human life and on certain cultural standards derived from Western tradition about the rightness of personal freedom. By continually using the argument that there should be *no* standards, some of the victimless crime proponents attack the basis of the system they invoke. For if we don't really have *some* idea of what is right and what is wrong, why object to prohibiting victimless crimes—or for that matter anything else?

That particular danger may seem rather abstract and remote, and though it is philosophically ominous, it is mentioned only in passing. A more immediate danger is the effect of the victimless crime campaign in terms of practical information. For as a result of the "alternative life style" argument, thousands and probably millions of American young people have been persuaded that certain practices are essentially innocent and harmless, when the facts of record on them are heavily the other way. By far the most serious example of this tendency is the nation's continuing brouhaha over the use of marijuana.

The Victims of Marijuana

Glamorizing marijuana has been a major project of the leftward counterculture for the past few years, especially favored by the young and certain adults attuned to drugs and anxious to convert the nation to their cause. As often occurs in such crusades, an interested minority has managed to make its version of the facts prevail against the vague suspicions of the majority whose attention is diverted elsewhere. Most explicit discussion of the matter appears to take for granted, for example, the alleged "facts" that pot is harmless, pleasant, less destructive than alcohol, and nonaddictive—the usual themes of the pot promoters.*

An emerging body of data makes it plain, however, that these supposedly factual statements are profoundly mistaken, and that millions of Americans thus assured that "grass" can't possibly hurt them are being badly led astray. There is considerable medical

---

* Thus the Consumers Union, paraphrasing and endorsing the findings of the Canadian LeDain Commission: ". . . marijuana is not an addicting drug. Users do not develop tolerance in the classical sense—the kind of tolerance that leads to increasing the dosage. . . . Physical dependence on marijuana . . . has not been demonstrated. . . . The short-term physiological effects . . . 'are usually slight' . . ." On the comparison with alcohol, Consumers Union says: "A knowledgeable society, noting a few years ago that some of its members were switching from alcohol to a less harmful intoxicant, marijuana, might have encouraged that trend." (*Licit & Illicit Drugs,* Little Brown, 1972, pp. 460, 433.)

evidence that marijuana can hurt you very badly indeed, that its effects are often the reverse of pleasant, and that in many key respects it is more dangerous to health and sanity than alcohol.

We have, to begin with, the research compiled by Dr. Olav Braenden, head of the United Nations Narcotics Laboratory in Geneva, Switzerland, who appeared, in the fall of 1972, before a U.S. Senate committee. Dr. Braenden informed the senators of various international studies assessing the effects of marijuana (or "cannabis") and presented seven detailed reports that corroborated his testimony. Point for point, the Braenden data contested the view of pot-as-innocent-diversion.

He observed that marijuana consists of some fifty substances, the properties of which are not fully understood. A principal active ingredient is known in chemical shorthand as Delta-9-THC, and it develops that this substance, as well as other marijuana components, tends to accumulate in body tissue—which is not the case with alcohol. The result is that the potential toxic effects of the drug can build up over periods of use.

"I do not think there is anybody," Braenden testified, "who questions that cannabis is dangerous. The question is the degree of dangerousness. . . . I think there is a substantial difference between cannabis and alcohol in that alcohol is readily excreted from the body. It is not accumulated . . . as is the case with cannabis. . . . [Nicotine] does not accumulate either, as far as I know." [1]

Braenden further noted that available studies of marijuana show, among other effects, physical brain damage, personality change, vegetative torpor, and memory impairment. According to a Danish study, the impact of pot on driving reactions is greater than the impact of alcohol. Most seriously, Braenden observes that psychological effects of the drug include tendencies toward paranoia and in some cases toward psychosis.

These observations are seconded by the researches of Dr. W. D. Paton of the Department of Pharmacology at Oxford University, who tells us the active ingredients in pot ("cannabinoids") persist in the body and are therefore subject to cumulative build-up. The general effects, he says, are euphoria, a dropping of inhibitions, a loss of concentration and memory, and a general breakdown of mental function.

"The effects can also be unpleasant," Paton says, "especially in inexperienced subjects, particularly timelessness and the feeling of loss of control of mental processes. Feelings of unease, sometimes amounting to anguish, occur. . . . There is also, especially in the habitual user, a tendency toward paranoid thinking. High or habitual use can be followed by a psychotic state; this is usually reversible, quickly with brief periods of cannabis use, but more slowly after sustained exposure." Paton further discloses that dosages of cannabis have produced fetal deformities in animals, and that the effect is dose-related.[2]

These general observations were confirmed in great detail in a series of hearings conducted in early 1974 by the Senate Internal Security subcommittee. In these proceedings, twenty scientists who had conducted studies on the properties and effects of marijuana suggested that it does indeed accumulate in body tissue, that it can produce organic damage of a serious kind, and that it is considerably more harmful in these respects than alcohol, tobacco, or even LSD.

Dr. Julius Axelrod, who won the Nobel Prize for his research on the effect of drugs on the brain, testified that the principal active ingredient in marijuana is a toxic substance that accumulates in body tissue, especially in the brain. In animal experiments, he said, a single injection of THC caused only slight concentrations, but after repeated administration there was a gradual build-up in the fatty tissue of the brain.

Dr. Robert Heath, chairman of the Department of Psychiatry and Neurology at Tulane University, reported that such concentrations have deleterious effects on brain function. He discovered in animal studies that ingestion of marijuana at a rate corresponding to heavy use in human beings produced evidence of irreversible brain damage—of a sort that would take 25 or 30 years of chronic alcoholism to duplicate.

"When I first began to work with marijuana," Heath asserted, "I was much in keeping with the ideas that were prevalent in the scientific arena at that time that marijuana seemed to be a relatively innocuous agent. . . . But as I have gone on with the experiments observing the effects in humans . . . I began to feel that this is a very harmful drug. . . . This drug seems to produce real and significant damage and my data, I believe, substantiate the fact that this is a drug which has strongly deleterious effects with probably destructive effects on the brain in heavy users." [3]

That marijuana is considerably more harmful than alcohol was attested by Dr. Henry Brill, senior psychiatric member of the Shafer Commission on Marijuana and Drug Abuse, which gave an ambiguous go-ahead for the "decriminalization" of pot. Brill observed that "the chronic disabling effect of alcohol tends to become fully apparent after 10 to 20 or more years of excessive alcohol abuse, whereas in the case of cannabis, this slides in insidiously, and within two or three years an individual has problems, and it takes some technical and professional experience to realize where this came from. . . ." [4]

Accumulation of THC in the brain was also confirmed by Dr. Paton, who further noted that "administration of cannabis during the vulnerable period of pregnancy has been found to cause fetal death and fetal abnormality in three species of animals. The deformity includes lack of limbs—reduction deformity." [5] * The exact component of marijuana that caused this effect has yet to be isolated.

In this connection, one of the most startling disclosures in the hearings was that of Dr. Morton Stenchever, chairman of the Department of Obstetrics and Gynecology at the University of Utah. Stenchever testified that on the basis of his experiments, marijuana is responsible for human chromosome breakage, and thus affects the basic mechanism of inheritance. It is far more dangerous in this respect, he said, than LSD.

---

* Paton gave a useful summary of the differences between marijuana on the one hand and alcohol and tobacco on the other. Alcohol, he noted, is often taken for thirst-quenching purposes rather than psychic effect, is eliminated rapidly from the body, is not a cancer or mutation-inducing agent, has valid medical uses, and exacts a price for overuse in later life. Nicotine is taken as a relaxant, is noncumulative, is not cancer-producing if separated from tars, does not induce mutations, and again the price of overuse is paid in later life.

Marijuana, on the other hand, "is taken specifically . . . for its psychic action; it is cumulative and persistent; . . . experimentally it is teratogenic [producing fetal deformities]; psychotic phenomena may occur with a single dose; . . . the price for overuse is paid in adolescence or in early life."

According to the Utah scientist, chromosome breakage originally traced to LSD and widely publicized as a leading danger of that drug was apparently caused instead by marijuana. It turns out that the overwhelming majority of LSD users in the earlier study were also using pot, and Stenchever's laboratory researches employing strict controls show LSD alone does not induce a deviant level of chromosome breakage. Marijuana, however, does—at more than double the rate among nonusers.

Potential results of such breakage include fetal abnormalities of the type discussed by Paton and higher susceptibility to cancer. Cancer expert Cecile Leuchtenberger testified that marijuana use damages cell growth, can reduce the ability of the body to combat disease, and produces abnormalities in the amount of the genetic material, DNA.

Dr. Gabriel Nahas and his colleagues at Columbia University have produced additional clinical evidence that marijuana impairs cell division and weakens the body's defenses against disease. Comparing blood samples from 51 marijuana smokers with those of 81 nonsmokers, they found that the cell reproduction rate of the first group was 40 percent less than that of the second. This impairment affects white cells that combat viruses entering the body.

"We don't know yet the mechanism responsible for this inhibition," Nahas says. "Possibly it is connected with the tendency of [THC] . . . to inhibit DNA production. . . . We have observed that marijuana products accumulate in the germ cells of the testes and ovaries. It is therefore most urgent to find out to what extent long-term marijuana use will impair the genetic equilibrium and the DNA metabolism of these dividing germ cells and possibly affect adversely the offspring of the marijuana user." [6]

In his extensive study, *Marijuana, Deceptive Weed*, Nahas further confirms the researches alluded to above. He focuses with particular care on the matter of build-up in body tissue and notes that the result of this phenomenon is a higher tolerance for the drug and thus a craving for ever-stronger doses—directly contrary to the prevailing legends. He concludes that use of pot is "reinforcing," and therefore psychologically addictive, as is use of cocaine.

When larger doses are required to achieve a high and feed the user's sense of dependence, Nahas says, they can and do produce paranoid and psychotic reactions and the "disintegration of mental function." He observes that "panic reactions and acute toxic psychoses, especially in favorable settings, do occur, infrequently but also unpredictably." Despite the general reinforcing euphoria, the weed "can also precipitate an underlying psychosis. Prolonged daily use . . . is associated with mental and physical deterioration." [7]

In reaching these conclusions Nahas examines various arguments and studies deployed in behalf of marijuana, noting that surveys purporting to "clear" the drug were not controlled for dose-response ratios, which can be determined only by isolating the active ingredient and calculating how much of it is actually ingested. He asserts that all the relevant data show sufficient use of marijuana is very harmful indeed.

Dr. D. Harvey Powelson, research psychiatrist at the University of California and for eight years the director of psychiatric services for the student-health service there, confirms the harmful psychological effects of marijuana, and then some. Powelson testified before the Senate subcommittee that he had originally believed the drug to be harmless, but after treating hundreds of Berkeley students using pot, he reversed his opinion and now considers marijuana "the most dangerous drug we must contend with."

"The essence of the pattern," he said, "is that with small amounts of marijuana, approximately three joints of street grade, memory and time sense are interfered with. With regular usage the active principles cause more and more distorted thinking. The user's field of interest gets narrower and narrower as he focuses his attention on immediate sensation. . . . His ability to think sequentially diminishes. . . . As this happens, he depends more and more on pathological patterns of thinking. Ultimately all heavy users, that is daily users, develop a paranoid way of thinking." [8]

How bad the paranoid-to-psychotic reaction can become is suggested by the studies of two American psychiatrists, Harold Kolansky and William T. Moore of Philadelphia. Their findings in the *Journal of the American Medical Association* document numerous cases of intellectual disintegration and paranoid delusion, and several instances of psychosis and suicidal impulse, associated with marijuana. Almost invariably, stopping marijuana use brought substantial recovery, although there were lingering aftereffects.

Kolansky and Moore observe that habitual users "showed very poor social judgment, poor attention span, poor concentration, confusion, anxiety, depression, apathy, passivity, indifference, and, often, slowed and slurred speech. An alteration of conciousness which included a split between an observing and an experiencing part of the ego, an inability to bring thoughts together, a paranoid suspiciousness of others, and a regression to a more infantile state, were all very common."

Also of interest in the Kolansky-Moore researches was their experience with young people convinced that the drug was innocuous. They recount one instance in which a patient went to his college counselor and expressed misgivings about marijuana and "the counselor reassured him that the drug was harmless and that there was no medical evidence of difficulties as a consequence of smoking." [9] *

Countless young people, of course, have heard that message in recent years—if not directly from college advisers, then indirectly from the communications media, presidential commissions (most notably that headed up by former Pennsylvania Governor Raymond Shafer), and various other supposed authorities. On the emerging evidence, a substantial number of Americans are paying dearly for that counsel in diminished health and sanity.

In the light of these findings, what should be our attitude concerning marijuana? First of all, it is obvious that more research is needed, to elaborate on the findings cited above, settle disputed points, and in particular to lay to rest such crucial issues

---

* These researchers add that the normal problems of adolescence can be seriously intensified by marijuana, and that "when the adolescent is further exposed to equivocation by authorities in speech or writing on the innocence or dangers of marijuana, then his urge toward a drug solution for conflict may be enhanced. . . . Several of our patients had parents who talked to the adolescent of their own curiosity about the effects of marijuana, without emphasizing its dangers, or emphasized the discrepancies in the law, without insisting that the youngster must not use marijuana or other drugs because of the serious effects that would occur. We have found that equivocation by the parents has contributed to eventual drug experimentation."

as the chromosomal damage reported by Stenchever and Leuchtenberger. On the data reviewed, it appears that the drug is more harmful, not less, than alcohol, although less harmful of course than heroin. This would seem to indicate a legal status somewhere between the other two substances—which is more or less the position, in theory at least, that it currently occupies.

It has been argued that numerous young lives have been ruined by imposition of long jail sentences for smoking a little grass. In individual cases this is doubtless true and also unfortunate, given the massive propaganda campaign to which these young people have been subjected, arguing that marijuana is merely a pleasant diversion. By and large, however, the incidence of arrest and conviction for smoking marijuana is almost nil.* It is likely, indeed, that far more young lives have been ruined by smoking pot than by laws attempting to prevent them from smoking it.

That being so, it seems that the urgent need of the hour, considerably more important than what we do about the laws, is to reverse the propaganda campaign in behalf of marijuana. All those people who have promoted the pleasant fun of smoking pot should either refute the findings of Drs. Paton, Heath, Nahas, Stenchever, Kolansky, Moore, et al., or else come forth with public recantations. The mass communications media, which have been happily glamorizing pot as a symbol of the alternative life style, should make it their business to spread the story of its potential dangers to the American people.

If this were accomplished, the legal end of the matter could be handled with common sense and compassion for the unfortunates inveigled into using the stuff. If American adolescents were con-

---

* Although the absolute number of arrests has grown in keeping with the enormous increase in marijuana use, only a tiny percentage of the 24 million people who have at some time indulged themselves are ever arrested (189,000 state arrests in 1970). And among those arrested, as noted by the Shafer commission, "approximately 50 percent of the adults and 70 percent of the juveniles are not processed through the system; their cases are dismissed by the police, by the prosecutors, or by the courts. Ultimately less than 6 percent of all those apprehended are incarcerated, and very few of these sentences are for possession of small amounts for personal use." (Marijuana: A Signal of Misunderstanding, First Report of the National Commission on Marijuana and Drug Abuse, March 1972, p. 130.)

vinced that pot was toxic, they would have little impulse to try it, and there would be no more need for criminal laws to punish consumption of marijuana than there is for laws to punish the consumption of, say, poison toadstools. On libertarian grounds, indeed, the onus of the law ought to be on those who advertise and merchandise marijuana as a beneficial substance—which on the evidence is a species of fraud, and lethal fraud at that.*

However, efforts to change the laws in such a fashion should not be made until *after* the educational campaign about the dangers of marijuana has been accomplished, or at least well launched. At this stage, while pro-marijuana propaganda still suffuses the nation, changes in the laws are seen, for the most part correctly, as symbolic capitulations to the notion that the stuff is harmless. Such changes, without the educational campaign, will merely serve to encourage consumption, on the mistaken notion that the authorities have finally caved in to the validity of the marijuana arguments.

The Victims of Pornography

A second social issue on which the imperatives of common sense and the factual record appear to go directly contrary to the usual arguments is that of pornography and obscenity. This perennial subject of national concern was brought sharply into focus in the summer of 1973 by the Supreme Court's ruling that upheld the use of "community standards" in banning pornographic material. This ruling was widely construed as a restriction on our consti-

---

* A logical intermediary step would be to have sale and distribution of marijuana placed under the same rules as the sale of beneficial drugs, administered by the Food and Drug Administration. Under these rules, of course, one could not sell marijuana at all, since the FDA rule on drugs is that they cannot be marketed until they have been proved both safe and effectively beneficial. Clearly, no such finding is possible in the case of marijuana. It is a curiosity of our time that the same people who put the burden of proof on beneficial drugs before they can be sold would reverse that burden of proof in discussion of a harmful drug like marijuana. If you want to sell vitamins, you have to prove they *are* safe. But if somebody wants to halt the sale of marijuana, he has to prove it *isn't* safe.

tutional liberties—opponents viewing it as a malign infringement, supporters hailing it as a welcome put-down of licentious freedoms. Both assessments are off the mark.

The issue of obscenity is complex, and not every aspect of the Supreme Court's reasoning, or of certain arguments for banning obscenity that have been offered of late in conservative circles, seems valid. There is something rather chilling about the suggestion that society should use the coercive power of law to shape a public consensus of belief and attitude, a position fraught with danger for all our liberties. Who, after all, is to say what the consensus should consist of, and who is to be in charge of enforcing it? Notions of this type might be used to justify almost any kind of repression, and appear to be more congenial to liberal social planners than to conservatives.

The Supreme Court's ruling is correct for other reasons altogether—its attention to the matter of community effects, and its renewed concern for the American federal balance. On both counts its decision makes more sense than does the usual case in behalf of pornography, which consists of arguing that "no maid was ever ruined by a book" (or film), that pornography is of interest only to the private purchaser of it, and that the Supreme Court should therefore impose a single permissive standard for obscenity on every state and community in America.

The argument is weak throughout. For one thing, the notion that people's behavior toward other people is not influenced by what they read or see is patently anti-intellectual and contrary to experience. It assumes that ideas have no consequences in the world of action and that modes of writing and expression are meaningless—a premise that if logically extended would render nugatory the labors of countless ministers, teachers, philosophers, and writers of every description. Everyone acknowledges that encouragements to moral conduct and models of exemplary behavior can influence action; why assume that negative encouragements and models are not equally potent?

As argued in a recent volume called *The Case Against Pornography,* there is plentiful reason for believing that pornography does influence behavior in criminal directions by providing models of sadistic or otherwise deviant conduct. Psychologist Ernest van den Haag cites in this connection the famous "Moors" murder trial in which adults steeped in the works of de Sade tortured children to death. He observes that "pornography nearly always leads to sadistic pornography. By definition, pornography de-individualizes and dehumanizes sexual acts; by eliminating all the contexts it reduces people simply to bearers of impersonal sensations of pleasure and pain. This de-humanization eliminates the empathy that restrains us ultimately from sadism and non-consensual acts." [10]

A considerable body of survey evidence suggests that ideas, including pornographic ones, do have consequences. Pamela Hansford Johnson, whose *On Iniquity* rehearsed the "Moors" case at some length, recalls the extensive research of the Eisenhower Commission that found a correlation between violent behavior and exposure to theatrical scenes of violence on television. Miss Johnson quotes the commission's findings that "experimental studies on this question have found that observed violence stimulates aggressive behavior, rather than the opposite. . . . Violence on television encourages violent forms of behavior, and fosters moral and social attitudes about violence in daily life which are unacceptable in civilized society." [11]

Since deploring violence on television is moderately fashionable, the report of the Eisenhower Commission met with no appreciable protest from America's leftward intelligentsia. Indeed, crusades to put the squeeze on violent TV shows are cranked up periodically by congressional liberals (Senator John Pastore, D-R.I., being the most usual spokesman), precisely on the grounds that the behavior models supplied thereby exert a negative impact on the social order. Granted the difference between TV as a federally licensed activity highly accessible to young people and the private distribution of books and movies, the intellectual question is essentially the same: Are we seriously to believe that "Hawaii Five-O" can adversely influence public behavior, but that the rape and violence of *A Clockwork Orange* cannot?

As it happens, there are some persuasive clinical studies suggesting that immersion in pornographic literature has a definite correlation to criminal activity. These studies were conducted, strangely enough, for the President's Commission on Obscenity and Pornography, but the majority members of that commission ignored the findings of their own researchers in their yen to argue the innocence of porn. The data are assembled in a powerful dissent to the commission's findings filed by Father Morton Hill and Winfrey Link, and concurred in by Charles H. Keating Jr., all of whom had served as members of the panel.

The Hill-Link study, compiled by psychologist Victor Cline, systematically reviews the data gathered by commission researchers and finds repeated instances in which exposure to pornography is correlated to deviant conduct: a survey of 476 reformatory inmates that found high exposure to porn coincided with sexually deviant behavior and "affiliation with groups high in criminal activity and sex deviancy"; a study of 365 widely dispersed individuals that concluded that "exposure to pornography is the strongest predictor of sexual deviance among the early age of exposure subjects"; yet another study in which "the data clearly support the proposition that aggression against women increases when that aggression is instrumental to securing sexual stimulation (through seeing pornography)." [12]

Perhaps the most disturbing of these surveys is the so-called Goldstein study that examined nine separate groups of male subjects, including rapists. The study found that the rapists were the most highly excited by pornography, that 80 percent of them reported "wishing to try" the acts portrayed in pornographic material, and that 55 percent reported being "excited to sex relations by pornography." In another commission-sponsored survey, some 39 percent of sex offenders indicated that "pornography had something to do with their committing the sex offense that they were convicted of." [13] And so on and on.

These reports are not conclusive, of course, and certainly do not prove that pornography "caused" the crimes of which the subjects were convicted. There are too many factors involved in criminal conduct to make that kind of statement, and the respondents' desire to offload their behavior to some external factor could be a powerful motive in producing some of their answers. Still and all, the logic of the situation and the empirical data alike suggest that the notion of pornography's affecting only the willing consumer is moot. We have a basis for wondering just what the community effects may be, and little reason for concluding flatly that there are no community effects at all.

And in that event, the decision of the Supreme Court to remand the issue to the states and local communities is exactly right. For in the absence of a conclusive finding that pornography consumption is purely self-regarding, and therefore purely a "civil liberties" issue, there can be no federal mandate to usurp the powers of states and local communities in dealing with such matters. (Indeed, on the premises stated in Chapter 17 there would be no such mandate even if the issue were clearly one of in that direction the argument on this score need not be elaborated.)

Philosophical versus Constitutional Principles

A point of perennial confusion in "civil liberties" debate is the constant necessity of weighing two different elements in the libertarian structure of our government—the philosophical and the constitutional. The first of these indicates what relationships ought to prevail in our society, in a theoretical sense. The second indicates what relationships ought to prevail, as a matter of legal and constitutional order. One defines an abstract attitude, the other the intended rule of law by which our political affairs are supposed to be governed.

While closely related in America by philosophic origin and political development, these two approaches can be and frequently are quite different in their implications. For example, a consideration on theoretical grounds (and a look at the practical record) strongly suggests the U.S. Post Office would be better conducted if it were run by private business, and not by the Federal government. Yet no one could contend that the government's operation of the Post Office is *unconstitutional,* since authority for conducting such an agency is explicitly set forward in the Constitution itself.

That kind of difference is equally applicable in the present instance. As a philosophical matter we may conclude that no level of government ought to have an "established church," or prohibit the distribution of contraceptives, or ban the distribution of certain kinds of literature. Yet under our constitutional settlement, all these powers (now in whole or part denied) clearly resided in the states and were exercised by them to one degree or another. They originally had such powers in a constitutional sense, even though on theoretical grounds we conclude they should not have.

When these two sets of imperatives are in conflict, as frequently occurs, the normal tendency of every ideological faction is to subordinate the second to the first, to strike down the exercise of a constitutional power in the state by appealing to the abstract correctness of our philosophical position, and calling in the Federal judiciary as the agent of our wishes. The conservative Supreme Court of the nineteenth and early twentieth centuries did exactly this when it struck down state laws· regulating industry—decisions with which a *laissez-faire* economist would agree but which clearly denied to the states the police powers they possessed under the Constitution.

This procedure is as mistaken as it is natural. For it clearly contributes to the drift of our system away from the known rule of law to a situation of indeterminacy, and it just as clearly erodes the federal balance in which the powers of the states act as a counterpoise against the Federal government in Washington. As argued earlier, a system in which our rights are dependent on the subjective discretion of the Federal authorities rather than the guidelines of the Constitution is one in which all our freedoms are perpetually endangered. It seems fine when the authorities agree with us, but not so fine, as the liberals discovered under Nixon, when they do not.

It follows that, on libertarian grounds, we should *oppose* the continual invocation of the Federal courts to override the police powers of the states, even when the laws in question—on criminal procedure, apportionment, or pornography—may appear to have an anti-libertarian character. If the state laws are to be changed—and many of them need to be—they should be changed by actions within the states, and not by Federal decree.*

---

* The obvious exception to this rule occurs, of course, in instances where the Federal government has an explicit constitutional basis for its action—as in protecting the right to vote in Federal elections.

22
A Matter of Life and Death

When Warren Burger became Chief Justice of the United States and Nixon appointees began to fill the chairs of the nation's highest tribunal, it was assumed the revolutionary epoch in the interpretation of America's basic law had come to at least a temporary close. And in certain areas (such as school finance and criminal justice) it proved to be so. But in certain other areas the Burger court and the Nixon appointees showed they were ready to embark on constitutional excursions of their own, quite as revolutionary as anything attempted by their predecessors.

Most notable of the constitutional thunderbolts delivered by the Burger court was the abortion decision handed down on January 22, 1973. In this decree, the high court came down conclusively on the side of permissive abortion.* Speaking through Justice Harry Blackmun, the court said it was unable to determine whether the child in embryo was actually a person or not, and that therefore the child could properly be killed to suit the convenience of the mother. So elective abortion was constitutional.

---

* The vote was 7–2. Of the four Nixon appointees, only Justice William Rehnquist dissented.

On the court's analysis, the principal issue at stake in this discussion was the danger of the operation to the mother. When restrictive abortion laws were drafted, according to Blackmun, the operation was considered hazardous; now medical science had made it less so. After three months, however, the maternal mortality rate from abortion is as high as or higher than the mortality rate from childbirth, so after the first trimester of pregnancy the state may regulate abortions—albeit in a manner professedly enhancing the mother's "psychological" and "emotional" well-being. In the event, this has proved to be a license for elective abortion up to the moment of delivery.[1]

On this showing, the life of the child in embryo counts for nothing; the exclusive focus of concern is the health and well-being of the mother. The court professed to find the question of the fetus' personhood moot, but by decreeing that it could legally be extinguished in fact decided the matter with a good deal of finality. The legal reasoning was that the drafters of the Fourteenth Amendment didn't believe the child in embryo was a "person" and didn't intend to confer its protection on the fetus—and far be it from the court to enlarge upon the purposes of the drafters.

The court's further treatment of the subject, however, made it plain that this alleged show of strict construction was not a forthright statement of judicial attitude. For, when considering the convenience of the mother, the court extended to hitherto unimaginable lengths that invented "right of privacy" which even the supple intellect of Justice Douglas does not pretend to deduce from constitutional language, but simply posits as something the court has decided to protect. Where the life of the child in embryo is at stake, that is, the court is a model of judicial quiescence; but where the *convenience* of the mother is at stake, it is willing to roam afar in pursuit of rights nowhere envisioned by the drafters.

Is Abortion Libertarian?

Despite its logical and legal defects, the Blackmun decision has been widely acclaimed as a proper libertarian initiative. This view is in keeping with a general attitude in certain sectors of our society that having an abortion is a strictly "private" matter between a woman and her physician. One may argue instead that the effect of the ruling, and of permissive abortion, is the opposite of libertarian, and thus a premier example of that class of issues in which the conventional rhetoric inclines in one direction while the facts of the case are deployed in the other.

The Supreme Court's decision is typical in that it so blandly dismisses all claims to consideration by the unborn child. The abortion is treated as a one-way proposition involving the mother's "right to her own body" with no other rights involved in the discussion. The fetus is treated as an insentient "thing"—or is simply not mentioned at all. So long as the discussion is conducted in this way, of course, it is very easy to think of abortion as an expression of personal liberty that need not yield to somebody else's beliefs or values.

Considering the importance of this question in deciding the issue, it is remarkable how little attention abortionists give to what in fact the fetus *is*. Is it simply a mass of undifferentiated tissue? An egg? A blob of protoplasm? Most usually the question is passed over in silence, the fetus being defined out of existence by the simple device of not bothering to talk about it.

For those who claim to be speaking for modernity against the outmoded claims of religious fanatics, this is a most curious method of proceeding. The reason for it, however, is not so curious. For the truth is that the facts of medical science are all the other way, and the more we learn the more it becomes apparent that the fetus is not a "part of the mother's body" or a "blob of protoplasm" at all. The evidence is irresistible that what is being extinguished by abortion is the life of an individuated, though very tiny, human being—which makes the reluctance of the abortionists to focus on it a bit more understandable.

When conception occurs by the fertilization of the ovum, something altogether different from "the mother's body" comes into being. The new genetic structure thus created consists of 23 chromosomes from the father and 23 from the mother—a package that is distinct from every other human being in the world. In that package are contained all the attributes of a new individual, different from its father and mother alike. Given time and nutrition, the being thus created will grow into an adult person—with exactly the genetic characteristics that were established at conception. None of this is true of any "part of the mother's body," be it her fingernails, her teeth, or her appendix.

The genetic imprint, we now understand, is the root principle of human individuality—and it is interesting to note that the advance of modern science has confirmed and reconfirmed the view that fetal life is separate and individual. In very short order this genetic package blossoms into recognizable human shape—a point established very vividly by photographs that show aborted fetuses are in fact little babies, with perfectly articulated hands and feet and facial features. Through the science of fetology we know what others in centuries past did not: that active, sentient life exists in the womb, and that this life is fully and recognizably human from the earliest days of the child's existence.

Thus blood cells form at 17 days, and the baby's eyes begin to form at 19 days. At 30 days the primary brain is present, and ears and nasal organs have begun. At the end of six weeks, the baby has articulated thumbs and fingers, brain waves are observable, the heart is beating, and the stomach produces digestive juices. Milk teeth buds are present by six and a half weeks. The baby will respond to touching, and by the beginning of the ninth week will also move spontaneously. By the twelfth week he can move his thumb in opposition to his fingers. All of this is before the mother feels any movement from the unborn child.

Dr. Arnold Gesell, the noted child authority, observes that "when the embryo is only four weeks old, there is behavior patterning: the heart beats. In two more weeks slow back and forth movements in the arms and limbs appear. Before the twelfth week of uterine life the fingers flex in reflex grasps." [2] Dr. H. M. I. Liley is equally emphatic on the subject. The fetus, she says, is "neither a vegetable nor an acquiescent tadpole as some have conceived him to be in the past, but rather a tiny human being as independent as though he were lying in a crib with a blanket wrapped around him instead of his mother." [3] And she gives us this graphic description of fetal life as it exists only seven days after fertilization:

The young individual, in command of his environment and destiny with a tenacious purpose, implants in the spongy lining and with a display of physiological power suppresses

the mother's menstrual period. This is his home for the next
270 days and to make it habitable the embryo develops a
placenta and a protective capsule of fluid for himself. We
know that he moves with a delightful easy grace in his buoy-
ant world, that fetal comfort determines fetal position. He is
responsive to pain and touch and cold and sound and
light. . . . he gets hiccups and sucks his thumb. He wakes
and sleeps. He gets bored with repetitive signals but can be
taught to be alerted by a first signal for a second different
one. . . . This then is the fetus we know and indeed we
each once were. This is the fetus we look after in modern
obstetrics, the same baby we are caring for before and after
birth, who before birth can be ill and need diagnosis and
treatment just like any other patient.[4]

To reiterate, the baby in the womb *can feel pain*. In the practice of fetology, injections can be given to the unborn child—but
for this it must be sedated. Otherwise it would move away from
the needle. Dr. Liley observes that "when doctors first began
invading the sanctuary of the womb, they did not know that the
unborn baby would react to pain in the same fashion as a child
would. But they soon learned that he would. By no means a 'vegetable' as he has so often been pictured, the unborn knows perfectly well when he has been hurt, and he will protest it just as
violently as would a baby lying in a crib." [5]

Not exactly a blob of protoplasm—but rather easily recognizable human life. And it is this life that must be exterminated
to perform an abortion, which explains the reluctance of the
abortionists to have us dwell on the matter unduly. Indeed, in their
effort to divert attention from what in fact the fetus is, the abortionists have tried to develop a vocabulary of thinghood to describe
it. According to the *Wall Street Journal,* abortionists in New York
have encouraged the use of such phrases as "products of conception," rather than baby, to convey "maximum meaning with
minimal emotional overtones." [6] Unfortunately for this antiseptic
approach, some of these aborted "products of conception" are
born alive.

Dr. Jean Pakter of New York City's Bureau of Maternity
Services has reported that, under that state's permissive law (but

before the Supreme Court's even more permissive decision), more than 60 aborted fetuses were born showing signs of life. Of these almost all subsequently died; at this report, however, one was living with his parents, and another was hospitalized. It is altogether likely the number of live abortions in New York and elsewhere has been many times this stated figure, since it is routine practice in hysterotomy (Caesarean) abortions for babies to emerge from the womb trying to live and thereafter simply be permitted to die or dispatched by smothering.

The youngest children known to survive premature delivery have been between 20 and 25 weeks old. Dr. Andre Hellegers of Georgetown University says 10 percent of children born in this span will survive, and it is acknowledged that "viability" today is much earlier than in years past.[7] Viability is not a static concept, but a function of the medical art. As our techniques improve, the date of viability becomes progressively earlier. It is therefore illogical to set some arbitrary limit such as the end of the first trimester as if it were graven in stone as a permanent benchmark of viability. Even more to the point, of course, *all* babies are alive before they are aborted; the point of the abortion is, precisely, to kill them.

Concealed by all that antiseptic language about disposing of the "products of conception" is a rather gruesome business. The methods employed are all brutal, hysterotomy being perhaps the least so. The other methods include dilation and curettage, in which the baby is dismembered with a curved knife and then pulled out of the womb piece by piece; suction, in which the baby is sliced up into bits and pieces and then sucked out of the womb in a bloody mass; and saline injections, which simply poison the baby to death, inducing miscarriage.

Against this evidence, what are we to make of the libertarian argument for abortion? In the name of asserting the mother's "right to privacy," the abortionists and the Supreme Court are telling us the right of the fetus to life itself may be denied. In the scale of civil liberties, this is to subordinate the greater right to the lesser, since manifestly the right to life is prior to all others, and is so denominated in the Declaration of Independence. Unless we are allowed to live, we cannot enjoy the rights of free speech, property, religious association, privacy, or anything else.

Prior to recent medical discoveries concerning the reality of fetal life, it had been assumed in some court decisions that the unborn child was indeed a "part of the mother's body." But it is noteworthy that the trend of twentieth century jurisprudence had been moving away from this notion as the scientific evidence unfolded. Thus in the case of *Bonbrest v. Katz* (1946) the U.S. District Court for the District of Columbia permitted a recovery for prenatal injuries, rejecting an older finding that the child in the womb was simply an extension of the mother. The state of medical knowledge in the twentieth century, said the court, made it plain that "a living fetus cannot be considered integral to the mother scientifically and that legal doctrine should take this into account."

It is true that the fetus is in the womb, "but it is capable now of extrauterine life—and while dependent for its continued development on sustenance derived from its peculiar relationship to its mother, it is not a 'part' of the mother in the sense of a constituent element—as that term is generally understood. Modern medicine is replete with cases of living children being taken from dead mothers; indeed, apart from viability, a nonviable fetus is not part of its mother. . . . The law is presumed to keep pace with the sciences and medical science has certainly made progress since 1884 [date of the earlier decision that the child is a part of the mother]." [8]

Further development of this line of reasoning occurred in the case of *Kelly v. Gregory* (1953) in which it was held that "legal separability should begin where there is biological separability," and that the latter "begins at conception." Of similar tendency was the case of *Paul v. Milwaukee Automobile Association* (1959), in which the court denied that "a child is more a part of its mother before it becomes viable than after it is viable. It would be more accurate to say that the fetus from conception lives within the mother rather than as a part of her." [9]

This was a logical effort to assimilate the findings of modern science into the body of the law, and appeared to be fully in keeping with the notion that modern legalists are sensitive to "civil liberties" and eager to expand the ambit of constitutional rights. It was also in keeping with the growing awareness of the public as to what abortion is all about, as well as with the impressive results at the polls when the subject was put to a vote.* The Supreme Court, however, has at a stroke reversed all this and demonstrated rather plainly how precarious are our rights when the guarantees of law may be taken away at the discretion of men with power, and sweeping decisions may be imposed top-down on the entire American nation.

Even without all this, however, the libertarian case *against* abortion would seem to be conclusive. I for one think the evidence of the fetus' humanity is overwhelming, but let me concede for purposes of argument that I am wrong, and that the Supreme Court's professed agnosticism is justified. What is the proper libertarian conclusion? Quite obviously, under libertarian legal (and medical) principles, any doubt whatsoever should be resolved in favor of innocent life—not against it.

Under our system we do not bury someone because we aren't sure he is still alive, or execute someone because we aren't sure he is innocent. So long as any shadow of a doubt remains, the equation is resolved *in favor of life*. Exactly the same considerations apply in the case of abortion: If the fetus is not a person, then refusal to kill it incurs the evil of inconvenience to the mother. But if it *is* a person—and the court explicitly says it cannot determine that it *isn't*—the judges have virtually sanctioned a million murders annually.

The foregoing should be enough to suggest that what is at stake in the abortion debate is not simply someone trying to impose religious or ethical views on someone else as an exercise in theology. Quite clearly, we are dealing here with medical facts as to the existence of life. The genetic record and the evidence unearthed by the science of fetology are matters of fact, not faith. And the question of whether fetal life may be destroyed is no more a "religious" issue than the question of whether any life may be destroyed—which indeed has religious elements but is properly recognized in our society as a quintessential function of secular government.

While the immediate issues are matters of fact, it is obvious

---

* In some rather notable referenda conducted in Michigan and North Dakota in November 1972, voters rejected permissive abortion by margins of better than two to one.

a number of serious religious and ethical questions are enfolded in the abortion struggle. Certainly the drive for abortion has ethical overtones of the most glaring sort. It is manifestly a product of the permissive impulse in our society, and in some ways the most extreme development of that impulse. For what is being argued here is that people may indulge their sexual appetites at will, and then dispose of the consequences by killing the baby that is the result. It would be difficult to conjure up a more thoroughgoing scenario of self-indulgence, devoid of ethical or legal constraints.

Viewed from a different angle, the abortion drive and associated movements in our society have yet another sort of ethical meaning. One's attitude toward human life is the most basic of all social and cultural attitudes, which are ultimately determined by theological considerations. Judaeo-Christian societies have held that every human being is precious by virtue of his or her creaturehood and relationship to a personal God. Such ideas are foreign to pagan societies, which have viewed individuals as creatures of the state and evinced a considerable indifference to the value of human life. Abortion and infanticide were common practices in Greece and Rome, because these societies did not affirm the religious view that lends value and dignity to every human person. A similar indifference to life has been manifest in the modern totalitarian systems, also distinguished by their rejection of the Judaeo-Christian heritage.

It is apparent on any survey of the total record that what we are witnessing today in American society, in the drive for abortion and associated movements, is a resurgence of pagan and neo-pagan attitudes. As we have drifted further from our moorings in Judaic and Christian belief, we have also drifted away from our libertarian conceptions concerning the value of human life.

The "Right to Die"

The "new ethic" suggested by easy acceptance of abortion is already seeking conquests beyond the womb, beginning with the aged and infirm. No sooner had the Supreme Court's abortion decision taken hold than we were subjected to a drumfire of publicity about the "right to die," the advantages of mercy killing, and the subtle joys of "death with dignity." The predicted drive for euthanasia is spreading across America, exactly as anticipated by the opponents of abortion.

Thus we are treated to media puffery, including TV entertainments, about the undignified state of people kept alive by expensive hospital machinery, clearly suggesting the superior attractiveness of death. A nationally distributed news feature describes the outlook of an aged lady who "does not want to hang on, like too many of her friends, wired into tubes and respirators . . . in effect, a living mummy, a degradation of life, a defilement of death." [10] This lady has executed a "living will" that urges her family, friends, and physician to pull the plug and let her die if she reaches that condition.

Such notions are apparently spreading. The Euthanasia Society of America, which promotes the "living will" idea and advocates "passive euthanasia" (letting people die instead of killing them outright), claims a quantum jump of membership in recent years. The head of the organization reports the number of members has grown from 600 in 1969 to 50,000 in 1973, and that the "living will" procedure is catching on. She asserts that "we had a bride and groom the other day who wanted to sign the 'living will' as part of their mutual understanding, which I thought was very sweet." [11]

Acceptance of euthanasia is confirmed by the Gallup Poll, which shows a startling rise in the percentage of the American population that looks with favor on the idea of mercy killing. In 1950 the affirmative responses on the question came to 36 percent. In 1973 the proportion was up to 53 percent. The most notable rise in favorable answers occurred among those under 30 years of age. Two decades ago their "yes" response to mercy killing was only 30 percent; in 1973 it stood at an enormous 67 percent. Among those with college educations, the "yes" response has gone from 34 percent to 61.

As with abortion, the argument for mercy killing is being made by emotional exploitation of hard cases, such as terminal cancer patients stuck full of tubes, allegedly wanting to die but prevented from doing so by outmoded value systems. With abortion it was victims of rape or incest—statistically insignificant factors in the widespread slaughter of the unborn to suit the convenience of their parents.*

On that analogy, it is logical to suspect the euthanasia drive embraces similar motives. Who is really being considered in the demand for mercy killings? The victims who will be permitted to die or actively dispatched, or the friends and relatives who find the old and infirm to be an emotional and financial nuisance? Dr. Milton Helpern, chief medical examiner of New York City, thinks it's the latter. He opposes euthanasia and observes that it's "done for the convenience of the family. . . . It's the family that can't stand the suffering. A patient who's in a coma isn't in pain. It's the family who's in pain." [12] Such pain is quenched most readily by letting the patient slip away.

That the anti-life campaign implies a reversal of civilizational values at the deepest level is suggested by a remarkable editorial that appeared a few years back in the journal of the California Medical Association. This editorial states that the drive for abortion is in fact a rejection of the Judaeo-Christian social ethic at its very core—a direct assault on life itself. What is really being decided in the abortion debate, the editorial argues, is that some shall live while others die, and that it is up to physicians with their special expertise to assist in making these difficult choices.

"Since the old ethic has not yet been fully displaced," says the editorial, "it has been necessary to separate the idea of abortion from the idea of killing, which continues to be socially abhorrent. The result has been a curious avoidance of the scientific fact, which everyone really knows, that human life begins at conception and is continuous whether intra- or extra-uterine until death. . . . It is suggested that this schizophrenic sort of subterfuge is necessary because while a new ethic is being accepted the old one has not yet been rejected."

The editorial stresses the repudiation of Western religious values implicit in this procedure, observing that problems of pollution and population growth confront us "with the necessity of deciding what is to be preserved and strengthened and what is not,

---

* Exactly how widespread may be inferred from the fact that in New York State, in 1972, there were more abortions than live births—by a margin of 278,600 to 252,278.

and that this will of necessity violate the traditional Western ethic. . . . It will become necessary to place relative rather than absolute values on such things as human lives, the usage of scarce resources, and the various elements which are to make up the quality of life or living which is to be sought. This is quite distinctly at variance with the Judaeo-Christian ethic. . . ." [13]

The unborn, the old, the sickly and unfit—where, exactly, does the process stop? Every resident of the twentieth century with its gallery of totalitarian horrors can provide a ready answer to that question.

23
The
Social
Engineers

The introductory chapter of this volume argued that American liberalism by theory and practice necessarily leads on to the erosion of freedom. It does this in two interrelated ways. First, by its theory of explicit politics, it encourages resort to collectivist practice in which effective power is increasingly concentrated in the hands of the central government. Second, by its theory of value, it eliminates those standards and safeguards by which the exercise of power can be controlled, and destroys the ethical basis for affirming individual freedom. The net effect, it was suggested, was to create an enormous engine of coercion that could tyrannize without restraint over its human subjects.

It was further argued that similar notions have marked the totalitarian movements of this century. All have been distinguished, precisely, by the embrace of relativist-to-nihilist doctrine, an enormous concentration of power in the hands of the political state, and a callous disregard for the rights of the individual citizen. Western liberalism, it was suggested, could be defined as an attempt to find a halfway house between these horrors of modernity and traditional Western standards—to embrace the premises of the totalitarian regimes, while avoiding the results. The emergence of totalitarian practice in Western societies may be taken to signal the failure of this experiment—and hence the death of liberalism itself.

That the concentration of power is a major feature of the liberal program has been a principal burden of our argument, and needs no retelling here. We have further seen that the relativism of the liberal outlook has indeed eroded the restraints on the use of the power once established. On the liberal analysis, there can be no *a priori* limits on the deployment of governmental authority except the discretion of the people wielding it. The idea of fixed and knowable boundaries is obviously incompatible with evolutionary metaphysics, relativist notions of the "living Constitution," judicial realism, and the rest of it. Thus the principal features of the totalitarian societies are in place and fully visible, and they are continually reinforced and amplified by other elements of the liberal program.

From Liberalism to Authoritarianism

While the economic policy failures we have reviewed are not directly relevant here, they offer tangential points worth considering. First, the fact that the liberals continue to build Leviathan despite its manifest and many failures strongly suggests the power urge has become an end in itself—an all too familiar political syndrome. Second, since every failure becomes the pretext for another intervention that in turn will issue in another failure of its own, the process of consolidation becomes perpetual. Thus viewed, the case for intervention is self-enclosed and sealed against critique.

These two factors taken together suggest that, barring external correction, the liberal urge to absorb and deploy power will continue to its logical conclusion—which is the authoritarian state. And data indicating we are headed in this direction are profusely evident in our society. In the chapter immediately preceding, we have observed the most alarming symptom of this development— a growing indifference toward the value of human life. As liberalism has drifted further and further away from our traditional conceptions of human worth and individuality, we find a growing hostility not only to personal freedom but to the very concept of life itself.

A devaluated notion of human life has long been implicit, of course, in the environmentalist view that personal conduct for good or ill is the result of external forces, an idea repeatedly encountered in this volume. Assumptions of this type are evident in nearly all the controversial programs that have marred the recent history of public education. They are the basis of programs to abolish crime by abolishing poverty, and of other economic aspects of the welfare state. They are the fount of "rehabilitation-ist" penology (although, as we shall note, this embraces other components as well). Indeed, they are a major premise of liberal efforts in the realm of foreign policy—where it is assumed that people turn to Communism because of economic conditions, and that wars are caused by weapons.

This array of social assumptions follows directly and neces-sarily from the liberal view of humanity, nature, and the universe. The liberal outlook has characteristically assumed that human beings are products of the natural order of things, a higher form of animal, or a product of the random spread of energy in the universe. The degree to which this view of man has become ac-cepted in modern academic thought was suggested by the late Carl Becker, a respected liberal scholar.

Becker asserted that, for those who study "modern science," it is impossible "to regard man as the child of God for whom the earth was created as a temporary habitation. Rather we must regard him as little more than a chance deposit on the surface of the world, carelessly thrown up between two ice ages by the same forces that rust iron and ripen corn. . . . It has taken eight centuries to replace the conception of existence as divinely com-posed and purposeful drama by the conception of existence as a blindly running flux of disintegrating energy. . . ." [1]

If this viewpoint be accepted, a number of consequences seem to follow—and lead us inexorably in the direction of totalitar-ianism. The most obvious is the inference that, if people are essen-tially animals or objects in the natural order of things, why not treat them accordingly? We deal with animals and natural phe-nomena as objects of control and experimentation; if people are animals or natural phenomena, it follows that they are also available for control and experimentation. This simple but terrifying logic is now being worked out before our eyes in American society.

The further reaches of such thought may be found among the behaviorist social scientists, whose work is beginning to have some practical as well as theoretical results. Harvard's B. F. Skinner, for example, contends that human conduct is essentially a product of environmental influences, and that to get the kind of behavior we want we need merely change the "contingencies" to which humanity is subjected. He offers us a behaviorist blueprint for a tightly controlled, anthill society in which people will be manipulated through proper "reinforcement." [2]

Skinner's discussion is instructive on a number of counts. His beginning assumptions, on every subject, are the essence of conventional liberalism. He assumes, for example, that the major problems in the world are overpopulation, pollution, the depletion of resources, and so forth—the usual litany of liberal "crises." And his method of fashioning a response is equally orthodox. Social problems exist, he says, because of aversive environmental influences, so the obvious method of solving the problems is to change the environment.* Although Skinner is somewhat elliptical in saying *what* exactly is involved in all of this, his antiseptic prose style does yield up occasional hints:

> The real issue is the effectiveness of techniques of control. . . . Contingencies are accessible, and as we come to understand the relation between behavior and the environment, we discover new ways of changing behavior. The outlines of a technology are already clear. . . . behavior can be changed by changing the conditions of which it is a function. . . . A child is born into a culture as an organism is placed in an experimental space. Designing a culture is like designing an experiment; contingencies are arranged and effects noted. . . .

---

* "We shall not solve the problems of alcoholism and juvenile delinquency," he writes, "by increasing a sense of responsibility. It is the environment which is 'responsible' for the objectionable behavior, and it is the environment, not some attribute of the individual, which must be changed. . . . [We must accept] the fact that all control is exerted by the environment and proceed to the design of better environment rather than of better men."

It is not difficult to see what is wrong in most educational environments, and much has already been done to design materials which make learning as easy as possible and to construct contingencies, in the classroom and elsewhere, which give the student powerful reasons for getting an education.[3]

Skinner's conception of society is chilling, and the totalitarian implications are plain enough on the face of it. But nothing about it is more disturbing than the fact that it is merely an extension of the ordinary liberal outlook that already controls so many of our major institutions. Such social-engineering views are implicit in the environmentalist outlook, and they are beginning to manifest themselves in practical terms wherever the liberal influence is supreme.

Social Engineering in Education

In keeping with Skinner's own enthusiasms, notions of planning behavior on "scientific" premises have shown up most prominently in the schools, where the social engineers have been striving for decades to mold young people to their wishes. As one group of education professors put it, "a considerable amount of knowledge has been accumulated respecting the problem of inducing and controlling changes in human relations and in the structure of social institutions. . . . It is now possible, on the basis of this knowledge, to set the bold outlines of social engineering as it is applied to public education. . . ."[4] *

Preoccupation with schooling is an inevitable result of what might be described as "environmentalist regression," wherein the

---

* Education theorist Theodore Brameld, an energetic "progressive," stated the social-engineering theme more flatly still. What is required, Brameld said, is "a revitalized 'group mind,' functioning as both ends and means. . . . Discipline . . . becomes the agreed-upon acceptance of orderly procedures through which groups unite in systematic efforts to articulate and attain their goals. . . . [The minority], while free to advocate, criticize, and to persuade if possible, is required to accept whatever rules are deemed necessary to and established for group solidarity and accomplishment."

social planners are driven toward ever more desperate and potentially dangerous measures in an effort to rescue earlier failures. As we have noted, nearly all the accepted formulas for remaking humanity by tinkering with "conditions" have failed or are in the process of doing so—welfare outlays, public housing and slum clearance, penal rehabilitation, or whatever. None of it seems to have worked out as the planners said it was going to.

This history of failure has increasingly focused social-engineering energies on the schools. Looking at the shambles around them, the planners do not conclude that their premises are wrong, but that they have been getting into the act too late. By the time the public housing programs or penal "rehabilitation" can catch up with the adults affected, the damage has already been done. The miscreants are set in their ways. From this it is deduced that the intervention must begin earlier, when the raw material is still in formative condition.

It is in partial obedience to such notions that billions of dollars have been poured into public education to obtain better facilities, higher teacher salaries, augmented counseling, lower pupil-teacher ratios, and more innovative programs. But even here, it seems, the plan has gone awry. For it develops that all the billions spent on public education are no more effective than the billions spent for public housing or for welfare, and that, despite the enormous effort and the incredible outlay, American children are leaving the public school in something very like the condition in which they entered it.

This final failure of the environmentalist program is in one sense encouraging, in another profoundly disturbing. There is something hopeful in the discovery that the human substance with all its frailties, virtues, and idiosyncrasies so doggedly defies the efforts of the environmental planners. It is regrettable that learning skills have not been improved, that poverty continues, and that billions of dollars have been wasted in unsuccessful efforts to change these things, but surely there is a victory here for the human personality, which turns out to be quite different from the potter's clay of liberal imaginings.

The disturbing part is that the social engineers refuse to accept this unfavorable verdict. The failure of conventional public schooling as documented in the Coleman report, the researches of Christopher Jencks, and the writings of Daniel Moynihan, among others, has convinced a number of planners that the conventional formula isn't going to get the job done, but it has not in general convinced them the job should be abandoned. It has merely indicated that official intervention in the life of the child must begin *even earlier*—that the bad environmental effects are being imposed on the child by his parents, his neighborhood, and his peers before he ever gets to school, and that these effects must be eradicated.

As we saw in Chapter 11, this is the principal conclusion emerging from the Coleman report and from the various studies based on its findings. Coleman himself has stated the matter in no uncertain terms: "Altogether, the sources of inequality of educational opportunity appear to lie first in the home itself and the cultural influences immediately surrounding the home; then they lie in the schools' ineffectiveness to free achievement from the impact of the home, and in the schools' cultural homogeneity which perpetuates the social influences of the home and its environs." [5]

Summarizing several "reanalyses" of the Coleman data, Frederick Mosteller and Moynihan likewise observe: ". . . family inputs are far more powerful indicators of achievement than school inputs, and this is true for both races. . . . The most promising alternative would be to alter the way in which parents deal with their children at home. Unfortunately, it is not obvious how this could be done. Income maintenance, family allowances, etc., seem a logical beginning. . . . major attention should be given to the socioeconomic condition of the black family. . . . The logical course is to turn attention and resources to the period before the lowered level of competence sets in. As [Jerome] Kagan has it, the task is to change 'the ecology of the lower class child in order to increase the probability that he will be more successful in attaining normative skills.' " [6]

As noted, this is the actual (as opposed to legal) rationale for busing. The Negro child is to be transported away from his family as soon as possible in the day and returned as late as possible in the afternoon. He is to be immersed in white middle-class surroundings, and he is to be shuttled about continually to make certain he never attends a black-majority school. In effect, the environmentalists are setting out to rescue him from the influence of his own culture, and most especially from his home and parents. The object is to break the link between the child and his family and to maximize the influence exerted on him by the agents of the government in the schools.

This fixation with the schools, with getting authority over children at an early age, and with using such authority to remedy alleged defects in the family, is suggestive of totalitarian attitudes. Every culture is concerned, of course, about the education of its young. But in the totalitarian states such efforts have a special and characteristic twist. The object of the schooling here is to *change* the young people into something different from young people before them, and indeed quite different from people in general as they have hitherto been known to history. Without exception, these regimes have tried to replace the natural influence of the parent with the pervasive tutelage of the state. Hostility to traditional family relationships is thus a leading feature of totalitarian societies, and we have reason to be disturbed when it becomes a feature of our own.

Busing alone is so grave an assault on traditional conceptions of the family that it would in itself be a sufficient indicator of our troubles, but it is far from isolated. The preoccupation with family environment and the need for government to do something about it is threaded through the activities of countless planners, educationists, social workers, mental health lobbyists, and numerous other social-engineering types. These gentry also believe it is their duty to rescue children from their parents, and are pursuing this objective with utmost determination on a dozen different fronts.*

* Thus Arlene Skolnick, in an article entitled "Families Can Be Unhealthy for Children and Other Living Things," discusses the findings of a White House Conference on Children. In this discussion Ms. Skolnick observes that the family "is not a psychological necessity" and "is only a relatively recent development of Western society." She is of the opinion that "the myth of the family blinds us to dangers of our normal child-care practice. . . . The message [of the conference] states quite clearly that little children are in danger from their own parents." (*Psychology Today*, August 1971.)

The focus of this discussion was the "battered child" syndrome, an example frequently brought forward in discussions of parental delinquency. A bit of inquiry, however, shows us that this emotional appeal is but the entering wedge—that the concern of the planners is not simply

The identical idea is stressed, for instance, in the continuing battle in the public schools on the subject of "sex education." Public controversy on this topic usually features angry parents arrayed against school administrators and teachers, the former charging that children are being exposed to pornography, the latter responding that young people need to learn the facts of life if they are to avoid venereal disease and pregnancy. Neither of these contentions, however, gets at the basic issue. While the explicit nature of some sex education materials certainly raises serious questions, this factor is incidental to the underlying problems associated with the movement.

Examine enough of the literature in this business (widely promoted, incidentally, by the Department of Health, Education, and Welfare) and you discover certain interrelated and recurring notions. One is the idea that sex education should be taught, not simply in terms of fact, but according to certain value assumptions —which generally boil down to a belief that sexual indulgence is natural and healthy if it feels good and doesn't hurt any other person. Another is the idea that sex education can and should be used as a method of limiting population increase, and is indeed a kind of "social engineering" tool by which this objective may be attained.*

The combined effect of such instruction is to separate the idea of sexual activity from the idea of procreation—the first being perceived as good, healthy, and fun, the second as antisocial and to be avoided. While there is little doubt that such ideas have gained wide currency in our society, there is equally little doubt that many parents hold contrary opinions and don't want their children instructed in such a manner. Which brings us to the real

---

to prevent parental violence and brutality (which of course are punishable under existing law) but to prevent or remedy the general retrograde *influence* of the parents on the child, in which respect the emotional debunking of the "myth of the family" is of course most useful. This attitude is seen in a variety of contemporary issues—busing, sex education, child development, among others.

* A Planned Parenthood official calls sex education "an essential aspect of what might be termed total contraception. . . . This is a new aspect of human engineering." An HEW official refers to that agency's activities in this area as "social engineering on a large scale." (*Triumph,* October 1969.)

preoccupation of the sex education movement—the urgent need to do something about the parents.

The delinquency of parents is the most persistent theme of the sex education enthusiasts. As in the busing controversy, the parents are seen as part of the problem—in fact, the major part—rather than of the solution. It is up to the school to overcome the difficulties parents create for their own children. Thus one sex education proponent, Dr. Harold Lief of the University of Pennsylvania, informs us:

> All the evidence we have demonstrates that parents are very poor sex educators. Either their overriding concern with morality or their own hang-ups prevent them from talking about sex with comfort and ease. This, of course, is not true of some parents, but is true of the vast majority. . . . In terms of role modeling, unfortunately, there are too many parents whose own attitudes toward each other and whose own behavior with each other leave much to be desired, in terms of something that the child can really imitate and identify with.[7]

Such notions, stressed over and over in sex education battles, suggest the superior knowledge and judgment of the experts in the schools as opposed to the ignorant, fumbling parents back there at home.* The ultimate meaning of the sex education battle is thus the same as in the struggle over busing: an assertion by the government agents in the schools that they have an interest which supersedes the authority of the parent—in this case affecting not simply cognitive skills but involving the most intimate matters of emotional and psychological development.†

---

* Former U.S. Commissioner of Education James Allen has said that "the biggest problem in sex education is not the children but the damn parents." And a guideline used in New York public schools asserts: "It is definitely not recommended to do the unit on sex education on a 'parent permission' basis." (*Triumph,* November 1969.)

† This tendency has also been manifest in psychological tests administered to school children. In these tests students are asked to react to provocative statements, as a supposed method of revealing their psychological profiles. Many of the questions concern the most intimate matters of sexual attitude and conduct, religious belief and doubt, and relationship

The Child Developers

What is implicit in the battles over busing and sex education is made explicit in a third arena of contemporary debate—the issue of "child development." Over the past few years, a number of child development bills have been presented in Congress; one of them passed both the House and Senate before receiving a presidential veto. As in the other controversies, the public presentation on this issue is rather different from the deeper motives the "child developers" from time to time acknowledge.

Most often, legislation of this type is promoted on the theory that working mothers need day care centers to watch over junior while mama is on the job. All, supposedly, very noncontroversial. But if one examines the literature on this question and the content of the legislation itself, it is clear that something far more serious and grandiose is looming into view. What is actually sought is Federal authority over American children, beginning at the earliest possible age.

Such ideas have been kicking around in Federal planning circles for a number of years. The 1970 White House Conference on Children placed considerable stress on the need for Federal "development" efforts, and Project Headstart, launched in 1966, contained some developmental overtones. Though chiefly educational in nature, this preschool venture obviously conformed to the idea of getting children under Federal auspices, and in one official utterance was described as "a massive social experiment to explore ways of intervening into early developmental processes to improve the abilities, attitudes, health, and well-being of young children and their families." [8]

---

to one's parents. Samples of such test statements, placed in the *Congressional Record* by Rep. John Ashbrook (R-Ohio), include the following:

"My father is a tyrant. . . . I feel there's a barrier between me and my parents. . . . I'm ashamed of my parents' dress and manner. . . . I wonder if I'm normal in my sexual development. . . . I want to know about venereal disease. . . . I think about sex a good deal of the time. . . . I'm bothered by the thought of heaven and hell. . . . Is there a conflict between the Bible and my school subjects? . . . Is it wrong to deny the existence of God?"

In the child development legislation that got through Congress in 1971, "development" embraces just about everything that has to do with the physical, mental, and emotional well-being of the child.* Its benefits, moreover, are not to be limited to the welfare population or the working poor; they are explicitly intended, rather, to reach out into every echelon of society ("should be available as a matter of right to all American children").⁹

To this end the Federal government would solicit customers for governmental day care centers, and foster a massive network of child development councils, local policy councils, a national center for child development, and an "advocacy" system in which free-lance trouble-shooters set up in local communities would be empowered to inquire into and take "appropriate" action on alleged problems of children. (As the White House Conference had explained the matter, "every child, because of his immaturity, and legal disabilities, requires a skilled, experienced, and dedicated advocate whenever he is deprived of a home, schooling, medical care, property rights, entitlement or benefits." ¹⁰)

So again we encounter the idea that parents left to their own devices are incapable of raising children and government must step in and supply the necessary expertise. Child development proponent Jacob Javits (R-N.Y.) put the matter succinctly when he stated in the Senate: *We have recognized that the child is a care of the state.* State law recognizes it. Federal law has recognized it in many affirmative programs. This [the child development bill] is but the summation, the articulation, in a sophisticated way, of programs to deal with the care of children insofar as society is

---

* Just how thorough this intervention was meant to be is suggested by the Senate committee report on the bill which says it would authorize the Federal government "to involve itself in comprehensive physical and mental health, social and cognitive developmental services (including family consultation), special programs for minority groups, Indians, and bilingual children; specially designed programs (including after school, summer, weekend, and overnight programs); identification and treatment of physical, mental, and emotional problems . . . ; prenatal services to reduce malnutrition, infant and maternal mortality, and the incidence of mental retardation; . . . training in the fundamentals of child development for family members and prospective parents; use of child advocates to assist children and parents in securing full access to other services; and other activities."

interested in a sound, healthy, educated, and well cared for child." [11] (Italics added.)

"Environmental regression" in the child development movement is apparent in the repeated emphasis on corralling children at the earliest possible age. One instructive quote to this effect appeared in a journal of the National Education Association, stating in a forecast for the 1970s that "as non-school, pre-school programs begin to operate, educators will assume formal responsibility for children when they reach the age of two. . . ." [12] The nature of the problem was explained (and an even earlier matriculation suggested) by child development advocate Reginald Lourie, president of the Joint Commission on Mental Health for Children.

"There is plenty of evidence," Lourie said, "that by three, four, and five years of age, remedial programs are already too late for a great many children. When distortions are already built in, they often can make it impossible for these children to utilize the corrective remedial approaches and services that are made available. . . . *Therefore, the timing of appropriate intervention is crucial. In the first 18 months of life, the brain is growing faster than it ever will again. This is the time when it is most plastic and most available for appropriate experience and corrective intervention."* [13] (Italics added.)

This is all quite different, of course, from the up-front advertising in behalf of "child development" and would be offensive to many American parents if they knew about it. It is extremely doubtful that most Americans want the government launching "corrective interventions" into the psyches of infant children. Yet that is the direction in which we are being consistently shepherded, as witness the provisions of the 1971 legislation. This bill provided that parents would be "informed" and have "the opportunity to except such child therefrom" before that child *"shall be the subject of research or experimentation."* [14] How many people knew the Senate had passed a bill allowing for *any* kind of Federal experimentation with American children?

Is it farfetched to compare all this to the conduct of the twentieth century totalitarianisms? The *Jugend* (Hitler Youth) and the commune sought to make the child a ward of government, and to insulate him from potential diversionary influences in the home, in order to raise up a brand new breed of people. When a prominent U.S. senator informs us that "the child is a care of the state," when assorted experts suggest the child must be rescued from his family, and when planners declare their intention of remolding children according to official specifications, the analogy seems fairly plain.*

* One is reminded of Leopold Tyrmand's anecdote about life in Communist Poland. As Tyrmand tells it, a youthful mother calls at the state nursery after work to pick up her daughter. She is handed an infant, only to discover that the child she has been given is not her own. When she protests to the nurse she is told, in effect: What's the difference? You'll simply bring the child back in the morning anyway, won't you? So why bother about which one you take home? The point of the anecdote, that in matters where it really counts the child is the ward of the state, is becoming quite as applicable to our own society as it is to Tyrmand's Poland. (*The Rosa Luxemburg Contraceptives Cooperative*, Macmillan, 1972, p. 22.)

24
The New Totalitarians

The record examined in the preceding chapter illustrates the social-engineering desire to get control of other people's lives. It also illustrates, however, the troubles that our would-be planners have met along the way. Just about every effort to fashion mankind to some ideal pattern by fiddling with "conditions" has issued in egregious failure—and thus produced the phenomenon of environmental regression. In their ceaseless battle for control, the environmentalists must keep pushing back the age at which their human charges will be turned over to them—until we find ourselves discussing "corrective interventions" in the lives of infant children.

It would appear that the planners have compounded their original error. The demand for increased authority over American children would be objectionable anyway, but now we may add to its intrinsic demerits the fact that it also very probably isn't going to work. Even with their early access to the child, we have no evidence that the environmentalists can do what they say. Project Headstart, for example, is an acknowledged disappointment, and on the data available with respect to busing there is no reason to suppose that even this severe incursion into home and neighborhood has accomplished much by way of learning gains.

Looking at all this failure, even the most case-hardened environmentalist must begin to wonder if something hasn't gone amiss. At some point the suspicion must begin to dawn that the facile assertions of Professor Skinner are mistaken—that there are givens in the human constitution which do not arise from "contingencies," and which therefore will not make way before environmentalist placebos. It may just be that there is an intractable something there that cannot be changed environmentally no matter how many dollars are thrown in its direction, or how early in life the human guinea pigs are rounded up and submitted to the strictures of the plan.

The Genetic Endowment

That this is exactly the situation before us is the teaching of two recently controversial educational psychologists—Arthur Jensen of the University of California and Richard Herrnstein of Harvard. These researchers have published voluminous data on I.Q. tests and other measures of human variation and concluded that the failure of the environmentalist approach is perfectly predictable, since observable differences in intellectual performance are determined much more by heredity than by environment.

Approximately 80 percent of I.Q. differentials, according to Jensen, is the result of genetic endowment rather than environmental influence. And if that is so, it is clear enough why the environmental programs have so consistently failed. The social engineers who want to reshape humanity by these methods are already too late when the child is born—indeed, when it is conceived. The principal determinants of performance have been established by parental chromosomes, beyond the reach of HUD or HEW.

It is this factor, perhaps, that accounts for the furious anger directed at Jensen and Herrnstein by so many members of the social science fraternity. Much of this protest has been based on asserted grounds of "racism," since the findings of Jensen and Herrnstein would mean that observed differentials in Negro and

white I.Q. performance are genetically determined. And because
"I.Q." is a rather subjective measurement invented by white researchers, it is understandable that this whole discussion has stirred
resentment among blacks and others who see it as an attempted
proof of racial superiority—which it is not.*

The anger on this issue would have ensued, however, even
without the black-white cleavage in the country, for the rebuke to
environmentalism would have been plain enough in any event.
Environmentalism, after all, is the social scientists' religion, so that
what Jensen and Herrnstein have done is to commit a species of
heresy. For if their teachings are true, the social-engineering hope
of transforming everything by way of welfare programs, education,
and expenditure of tax money is doomed to failure. *Therefore* the
hypothesis must be false.

Since the facts of record on these programs suggest they are
indeed failures, and since the data mustered by Jensen and Herrnstein are fairly impressive,† the social-engineering types confront
an obvious dilemma, whose dimensions are slowly beginning to
dawn on them. For most of us, a realization of this sort would
suggest the whole presumptive business of remaking other people
should be abandoned. If we can't remold our fellow beings by
fooling around with the environment, the logical conclusion would
seem to be to stop trying.

The conclusion of the social-engineering mentality, however, is
altogether different. In certain circles, at least, the reasoning appears to be that, if human attributes are chiefly determined by the
genetic constitution and not by the environment, then we must
control the genetic constitution. Rather than dropping anything,
therefore, we must press on to new and even grander visions of
control. We must take hold of existence itself, and by control of
life, death, procreation, the biological processes of our subjects,
and ultimately the genetic endowment as such, finally produce the
kind of human beings we want.

---

* The subjective character of I.Q. measurement is acknowledged (and discussed at some length) by both Jensen and Herrnstein.

† Most of the social scientists who were asked by the *Harvard Educational
Review* to answer Jensen's controversial article on this subject (*HER,*
June 1969) acknowledged the essential correctness of his facts. The argu-
ment was over how, exactly, they should be construed.

Biological Engineering

It is in the context of biological control that the uproar about population, abortion, and euthanasia examined in chapters 14 and 22 becomes especially forbidding. Much of this discussion, as we have seen, is premised on the idea that we have too many people in our nation, or the world, and that the object of our concern should be to limit the numbers being born—through abortion, sterilization, or some kind of enforced contraception.*

The overtones of this campaign are themselves disturbing, but there is more. For we discover in the populationist outcry, and most especially in the campaign for abortion (and now for euthanasia), a further suggestion: that we should be concerned not merely with the number of people being born, but with the *kind* of people being born. If we didn't have all these defectives or unloved children, or children coming from the wrong kind of homes, or people with low I.Q.s, or welfare families, or whatever—why, then, the whole problem would be solved. Why not, therefore, control the very matter of life itself?

The direction in which we are heading in such questions is indicated by one seemingly innocuous bit of political jargon. This is the repeated statement in discussions of environmental problems, population, abortion on demand, and various other issues, that our nation should concern itself with the "quality" rather than the "quantity" of life.

On first appraisal, perhaps, this formula sounds appealing. Who among us doesn't want to upgrade the conditions in which

---

* Dr. Garret Hardin, a well-known spokesman on questions of population and environmental pollution, tells us that eventually compulsion will have to be used to get our breeding habits in proper order. "In the long run," says Dr. Hardin, "a purely voluntary system of birth control cannot achieve the goal of national (or international) population control. In the long run, some form of community coercion—gentle or severe, explicit or cryptic—will have to be employed. In the long run.

"Community control of breeding is so revolutionary an idea that we cannot institute it immediately. For the near future, we will have to look toward voluntarism and persuasion to help create a climate of opinion that can some day support stronger measures." (*California Medicine,* November 1970.)

we live out our earthly existence? The problem is that the "quality
of life" refrain has a special—and ominous—meaning beyond this
common hope. What is meant by it is that some lives are preferable
to others, and thus deserve a special kind of preference. Conversely, there are other kinds of human life that simply aren't
worth all the pain and trouble—and people condemned to such
existence would be better off if they were not alive at all.

These notions appear most plainly in debate over abortion and
euthanasia. In the former case, we are told unborn children who
are deformed, retarded, or simply "unwanted" should be exterminated in the mother's womb. In the latter, we are informed in no
uncertain terms that various people in terminal stages of illness or
otherwise "incapable of rational existence" (a standard phrase in
euthanasia legislation) would be better off if we simply let them
die. And, as Dr. Robert Morison puts it, "we have to do this on the
basis of some judgment on the *quality of the life* in question." [1]
(Italics added.)

What is emerging here, quite plainly, is a eugenic mentality—a
belief that we ought to have certain types of people and not others,
and that we must take measures to get the type we want. That this
attitude has been adopted in fairly influential circles is suggested
by the statement of Dr. Bentley Glass, former president of the
Association for the Advancement of Science. Dr. Glass foresees a
time when we shall affirm "the right of every child to be born
with a sound physical and mental constitution, based on a sound
genotype." He adds to this the further insight that *"no parents in
that future time will have a right to burden society with a mal-
formed or mentally incompetent child."* [2] (Italics added.) *

Such attitudes, I think, are an obvious concomitant of the drive
for permissive abortion and blissful euthanasia. Once decide that

---

* Not far distant from these ideas are the notions of Dr. William Shockley,
who received the Nobel Prize for his work in developing the transistor.
Dr. Shockley proposes to offer subsidies to people of low I.Q. or otherwise considered defective to accept voluntary sterilization. Because Shockley accepts and propounds the genetic view of human differentiation, his
teachings have been identified as "conservative." It should be apparent
on what has been said before that in his social recommendations he is a
pluperfect social engineer who knows "scientifically" what is good for
us and is eager to promulgate his plan.

there is such a thing as a life that isn't worth living, and the Glass approach ensues quite naturally. There are other concomitants as well—all pointing in the same direction. We see about us, for example, proliferating signs that human beings are increasingly viewed as laboratory animals, to be treated as experimental guinea pigs and subjected to the most dehumanizing procedures in the interests of "science." *

One of the more ghastly examples in this genre is the practice of fetal experimentation, in which unborn children in certain instances are treated very much like laboratory animals. In some cases the fetuses are experimented on while they are still in the womb. In others, they have been kept alive outside the womb so that scientists can test their reactions and do tissue research. *Newsweek* magazine informs us that "researchers" have "voiced serious concern over any legislation that would unduly curb fetal research. Such research is vital, they argue, to gain insights into a broad range of problems, including prematurity, mental retardation, and many other disorders affecting children." [3]

The experimentation in dispute is avowedly "non-therapeutic" —predicated not on the interest of the fetus itself, but on the idea that such experimentation will help us find out more about early life processes, disease prevention, and so on. (There is no serious objection, of course, to medical efforts undertaken to strengthen or cure the unborn child). The logic here is that the fetus scheduled for abortion is going to die anyway, so that we are justified in trying out on it new and possibly dangerous techniques that we would not attempt on a mature adult, or on a child that has had the good fortune to have been born and is therefore legally alive.†

The lengths to which such practices can go is illustrated by developments in Great Britain. A furor was aroused in England

---

* In the euthanasia debates in Britain a number of such examples were cited. Lord Denman, for one, asserted in 1936 that "horses and dogs were put down painlessly—only human beings had to suffer to the end." Lord Chorley repeated the argument in 1950: "Animals in suffering were put down—why not humans?" The Earl of Huntingdon, we are informed, "supported the notion, repeating the argument from the comparison with animals."

† A proponent of fetal experimentation, Dr. Richard Berhman of Columbia, explained the matter this way in congressional hearings on the subject: "The health and welfare of our children and of our children's children is

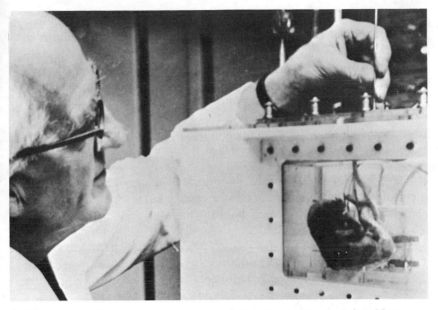

Experimentation with a live fetus. (The Cambridge Evening News, *Cambridge, England*)

by news that abortion clinics were selling live aborted fetuses for research. One of the researchers who worked with a live fetus, Dr. Lawrence Lawn of Cambridge, explained that "we are simply using something which is destined for the incinerator to benefit man-kind. Of course we would not dream of experimenting with a viable child. We would not consider that to be right." A spokes-man for an abortion clinic likewise stated that, under English law, "a fetus has to be 28 weeks to become legally viable. Earlier than that it is so much garbage." [4]

Certain types of behavior-altering experimentation *are* being conducted with born children and adults. Efforts to effect changes

---

currently being placed in serious jeopardy by efforts to prohibit or signifi-cantly limit research on fetuses. . . . Individual decisions must be placed in a time scale that measures their impact not only on the individual living today but also what a particular decision will mean to the child or adult 20 or 50 years later, and what it implies for other individuals living at this time, as well as for future generations." (*National Right to Life News,* September 1974.)

in learning ability, temperament, and behavior through physical alterations of consciousness have, for example, been documented in our schools and our penal institutions. Schools have used mind-altering drugs to make some children more tractable and tranquil. At hearings conducted by the House Privacy subcommittee in September 1970, witnesses from the Department of Health, Education, and Welfare testified that as many as 200,000 American school children were receiving amphetamine and stimulant therapy, and that possibly another 100,000 were being given tranquillizers and anti-depressants.

Some educators frankly envision further use of behavior-modification drugs and drugs to induce certain kinds of learning experience. What the future may hold in this regard is suggested by an article in a National Education Association publication that tells us that "biochemical and psychological mediation of learning is likely to increase. New drama will play on the educational stage as drugs are introduced experimentally to improve in the learner such qualities as personality, concentration and memory." [5]

One particularly horrific species of biological engineering that has made its appearance in schools and prisons is a phenomenon called "psychosurgery." Dr. Peter Breggin of the Center for the Study of Psychiatry has documented in some detail the increasingly widespread campaign in a number of public institutions and in certain areas of private medical practice to alter patterns of human consciousness and behavior by the use of surgery, drugs, and other mind-bending procedures. Breggin, himself a practicing psychiatrist, cites case histories of people blinded by pre-frontal lobotomies, children whose brains have been coagulated by electroshock, and prisoners submitted to mutilating operations.

"The revival of lobotomy and psychosurgery," Breggin writes, "is a part of the increasing interest in finding mental health and medical-technological solutions to our personal and political problems. Dozens of medical centers are involved, and a new wave of operations has begun with an estimated 1,000 operations a year, mostly on women diagnosed as 'neurotic' with anxiety, depression and other symptoms. . . . The psychosurgery of violence has been attached directly to political aims, including the control of ghetto riots." [6]

Projects to alter human behavior by use of surgery, electroshock, and mind-altering drugs have been funded by the National Institute of Mental Health, the Law Enforcement Administration, and other Federal agencies. In California penal institutions prisoners have been subjected to psychosurgery operations and drug injections. A prominent physician in Mississippi has conducted about 30 brain operations on children to correct "erratic hyper-sensitiveness, aggressiveness, and emotional instability," which made them "a detriment to themselves and to society." A concerted outcry has caused the suspension of Federal funding for such activities, but it is chilling to think that they should have been funded at all.

These programs are distressing enough, but they are relatively mild compared to what is being promoted in some of our social-engineering circles. A number of our scientific planners are not content with manipulating or ending the biological processes of life once it is in existence. They want to go further to create new life according to plan, and to terminate it when its development doesn't suit the proper social blueprint. And this particular movement, sad to say, is very far advanced in our society.

"Test Tube Babies"

The feasibility of "decanting" test tube babies à la Aldous Huxley's *Brave New World* has for several years been celebrated not only in technical journals but in certain segments of the popular press. For a generation or so it has been technically feasible to achieve human fertilization *in vitro* (that is, in a test tube or other laboratory glass) by forming a laboratory culture in which eggs and sperm cells may unite. From such experiments human embryos have been bred up to the so-called "blastocyst" stage at about seven or eight days of life, at which time in the normal course of events the embryo would be implanted on the wall of the uterus.

Successful implantation of test tube babies has already been achieved in England, according to Douglas Bevis of Leeds University. Bevis explains that "so many have been attempted that by the law of averages some have come through." [7] Such developments have the scientific engineers breathless with anticipation. For the combination of these embryo-ranching techniques, advanced methods for determining some genetic characteristics, and easy access to abortion opens up the prospect of breeding people as one breeds plants: Grow them, test them, keep the ones you like, and throw the others away.

The possibilities arising from all this are of course numerous. An article in the *Wall Street Journal* discusses a relatively simple version of embryo-ranching that relies on natural processes of gestation and is fully possible with existing law and scientific technique. By amniocentesis, the *Journal* notes, it is now feasible to discover the sex of the child in embryo at a relatively early stage. Parents may therefore keep the children that are of the sex they prefer, and abort those who are not. Dr. Thomas Schelling of Harvard informs us that "we must try to get ready for this, and consider just how we want to accommodate to it.[8]

More sophisticated variations on the theme include using artificial implantation to permit childbirth to women who otherwise cannot have children. An embryo from one woman's body, for example, might be transferred for health reasons to the body of another. At a more practical level, a popular magazine article has suggested that "a completely healthy young woman, reluctant to remove herself from a rewarding career for even a few months, might still produce a child by *hiring* another woman to carry her embryo to term." [9]

Dr. Glass, for his part, believes that laboratory growth of embryos has opened up new vistas of genetic planning. "Sex determination of the embryos is possible before implantation," he says, "and embryos with abnormal chromosome constitutions can be discarded. By checking the sperm and egg donors with a battery of biochemical tests, matching of carriers of the same defective gene can be avoided, *or the defective embryos themselves can be detected and discarded.*" [10] (Italics added.)

We have already proceeded at least part of the way down this Orwellian road: *Time* suggests that, with the advent of genetic counseling and supposedly mounting population troubles, "those with defective genes could become, in effect, second-class citizens, a caste of genetic lepers." *Time* notes that women carrying unborn mongoloid children are nowadays encouraged to abort, and that "already a number of medical planners are pointing up the cost-effectiveness of abortion in those cases." [11]

Even these notions are relatively mild, however, compared to what a really good social engineer is able to conjure up. Among a number of the "new biologists," the current emphasis is on actually creating new human beings of a desired type. By *in vitro* fertilization embryos may be generated in profusion, using different genetic mixes from various types of donors. As suggested by Dr. Glass, these can be artificially implanted and "grown" until the desired type of human being is produced. There are, of course, risks—like, maybe, producing monsters, as has occasionally happened in animal experimentation. But if any of these develop we simply abort them (if we can discover them in time) and keep on trying. Simple enough.

Above and beyond this ghastly prospect lies another—the technique of "cloning," or asexual reproduction. This is a method by which a cell from an adult human being is substituted for the nucleus of an unfertilized egg, then permitted to grow into an embryo. The characteristics of the resulting individual will be genetically identical to those of the adult cell donor—and this person will be an exact replica of his twin-parent. This technique, it is supposed, could permit us to replicate an indefinite number of Beethovens, Michelangelos, or Bentley Glasses, if we can get hold of the requisite cell material.

Lest these visions be dismissed as science fiction, be assured that such efforts are going on in laboratories in the United States, England, and other nations. Moreover, the eugenic mentality and the notion that human beings are essentially aspects of animal nature, to be bred and otherwise treated as one deals with laboratory animals, are spreading quite widely in Western society, on the heels of permissive abortion and euthanasia. The rather straightforward logic of it seems to be that where there is a license to kill, *a fortiori* there must be a license to breed and to experiment.

That the ideas we have been rehearsing are not limited to a few isolated scientists here and there but have spread out into general discourse may be seen in the writings of novelist-polemicist Gore Vidal. This prominent liberal writer has put the whole farrago of populationist notions together in coherent fashion, arguing that we should have an "authority with a capital A" to determine who should and should not be allowed to have children:

> Only certain people would be allowed to have children.
> Nor is this the hardship that it might at first appear. Most

people have no talent for bringing up children and they usually admit it—once the damage is done. . . . The right to unlimited breeding is not a constitutional guarantee. If education and propaganda failed, those who violated the birth control restrictions would have to pay for their act as for any other criminal offense. I suspect that, eventually, the whole idea of parenthood will vanish, when children are made impersonally by the laboratory insemination of ova. . . .

I would favor an intelligent program of eugenics, that would decide which genetic types would be continued and which allowed to die off. It's within the range of our science to create, very simply, new people physically healthier and intellectually more competent than ourselves. After all, we do it regularly, in agriculture and in the breeding of livestock, so why not with the human race? [12]

If all this sounds vaguely familiar, it should. Compare the following:

The state has to make the child the most precious possession of the people. It has to take care that only the healthy beget children, that there is only one disgrace: to be sick and to bring children into the world despite one's own deficiencies; but one highest honor: to renounce this. . . . It has to put the most modern medical means at the service of this knowledge. It has to declare unfit for propagation everybody who is physically ill and has inherited a disease and it has to carry this out in practice. . . .

By education it has to teach the individual that it is not a disgrace but only a regrettable misfortune to be sick and weakly, but that it is a crime and therefore at the same time a disgrace to dishonor this misfortune by one's egoism by burdening it again upon an innocent being. . . . The state has finally to succeed in bringing about that nobler era when men see their care no longer in the better breeding of dogs, horses, and cats, but rather in the uplifting of mankind itself. [13]

These are, of course, the words of Adolf Hitler.

The repeated analogies of people to animals, the experimenting, the eugenics—none of it should really surprise us. It is all quite congruent with that "modern" view of humanity which discards the metaphysics of Judaic and Christian revelation and asserts that human beings are simply higher animals or products of the natural flux of things. If, in fact, humanity is simply a "chance deposit" cast up on the shore of earth by "the same forces that rust iron and ripen corn," if people are that and nothing more, then the abyss of genetic engineering, cloning, and elimination of the unfit is opened up before us.

Epilogue
What Is
to Be Done?

The argument of this book has been that twentieth-century liberalism has failed, and most of our discussion has been an effort to document this failure. Specifically, it has been contended that the liberal urge-to-regulate is almost always counterproductive—creating problems instead of curing them and working hardship on the people it is supposed to help. Even more disturbing, perhaps, we find that the resulting concentrate of power, combined with liberalism's slipping value metaphysics, has led us steadily toward authoritarian practice.

To argue thus, however, is only the beginning of wisdom and not the end of it. If one concedes that the foregoing statements are true or nearly so—as an increasing number of people from many different vantage points are beginning to do—the normal and proper question becomes what, if anything, might be done about it. Granted that government outlays help the relatively affluent, or that social security is regressive, or that economic regulations hurt consumers—what then? What steps may be taken to effect a remedy?

Such questions are grave enough in any event, but to our

friends on the left they are downright embarrassing. There is, of course, no shortage of conventional liberals who shrug off all evidence of failure, but for a growing number of leftward scholars the scandal has become impossible to ignore. Some of these (Irving Kristol, Daniel Moynihan, Nathan Glazer) have attacked the regulatory formula as such and begun to work their way toward de-centralist solutions. But others (Michael Harrington, Arnold Kaufman) have chosen to stand by their ideological guns, to devise responses to collectivist failure somehow congruent with collectivist dogma. From this intriguing problem in dialectics arises what is known as the "radical" critique of the liberal welfare state.

The Radical Solution: Total Collectivism

The essence of the radical response is to find the difficulty not in the regulations but in the people regulated. Recognizing that the liberal system has gone awry, the radical traces the problem to the remaining vestiges of capitalistic influence: So long as our economy is mixed between public service functions and the remnants of free enterprise, the wily capitalists will control the machinery to their advantage. It is concluded that we cannot tarry in our halfway condition, but must go all the way to a collectivized economy—suppressing capitalism totally. Once this is accomplished, the counterproductive and regressive features of the existing set-up will disappear.

Through a good deal of repetition, this sort of analysis has achieved a certain currency in what were recently known as "new left" circles, in quasi-Marxist publications, and even in the popular media. For that reason, and because it appears to be the only explanation of regulatory failure that can be deduced from collectivist premises, it is worth a bit of examination. So let us consider for a moment the likelihood that business interests, rather than governmental ones, are responsible for the problems of the regulatory system.

The threshold distinction in considering this matter is that suggested in Chapter 7: the differences between government power on the one hand and business influence on the other. The *modus operandi* of government is coercive, forcing people to do things they would not do freely of their own volition. The *modus operandi* of business is consensual, achieving its effects through contract, voluntary exchange, persuasion. To confuse these types of behavior—to suggest, indeed, that volitional arrangements are *more* objectionable than compulsory ones—is to turn the logic of history and common sense abruptly on its ear.

It is true that the political power of government and the financial power of business can be combined; examples of this tendency have been a major theme of this book. But the point of such convergence is, precisely, the introduction of compulsion into the realm of exchange—using coercive power to exalt some element in the business community, extend subsidies or protections, suppress competitors. The operative evil in the amalgam is the resort to force, which radicals now propose by way of remedy to magnify still further.

Those who equate the powers of business and government tell us that the relationship cuts both ways: Just as government intervenes in business, so business through political contributions or outright bribes has intervened in government. This is, as noted, a point of "reformist" advocacy in the aftermath of Watergate, and true as far as it goes. But discussions of this type routinely ignore the fact that what business interests are trying to do in all such cases is to affect the deployment of government compulsion in some fashion. That is always the payload, and without it there would be no reason for this species of political interest in the business community, or in any other.

This "reformist" argument, moreover, badly tilts the issue in favor of the collectivists, since it assumes that the regressive features of the liberal system are associated *only* with its capitalistic, or business-oriented, components. The facts are otherwise. We have noted cases in which distinctly different interests have used the influence system to their advantage as well—labor unions, government employes, and academicians at various levels. The regulatory system may be used by any interest group that has sufficient leverage, and the requisite skills for getting leverage are not specifically business skills at all.

Or consider the matter from the other direction. The characteristic manner in which the influence system works to assist a given businessman in, say, the transportation field is to provide an exclusive franchise or license and to block out entry by competitors. This permits the favored business interest to charge higher than market prices and thus to bilk consumers—a prototypical case of "capitalist" evil to which the radical (in this case quite properly) objects. But who, we may ask, are the competitors banished from the marketplace? The answer, of course, is that they are *also* capitalists, or businessmen, and that they too are injured by the collusive arrangements in question.*

The net of it is that certain beneficiaries of the influence system manifestly are not "capitalists," while certain victims of it manifestly *are*. These considerations should be enough to suggest that the generic evil is not the business component as such, but the deployment of force by any interest group in what ought to be a voluntary system. It is the use of compulsion, and the resulting build-up of constrictions and rigidities preventing entry, denying opportunity, and favoring the politically influential, that are the source of the difficulty.

What the radical solution thus comes down to is an intensification of the real problem as an alleged answer to an imaginary one,

---

* To encompass these problems, the radical critique will on occasion broaden the concept of "capitalism" to mean the acquisitive instinct generally: The evil in the regulatory system is seen as the quest for private gain, however defined, and the solution becomes a matter of eliminating this element from the regulatory equation. But this variation is no more persuasive than what has gone before. For one thing, abolishing the acquisitive instinct in humanity is quite clearly a religious and ethical matter and not a political one. There is no political formula for achieving this objective, and no society known to history excepting small religious communities in which it has been remotely approximated. To posit this as a condition requisite to making a political system work is to say that we shall be able to run our practical affairs in tolerable order only *after* we have ascended into ethical nirvana. It is to make the lesser miracle contingent on the greater, and constitutes a confession that the political formula in question is a simplistic fantasy.

At a more mundane level, we may add that the acquisitive instinct, whatever one may think of it in ethical terms, is not the source of our economic problems anyway. After all, the consumers injured by irrational regulation, the workers blocked from employment, and the businessmen prohibited from competing—all these have their acquisitive instincts too, but are foiled in the attempt to exercise them by the constrictions built into our economy. If *these* acquisitive impulses were permitted access to the marketplace, the economic evils considered would not exist.

invoking total compulsion as a supposed remedy for partial compulsion. On the logic of that transition, as well as on the hideous social and economic record of systems in which this particular solution has been attempted, we may safely predict that the radical formula will produce an immensely greater sum of human suffering and economic want than may be discovered in the existing situation.

The answer to our regulatory problems cannot, in short, be sought by imposing further regulation, whether piecemeal as suggested by conventional liberals or wholesale as suggested by the radicals. It can be discovered only by moving, wherever possible, in the opposite direction—away from compulsory arrangements toward volitional ones. We shall correct the nation's growing economic problems and safeguard our political liberties not by regulating, but by de-regulating. Such, in general, is the view advanced by libertarians and conservatives, and the view adopted in this volume.

Some Conservative Proposals

The call for de-regulation must be qualified a bit by recalling the statement of the objects of government set forward in Chapter 1. To phrase the matter more exactly, the conservative believes our effort should be to reestablish the American system on its proper foundations: to ensure that it does effectively and well those things it is supposed to do, and refrains from doing those things it is not. This means a strengthening of government in certain areas, along with a considerable reduction of its power in others.

Some further qualifications should also be noted. Most obviously, one cannot approach a heavily regulated economic system as though it were *tabula rasa,* throwing out the regulations and subsidies overnight. For one thing, there are so many vested interests with stakes in the existing arrangement that any effort at de-regulation in almost any field will encounter powerful resistance. This should not of course prevent one from saying what the proper solution might be in any given case, even if it is politically unattainable. But for those who are interested in practical improvement, this factor will necessarily focus attention on intermediary steps by which the desired objective may be approached.

There are other prudential considerations. In some cases, if the conservative could simply will it, he would be justified in saying a given intervention or subsidy should be abolished outright. But he would be wrong to seek such immediate changes, even if it were possible to get them, in cases where the result would be extremely injurious to many innocent parties. So many people have laid plans on the basis of the existing economic structure and so many are dependent on given programs (such as Social Security) that a wholesale uprooting would cause enormous hardship.

These factors suggest the virtue of a gradualist or decrementalist approach—devising linkages by which it is possible to move from compulsory arrangements to voluntary ones. Such Fabianism-in-reverse is also recommended by the conservative's awareness that a theoretical formula, attractive on the drawing board, can work out rather differently in practice. An experimental attitude will make allowance for this fact, permitting adoption of other techniques if the original ones do not succeed. Consideration of some specific problem areas examined in the preceding chapters will suggest the manner in which a decrementalist formula might be attempted:

1. *Employment.* We have noted evidence that massive unemployment in the central cities among adolescent blacks is closely linked to increases in the statutory minimum wage. An obvious remedy for this problem would be to eliminate the minimum altogether, and many market economists propose exactly that. Given the existing political climate, however, this hardly seems feasible. The indicated step therefore, which might have a chance of making it through Congress, is enactment of a "youth wage," permitting adolescents to obtain employment at some fraction of the Federal minimum—two-thirds, one-half, or whatever.

This step would not eliminate the unemployment problem entirely (there are other sources of unemployment and other groups besides teen-agers for whom the statutory minimum has an adverse effect), but it would be a start. And once the start is made and the results can be properly noted, an empirical base will exist for exporting the idea into other sectors of the economy and thus for easing the economic hardship imposed on marginal workers generally by the minimum.

2. *Housing.* Here is an area where it would be possible to achieve considerable improvement simply by canceling out a number of existing programs. In particular, a great deal of good might be accomplished if any new programs of Federal urban renewal and public housing were simply scrubbed from the books. If urban renewal and related programs could be prevented from destroying livable low-income housing, many of the characteristic problems of the big-city "ghetto" might be avoided.

Pending readiness for sweeping changes (there *have* been some partial restraints), intermediary measures seem advisable. One such measure generally favored by conservatives, as well as some radicals, is the requirement that before any urban renewal program is attempted, the people in the affected neighborhood be given a chance to vote on it in a referendum. This is hardly an ironclad assurance against abuse, but it would give the otherwise voiceless citizens (usually blacks) in the central cities a say-so in their own affairs.

Conservatives and market economists in recent years have come up with a number of other proposals that could conceivably alter the situation for the better. One proposal worth considering is to eliminate taxes on structural improvements on property, since these added levies discourage efforts to upgrade the appearance and livability of inner city buildings. An even more far-reaching proposal is offered by economist-lawyer Bernard Siegan, who concludes from an intensive study of zoning ordinances impeding new construction that this practice should be eliminated, permitting market arrangements rather than political ones to dictate the pattern of residential and commercial development.

3. *Transit.* We have already noted in passing some major steps that can and should be taken in an effort to revivify the transit business in this country. The key consideration here, quite simply, is to break up monopoly situations created by governmental licensing at whatever level, to allow competitors into the field as freely as possible (subject to minimal safety requirements), and to permit price competition to operate in this area as in any other.

For those who claim market prices for bus or taxi service would be too high for the elderly or indigent, three answers suggest themselves. First, there is no good reason for supposing the market is any less qualified (or government any more so) to provide cost-efficient transportation services than it is to provide any other. Second, it is not at all certain the fare structure resulting from a highly competitive and innovative transit business would be *higher* than the existing structure; indeed, as we have seen, it is rather clear in many instances that the case would be decidedly otherwise. And third, if it is determined that certain indigent members of the society could not avail themselves of such services under market conditions, there is a better method of dealing with the problem than extensive governmental involvement with or ownership of transit systems: namely, to permit the market to operate but to give indigent passengers vouchers or travel stamps with which to pay their way.

4. *Education.* Chapter 11 suggested a kind of negative answer to the problems generated by the educationists and spenders: Keep finance of the public schools as much as possible at the local level, rather than permitting the burden (and the control) to be transferred to higher reaches of government, where it would be remote from popular influence and therefore guaranteed to get increasingly expensive. But that particular kind of counsel does little to correct a myriad of other problems in the schools—declining achievement levels, busing, sex education disputes, textbook wrangles, and so on.

On reflection, it is not astonishing that our public schools should be afflicted by such difficulties. The American nation, after all, is enormously diverse, while our system of public education is fairly uniform and rigid, a Procrustean attempt to fit a people of widely differing cultures, aptitudes, and interests into a single mold. Small wonder that parents and taxpayers—from inner city black neighborhoods to white and middle class suburbia—have expressed their disenchantment with the current state of public education.

These considerations suggest that if there is to be any hope of rescuing the public schools it will have to come through some infusion of diversity and competition into what is essentially a monopoly situation. This may best be achieved by institution of the so-called voucher system. Under this system, parents would be given a certificate with which to purchase their children's education, at any school within a broad framework of accreditation.

This approach would encourage new suppliers to enter the field, submit the schools to the discipline of competition, and give parents greater influence in the education of their children. Preliminary experiments with the voucher concept (conducted by the Department of Health, Education, and Welfare) indicate high levels of parental and teacher satisfaction, and suggest that the idea should be investigated more intensively.

5. *Energy*. This problem area could be greatly improved if it were simply de-regulated across the board, as rapidly as possible. Specific steps that should be taken include: (1) A complete de-regulation of energy prices by the Federal Energy Administration (which took over this counterproductive function from the Cost of Living Council); (2) Continued de-regulation of natural gas prices in particular, permitting them to seek their market level; (3) A go-ahead on offshore drilling for petroleum on the North American continental shelf; (4) Elimination of the stringent air-pollution control requirements mandated for future adoption by automobiles and industry.

These steps would vastly improve our access to energy supplies and the usability of those we have. In addition, a master reform is needed in the realm of environmental regulation, where government officials have been imposing single-purpose regulations aimed at getting zero pollution with little regard for economic consequences. What is obviously needed is to right this equation: to require that before any agency can impose an environmental restraint, it must file an "economic impact statement"—indicating to what extent the restraint will limit energy or other supplies, its side effects on other natural resources, its impact on consumption and prices, and the number of people who might be unemployed as a result. Only if these economic costs were considered acceptable could the program go into effect. If the agency under-calculated such costs an equivalent sum would be subtracted from its operating budget for the following year or years.

6. *Welfare*. The urgent need in this department (as in several others) is to do exactly the opposite of what we have been doing, and are constantly urged to do even more of. We need to de-federalize welfare rather than to federalize it. So long as costs in whole or major part be offloaded to some higher level of government, states and local communities have small incentive to get

these expenditures under control. To the extent that these jurisdictions must bear their own costs, we can be certain they will move with reasonable dispatch to put their affairs in order.

The feasibility of such reform was demonstrated in 1973 by U.S. Welfare Commissioner Robert Carleson, who encouraged the states to tighten up procedures and gave them financial and legal leeway in which to do so. The result was that certain states and local communities went after freeloaders and runaway papas, and welfare caseloads, for the first time in years, actually declined. This record could be improved still further if the welfare problem *in toto* were dumped back into the laps of the states—letting them pay their own bills, thereby reaping the benefits of prudence and paying the costs of profligacy.

7. *Health.* Similar considerations apply in the case of soaring health care expenditures. The crying need is to get the Federal government as far as possible out of the practice of medicine, and the obvious place to begin is with the Medicaid program. On present cost projections, it would pay many states to get out of Medicaid altogether, thereby eliminating Federal rules and guidelines that induce an increasing level of expenditure. Once engaged in independent programs and required to pay their own bills, the states will tailor requirements to their own abilities and needs. This will lower costs to taxpayers and correspondingly reduce the flood of monetary demand that has forced the medical price index into such a giddy climb.

On another front, there is little doubt that the quality of health care available to Americans could be vastly improved if the counterproductive "safe and effective" regulations of the Food and Drug Administration were changed back to the "safe" criterion that existed in 1962. Under that standard, many beneficial drugs currently blocked from the market until proven "effective" would be available—providing more and better medication to American citizens and tending to push down prices. On the latter point, considerable research has demonstrated that advertising of prescription drugs, barred in many states, also results in lower prices; prohibitions on such advertising should be removed.

8. *Social Security.* The other part of the medical expenditure explosion, the Medicare program, cannot be treated without considering the increasingly hazardous condition of the Social Security

system of which it is a part. Something will have to be done about Social Security fairly soon, and the fate of Medicare will be directly affected by whatever is done. As Social Security presently operates, every increase in payroll taxes to pay existing debts piles up additional obligations for the future—a pyramid club procedure that must eventually end in total bankruptcy.

One proposal that gives some hope of getting out of this quagmire runs as follows: (1) Convert the Social Security program to a system of bonds—purchased by workers through payroll deductions as are savings bonds, fully transferrable and redeemable at retirement; (2) Give workers the option of getting out of the program by spending the equivalent amount on private bonds or annuities (a much better deal financially). If properly handled, this approach should encourage new employes to switch to private coverage, which is cheaper and provides better benefits.

To the extent that this was accomplished, the exponential piling up of future obligations under the present formula would be curtailed, and we could set about retiring the enormous indebtedness of the system. The revenues subtracted by the opting out of younger workers would, of course, have to be made up from general revenues, but this would be nowhere near as expensive in the long run as the existing set-up. Most significantly, it would not be an open-ended drain on general revenues, since the amount of money to be made up would be strictly tied to worker withdrawals, which in turn would reduce the long-run obligations of the system. The alternative is to pile up billions of dollars in obligations that will ultimately draw on general revenues anyway, at much higher levels and with no inherent limitations.

9. *Inflation.* Closely related to these financial problems is inflation, which raises the cost of everything, pushes up Social Security payouts on an endless escalator, and works a particular hardship on the elderly receiving Medicare and other similar payments. The greatest service the Federal government could render such people—and the rest of us—is simply to stop inflating the currency. The problem, of course, is how to achieve this most desirable objective.

The obvious need of the hour is to place the money supply beyond the manipulative power of inflationists—a goal that clearly has not been achieved through the Federal Reserve System. The best way of doing this would be to reestablish the gold standard, disparaged by the inflationists precisely because it renders the money supply somewhat immune to manipulation. The recent revival of interest in gold suggests this solution is not impossible, but it must at this juncture be accounted remote. Failing its adoption, the best alternative is that suggested by Milton Friedman: Require the Federal Reserve by statute to expand the money supply at a drastically slower rate, roughly equivalent to the annual increase in the volume of production.

10. *Tax reform.* The principal reform that is needed in the realm of taxation is to control the total amount of money that can be taken from American citizens of whatever income level. This consideration is far more important than exemptions, deductions, loopholes, and so on, which as usually discussed are simply diversions from the fundamental issue of government's enormous total take. The closest approach to this objective yet devised is the constitutional amendment promoted in 1973 by former Governor Ronald Reagan of California, which sought to freeze the total tax burden as a percentage of personal income and then to roll that level back over a period of years. Similar proposals have been advanced in other states, and a Federal version has been introduced into Congress by Representative Jack Kemp (R-N.Y.).

While the aggregate burden is the major issue, adjustments are possible as well in the way the burden is distributed. Friedman, for one, has suggested setting a much lower Federal income tax rate, but eliminating many exemptions and deductions. As for state and local taxes, suffice it here to reiterate the point set forward in Chapter 8: It is generally preferable to have local functions financed by local property taxes rather than by statewide general taxes, because the local method of finance imposes needed limitations on the spenders.

11. *Civil liberties.* We need a single standard for the protection of our civil liberties, which means, in essence, adherence to the Constitution rather than submission to the discretionary enthusiasms of liberal ideologues. There will always be human variation in interpreting the meaning of the Constitution or any other written document, but that variation is quite different from the enunciated doctrine of the liberals—that the Constitution means exactly what they wish it to mean in any given set of circumstances.

This calculated erosion of our fundamental law must be reversed if libertarian guarantees are to be secure.

To affirm this single standard it is necessary to reject attempts at elasticization from whatever source—be it liberal or conservative. It is just as wrong for conservatives to interpret away the First or Fourth Amendments (free speech, protection against wiretapping) as it is for liberals to interpret away the Tenth (states' rights), or to employ a species of constitutional jiu-jitsu to use restraints on Federal power as a means of extending it, as in the prayer or pornography cases. Either we have a Constitution or we do not; if not, everyone's civil liberties will ultimately depend on the discretion of the people wielding power.

12. *Law enforcement.* Protection of civil liberties implies, as previously noted, sufficient attention to the functions that government is supposed to perform, as well as preventing it from entering areas where it is prohibited. Most essential of the areas of required performance is the matter of law enforcement. Liberals have succeeded in projecting this as a strictly two-dimensional equation—the force of government on the one hand versus the criminal defendant on the other· a way of viewing the matter that effectively marshals libertarian sentiment in behalf of criminals.

This formulation, however, omits the person whose well-being should concern us if we are authentically interested in protecting human liberty—the victim of crime. To the extent that proper law enforcement is weakened, government has defaulted its basic mission and subjected countless people to the depredations of violent criminals, thereby diminishing the level of human freedom. We need to reestablish certain minimal safeguards in this area: The discredited notion of "rehabilitation," permitting violent criminals to be released again and again into society, must be abandoned; effective sanctions like capital punishment must be invoked; and legal protections for victims—such as a recently proposed Victims Rights Commission—should be brought to bear to restore the law enforcement equation to its proper balance.

13. *Victimless crimes.* According to the intentions of America's founders, matters of basic law enforcement should be handled by the states and local communities. That insight, as stated in Chapter 21, is particularly relevant to the question of "victimless crimes"—drugs, pornography, and the like. As noted, the essen-

tial need in the vexed case of marijuana is to reverse the momentum of advocacy and propaganda—to undo the notion that marijuana is harmless, or no worse than alcohol, or whatever. Once the emerging facts about marijuana are widely communicated, the need to maintain criminal penalties against its use will be diminished.

In the question of pornography, potential neighborhood effects support the normal constitutional presumption in favor of leaving the matter to the states. Interestingly enough, the Supreme Court decision pointing in this direction has issued in a partial vindication of those who take the states' rights approach *and* of those who argue that pornography, under relatively *laissez-faire* conditions, will eventually run its course. There has been no wave of repression in the states, and in many communities the pornography industry continues to operate on a fairly wide-open basis. Reports as of late 1974, however, indicated that many porno houses were doing sluggish business and were having to close up shop for purely economic reasons.

14. *Population issues.* The best thing to do about the issue of population in America is—nothing. There are areas of dispute, however, impinging on the "population" question broadly construed, where corrective action is needed. Counterproductive economic regulations should be removed to permit improved production and a greater degree of social mobility. By providing economic satisfaction to consumers and easing problems of congestion in the larger urban centers, we could solve the greater part of what is incorrectly perceived as a "population" problem.

The necessity of such actions is even more obvious in the underdeveloped nations, where the pressing need is to obtain improved production through higher energy inputs, use of fertilizers and insecticides, and removal of economic constraints that inhibit enterprise. Needless to say, resort to abortion is an unacceptable method of dealing with "population" matters—both because it is intrinsically wrong on libertarian moral premises and because it in fact does not address the authentic problem in this area.

Two specific measures in this category are recommended from the conservative standpoint. A skewing of population patterns toward illegitimacies may be prevented by reforming the welfare system—ceasing to provide cash bonuses for illegitimate children and tracking down runaway papas and making them support their children. Second, to avert the false and anti-libertarian solution of permissive abortion, Congress should pass a human life amendment protecting the life of the unborn child. Such an amendment would also fend off the growing movement for mercy-killing, or euthanasia.

15. *Social engineering*. The principal corrective measure that is needed in the realm of social engineering is a much greater public awareness that it is going on. This alone should produce a systematic effort to get the activity stopped. On libertarian premises, social engineering is the very definition of authoritarian practice that it should be our consuming interest to avoid. As we have seen, such measures do not work, but even if they did they should be opposed on libertarian ethical grounds—indeed, opposed more vehemently still, since to the extent such practices succeed they pose an even greater threat to human freedom.

Because the principal thrust of social engineering activity has occurred in public education, the voucher experiment becomes in this respect a potentially crucial safeguard. Among its other virtues, the voucher system would diffract homogenizing impulses in the schools, bar attempts at top-down control, and enhance parental sovereignty *vis à vis* the "experts"; such a system, on every major count, would run directly contrary to the program of the engineers. On the populationist front, meanwhile, the passage of the human life amendment would be a stinging setback for those who have been meditating schemes of biological control.

16. *Foreign policy*. As in the realm of law enforcement, the urgent need in the realm of foreign policy is to revive the performance of our government in an area where it is supposed to act with energy and promptness. In pursuit of this revival, the best thing that could be done is simply to *stop* doing a great deal of what we are doing: Stop trading with and strengthening the enemy, stop weakening our defenses, stop subordinating our legitimate national interests to the vague and often preposterous imperatives of "world opinion" as sounded in the United Nations.

The legitimate purpose of our government in foreign affairs, as we have seen, is to defend the people of the United States from the incursions of hostile foreign powers. Adherence to such a standard requires a correct perception of the enemy, and intelligent deployment of our energies and resources to strengthen ourselves against that enemy. This means not only a realistic defense program and a refusal to build up the Soviet economy, but support for an alliance of non-Communist and anti-Communist states against the threat of Communist aggression.

Such an alliance, in place of the feckless United Nations, could include the nations of Western Europe, Canada, friendly nations in Latin America, certain of the saner Middle Eastern states, Japan, the Philippines, South Korea, South Vietnam, and the anti-Communist nations of the Asian littoral. Also, it would include those nations that are presently harassed and proscribed by the United Nations: Israel, Taiwan, South Africa, Rhodesia, Portugal.

This is an impressionistic rendering of the issues, with no pretension to completeness. It is not suggested that these proposals would work out to perfection, that all conservatives would endorse them equally, or that they exhaust the possibilities of corrective action. They are set forward merely to indicate the potential thrust of a conservative reform, employing a number of specifics advanced in recent years by conservative and libertarian spokesmen.

No such proposals have any prospect of success, moreover, unless they occur within the context of other and even larger changes. Most obviously, few of these measures will be attempted, much less be carried through to completion, until there are major alterations in the political landscape. In general, changes in government policy are voted by Congress or enacted by the executive —and few initiatives of the sort considered in this chapter are likely to occur with the kind of public officials returned to office in recent years.

Beyond these more immediate political considerations lie questions of long-range structural reform—restoring the balance among the executive, the legislature, and the judiciary; between the Federal government and the states; and between governments in general and the beleaguered private citizen. Changes such as these, if they are ever to occur, will be the work of generations, and would be much more difficult to achieve than the rather modest policy goals set forward above.

Finally, there remains the master difficulty of them all. There is little likelihood that America can regain its vigor as a free society, cure its economic ills, or correct its political disorders, if it continues to drift in metaphysical confusion. We therefore end as we began, in the awareness that our political troubles arise from the deeper realms of ethics and religion. No political program can remedy our problems in this area, which lie beyond the scope of the present limited, topical volume. Fortunately, the book that explains this ultimate subject has already been written, and enjoys a general circulation.

Notes

INTRODUCTION: THE DEATH OF LIBERALISM

1. Lionel Trilling, *The Liberal Imagination* (Doubleday, Anchor Books, 1954), p. 5.
2. Harry A. Overstreet, *The Great Enterprise* (W. W. Norton, 1952), p. 115.
3. J. Salwyn Schapiro, *Liberalism: Its Meaning and History* (D. Van Nostrand, 1958), p. 9.
4. Joseph S. Clark, "Can the Liberals Rally?" *Atlantic Monthly,* July 1953.
5. Robert Theobald, *The Challenge of Abundance* (Mentor Books, 1962), pp. 108, 109, 116–17.
6. *New York Times,* June 11, 1962.
7. Kenneth R. Minogue, *The Liberal Mind* (Vintage Books, 1968), pp. 1–13.
8. Max Lerner, ed., *The Mind and Faith of Justice Holmes* (Modern Library, 1943), pp. 415–16.
9. Max Lerner, ed., *Essential Works of John Stuart Mill* (Bantam Books, 1961), p. 418.
10. Christopher Dawson, *Religion and Culture* (Meridian Books, 1958), p. 22.

CHAPTER 1: THE AMERICAN DESIGN

1. Gertrude Himmelfarb, ed., *Essays on Freedom and Power* (Meridian Books, 1955), p. 175.
2. George A. Peek, Jr., ed., *The Political Writings of John Adams* (Liberal Arts Press, 1954), p. 165.
3. Alexander Hamilton, John Jay, and James Madison, *The Federalist* (Modern Library, 1937), p. 320.
4. Ibid., p. 303.
5. Quoted in R. L. Ashley, *The American Federal State* (Macmillan, 1902), p. 104.
6. *The Federalist,* p. 337.
7. James Bryce, *The American Commonwealth* (Macmillan, 1891), vol. 1, pp. 411–12.

CHAPTER 2: THE DESTRUCTION OF THE AMERICAN DESIGN

1. John Dewey, *Individualism Old and New* (Capricorn Books, 1962), p. 112.
2. Howard Zinn, ed., *New Deal Thought* (Bobbs-Merrill, 1966), p. 10.
3. Dewey, *Individualism*, pp. 116–19.
4. Zinn, *New Deal Thought*, p. 89.
5. John Kenneth Galbraith, *The Affluent Society* (Houghton Mifflin, 1958), p. 253.
6. John Kenneth Galbraith, *Economics and the Public Purpose* (Houghton Mifflin, 1973), pp. 277–78.
7. Arthur M. Schlesinger, Jr., "The Shape of National Politics to Come," mimeographed, 1960, pp. 8, 10.
8. Joseph S. Clark, "Staffing Freedom," reprint from the National Civil Service League, n.d.
9. Edward Reed, ed., *Challenges to Democracy* (Frederick A. Praeger, 1963), p. 148.
10. Quoted in *Congressional Quarterly*, September 18, 1964.
11. Reed, *Challenges to Democracy*, p. 101.
12. Quoted in James Burnham, *The Suicide of the West* (John Day, 1964), p. 90.
13. United States v. Butler, 297 U.S. 1, 66 (1936).
14. Quoted in Carl Brent Swisher, *The Growth of Constitutional Power in the United States* (University of Chicago Press, 1963), p. 77.
15. Quoted in Alpheus T. Mason, *The Supreme Court from Taft to Warren* (W. W. Norton, 1964), p. 15.
16. Rexford G. Tugwell, "Rewriting the Constitution," *The Center Magazine,* publication of the Center for the Study of Democratic Institutions, vol. 1, no. 3, March 1968.

CHAPTER 3: THE POWER IN THE PRESIDENT

1. Arthur M. Schlesinger, Jr., *The Imperial Presidency* (Houghton Mifflin, 1973), p. ix.
2. Arthur M. Schlesinger, Jr., *A Thousand Days* (Houghton Mifflin, 1965), pp. 707–08.
3. Walter Lippmann, *The Public Philosophy* (Mentor Books, 1956), pp. 50, 53, 137.
4. J. William Fulbright, "American Foreign Policy in the 20th Century Under an 18th-Century Constitution," *Cornell Law Quarterly,* Fall 1961, vol. 47, no. 1.
5. Quoted in Rexford G. Tugwell and Thomas E. Cronin, *The Presidency Reappraised* (Frederick A. Praeger, 1974), p. 38.
6. Wilfred E. Binkley, *President and Congress* (Vintage Books, 1962), p. 263.
7. Quoted in Arthur M. Schlesinger, Jr., *The Crisis of the Old Order* (Houghton Mifflin, 1957), p. 39.

8. Alfred de Grazia, ed., *Congress: The First Branch of Government* (Doubleday, Anchor Books, 1967), pp. 72–73.

9. Binkley, *President and Congress,* p. 301.

10. James MacGregor Burns, *Roosevelt: The Soldier of Freedom* (Harcourt Brace Jovanovich, 1970), pp. 33–63.

11. Ibid., pp. 98–167. For a revisionist treatment of these events, see Benjamin Colby, *'Twas a Famous Victory* (Arlington House, 1974).

12. James Burnham, *Congress and the American Tradition* (Henry Regnery, 1959), p. 150.

13. James MacGregor Burns, *Presidential Government* (Houghton Mifflin, 1965), pp. 319–21.

14. Dwight D. Eisenhower, *Mandate for Change* (Doubleday, 1963), p. 597.

15. *New York Times,* May 17, 1954.

16. Clark R. Mollenhoff, *Despoilers of Democracy* (Doubleday, 1965), p. 33.

17. Ibid., p. 34.

18. For a point-by-point comparison of the Otepka and Watergate cases, see M. Stanton Evans, "A Case of Political Bugging," *Human Events,* July 16, 1973.

19. Burns, *Presidential Government,* pp. 329–30.

CHAPTER 4: THE DECLINE OF CONGRESS

1. *United States Government Organization Manual, 1972/73,* Office of the Federal Register, National Archives and Records Service, General Services Administration.

2. *The American Almanac,* 1974 (Grosset & Dunlap), p. 403 (data based on *Statistical Abstract of the United States*).

3. Tax Foundation, *Facts and Figures on Government Finance,* 17th biennial ed. (Tax Foundation, Inc., 1973), p. 82.

4. Stephen K. Bailey, *The New Congress* (St. Martin's Press, 1966), pp. 30, 32.

5. Joseph P. Harris, *Congressional Control of Administration* (Doubleday, Anchor Books, 1965), p. 227.

6. Ibid., pp. 314–15.

CHAPTER 5: THE COURT AND THE CONSTITUTION

1. Clifton Brock, *Americans for Democratic Action* (Public Affairs Press, 1962), p. 7.

2. Robert H. Jackson, *The Struggle for Judicial Supremacy* (Vintage Books, 1941), pp. xii, xiv.

3. Mason, *Supreme Court,* p. 94.

4. Leonard Levy, ed., *Judicial Review and the Supreme Court* (Harper Torchbooks, 1967), pp. 16, 73.

5. Irving Brant, *Storm Over the Constitution* (Bobbs-Merrill, 1936), pp. 125, 241, 244–45.
6. Lerner, *Justice Holmes,* p. 50.
7. Mason, *Supreme Court,* p. 118.
8. Charles L. Black, *The People and the Constitution* (Spectrum Books, 1960), p. 168.

CHAPTER 6: THE GROWTH OF GOVERNMENT

1. "Big Government: Is It Out of Hand?" *U.S. News and World Report,* March 24, 1969.
2. *Facts and Figures on Government Finance,* p. 33.
3. Ibid.
4. Ibid., p. 25.
5. Henry Hazlitt, *The Conquest of Poverty* (Arlington House, 1973), p. 94.
6. *Facts and Figures on Government Finance,* p. 21.
7. "You're On Your Own Now," *Indianapolis News,* May 10, 1971.
8. "U.S. Income Taxes Too High, 65% Say," *Indianapolis Star,* April 12, 1973.
9. Quoted in *Battle Line,* publication of the American Conservative Union, September 1971.
10. Executive Office of the President, Office of Management and Budget, *The Federal Budget in Brief, Fiscal Year 1974,* p. 32; and *The Federal Budget in Brief, Fiscal Year 1975,* p. 54.
11. Roger A. Freeman, "National Priorities in the Decade Ahead," *Intercollegiate Review,* Winter-Spring 1972, p. 16.
12. Charles L. Schultze et al., *Setting National Priorities: The 1973 Budget* (Brookings Institution, 1972), p. 42.
13. Ibid., pp. 10–11.
14. *Facts and Figures on Government Finance,* p. 31.
15. *Battle Line,* April 1973.

CHAPTER 7: THE REGRESSIVE STATE

1. William F. Buckley, Jr., *Four Reforms* (G. P. Putnam's Sons, 1973), pp. 31–40.
2. *Facts and Figures on Government Finance,* p. 24; and "50 Richest Counties Found in Suburbs," *New York Times,* September 19, 1972.
3. *The American Almanac,* 1974, p. 335.
4. Roger A. Freeman and John A. Lynch, *Financing the Schools* (American Enterprise Institute, 1972), p. 11.
5. Daniel P. Moynihan, *Coping: On the Practice of Government* (Random House, 1973), p. 376.
6. Murray N. Rothbard, *For a New Liberty* (Macmillan, 1973), pp. 155–56.

7. "Who Will Foot the Bill for Social Security Raises?" *U.S. News and World Report,* November 26, 1973.

8. "Social Security: Promising Too Much to Too Many?" *U.S. News and World Report,* July 15, 1974.

9. Ibid.; also Roger Leroy Miller, "Social Security: The Cruelest Tax," *Harper's,* May 1974; and "New Changes in Social Security Laws," *U.S. News and World Report,* January 29, 1973.

10. "How Long Can a Tax Increase Be Avoided?" *U.S. News and World Report,* October 1, 1973.

11. *U.S. News and World Report,* November 26, 1973.

12. Rothbard, *For a New Liberty,* p. 182.

13. Ibid., p. 183.

CHAPTER 8: THE ROAD TO TAX REFORM

1. Joseph A. Pechman and Benjamin A. Okner, *Who Bears the Tax Burden?* (Brookings Institution, 1974), pp. 64–65.

2. *Battle Line,* May 1972.

3. Roger A. Freeman, *Tax Loopholes: The Legend and the Reality* (American Enterprise Institute, 1973, pp. 22, 25, 29.

4. *The Public Interest,* Summer 1972, p. 9.

5. Ibid.

6. Freeman and Lynch, *Financing the Schools,* p. 14.

7. Schultze, *The 1973 Budget,* pp. 326, 322.

8. Ibid., p. 326.

9. Charles E. McClure, Jr., with Norman Ture, *Value Added Tax. Two Views* (American Enterprise Institute, 1972), p. 57.

10. *The Root of the Opposition,* National Education Association, n.d.

11. Moynihan, *Coping,* p. 371.

CHAPTER 9: THERE IS NO URBAN CRISIS

1. "Black Youths' Unemployment Rate Is 'Disaster,'" *Indianapolis News,* July 5, 1973.

2. John M. Peterson and Charles T. Stewart, Jr., *Employment Effects of Minimum Wage Rates* (American Enterprise Institute, 1969), p. 155.

3. Ibid., p. 13.

4. Ibid., p. 9.

5. Quoted in *Congressional Record,* July 18, 1973, p. S13841.

6. "Housing Lack Is Stressed by Romney," *Indianapolis News,* July 25, 1969.

7. "The Absurd Issue of Open Occupancy," *The Center Diary,* publication of the Center for the Study of Democratic Institutions, 18, May–June 1967.

8. John C. Weicher, *Urban Renewal: National Program for Local Problems* (American Enterprise Institute, 1972), p. 6.

9. *The Public Interest,* Spring 1972, p. 79.

412

10. Richard Craswell, *The Failure of Federal Housing* (American Conservative Union, 1974), p. 8.
11. *The Public Interest,* Summer 1969, p. 131.
12. Harrison G. Wehner, Jr., *An Economic Evaluation of HUD's Principal Housing Subsidy Programs: Sections 235 and 236* (American Enterprise Institute, 1973), p. 6.
13. Quoted by Welfeld in *The Public Interest,* Spring 1972, p. 90.
14. *The Public Interest,* Summer 1973, p. 35.
15. James Q. Wilson, ed., *The Metropolitan Enigma* (United States Chamber of Commerce, 1967), p. 165.

CHAPTER 10: SICK TRANSIT

1. John H. Frederick, *Improving National Transportation Policy* (American Enterprise Association, 1959), pp. 18–19.
2. "The Railroad Crisis," *Congressional Quarterly,* May 22, 1973.
3. Robert Fellmeth et al., *The Interstate Commerce Omission,* the Ralph Nader Study Group Report on the Interstate Commerce Commission and Transportation (Grossman Publishers, 1970), p. 145.
4. Mary Bennett Peterson, *The Regulated Consumer* (Nash Publishing, 1971), p. 198.
5. "CAB Is Enthusiastic Backer of Moves to Trim Airline Service, Increase Fares," *Wall Street Journal,* August 13, 1974.
6. "Crusty CAB Is in Restraint of Flight," *Los Angeles Times,* September 2, 1973.
7. *Once Upon a Time* (Campus Studies Institute, 1974), p. 10.
8. Fellmeth, *The Interstate Commerce Omission,* pp. 120–21.
9. Ibid., p. 130.
10. Ross D. Eckert and George W. Hilton, "The Jitneys," *The Journal of Law and Economics,* vol. 15, no. 2, October 1972, pp. 293–325.

CHAPTER 11: SOME MYTHS OF LIBERAL EDUCATION

1. Department of Health, Education and Welfare, *Equality of Educational Opportunity,* 1966, p. 21.
2. Frederick Mosteller and Daniel P. Moynihan, eds., *On Equality of Educational Opportunity* (Vintage Books, 1972), pp. 8, 10, 69.
3. Ibid., p. 15.
4. Christopher Jencks et al., *Inequality: A Reassessment of the Effect of Family and Schooling in America* (Basic Books, 1972), pp. 23, 95, 106, 109, 256.
5. *Congressional Record,* February 6, 1964, p. H2280.
6. *Equality of Educational Opportunity,* p. 20.
7. Ibid., p. 22.
8. *The Public Interest,* Summer 1966, p. 74.
9. United States Commission on Civil Rights, *Racial Isolation in the Public Schools,* 1967, vol. 1, p. 193.
10. *The Public Interest,* Summer 1972, pp. 99–106.

11. Jeffrey J. Leech, "Busing as a Judicial Remedy: A Socio-Legal Reappraisal," *Indiana Law Review*, vol. 6, no. 4, 1973.

CHAPTER 12: THE CAUSE AND CURE OF INFLATION

1. Quoted in Henry Hazlitt, *The Failure of the New Economics* (D. Van Nostrand, 1959), p. 396.
2. *Battle Line*, October 1973.
3. Paul A. Samuelson, *Economics: An Introductory Analysis* (McGraw-Hill, 1955), p. 252.
4. David Levy, *The Cause and Cure of Inflation* (American Conservative Union, 1973), p. 2.
5. *Facts and Figures on Government Finance*, p. 66.
6. "Food Facts," *Indianapolis News*, March 12, 1973.

CHAPTER 13: GOVERNMENT CAN BE HAZARDOUS TO YOUR HEALTH

1. Edward M. Kennedy, "National Health Insurance and Health Security," reprint from *Congressional Record*, August 27, 1970.
2. Marvin H. Edwards, *Hazardous to Your Health* (Arlington House, 1972), pp. 40–44.
3. Ibid., pp. 92, 103.
4. Harry Schwartz, *The Case for American Medicine* (David McKay, 1972), pp. 9–10.
5. *Source Book on Health Insurance Data, 1973–74* ed. (Health Insurance Institute), pp. 18–19; and Rita R. Campbell and W. Glenn Campbell, *Voluntary Health Insurance in the United States* (American Enterprise Association, 1960), p. 1.
6. Schwartz, *American Medicine*, p. 40.
7. *Indianapolis News*, November 3, 1970.
8. *New York Times*, December 24, 1973.
9. Message to Congress, February 6, 1974; text in *Congressional Quarterly*, February 9, 1974, p. 254.
10. Schwartz, *American Medicine*, p. 116.
11. Herbert E. Klarman, "Major Public Initiatives in Health Care," *The Public Interest*, Winter 1974, pp. 109, 112.
12. Ibid., p. 110.
13. Edwards, *Hazardous to Your Health*, p. 240; and *Indianapolis News*, January 16, 1974.
14. Edwards, *Hazardous to Your Health*, p. 250.
15. Walter S. Ross, "The Medicine We Need—But Can't Have," *Reader's Digest*, October 1973.
16. Milton Friedman, "Frustrating Drug Advancement," *Newsweek*, January 8, 1973.
17. *Medical Economics*, August 6, 1973.
18. Ibid.

CHAPTER 14: THE POPULATION SCARE

1. Donella H. Meadows et al., *The Limits to Growth* (Universe Books, 1972), p. 190.
2. *Indianapolis News,* December 8, 1973.
3. Charles Rice, "Are We Faced with a Population Explosion?" Manion Forum radio broadcast, January 17, 1971.
4. "Too Many Americans?" *U.S. News and World Report,* February 15, 1971.
5. Ibid.
6. George Grier, *The Baby Bust* (Washington Center for Metropolitan Studies, 1972), p. 9.
7. Ibid., p. 74.
8. Ibid.; and Barry Kramer, "Why America's Birth Rate Is Falling," *Wall Street Journal,* February 1, 1974.
9. *The American Almanac,* 1974, p. 25.
10. Ibid., p. 6.
11. Kramer, "America's Birth Rate"; and Grier, *The Baby Bust,* p. 73.
12. R. Ederer, "Overpopulation Mythology," *Life in America,* June 1971.
13. Colin Clark, "Starvation or Plenty?" *Triumph,* February 1971.

CHAPTER 15: FRIENDS OF EARTH, ENEMIES TO MAN

1. Melvin J. Grayson and Thomas R. Shepard, Jr., *The Disaster Lobby* (Follett Publishing Co., 1973), p. 49.
2. Charles H. Connolly, *Air Pollution and Public Health* (Dryden Press, 1972), p. 191; and Grayson and Shepard, *The Disaster Lobby,* pp. 48–49.
3. Grayson and Shepard, *The Disaster Lobby,* pp. 50–52.
4. Ibid., p. 52.
5. Connolly, *Air Pollution,* p. 32.
6. Ibid., pp. 74, 79.
7. Grayson and Shepard, *The Disaster Lobby,* pp. 53–54.
8. Connolly, *Air Pollution,* pp. 251–53.
9. Ibid., pp. 83, 84.
10. "Leaded Gasoline: Current Status," *Ethyl Digest,* publication of Ethyl Corp., 1973, p. 39.
11. *Bloomington* (Ind.) *Courier-Tribune,* November 7, 1973.
12. Statement issued through the Department of Health, Education and Welfare, September 15, 1971.
13. Environmental Protection Agency, *Hearing Examiner's Recommended Findings, Conclusions and Orders,* 40 CFR 164.32, April 25, 1972.
14. Grayson and Shepard, *The Disaster Lobby,* p. 36.
15. *Human Events,* June 17, 1972.

CHAPTER 16: THE ENERGY CRISIS

1. Lawrence Rocks and Richard P. Runyon, *The Energy Crisis* (Crown Publishers, 1972), pp. 33–39.

2. Paul Wollstadt with Frank Ikard, "Factors Affecting Energy Supply and Demand," American Petroleum Institute, December 5, 1973.
3. Richard C. Sparling et al., *Financial Analysis of a Group of Petroleum Companies, 1972,* Energy Economics Division, Chase Manhattan Bank, August 1973.
4. Ibid.
5. Wollstadt, "Energy Supply."
6. Rocks and Runyon, *The Energy Crisis,* p. 22.
7. Wollstadt, "Energy Supply."
8. Ibid.
9. Quoted in *Battle Line,* November 1973.
10. Senate Committee on Interior and Insular Affairs, *Federal Energy Organization,* staff analysis prepared at the request of Senator Henry M. Jackson, March 5, 1973.
11. Sparling et al., *Petroleum Companies.*
12. Quoted in *Human Events,* January 5, 1974.
13. "The Profits Boom Shows Its Age," *Business Week,* November 10, 1973.
14. Wollstadt, "Energy Supply."
15. Sparling et al., *Petroleum Companies.*

CHAPTER 17. LIBERALISM AND CIVIL LIBERTIES

1. Mason, *Supreme Court,* p. 185.
2. United States v. Darby, 312 U.S. 100 (1941).
3. Mason, *Supreme Court,* p. 107.
4. Concurring opinion in Roe v. Wade, Doe v. Bolton, January 22, 1973.
5. See Willmoore Kendall, "The Bill of Rights and American Freedom," in Frank S. Meyer, ed., *What Is Conservatism?* (Holt, Rinehart and Winston, 1964), pp. 41ff.
6. Quoted in Laurentz B. Frantz, "Is the First Amendment Law?" in Leonard Levy, ed., *Judicial Review and the Supreme Court* (Harper Torchbooks, 1967), p. 156.

CHAPTER 18: HOW TO SILENCE DISSENT

1. *The Federalist,* p. 512.
2. Quoted in decision of Federal Communications Commission on application of Brandywine-Main Line Radio for renewal of license for stations WXUR and WXUR-FM, Media, Pa., July 7, 1970.
3. Letter to Dr. Carl McIntire from George K. Culbertson, president and general manager, station KONI, Spanish Fork, Utah, August 14, 1967.
4. James Ring Adams, "Doctoring Up TV Commercials," *Wall Street Journal,* March 27, 1974.
5. Nicholas Johnson, *How to Talk Back to Your TV Set* (Bantam Books, 1970), p. 172.
6. Ibid., p. 174.
7. Quoted in *Editor and Publisher,* June 29, 1974.
8. *Indianapolis News,* November 2, 1973.

9. "The Radical Right in America Today," text provided by Andrew F. Oehmann, Executive Assistant to the Attorney General, July 11, 1963.

CHAPTER 19: FREEDOM AND FOREIGN POLICY

1. *The Federalist,* pp. 87–88.
2. Winton U. Solberg, ed., *The Federal Convention and the Formation of the Union of the American States* (Liberal Arts Press, 1958), p. 107.
3. *The Federalist,* p. 142.
4. Quoted in Burnham, *The Suicide of the West,* pp. 176–77.
5. *U.S. News and World Report,* May 30, 1966.
6. N. H. Magan and Jacques Katel, eds., *Conquest Without War* (Pocket Books, 1961), p. 49.
7. Quoted in Richard V. Allen, *Peaceful Coexistence: A Communist Blueprint for Victory* (American Bar Association, 1966), p. 19.
8. *Who Is the Imperialist?* (AFL-CIO, June 1971).
9. Vincent P. Rock, *A Strategy of Interdependence* (Charles Scribner's Sons, 1964), p. 33.
10. James Roosevelt, ed., *The Liberal Papers* (Doubleday, Anchor Books, 1962), p. 111.
11. Donald G. Brennan, "When the SALT Hit the Fan," *National Review,* June 23, 1972.
12. "SALT: A Lecture by Dr. Kissinger," *Washington Sunday Star,* June 18, 1972.
13. Statement of Deputy Secretary of Defense David Packard before the Subcommittee on Arms Control, Senate Committee on Foreign Relations, July 13, 1971.
14. Edward Reed, ed., *Pacem in Terris* (Pocket Books, 1965), p. 82.

CHAPTER 20: CRIME WITHOUT PUNISHMENT

1. *The Challenge of Crime in a Free Society,* report by the President's Commission on Law Enforcement and Administration of Justice, 1967, p. 22; and *The American Almanac,* 1974, p. 146.
2. *The American Almanac,* 1974, pp. 226, 227, 323, 328.
3. Ibid., p. 146.
4. *Crime in the United States,* the uniform annual crime report of the Federal Bureau of Investigation, 1972, p. 36.
5. M. Stanton Evans and Margaret Moore, *The Lawbreakers* (Arlington House, 1968), p. 129.
6. Robert L. Martinson, "Can Corrections Correct?" *The New Republic,* April 8, 1972.
7. Paper presented before the American Corrections Association, April 1974.
8. Gordon Tullock, "Does Punishment Deter Crime?" *The Public Interest,* Summer 1974, p. 105.

9. *Human Events,* July 13, 1974.
10. Tullock, "Does Punishment Deter Crime?" p. 106.
11. *Crime in the United States,* 1972, pp. 36, 47.
12. *Crime in the United States,* 1964, p. 27.
13. *The American Almanac,* 1974, p. 150; and *Crime in the United States,* 1972, p. 9.

CHAPTER 21: THE VICTIMS OF VICTIMLESS CRIME

1. Senate Committee on the Judiciary, Subcommittee on Internal Security, *Hearings, World Drug Traffic and Its Impact on U.S. Security,* Sept. 18, 1972, pp. 204, 205.
2. Ibid., p. 211.
3. Senate Committee on the Judiciary, Subcommittee on Internal Security, *Hearings, Marijuana-Hashish Epidemic and Its Impact on United States Security,* May 9–June 13, 1974, p. 62.
4. Ibid., p. 34.
5. Ibid., p. 74.
6. Statement issued through Columbia University College of Physicians and Surgeons, January 25, 1974.
7. Gabriel G. Nahas, *Marijuana—Deceptive Weed* (Raven Press, 1973), p. 249.
8. *Marijuana-Hashish Epidemic and . . . U.S. Security,* pp. 21–22.
9. *World Drug Traffic and . . . U.S. Security,* pp. 239, 243.
10. David Holbrook, ed. *The Case Against Pornography* (The Library Press, 1973), pp. 163–64.
11. Ibid., pp. 201–02.
12. *The Report of the Commission on Obscenity and Pornography* (Bantam Books, 1970), pp. 466–69.
13. Ibid., pp. 470–71.

CHAPTER 22: A MATTER OF LIFE AND DEATH

1. Roe v. Wade, Doe v. Bolton, January 22, 1973.
2. Quoted by Committee for the Preservation of Life in a brief submitted to United States District Court, Southern District of Indiana, IP 70-C-217.
3. Ibid.
4. Quoted in Dr. and Mrs. J. C. Willke, *Handbook on Abortion* (Hiltz Publishing, 1973), pp. 22–23.
5. Committee for the Preservation of Life, brief IP 70-C-217.
6. David C. Anderson, "Abortion and Life's Intrinsic Value," *Wall Street Journal,* April 7, 1972.
7. Willke, *Handbook on Abortion,* p. 20.
8. Committee for the Preservation of Life, brief IP 70-C-217.
9. Ibid.

10. *Indianapolis Star,* August 19, 1973.
11. *Kansas City Star,* August 7, 1973.
12. Ibid.
13. "A New Ethic for Medicine and Society," *California Medicine,* September 1970.

CHAPTER 23: THE SOCIAL ENGINEERS

1. Carl L. Becker, *The Heavenly City of the Eighteenth Century Philosophers* (Yale University Press, 1932), pp. 14–15.
2. B. F. Skinner, *Beyond Freedom and Dignity* (Alfred A. Knopf, 1972), pp. 3–43.
3. Ibid., pp. 74, 149, 153, 156–57.
4. *National Review Bulletin,* October 14, 1969.
5. James S. Coleman, "Equal Schools or Equal Students?" *The Public Interest,* Summer 1966, pp. 73–75.
6. Mosteller and Moynihan, *Educational Opportunity,* pp. 39, 43, 49.
7. *Sexual Behavior,* August 1971.
8. Quoted in Connaught Coyne Marshner, *Federal Child Development: What's Developing?* (Heritage Foundation, 1974), p. 26.
9. S. 2007, Sec. 501, *Congressional Record,* September 9, 1971, p. S14033.
10. Quoted in Marshner, *Federal Child Development,* p. 10.
11. *Congressional Record,* September 9, 1971, p. S14013.
12. "Forecast for the 1970s," *Today's Education,* January 1969.
13. Letter to Representative John Brademas, quoted by the Emergency Committee for Children, May 28, 1971.
14. S. 2007, Sec. 587, *Congressional Record,* September 9, 1971, p. S14040.

CHAPTER 24: THE NEW TOTALITARIANS

1. *Indianapolis Star,* August 19, 1973.
2. Quoted by Leon R. Kass, "Making Babies—The New Biology and the 'Old' Morality," *The Public Interest,* Winter, 1972, p. 37.
3. "Row Over Fetal Research," *Newsweek,* June 24, 1974.
4. Quoted in Willke, *Handbook on Abortion,* p. 136.
5. "Forecast for the 1970s."
6. *Human Events,* May 5, 1973.
7. *Indianapolis Star,* July 16, 1974.
8. Alan L. Otten, "Boy or Girl?" *Wall Street Journal,* June 20, 1974.
9. *Look,* May 18, 1971.
10. Kass, "Making Babies," pp. 37–38.
11. Quoted in M. Stanton Evans, "The Death of Liberalism," in Dorothy Buckton James, ed., *Outside, Looking In* (Harper & Row, 1972), p. 27.
12. Ibid., p. 30.
13. Adolph Hitler, *Mein Kampf* (Reynal and Hitchcock, 1939), pp. 608, 609, 610.

Index